THE ANNOTATED
GILBERT AND SULLIVAN: 2

Ian Bradley was born in 1950 in Berkhamsted, Hertford-shire, and educated at Tonbridge School and New College, Oxford, where he obtained a First Class Honours degree in modern history. He stayed on at Oxford to complete a doctoral thesis on early nineteenth-century politics. After a brief period with the B.B.C. he joined the staff of *The Times* where he spent five years writing on political, historical and educational topics. Since 1982 he has combined free-lance writing and school teaching.

He is the author of six books, ranging in their subject matter from Victorian Evangelicalism to the birth of the Social Democratic Party. He is now working on a philosophical study of the British Liberal tradition and its relevance to the emerging post-industrial society.

Ian Bradley has been a Gilbert and Sullivan addict ever since he was taken by his parents to the Savoy Theatre as a small boy to see a performance of *Iolanthe*. Among his other loves are spa towns, remote railway stations, fishing ports, Scotland and the American Mid-West. Penguin also publish a companion volume of annotated Gilbert and Sullivan containing *H.M.S. Pinafore, The Pirates of Penzance, Iolanthe, The Mikado,* and *The Gondoliers*.

THE ANNOTATED
GILBERT
AND
SULLIVAN: 2

Introduced and edited by Ian Bradley

PENGUIN BOOKS

Penguin Books Ltd, Harmondsworth, Middlesex, England
Penguin Books, 40 West 23rd Street, New York, New York 10010, U.S.A.
Penguin Books Australia Ltd, Ringwood, Victoria, Australia
Penguin Books Canada Ltd, 2801 John Street, Markham, Ontario, Canada L3R 1B4
Penguin Books (N.Z.) Ltd, 182–190 Wairau Road, Auckland 10, New Zealand

This edition first published 1984

Made and printed in Great Britain by
Hazell Watson & Viney Ltd
Set in Palatino

CONTENTS

PREFACE

Kind comments from both critics and readers of my book *The Annotated Gilbert and Sullivan*, published by Penguin in 1982, have encouraged me to produce a second volume covering the rest of the major Savoy Operas. Like the first work, this book is offered as a source of innocent merriment and, I hope, of some interesting information and not as an academic treatise.

Sadly, it has proved impossible for reasons of space to include all the works on which Gilbert and Sullivan collaborated, and *Thespis*, *The Grand Duke* and *Utopia Limited* have had to be left out. However, these two volumes include all the operas which are still regularly performed.

As in the earlier book, the texts printed on the right-hand pages are those used by most amateur and professional companies performing the operas today. They are also the versions in which the operas were performed most recently by the D'Oyly Carte Opera Company before its sad demise in February 1982.

Once again, I have several debts of gratitude to record. The first must be to Dame Bridget D'Oyly Carte, who opened her archives to me and proved a fund of information on production points. Peter Riley, now general manager of the Bristol Hippodrome, shared with me his extensive knowledge of D'Oyly Carte practices and folklore.

In compiling this volume I have had the benefit of a source which was not available to me when I was working on the earlier book, namely the papers of J. M. Gordon, who joined the D'Oyly Carte Company in 1883 to play the Colonel in *Patience* and eventually left it fifty-six years later. I am most grateful to their present owner, Mrs D. W. S. Benney, for letting me look at them.

I have also benefited enormously from the critical comments and corrections of Michael Walters, a far greater expert on Gilbert and Sullivan than I can ever hope to be, who was kind enough to read through all my notes in typescript and saved me from several howlers.

My grateful thanks are also once again extended to the Royal General Theatrical Fund Association, the owner of the subsisting copyright in Sir W. S. Gilbert's unpublished writings, for allowing me to quote from lines in the Lord Chancellor's licence copies of the operas and from unpublished letters.

In addition to the books which I mentioned at the end of the preface to the earlier volume, I have derived much pleasure and information from two recently published works: *George Grossmith* by Tony Joseph, privately published and available from the author at 55 Brynland Avenue, Bristol, and *The Lost Stories of W. S. Gilbert*, edited by Peter Haining (Robson Books, London, 1982).

As before, I would also like to record my thanks to John Denny, my editor at Penguin, Judith Wardman, my copy-editor, and, last but not least, to my parents, who read the manuscript and made many useful comments and corrections. For the errors which remain I alone am responsible.

TRIAL
BY
JURY

DRAMATIS PERSONÆ

THE LEARNED JUDGE
THE PLAINTIFF
THE DEFENDANT
COUNSEL FOR THE PLAINTIFF
USHER
FOREMAN OF THE JURY
ASSOCIATE
FIRST BRIDESMAID

TRIAL BY JURY

Trial by Jury is the earliest work by Gilbert and Sullivan which is still performed today. It was not, in fact, their first joint enterprise. They had collaborated in 1871 on an opera called *Thespis, or the Gods Grown Old*, which had been commissioned by John Hollingshead, the owner and manager of the Gaiety Theatre. However, the musical score of this work does not survive.

After *Thespis*, which was staged at the Gaiety, the librettist and composer had gone their separate ways – Gilbert to write plays and Sullivan to compose church music, songs and ballads. That their remarkable talents were brought together again four years later was due partly to accident and partly to the vision and imagination of Richard D'Oyly Carte, theatrical manager and impresario.

In 1875 Carte put on Jacques Offenbach's comic opera *La Périchole* at the Royalty Theatre in Dean Street, Soho, where he was manager. It seems that he originally hoped that the one-act French work would be accompanied by a two-act opera composed by Arthur Sullivan. However, this was not ready in time for the opening night on 30 January and Carte hastily substituted a domestic comedy. Meanwhile, he looked around for another short musical piece which would complete the bill and provide a popular evening's entertainment.

One story has it that W. S. Gilbert happened to walk into Carte's office one day early in January, another that the two men met in the street. However it came about, their meeting was fruitful. Gilbert already had a one-act operetta up his sleeve, the libretto of which he had shown to Carte the previous summer. It was to prove the ideal companion to *La Périchole*.

Gilbert had first sketched out the bare bones of *Trial by Jury* in the 11 April 1868 issue of *Fun*, a magazine to which he regularly contributed humorous verse. In 1873 he extended it into a full-scale libretto at the suggestion of Carl Rosa, the opera impresario, who wanted to set it to music and stage it with his wife, Euphrosyne Parepa-Rosa, appearing in the leading role as the plaintiff. However, the project was abandoned when Madame Rosa suddenly died in January 1874.

11

When he talked to Gilbert in January 1875, Carte suggested that Sullivan would be the ideal person to set *Trial by Jury* to music. So Gilbert trudged through the snow to the composer's rooms in Albert Mansions, Battersea, clutching the libretto in his frozen hands. Over a blazing fire, Sullivan recalled, 'He read it through to me in a perturbed sort of way with a gradual crescendo of indignation, in the manner of a man considerably disappointed with what he had written. As soon as he had come to the last word he closed the manuscript up violently, apparently unconscious of the fact that he had achieved his purpose so far as I was concerned, inasmuch as I was screaming with laughter the whole time.' Sullivan immediately agreed to set the piece to music, and this he did in less than three weeks.

Trial by Jury opened at the Royalty Theatre on 25 March in a triple bill with *La Périchole* and the bewilderingly named farce, *Cryptoconchoid Syphonostomata*. The 'dramatic cantata', as it was described on the programme, was an immediate success, winning rapturous acclaim from audiences and critics alike. It continued at the Royalty until 18 December, and then in January 1876 transferred to the Opéra Comique theatre just off the Strand, with a further season at the Royal Strand Theatre in the spring of 1877. Altogether, it was performed about 300 times in its first two years.

Although it is much shorter than Gilbert and Sullivan's later works, lasting only about forty-five minutes, and although it differs from the rest in having only one act and lacking any spoken dialogue, *Trial by Jury* otherwise has all the distinctive features of the Savoy Operas which were to follow it. There is the gentle mockery of British institutions – in this case, of course, the legal system – the central role for the chorus, and the juxtaposition of rollicking patter song and tender romantic aria. There is also the extraordinary rapport between librettist and composer. As *The Times* observed in its review of the first night: 'It seems, as in the great Wagnerian operas, as though poem and music had proceeded simultaneously from one and the same brain.'

For Gilbert the legal world was an obvious subject to burlesque. He himself had practised as a barrister, though not very successfully, before turning full-time to writing, and therefore had had plenty of opportunity to observe the quaint customs of English legal procedure. Sullivan also found that the pomp and ritual of the law afforded him splendid scope for musical jokes, as in his parody of Handel for the entrance of the Judge.

Trial by Jury has long been a favourite with schools and amateur societies. The staff of the Dragon School in Oxford have a tradition of performing it every three years with the headmaster as the Judge. It also continues to be very popular with audiences. A recording made by Decca with the D'Oyly Carte Opera Company in 1975 to mark the centenary of the first performance was top of the record industry's 'Classical Pops' chart. In 1978 a gala performance attended by the Queen Mother was given in the hall of the Middle Temple to mark the one-hundredth concert given by the Bar Theatrical Society; and the operetta was performed in full costume during the 1982 Proms season. For a long time the D'Oyly Carte Company performed it in a double bill with either *The Pirates of Penzance* or *H.M.S. Pinafore*, but, sadly, financial constraints caused it to be dropped from the repertoire in 1975.

There is one further point of interest worth noting about *Trial by Jury*. It seems to have been the only one of the Savoy Operas in which Gilbert himself ever appeared. On at least two occasions, at benefit matinées for Nellie Farren in 1898 and for Ellen Terry in 1906, the tone-deaf librettist played the part of the Associate, the legal official who sits at a desk below the Judge's bench throughout the entire performance and never utters a single word.

1–2 *Scene*: The D'Oyly Carte prompt-book for the 1884 revival of *Trial by Jury*, which Gilbert supervised, amplifies the rather bare description of the scene given in the libretto: 'The Bench faces the audience and extends along the back of the Court. The Judge's desk centre, with canopy overhead, Jury-box right, Counsel's seats left'. In a real courtroom, counsel would normally sit facing the judge, as it were in the orchestra pit. It is said that Gilbert modelled his courtroom on the old Clerkenwell Sessions House in which he had himself appeared during his career as a barrister.

A printed note at the beginning of the libretto used for the 1884 revival also has some useful advice on costumes: 'Modern dresses, without any extravagance or caricature. The defendant is dressed in bridal dress. The plaintiff as a bride. The bridesmaids as bridesmaids. The Judge, Counsel and Usher etc. should be as like their prototypes at Westminster as possible.'

3–10 *Hark, the hour of ten is sounding*
This opening chorus appeared in Gilbert's original short sketch of *Trial by Jury* in *Fun* in April 1868, the only difference from the present version being that there the second line ran 'Hearts with anxious hopes are bounding'.

8 *subpœna*: A writ commanding a person's attendance in a court of justice. The Latin words *sub poena* ('under penalty') are the first words of the writ.

9 *Edwin, sued by Angelina*: These names were first linked in a poem, 'The Hermit, or Edwin and Angelina', written in 1764 by Oliver Goldsmith, and included in *The Vicar of Wakefield*. The names were also used for a newly married couple, Edwin and Angelina Brown, in a series entitled 'Letters from a Young Married Lady' which appeared in the magazine *Fun* in the 1860s.

11 *Enter Usher*: An usher is a court official who shows people to their seats and leads judges into court. In *Iolanthe*, Strephon speaks of being led by a servile usher into Chancery Lane after an audience with the Lord Chancellor (Act I, line 147).

21 *the plaintiff*: The complainant, one who brings a suit into a court of law.

SCENE. – *A Court of Justice. Barristers, Attorneys, Jurymen and Public discovered.*

CHORUS.

Hark, the hour of ten is sounding;
Hearts with anxious fears are bounding,
Hall of Justice crowds surrounding,   5
    Breathing hope and fear –
For to-day in this arena,
Summoned by a stern subpœna,
Edwin, sued by Angelina,
    Shortly will appear.   10

(*Enter* USHER.)

SOLO – USHER.

Now, Jurymen, hear my advice –
All kinds of vulgar prejudice
    I pray you set aside:
With stern judicial frame of mind   15
From bias free of every kind,
    This trial must be tried.

CHORUS.

From bias free of every kind,
This trial must be tried.

(*During Choruses,* USHER *sings fortissimo, 'Silence in Court!'*)   20

USHER.

Oh, listen to the plaintiff's case:
Observe the features of her face –
    The broken-hearted bride.

29 *The . . . defendant*: A person sued in a court of law who defends the charge brought against him or her.

35 *Enter Defendant*: In the first edition of the libretto this stage direction read: '*Enter* DEFENDANT *with guitar*'. In early performances the Defendant accompanied himself on the guitar in his song 'When first my old, old love I knew'.

36 *Court of the Exchequer*: The Court of Exchequer was a common-law court which traced its origins back to the reign of Edward I and which dealt with revenue cases. It no longer existed in 1875, having been merged with two other medieval courts under the terms of the 1873 Judicature Act to form the Queen's Bench Division of the High Court. It would never in any case have dealt with actions for breach of promise. The defendant's anachronistic and legal lapses can perhaps be pardoned, however – there aren't many courts which rhyme with 'pecker'.

38 *Be firm . . . my pecker*: 'Pecker' means mouth, so this expression could be taken to mean either 'preserve a stiff upper lip' or 'keep your chin up'. It probably implies a combination of both. The phrase 'keep your pecker up' means don't get low and down-hearted. In the first edition of the libretto this line was 'Be firm, my moral pecker', recalling a phrase from one of Gilbert's *Bab Ballads*, 'The Haughty Actor':

> Dispirited became our friend –
> Depressed his moral pecker –

Condole with her distress of mind:
From bias free of every kind, 25
This trial must be tried!

CHORUS.

From bias free, etc.

USHER.

And when amid the plaintiff's shrieks,
The ruffianly defendant speaks –
Upon the other side; 30
What *he* may say you needn't mind –
From bias free of every kind!
This trial must be tried!

CHORUS.

From bias free, etc.

(*Enter* DEFENDANT.) 35

RECITATIVE – DEFENDANT.

Is this the Court of the Exchequer?

ALL.

It is!

DEFENDANT (*aside*).

Be firm, be firm, my pecker,
Your evil star's in the ascendant!

ALL.

Who are you? 40

DEFENDANT.

I'm the Defendant!

CHORUS OF JURYMEN (*shaking their fists*).

Monster, dread our damages.
We're the jury,
Dread our fury!

49 *You're at present in the dark*: In the early copy of the libretto sent to the Lord Chamberlain for licensing, the jurymen's chorus 'Oh, I was like that when a lad!' (lines 75–87) follows directly after this line, without the intervening chorus, 'That's a very true remark', and the Defendant's song, which occur in all published editions of the libretto.

57–74 *When first my old, old love I knew*
A note by Rupert D'Oyly Carte in a 1935 copy of the libretto records that in early productions, the Defendant tuned his guitar at the beginning of this song, with appropriate noises being made by the strings in the orchestra. This bit of business was later dropped.

58 *My bosom welled with joy*: The first edition of the vocal score has 'swelled with joy', but the libretto has always had 'welled'.

61 *No terms seemed too extravagant*: Another discrepancy between libretto and vocal score. The first edition of the former has 'No terms seemed extravagant', but the latter has from the first had the additional 'too', which scans better and is now found in all editions of the libretto.

65 *Tink-a-Tank*: This strange expression is supposed to be the nearest vocal approximation to the noise made by the plucking of guitar strings. The 1884 prompt-book mentioned above indicates that 'At "Tink-a-Tank" the Jury affect to be playing a guitar – the right hand and foot going together – the man at the right corner affects the tamborine and the one on the left the bones'. Thus the gentlemen of the jury transform themselves into a troupe of nigger minstrels.

DEFENDANT.

Hear me, hear me, if you please,   45
   These are very strange proceedings –
For permit me to remark
   On the merits of my pleadings,
You're at present in the dark.

(DEFENDANT *beckons to* JURYMEN *– they leave the box*   50
  and gather round him as they sing the following):

   That's a very true remark –
     On the merits of his pleadings
   We're entirely in the dark!
   Ha! ha! Ho! ho!   55
   Ha! ha! Ho! ho!

SONG – DEFENDANT.

When first my old, old love I knew,
   My bosom welled with joy;
My riches at her feet I threw –
   I was a love-sick boy!   60
No terms seemed too extravagant
   Upon her to employ –
I used to mope, and sigh, and pant,
   Just like a love-sick boy!
     Tink-a-Tank – Tink-a-Tank.   65

But joy incessant palls the sense;
   And love, unchanged, will cloy,
And she became a bore intense
   Unto her love-sick boy!
With fitful glimmer burnt my flame,   70
   And I grew cold and coy,
At last, one morning, I became
   Another's love-sick boy.
     Tink-a-Tank – Tink-a-Tank.

CHORUS OF JURYMEN (*advancing stealthily*).

Oh, I was like that when a lad!   75
   A shocking young scamp of a rover,
I behaved like a regular cad;
   But that sort of thing is all over.

85 *Singing so merrily – Trial-la-law*: This refrain appeared in Gilbert's original sketch of *Trial by Jury* in *Fun*, although in that version it was given to attorneys and barristers rather than jurymen. The following choruses for the two branches of the legal profession came straight after the opening chorus in the *Fun* version:

CHORUS OF ATTORNEYS.

Attorneys are we
And we pocket our fee,
Singing so merrily, 'Trial la law!'
With our merry *ca. sa.*,
And our jolly *fi. fa.*,
Worshipping verily Trial la law!
Trial la law!
Trial la law!
Worshipping verily Trial la Law!

CHORUS OF BARRISTERS.

Barristers we
With demur and plea,
Singing so merrily, 'Trial la law!'
Be-wigged and be-gowned
We rejoice at the sound
Of the several syllables 'Trial by law!'
Trial la law!
Trial la law!
Singing so merrily, 'Trial la law!'

89 *Silence in Court*: This brief recitative for the Usher was also in the original *Fun* sketch, following on from the barristers' chorus above. After it, however, there was no chorus or song for the Judge, and Gilbert went straight on to the recitative and aria for the Counsel for the Plaintiff (lines 235–65).

93–102 *All hail, great Judge*
In this chorus, and in the passage for the Judge and chorus which precedes 'When I, good friends, was called to the bar', Sullivan deliberately imitated the florid fugal style of Handel. There is another splendid parody of Handelian style in the song 'This helmet, I suppose' in Act III of *Princess Ida*.

101 *Reversed in banc*: 'In banc' is a legal phrase meaning on the bench and is applied to sittings of a superior court of common law. So this phrase means 'reversed by a full bench of judges in a higher court'.

104 *Breach of Promise*: Until 1970 women could, and did, take men to court for breaking off engagements. A contract to marry was as binding in law as any other contract, and therefore the party who broke it was liable for damages. The most famous action for breach of promise in Victorian literature was, of course, that brought by Mrs Bardell against Mr Pickwick in Charles Dickens's *The Pickwick Papers*. In that case, judgment was given for the plaintiff, and Mr Pickwick had to pay damages of £750.

I am now a respectable chap
    And shine with a virtue resplendent,   80
And, therefore, I haven't a scrap
    Of sympathy with the defendant!
        He shall treat us with awe,
        If there isn't a flaw,
Singing so merrily – Trial-la-law!   85
Trial-la-law – Trial-la-law!
Singing so merrily – Trial-la-law!

(They enter the Jury-box.)

RECITATIVE – USHER (*on Bench*).

    Silence in Court!
Silence in Court, and all attention lend.   90
Behold your Judge! In due submission bend!

(Enter JUDGE *on Bench.)*

CHORUS.

    All hail, great Judge!
        To your bright rays
    We never grudge   95
        Ecstatic praise.
           All hail!
    May each decree
        As statute rank
    And never be   100
        Reversed in banc.
           All hail!

RECITATIVE – JUDGE.

For these kind words accept my thanks, I pray.
A Breach of Promise we've to try to-day.
But firstly, if the time you'll not begrudge,   105
I'll tell you how I came to be a Judge.

ALL.

He'll tell us how he came to be a Judge!

JUDGE.

Let me speak!

111–54 *When I, good friends, was called to the bar*
This is the first of Gilbert and Sullivan's inimitable patter songs (not counting three early examples of the genre in *Thespis*, of which the music has not survived), and it introduces the first in a long line of comic figures which was to include a sorcerer, a First Lord of the Admiralty, a modern Major-General and a Lord High Executioner. It was not surprising that Gilbert should begin with a judge. As a former barrister himself, he had been able to examine that particular species at close quarters. He was, of course, to create another comic role from the legal world in *Iolanthe*. Indeed, the Lord Chancellor's song 'When I went to the Bar as a very young man' has very close similarities with this song (see the notes to lines 465–96 of *Iolanthe*, Act I, in *The Annotated Gilbert and Sullivan*).

The part of the Judge in *Trial by Jury* was created by Fred Sullivan, the composer's brother. He was a great success in the role, which he played throughout the opening season at the Royalty Theatre and for part of the 1876 season at the Opéra Comique. However, he became seriously ill and died at the age of thirty-six in January 1877. During Fred's last illness Arthur sat by his bedside reading verses by Adelaide Anne Procter. One of these verses, 'The Lost Chord', he later set to music, and it became perhaps the most popular of all Victorian drawing-room ballads. Fred Sullivan's role as the Judge was taken over by W. S. Penley, who later achieved fame as creator of the title role in the play *Charley's Aunt*.

115 *a swallow-tail coat*: A coat with a forked tail like that of a swallow.

116 *A brief*: A summary of the relevant facts and points of law in a case drawn up for a barrister, usually by a solicitor.
a booby: A dull, stupid fellow, especially one who allows himself to be imposed upon. The word is also used for the boy who comes bottom of the class and for a species of gannet thought to be particularly stupid.

120 *Westminster Hall*: Before the present Law Courts in the Strand came into use in 1882, the Common Law Courts were housed in Westminster Hall adjoining the Houses of Parliament.

132 *the Bailey and Middlesex Sessions*: The Bailey, referred to in line 141 as 'Ancient Bailey', is, of course, the Old Bailey, built in 1539 on Cheapside in the City of London, and established in 1834 as the Central Criminal Court in England and Wales. It is mentioned as such near the end of Act II of *The Pirates of Penzance* (see the note to line 564). Sessions were courts held four times a year in a county or other administrative area and having limited civil and criminal jurisdiction. They are now called Crown Courts. The Middlesex Sessions, where Gilbert himself had practised and which he made the subject of an early poem in *Fun* magazine, were held in a building in Parliament Square, London, opposite the Houses of Parliament.

135 *She may very well pass for forty-three*: Gilbert had a thing about women in their forties. Poor Ruth in *The Pirates of Penzance* is mocked by Frederic for being forty-seven (see the note to Act I, line 172), while Marco is warned by Gianetta in *The Gondoliers* not to address any lady less than forty-five (see the note to Act I, line 934).

ALL.

Let him speak, etc.
Hush! hush! He speaks. 110

SONG – JUDGE.

When I, good friends, was called to the bar,
    I'd an appetite fresh and hearty,
But I was, as many young barristers are,
    An impecunious party.
I'd a swallow-tail coat of a beautiful blue – 115
    A brief which I bought of a booby –
A couple of shirts and a collar or two,
    And a ring that looked like a ruby!

CHORUS.

He'd a couple of shirts, etc.

JUDGE.

In Westminster Hall I danced a dance, 120
    Like a semi-despondent fury;
For I thought I should never hit on a chance
    Of addressing a British Jury –
But I soon got tired of third-class journeys,
    And dinners of bread and water; 125
So I fell in love with a rich attorney's
    Elderly, ugly daughter.

CHORUS.

So he fell in love, etc.

JUDGE.

The rich attorney, he jumped with joy,
    And replied to my fond professions: 130
'You shall reap the reward of your pluck, my boy,
    At the Bailey and Middlesex Sessions.
You'll soon get used to her looks,' said he,
    'And a very nice girl you will find her!
She may very well pass for forty-three 135
    In the dusk, with a light behind her!'

147 *the Gurneys*: A well-known Quaker banking family which hailed originally from Norwich. The London branch of the bank, Overend, Gurney and Co., failed in 1866, but the Norwich branch prospered and was taken over by Barclays in 1896.

148 *An incubus*: Defined by the *Oxford English Dictionary* as a person or thing that weighs upon and oppresses like a nightmare. It sounds a more appropriate image for the Lord Chancellor in *Iolanthe* to use in his nocturnal wanderings.

CHORUS.

She may very well, etc.

JUDGE.

The rich attorney was good as his word;
　The briefs came trooping gaily,
And every day my voice was heard　　　　　　140
　At the Sessions or Ancient Bailey.
All thieves who could my fees afford
　Relied on my orations,
And many a burglar I've restored
　To his friends and his relations.　　　　　　145

CHORUS.

And many a burglar, etc.

JUDGE.

At length I became as rich as the Gurneys –
　An incubus then I thought her,
So I threw over that rich attorney's
　Elderly, ugly daughter.　　　　　　　　　　150
The rich attorney my character high
　Tried vainly to disparage –
And now, if you please, I'm ready to try
　This Breach of Promise of Marriage!

CHORUS.

And now if you please, etc.　　　　　　　　155

JUDGE.

For now I'm a Judge!

ALL.

And a good Judge too!

JUDGE.

Yes, now I'm a Judge!

ALL.

And a good Judge too!

160 *Though all my law be fudge*: In the first edition of the libretto this line went: 'Though all my law is fudge'. That version is still retained in the current Macmillan edition of the Savoy Operas.

164 *a job*: A colloquial expression for a transaction in which duty or the public interest is sacrificed for the sake of private advantage.

169 *a nob*: An important personage. It probably derives from the oriental word 'nabob'.

172 *Enter Counsel*: Counsel is the name given to a barrister or barristers when engaged in the direction or conduct of a case in court.

175 *Kneel, Jurymen, oh, kneel*: A favourite joke among the members of the D'Oyly Carte chorus was to ask 'Who's playing Juryman O'Neill tonight?'

JUDGE.

Though all my law be fudge,　　　　　　　160
Yet I'll never, never budge,
But I'll live and die a Judge!

ALL.

And a good Judge too!

JUDGE (*pianissimo*).

It was managed by a job –

ALL.

And a good job too!　　　　　　　165

JUDGE.

It was managed by a job!

ALL.

And a good job too!

JUDGE.

It is patent to the mob,
That my being made a nob
Was effected by a job.　　　　　　　170

ALL.

And a good job too!

(*Enter* COUNSEL *for* PLAINTIFF. *He takes his place in
front row of Counsel's seats.*)

RECITATIVE – COUNSEL.

Swear thou the Jury!

USHER.

Kneel, Jurymen, oh, kneel!　　　　　　　175

185 *That we will well and truly try*: The first edition of the libretto has a longer stage direction
at this point: '*All rise with the last note, both hands in air*'. The libretto goes on with a two-
line recitative for the Usher:

> This blind devotion is indeed a crusher –
> Pardon the tear-drop of a simple usher:

These two lines did not appear in the edition of the libretto issued for the 1884 revival.
A note by Rupert D'Oyly Carte in 1935 indicates that they were never, in fact, set to
music by Sullivan and had never been sung.

In the licence copy sent to the Lord Chamberlain the Usher's recitative is followed
by this ballad for the Foreman of the Jury, which was cut out before the first
performance:

> Oh, do not blush to shed a tear
> This is your foreman's prayer.
> For if you really feel it *here* (pointing to his heart)
> Why not express it *there* (pointing to his eye)
> The tears that to your eyelid start
> Do not attempt to dry
> Your eye is but your outer heart
> Your heart is all your eye!

The Counsel's recitative 'Where is the Plaintiff?' then followed as now.

189 *Oh, Angelina*: The summoning of Angelina is accomplished with much echoing of
voices around and outside the courtroom. A note in the prompt-book for the 1884
revival directs: 'The Usher trips à la fairy to right and calls "Angelina" and listens for
echo and then trips across stage to left and calls "Angelina" again and listens for echo.
Then trips to centre of stage and strikes attitude of welcome as bridesmaids enter.' In
D'Oyly Carte productions, the 'echo' was performed by the Defendant singing with
his back to the audience.

191 *Enter the Bridesmaids*: The original stage direction for this entrance in the first-edition
libretto read: '*Enter the* BRIDESMAIDS, *each bearing two palm branches, their arms crossed
on their bosoms, and rose-wreaths in their arms*'.

196 *Take, oh take these posies*: In some editions, this line appears as 'Take, oh maid these
posies'.

(*All the* JURY *kneel in the Jury-box, and so are hidden from audience.*)

USHER.

Oh, will you swear by yonder skies,
Whatever question may arise,
'Twixt rich and poor, 'twixt low and high,
That you will well and truly try?

180

JURY (*raising their hands, which alone are visible*).

To all of this we make reply,
To all of this we make reply,
By the dull slate of yonder sky:
That we will well and truly try.
    (*All rise with the last note.*)

185

RECITATIVE – COUNSEL.

Where is the Plaintiff?
Let her now be brought.

RECITATIVE – USHER.

Oh, Angelina! Come thou into Court!
    Angelina! Angelina!!

190

(*Enter the* BRIDESMAIDS.)

CHORUS OF BRIDESMAIDS.

Comes the broken flower –
    Comes the cheated maid –
Though the tempest lower,
    Rain and cloud will fade!
Take, oh take these posies:
    Though thy beauty rare
Shame the blushing roses,
    They are passing fair!
      Wear the flowers till they fade;
      Happy be thy life, oh maid!

195

200

(*The* JUDGE, *having taken a great fancy to* FIRST BRIDESMAID, *sends her a note by* USHER, *which she reads, kisses rapturously, and places in her bosom. Enter* PLAINTIFF.)

205 *the season vernal*: Spring. 'Vernal' comes from the Latin *vernalis* ('of the spring').

209, 211 *Time may do his duty . . . Winter hath a beauty*: This is the first of no fewer than fifteen occasions, exclusive of repetitions, when the words 'duty' and 'beauty' are rhymed in the Savoy Operas. This is the only such rhyming in *Trial by Jury*. *H.M.S. Pinafore* holds the record with four separate songs in which the words are rhymed (see the note to Act I, lines 247–58).

218 *Wear the flowers*: The first-edition libretto had the following stage direction at this point: '*During chorus* ANGELINA *collects wreaths of roses from* BRIDESMAIDS *and gives them to the* JURY, *who put them on and wear them during the rest of the piece.*'

221 *Ah, sly dog*: Gilbert used this refrain in his original sketch for an operetta in *Fun* in 1868 (see the note to line 385 below).

SOLO – Plaintiff.

O'er the season vernal,   205
　Time may cast a shade;
Sunshine, if eternal,
　Makes the roses fade!
Time may do his duty;
　Let the thief alone –   210
Winter hath a beauty,
　That is all his own.
　　Fairest days are sun and shade:
　　I am no unhappy maid!

(*The* Judge *having by this time transferred his admiration to* Plaintiff, *directs*   215
Usher *to take the note from* First Bridesmaid *and hand it to* Plaintiff,
who reads it, kisses it rapturously, and places it in her bosom.)

Chorus of Bridesmaids.

Wear the flowers, etc.

Judge.

Oh, never, never, never, since I joined the human race,
Saw I so exquisitely fair a face.   220

The Jury (*shaking their forefingers at him*).
Ah, sly dog! Ah, sly dog!

Judge (*to* Jury).

How say you? Is she not designed for capture?

Foreman (*after consulting with the* Jury).

We've but one word, my lord, and that is – Rapture!

Plaintiff (*curtseying*).

Your kindness, gentlemen, quite overpowers!

Jury.

We love you fondly and would make you ours!   225

The Bridesmaids (*shaking their forefingers at* Jury).
Ah, sly dogs! Ah, sly dogs!

228–33 *Monster! Monster! dread our fury!*
The first edition of the libretto did not contain this chorus, which was certainly sung in the 1884 revival, if not before.

235 *May it please you, my lud*: The Counsel's recitative and aria appeared in almost exactly their present form in Gilbert's early *Fun* sketch, where they followed straight on from the entrance of the Judge into court.

243 *He deceived a girl*: In the licence copy this is printed as 'Or deceive a girl'. The *Fun* version, however, is as now.

JURY.

We love you fondly, and would make you ours!

(*Shaking their fists at the* DEFENDANT.)

Monster! Monster! dread our fury!
There's the Judge and we're the Jury,
Come, substantial damages!   230
Substantial damages!
Damages!
Dam—

USHER.

Silence in Court!

RECITATIVE – COUNSEL *for* PLAINTIFF.

May it please you, my lud!   235
Gentlemen of the jury!

ARIA.

With a sense of deep emotion,
  I approach this painful case;
For I never had a notion
  That a man could be so base,   240
Or deceive a girl confiding,
Vows, *etcetera*, deriding.

ALL.

He deceived a girl confiding,
Vows, *etcetera*, deriding.

(PLAINTIFF *falls sobbing on* COUNSEL'S *breast and remains there.*)   245

COUNSEL.

See my interesting client,
  Victim of a heartless wile!
See the traitor all defiant
  Wear a supercilious smile!
Sweetly smiled my client on him,   250
Coyly woo'd and gently won him.

255 *Camberwell*: A rather undistinguished lower-middle-class suburb of London which grew up in the mid-Victorian period.
256 *Peckham*: Camberwell's neighbour to the south, further away from the centre of the capital, even less distinguished and decidedly working-class. Both Camberwell and Peckham, it should in fairness be pointed out, are now becoming 'gentrified' and, if not quite Arcadian, then certainly Bohemian.
   an Arcadian Vale: Arcadia, a mountainous area in central Peloponnesus, was regarded by the ancient Greeks as the ideal region of rural contentment and pastoral simplicity. Act I of *Iolanthe* is set in an Arcadian landscape.
257 *otto*: A scent known as 'attar of roses', distilled from rose petals and obtained from the Balkan states.
258 *Watteau*: Antoine Watteau (1684–1721) was a French painter who specialized in idyllic pastoral scenes.
259 *Breathing concentrated otto*: The *Fun* sketch, the licence copy, the first edition of the libretto and the current Macmillan edition of the Savoy Operas all render this line: 'Bless us, concentrated otto!'
260 *Picture, then, my client naming*: The 1884 prompt-book directs that at this point 'Plaintiff coquets with jury'. On the word *'trousseau'*, she shows a pair of pink stockings, and at the Counsel's 'Cheer up, my pretty', she staggers into his arms.
265 *trousseau*: A bride's outfit of clothes, household linen etc. From the French word *trousse*, meaning a bundle.

272 *Is plain to see*: In the first edition of the libretto and in most Chappell editions, this line reads 'Is plain to me'. It appears in that form also in the Oxford University Press World's Classics edition.

274 *Recline on me*: In the licence copy, and in some editions of the libretto, though not the first one, this line appeared as 'Lean on me'.

ALL.

Sweetly smiled, etc.

COUNSEL.

Swiftly fled each honeyed hour
 Spent with this unmanly male!
Camberwell became a bower,   255
 Peckham an Arcadian Vale,
Breathing concentrated otto! –
 An existence *à la* Watteau.

ALL.

Breathing concentrated otto! etc.

COUNSEL.

Picture, then, my client naming,   260
 And insisting on the day:
Picture him excuses framing –
 Going from her far away:
Doubly criminal to do so,
For the maid had bought her *trousseau*!   265

ALL.

Doubly criminal, etc.

COUNSEL (*to* PLAINTIFF, *who weeps*).

Cheer up, my pretty – oh, cheer up!

JURY.

Cheer up, cheer up, we love you!

(COUNSEL *leads* PLAINTIFF *fondly into Witness-box; he takes a tender leave
of her, and resumes his place in Court.* PLAINTIFF *reels as if about to faint.*) 270

JUDGE.

That she is reeling
 Is plain to see!

FOREMAN.

If faint you're feeling
 Recline on me!

278 *Oh, perjured lover*: Although this phrase appeared in the licence copy, it was not in the first published edition of the libretto, and when it did first appear in print, it was in the form 'Oh, perjured monster'.

286 *From far Cologne*: *Eau de Cologne* is a perfumed spirit which was invented by Johann Maria Farina, an Italian chemist who settled in Cologne in 1709. The recipe prescribes twelve drops of each of the essential oils (bergamot, citron, neroli, orange and rosemary) with one drum of Malabar cardamoms and a gallon of rectified spirits, all of which are distilled together. Guaranteed to restore fainting plaintiffs to their senses.

294–318 *Oh, gentlemen, listen, I pray*

The Defendant's song was apparently written at the last minute. It does not appear in the copy of the libretto sent to the Lord Chamberlain for licensing a week or so before the first performance. Instead there is a gap with the word 'Song' above it.

The prompt-book for the 1884 revival has the following stage direction at the beginning of this song: *'As Defendant begins to sing the Jury turn their backs and read newspapers'*.

(*She falls sobbing on to the* FOREMAN'S *breast.*) 275

PLAINTIFF (*feebly*).

I shall recover
If left alone.

ALL (*shaking their fists at* DEFENDANT).

Oh, perjured lover,
Atone! atone!

FOREMAN.

Just like a father   280
I wish to be.   (*Kissing her.*)

JUDGE (*approaching her*).

Or, if you'd rather,
Recline on me!

(*She jumps on to Bench, sits down by the* JUDGE, *and falls sobbing on his breast.*)

COUNSEL.

Oh! fetch some water   285
From far Cologne!

ALL.

For this sad slaughter
Atone! atone!

JURY (*shaking fists at* DEFENDANT).

Monster, dread our fury –
There's the Judge, and we're the Jury!   290
Monster, monster,
Dread our fury.

USHER.

Silence in Court!

SONG – DEFENDANT.

Oh, gentlemen, listen, I pray,
Though I own that my heart has been ranging,   295

306 *Consider the moral*: The 1884 stage direction as the bridesmaids rush forward at this point is: '*Jury turn and show the greatest affection – but repeat the business with papers as Defendant sings*'.

310 *To turn his attention to dinner*: The first edition of the libretto and the current Macmillan edition render this line as 'To turn your attention to dinner'.

312 *To look upon him as a glutton*: In the first-edition libretto and the Macmillan edition, this line is: 'That you could hold him as a glutton'.

315 *But this I am willing to say*: The first-edition libretto has 'But this I am ready to say'. In this case, the Macmillan edition has been brought up to date.

316 *If it will appease her sorrow*: In the first-edition libretto, 'If it will appease their sorrow'.

319 *But this he is willing to say*: The stage direction in the 1884 prompt-book at this point was: 'Defendant again remonstrates with the Judge who dips his pen in ink and throws ink in Defendant's eye'.

In the first edition of the libretto, and, therefore, possibly in early performances of the opera, there were no refrains for the chorus in this song. The second verse ended with the line 'Determines to tackle the mutton', after which the Defendant repeated 'Consider the moral, I pray'. He then had a third verse, cut out by the time of the 1884 revival, which went as follows:

> Oh, beware a dilemma so strange,
>   It will soon play the deuce with your dollars,
> It will soon be illegal to change
>   Your money, your mind, or your collars;
> A singer must sing the same song
>   From the time of his youth to his latter days;
> 'Twill be eight o'clock all the day long,
>   And the week will be nothing but Saturdays!
>   But this I am ready to say,
>   If it will appease their sorrow,
>   I'll marry one lady to-day,
>   And I'll marry the other to-morrow!

323 *Burglaree*: It would be more accurate, and would provide just as good a rhyme, for the Defendant to have said 'Bigamee' at this point.

The 1884 prompt-book has a further stage direction here: 'The Judge now requests the Plaintiff to go down – she refuses but he insists – she then goes reluctantly a couple of paces and then rushes back and sticks pen in Judge's wig – she then comes down and flirts with the Jury and the Usher'.

325 *the reign of James the Second*: Men of learning, like the Judge, will need no prompting on this, but others may care to be reminded that James II ruled from 1685 to 1689, when he was supplanted by William of Orange in the Glorious Revolution.

Of nature the laws I obey,
  For nature is constantly changing.
The moon in her phases is found,
  The time and the wind and the weather,
The months in succession come round,   300
  And you don't find two Mondays together.
  Ah! Consider the moral, I pray,
    Nor bring a young fellow to sorrow,
  Who loves this young lady to-day,
    And loves that young lady to-morrow.   305

BRIDESMAIDS (*rushing forward, and kneeling to* JURY).

  Consider the moral, etc.

You cannot eat breakfast all day,
  Nor is it the act of a sinner,
When breakfast is taken away,
  To turn his attention to dinner;   310
And it's not in the range of belief,
  To look upon him as a glutton,
Who, when he is tired of beef,
  Determines to tackle the mutton.
  But this I am willing to say,   315
    If it will appease her sorrow,
  I'll marry this lady to-day,
    And I'll marry the other to-morrow!

BRIDESMAIDS (*rushing forward as before*).

  But this he is willing to say, etc.

RECITATIVE – JUDGE.

That seems a reasonable proposition,   320
To which, I think, your client may agree.

COUNSEL.

But, I submit, m'lud, with all submission,
To marry two at once is Burglaree!

  (*Referring to law book*)

In the reign of James the Second,   325
It was generally reckoned
As a rather serious crime
To marry two wives at one time.

330 *Oh, man of learning*: At this point the licence copy continues with the following passages for the Judge, Usher and chorus, none of which was ever performed or probably even set to music:

RECITATIVE – Judge.

We do not deal with artificial crime,
Nor do we wish barbaric law to borrow.
Besides, he does not say two at one time –
He says, 'One wife today – one wife tomorrow'.

All.   Oh, Judge discerning!

SOLO – Usher.

His lordship's always quits
   In points like this contesting.
This keen exchange of wits
   Is always interesting.
These epigrams so bright,
   Like stars in autumn falling,
Relieve with points of light
   The Usher's gloomy calling.

Chorus.   His Lordship's always right, etc.

(*During this* Usher *cries* 'Silence in Court').

Judge.   If you're quite finished will you kindly state
                There is another verse, but that can wait.

The licence copy then continues with the quartet 'A nice dilemma', as now.

340 *A nice dilemma*: At this point the 1884 prompt-book directs: 'Each of the principals singles out an imaginary person in the stalls and sings to them – but not offensively'.

(*Hands book up to* JUDGE, *who reads it.*)

ALL.

Oh, man of learning! 330

QUARTET.

JUDGE.

A nice dilemma we have here,
That calls for all our wit,
For all our wit:

COUNSEL.

And at this stage, it don't appear
That we can settle it. 335

DEFENDANT (*in Witness-box*).

If I to wed the girl am loth
A breach 'twill surely be –

PLAINTIFF.

And if he goes and marries both,
It counts as Burglaree!

ALL.

A nice dilemma, etc. 340

DUET – PLAINTIFF *and* DEFENDANT.

PLAINTIFF (*embracing him rapturously*).

I love him – I love him – with fervour unceasing,
    I worship and madly adore;
My blind adoration is always increasing,
    My loss I shall ever deplore.
Oh, see what a blessing, what love and caressing 345
    I've lost, and remember it, pray,
When you I'm addressing, are busy assessing
    The damages Edwin must pay!
    Yes, he must pay!

350 *I smoke like a furnace*: Here the 1884 direction is: 'As Defendant begins to sing the Jury suddenly disappear. The Ladies and Barristers get up to see where they have gone'. The jurymen then rise again at the end of the song.

358 *Yes, he must pay*: This line was not in either the licence copy or the first published edition of the libretto. In the former, the Defendant continues his song as follows:

> Oh, let this Jury know
> What ought they for to do!

This leads straight into the Judge's *recitative*, 'The question, gentlemen – is one of liquor'. The first edition has the jury's 'We would be fairly acting,/But this is most distracting' but does not have their next two lines, nor the public's 'She loves him and madly adores him'. These were added after the first night. These are also missing from the current Macmillan edition.

368 *He says, when tipsy, he would thrash and kick her*: In the first-edition libretto this line was 'If he, when tipsy, would assault and kick her'.

DEFENDANT (*repelling her furiously*).

I smoke like a furnace – I'm always in liquor,   350
    A ruffian – a bully – a sot;
I'm sure I should thrash her, perhaps I should kick her,
    I am such a very bad lot!
I'm not prepossessing, as you may be guessing,
    She couldn't endure me a day;   355
Recall my professing, when you are assessing
    The damages Edwin must pay!

PLAINTIFF.

Yes, he must pay!

    (*She clings to him passionately; after a struggle, he
      throws her off into arms of* COUNSEL.)   360

JURY.

    We would be fairly acting,
    But this is most distracting!
    If, when in liquor, he would kick her,
    That is an abatement.

PUBLIC.

    She loves him and madly adores him, etc.   365

RECITATIVE – JUDGE.

The question, gentlemen – is one of liquor;
    You ask for guidance – this is my reply:
He says, when tipsy, he would thrash and kick her,
    Let's make him tipsy, gentlemen, and try!

COUNSEL.

    With all respect   370
    I do object!

PLAINTIFF.

    I do object!

DEFENDANT.

    I don't object!

378 *I can't sit up here all day*: In the first edition, 'I can't stop up here all day'. The licence copy, however, has the present version.

379 *I must shortly get away*: Here, the first edition has 'I must shortly go away', although once again the licence copy is as now.

382 *Gentle, simple-minded Usher*: This and the next line were not in the first-edition libretto although they were in the licence copy.

385 *I will marry her myself*: The last two lines of the Judge's song occur in Gilbert's original *Fun* sketch, the final passage of which is as follows:

SOLO – JUDGE.

In the course of my career
As a judex sitting here,
Never, never, I declare,
Have I seen a maid so fair!

ALL.   Ah! Sly dog!

See her sinking on her knees
In the Court of Common Pleas –
Place your briefs upon the shelf
I will marry her myself!
(*He throws himself into her arms.*)

ALL.   Ah! Sly dog!

RECITATIVE – JUDGE.

Come all of you – the breakfast I'll prepare –
Five hundred and eleven, Eaton Square.

FINAL CHORUS.

Trial la law! Trial la law!
Singing so merrily, Trial la law!

The licence copy continues in a rather different vein after the line 'I will marry her myself':

PLAINTIFF. Oh, rapture!
DEFENDANT.   Oh rapture!
BOTH.   Oh, joy unalloyed!
JUDGE. With this rapture,
PLAINTIFF.   This capture,
BOTH.   I am overjoyed!

ALL.   Oh, joy unbounded, etc.

388–420 *FINALE*

The finale of *Trial by Jury* has undergone a number of important changes since Gilbert first conceived it, not least in the introduction of a Grand Transformation Scene in the best pantomime tradition.

In the licence copy, lines 413–20 are rendered as follows:

JUDGE.   Though defendant is a snob,
ALL.   And a great snob too.
JUDGE.   A wretched little snob,
ALL.   And a great snob too.
JUDGE.   Though defendant is a snob,
                               I'll reward him from my fob,
                               Then I'll go and do the job.
ALL.   And a good job too!

ALL.

With all respect
We do object! 375

JUDGE (*tossing his books and papers about*).

All the legal furies seize you!
No proposal seems to please you,
I can't sit up here all day,
I must shortly get away.
Barristers, and you, attorneys, 380
Set out on your homeward journeys:
Gentle, simple-minded Usher,
Get you, if you like, to Russ*her*;
Put your briefs upon the shelf,
I will marry her myself! 385

(*He comes down from Bench to floor of Court.
He embraces* ANGELINA.)

FINALE.

PLAINTIFF.

Oh, joy unbounded,
With wealth surrounded,
The knell is sounded 390
Of grief and woe.

COUNSEL.

With love devoted
On you he's doated.
To castle moated
Away they go. 395

DEFENDANT.

I wonder whether
They'll live together
In marriage tether
In manner true?

USHER.

It seems to me, sir, 400
Of such as she, sir,
A judge is he, sir,
And a good judge too.

The first-edition libretto ends at line 412, as does the current Macmillan edition of the Savoy Operas, although the earliest vocal score has lines 413–20 as they are now sung, except that lines 417 and 418 are given to the Judge (the latter being 'I'll reward him from my fob') rather than to the chorus.

The first-edition libretto ends with the stage direction 'JUDGE *and* PLAINTIFF *dance back, hornpipe step, and get on to the Bench –* the BRIDESMAIDS *take the eight garlands of roses from behind the Judge's desk and draw them across floor of Court, so that they radiate from the desk. Two plaster Cupids in bar wigs descend from flies. Red fire.'*

A much more elaborate transformation scene was introduced into the finale for the 1884 revival. Indeed, two surviving prompt-books from that year in the D'Oyly Carte archives have different versions of this scene. One directs that it begins at line 405: 'At "Yes, I am a Judge" the Bridesmaids clap their hands à la Minstrels, Judge and Plaintiff dance hornpipe steps. For final picture Plaintiff gets on the Judge's back à la fairy – the two Bridesmaids with counsel and Defendant fall right and left – while the remaining Bridesmaids kneel with their arms over their heads. Cupids lowered a little before curtain.'

The other prompt-book has the following even more elaborate directions for what it calls the 'Trick Change':

> At the last 'And a good Judge too!' [line 412], the gong is struck for the trick change to fairyland. The canopy revolves. The fan pieces behind judge fall. Two revolving pieces on either side of Judge come round. The Rise comes up and covers Bench front. The Judge and associate's desks open. The Chamber flats are broken and taken away and wings pushed on. Cloth in front of benches and Jury box are let down and masking for same pushed on. The Jurymen, Counsel and Ladies have blue bells which they hold over Bridesmaids for final picture. At 'Yes, I am a Judge' the Bridesmaids clap their hands à la Minstrels. For final picture the Plaintiff gets on the Judge's back, the two Bridesmaids with Counsel and Defendant fall right and left while the remaining Bridesmaids kneel with their arms over their heads. Red fire.

The transformation scene was apparently abandoned in the 1920s because of the damage sustained by the plaster cupids while the Company was on tour.

ALL.

Oh, joy unbounded, etc.

JUDGE.

Yes, I am a Judge.   405

ALL.

And a good Judge too!

JUDGE.

Yes, I am a Judge.

ALL.

And a good Judge too!

JUDGE.

Though homeward as you trudge,
You declare my law is fudge,   410
Yet of beauty I'm a judge.

ALL.

And a good Judge too!

JUDGE.

Though defendant is a snob.

ALL.

And a great snob too!

JUDGE.

Though defendant is a snob.   415

ALL.

And a great snob too!
Though defendant is a snob,
He'll reward him with his fob.
So we've settled with the job,
And a good job too!   420

CURTAIN

THE SORCERER

DRAMATIS PERSONÆ

SIR MARMADUKE POINTDEXTRE (*an Elderly Baronet*)
ALEXIS (*of the Grenadier Guards – his Son*)
DR DALY (*Vicar of Ploverleigh*)
NOTARY
JOHN WELLINGTON WELLS (*of J. W. Wells & Co., Family Sorcerers*)
LADY SANGAZURE (*a Lady of Ancient Lineage*)
ALINE (*her Daughter – betrothed to Alexis*)
MRS PARTLET (*a Pew-opener*)
CONSTANCE (*her Daughter*)
Chorus of Villagers.

ACT I. – Exterior of Sir Marmaduke's Mansion. Mid-day.
(Twelve hours are supposed to elapse between Acts I and II)
ACT II. – Exterior of Sir Marmaduke's Mansion. Midnight.

THE SORCERER

Following the success of *Trial by Jury* Richard D'Oyly Carte was determined to keep Gilbert and Sullivan together to establish an English school of light opera to rival the French *opéra comique* style of Offenbach. This was to take some time, however. His librettist and composer initially went their separate ways, Gilbert to write more plays and contemplate a collaboration with Carl Rosa, and Sullivan to take up first the directorship of the Glasgow Orpheus Choir and then the principalship of the National Training School of Music (now the Royal College of Music).

D'Oyly Carte persisted in his scheme. Having been informed by Gilbert that there would need to be payment in advance before any new operas were written, he recruited four backers for a new Comedy Opera Company. They were Frank Chappell and George Metzler, both music publishers, Collard Augustus Drake, an associate of Metzler's, and Edward Hodgson Bayley, who was known as 'Water cart Bayley' because he owned the vehicles which sprinkled water over the dusty streets of London. With these four men as co-directors, the Comedy Opera Company was set up in 1876.

Carte now had the money to tempt Gilbert and Sullivan into further collaborations. For their first joint full-length work Gilbert resurrected the basic plot from a story which he had written for the *Graphic*. 'An Elixir of Love', as it was called, was about the effects of a magic love potion sold by a London firm of magicians to a country curate for distribution among his parishioners. Changing the professions of the central characters around slightly, Gilbert expanded this story into a libretto for a two-act operetta entitled *The Sorcerer*.

The comic and dramatic possibilities of a plot based on the use of a love potion had an extraordinary appeal to Gilbert. The theme is found in one of his *Bab Ballads*, 'The Cunning Woman', and in his first play, *Dulcamara*, which was a burlesque of Donizetti's famous opera *L'Elisir d'amore*. In later years he was constantly trying to interest Sullivan in another collaboration based on a story about a magic lozenge. The composer would have none of it, however, and when eventually, in 1892, Gilbert did produce another opera on this theme, *The Mountebanks*, it was with music by Alfred Cellier.

51

Love potions and their often unexpected effects have, of course, been a favourite theme of operatic librettists and composers. They figure prominently in Auber's *Le Philtre* and Wagner's *Tristan und Isolde* as well as in Donizetti's well-known work mentioned above. *The Sorcerer* provided Sullivan with some splendid opportunities to parody the operatic tradition, particularly in the incantation scene towards the end of Act I.

Richard D'Oyly Carte gave Gilbert a free hand in casting the new opera. In picking those who were to be the first principals of the new company, he deliberately avoided well-known names and instead chose those whom he could mould to fit his own conception of the characters. For the sorcerer he picked a little-known piano entertainer and former police court reporter called George Grossmith.

Grossmith, who had no pretensions to being an opera singer, was amazed when he was offered the role. 'I should have thought you would have required a fine man with a fine voice,' he observed to Gilbert. 'No, that is just what we don't want' was the emphatic reply.

For the stately Lady Sangazure, Gilbert chose Mrs Howard Paul, who ran a touring troupe of actors and singers. Mrs Paul, who helped to persuade Grossmith to join the new company, also insisted that Gilbert should take on one of her young protégés, Rutland Barrington. Like Grossmith, he was no opera singer, but his personality and style fitted the bill exactly: 'He's a staid, stolid swine, and that's what I want,' said Gilbert. Grossmith and Barrington were both, of course, to go on to become stalwarts of the D'Oyly Carte Company, creating nearly all of the great comic baritone and bass-baritone roles in the Savoy Operas.

The Sorcerer opened on 17 November 1877 at the Opéra Comique Theatre just off the Strand, which Carte had leased as the temporary first home for his new company. It ran for 178 performances until 24 May 1878. When first performed, it had no overture: Sullivan simply used the dance movement from his incidental music to Shakespeare's *King Henry VIII*. A proper overture was written for the opera's revival in 1884, when substantial changes were also made to the opening of the Second Act.

The Sorcerer remained in the D'Oyly Carte repertoire until June 1939. During the Second World War the scenery and costumes for the production were destroyed in an air-raid, and the opera was not performed again until 29 March 1971, when a new production by Michael Heyland, designed by Sir Osbert Lancaster, opened at the Palace Theatre, Manchester. It remained intermittently in the repertoire until the company closed in 1982. Like some of the other lesser-known Savoy Operas, *The Sorcerer* has never received a professional production other than by the D'Oyly Carte, and one wonders about its future now that the company has gone.

It will certainly be a great pity if it gradually fades away. *The Sorcerer* contains two of W. S. Gilbert's best-drawn characters, the soulful Dr Daly, who is, incidentally, the only clergyman in the Savoy Operas, and the flashy but ultimately tragic figure of John Wellington Wells. Sir Arthur Sullivan's music is delightful and guaranteed to weave a magic spell over all those who hear it, if not actually to make them fall instantly in love with their next-door neighbours.

1 *Scene*: The first edition of the libretto gave a rather fuller description of the scene for Act I: '*Garden of Sir Marmaduke's Elizabethan Mansion. The end of a large marquee, open, and showing portion of a table covered with white cloth, on which are joints of meat, tea pots, cups, bread and butter, jam, etc. A park in the background, with spire of church seen above the trees.*' Sir Osbert Lancaster followed these directions in designing his set for the 1971 D'Oyly Carte revival. He also put a few deer into Sir Marmaduke's park.

    The first edition of the libretto also gives the date of the action of *The Sorcerer* as 'the present day' and describes the chorus as 'peasantry' rather than 'villagers'.

10 *Pointdextre*: Gilbert deliberately used a heraldic term for the surname of his aristocratic heroine. The dexter point is the top right-hand corner of a coat of arms as carried by its bearer, i.e. the top left-hand corner as seen by a spectator.

11 *Sangazure*: Another carefully chosen surname – literally translated from the French, *sangazure* means 'blue blood', which, as we know from *Iolanthe* (see the note to Act I, line 394), is an indication of high or noble birth. Gilbert had used the name before in a short story called 'Diamonds' which appeared in *Routledge's Christmas Annual* for 1867. The central figure of the story was the Earl of Sangazure, K.G., the Lord Lieutenant of the county of Turniptopshire and honorary colonel of the local yeomanry.

16 *Mrs Partlet*: Yet another name designed to fit the character who bears it. Partlet was frequently used as the name for a hen, as in Chaucer's *Nun's Priest's Tale*, and it cannot be denied that Mrs Partlet has a certain slightly clucking quality about her.

    A word is needed about her strange-sounding occupation as given in the list of *Dramatis personæ*: a pew-opener went up and down the aisles of churches opening the private boxed pews which were rented by wealthy members of the congregation.

ACT I

SCENE. – *Exterior of Sir Marmaduke's Elizabethan Mansion.*

CHORUS OF VILLAGERS.

Ring forth, ye bells,
   With clarion sound –
Forget your knells,
   For joys abound.
Forget your notes
   Of mournful lay,
And from your throats
   Pour joy to-day.

For to-day young Alexis – young Alexis Pointdextre   10
   Is betrothed to Aline – to Aline Sangazure,
And that pride of his sex is – of his sex is to be next her,
   At the feast on the green – on the green, oh, be sure!
      Ring forth, ye bells, etc.

         (*Exeunt the men.*)   15

(*Enter* MRS PARTLET *with* CONSTANCE, *her daughter.*)

RECITATIVE.

MRS P. Constance, my daughter, why this strange depression?
   The village rings with seasonable joy,
   Because the young and amiable Alexis,
   Heir to the great Sir Marmaduke Pointdextre,   20
   Is plighted to Aline, the only daughter
   Of Annabella, Lady Sangazure.
   You, you alone are sad and out of spirits;
   What is the reason? Speak, my daughter, speak!

CON.   Oh, mother, do not ask! If my complexion   25
   From red to white should change in quick succession,

31 *must ne'er be known*: At this point the first-edition libretto has a continuation of the recitative for Mrs Partlet and her daughter:

MRS P.   My child, be candid – think not to deceive
           The eagle-eyed pew opener – You love!
CON. (*aside*). How guessed she that, my heart's most cherished secret?
      (*aloud*). I *do* love – fondly – madly – hopelessly!

Constance's aria 'When he is here' then follows.

34–49 *When he is here*
Although it was cut from libretti in the 1920s, a second verse to this aria still appears in the current edition of the vocal score and was sung in the last D'Oyly Carte recording of *The Sorcerer* in 1966:

> When I rejoice,
>   He shows no pleasure.
> When I am sad,
>   It grieves him not.
> His solemn voice
>   Has tones I treasure –
> My heart they glad,
>   They solace my unhappy lot!
> When I despond,
>   My woe they chasten –
> When I take heart,
>   My hope they cheer;
> With folly fond
>   To him I hasten –
> From him apart,
>   My life is very sad and drear!

In early productions, the women did not leave the stage until after the end of Constance's aria.

53 *He is here*: In the original libretto, Dr Daly makes his entrance at this point.

And then from white to red, oh, take no notice!
If my poor limbs should tremble with emotion,
Pay no attention, mother – it is nothing!
If long and deep-drawn sighs I chance to utter,   30
Oh, heed them not, their cause must ne'er be known!

(MRS PARTLET *motions to* CHORUS *to leave her with* CONSTANCE. *Exeunt Ladies of* CHORUS.)

ARIA – CONSTANCE.

When he is here,
    I sigh with pleasure –   35
When he is gone,
    I sigh with grief.
My hopeless fear
    No soul can measure –
His love alone   40
    Can give my aching heart relief!
When he is cold,
    I weep for sorrow –
When he is kind,
    I weep for joy.   45
My grief untold
    Knows no to-morrow –
My woe can find
    No hope, no solace, no alloy!

MRS P.   Come, tell me all about it! Do not fear –   50
         I, too, have loved; but that was long ago!
         Who is the object of your young affections?
CON.   Hush, mother! He is here! (*Looking off.*)
MRS P.   (*amazed*).   Our reverend vicar!
CON.   Oh, pity me, my heart is almost broken!   55
MRS P.   My child, be comforted. To such an union
         I shall not offer any opposition.
         Take him – he's yours! May you and he be happy!
CON.   But, mother dear, he is not yours to give!
MRS P.   That's true indeed!   60
CON.   He might object!
MRS P.   He might.
         But come – take heart – I'll probe him on the subject.
         Be comforted – leave this affair to me. (*They withdraw.*)

65 *Enter Dr Daly*: Dr Daly is the only clergyman to appear in the Savoy Operas, unless one counts the ghost bishop in *Ruddigore* or Pooh-Bah, who, among his many other sinecures, holds the position of Archbishop of Titipu. There was originally to have been two rival curates in *Patience*, but Gilbert decided to make them aesthetes instead. Dr Daly is a saintly figure, and perhaps the most endearing of all the characters in the G. & S. repertoire. The role was created by Rutland Barrington, whose father was a clergyman. A first-night review commented: 'Mr Barrington is wonderful. He always manages to sing one-sixteenth of a tone flat; it's so like a vicar'. The last D'Oyly Carte principal to play Dr Daly was Kenneth Sandford. For many Savoyards, including the present author, it was undoubtedly his greatest role.

In Michael Heyland's production, Dr Daly made his entrance on an old lady's bicycle. The idea for this came during rehearsals for the new production in Stratford-on-Avon in the autumn of 1970. The landlady with whom Jimmy Marsland, then the D'Oyly Carte staff producer, was staying, Mrs Buckingham, had an ancient bicycle in her shed which she had been trying to get rid of for some time. Marsland and Peter Riley, then the company's stage manager, took a look at it and decided it would make the perfect 'prop' to accompany Kenneth Sandford's entrance. Mrs Buckingham was more than pleased with the bunch of flowers she received in return. Her bicycle appeared on stage for more than ten years and also served as a convenient form of transport for stage-hands sent out to buy last-minute props. It is now stored, with the rest of the D'Oyly Carte costumes and props, in a warehouse in Camberwell.

After dismounting, Kenneth Sandford would walk over to the veranda in front of Sir Marmaduke's mansion and pick a flower, which he then smelled soulfully, the scent reminding him of love long ago. At an early performance of the new 1971 production Dame Bridget D'Oyly Carte was horrified to see that the flower he picked was a clematis – a variety that has no smell. In subsequent performances the dreamy parson always picked a rose.

75 *Forsaking even military men*: Shades of *Patience*, where the rapturous maidens forsake the officers of the 35th Dragoon Guards for the subtler attractions of Reginald Bunthorne and Archibald Grosvenor. The situation described in this song – of the idolization of young clergymen by their female parishioners – was at one stage to have been the basis of *Patience* before it was turned into a satire on the aesthetic movement.

84 *gilded dukes and belted earls*: The House of Lords was known as the Gilded Chamber, so 'gilded' is an appropriate adjective to use to denote nobility. In *H.M.S Pinafore* (Act I, line 214) Captain Corcoran asks Josephine if her heart is given to 'some gilded lordling'. The phrase 'belted earl' refers to the belt and spurs with which knights and others were invested when raised to their titles. In American usage a belted earl is a person who claims noble birth.

92 *she is nearly eighteen*: At seventeen Constance and Elsie Maynard in *The Yeomen of the Guard* share the distinction of being the youngest characters in the Savoy Operas whose age is actually mentioned. Patience is eighteen, and Phyllis in *Iolanthe* nineteen. There is strong evidence for suggesting that Yum-Yum is even younger, at sixteen (see *The Mikado*, Act I, line 333).

(*Enter* Dr Daly. *He is pensive and does not see them.*)   65

RECITATIVE – Dr Daly.

The air is charged with amatory numbers –
  Soft madrigals, and dreamy lovers' lays.
Peace, peace, old heart! Why waken from its slumbers
  The aching memory of the old, old days?

BALLAD.

Time was when Love and I were well acquainted.   70
  Time was when we walked ever hand in hand.
A saintly youth, with worldly thought untainted,
  None better-loved than I in all the land!
Time was, when maidens of the noblest station,
  Forsaking even military men,   75
Would gaze upon me, rapt in adoration –
  Ah me, I was a fair young curate then!

Had I a headache? sighed the maids assembled;
  Had I a cold? welled forth the silent tear;
Did I look pale? then half a parish trembled;   80
  And when I coughed all thought the end was near!
I had no care – no jealous doubts hung o'er me –
  For I was loved beyond all other men.
Fled gilded dukes and belted earls before me –
  Ah me, I was a pale young curate then!   85

(*At the conclusion of the ballad,* Mrs Partlet *comes
forward with* Constance.)

Mrs P. Good day, reverend sir.

Dr D. Ah, good Mrs Partlet, I am glad to see you. And your little
daughter, Constance! Why, she is quite a little woman, I declare!   90

Con. (*aside*). Oh, mother, I cannot speak to him!

Mrs P. Yes, reverend sir, she is nearly eighteen, and as good a girl as
ever stepped. (*Aside to* Dr D.) Ah, sir, I'm afraid I shall soon lose her!

Dr D. (*aside to* Mrs P.). Dear me, you pain me very much. Is she
delicate?   95

Mrs P. Oh no, sir – I don't mean that – but young girls look to get
married.

Dr D. Oh, I take you. To be sure. But there's plenty of time for that. Four
or five years hence, Mrs Partlet, four or five years hence. But when the time
does come, I shall have much pleasure in marrying her myself –   100

123 *puling*: Whining, crying in a querulous or plaintive tone.

125 *Enter Sir Marmaduke and Alexis*: In early productions of *The Sorcerer* Alexis appeared in the uniform of a Grenadier Guards officer in the First Act, and in regimental mess dress in the Second. Sir Osbert Lancaster decided, however, that as there was no mention of Alexis' military career in the opera (the only reference being in the list of *Dramatis personæ*), and as he was not with friends or colleagues from the regiment, he should be given ordinary civilian clothing. In the 1971 D'Oyly Carte production, Alexis and Sir Marmaduke made their entrance with croquet mallets as though they were in the middle of a game on the mansion lawns.

135 *May fortune bless you*: The exchange between Dr Daly and Sir Marmaduke, which is carried on to the accompaniment of a stately minuet, is, of course, a skit on the excessively polite and formal style of conversation associated with the late eighteenth- and early nineteenth-century aristocracy.

CON. (*aside*). Oh, mother!

DR D. To some strapping young fellow in her own rank of life.

CON. (*in tears*). He does *not* love me!

MRS P. I have often wondered, reverend sir (if you'll excuse the liberty), that *you* have never married.　　　　　　　　　　　　　　　105

DR D. (*aside*). Be still, my fluttering heart!

MRS P. A clergyman's wife does so much good in a village. Besides that, you are not as young as you were, and before very long you will want somebody to nurse you, and look after your little comforts.

DR D. Mrs Partlet, there is much truth in what you say. I am indeed　110 getting on in years, and a helpmate would cheer my declining days. Time was when it might have been; but I have left it too long – I am an old fogy, now, am I not, my dear? (*to* CONSTANCE) – a very old fogy, indeed. Ha! ha! No, Mrs Partlet, my mind is quite made up. I shall live and die a solitary old bachelor.　　　　　　　　　　　　　　　115

CON. Oh, mother, mother! (*Sobs on* MRS PARTLET's *bosom*.)

MRS P. Come, come, dear one, don't fret. At a more fitting time we will try again – we will try again.

(*Exeunt* MRS PARTLET *and* CONSTANCE.)

DR D. (*looking after them*). Poor little girl! I'm afraid she has something　120 on her mind. She is rather comely. Time was when this old heart would have throbbed in double-time at the sight of such a fairy form! But tush! I am puling! Here comes the young Alexis with his proud and happy father. Let me dry this tell-tale tear!

(*Enter* SIR MARMADUKE *and* ALEXIS.)　　　　　　　125

RECITATIVE.

DR D.　　Sir Marmaduke – my dear young friend, Alexis –
　　　　On this most happy, most auspicious plighting –
　　　　Permit me, as a true old friend, to tender
　　　　My best, my very best congratulations!

SIR M.　Sir, you are most obleeging!　　　　　　　　130

ALEXIS.　　　　　　　　　　Dr Daly,
　　　　My dear old tutor, and my valued pastor,
　　　　I thank you from the bottom of my heart!

(*Spoken through music.*)

DR D.　May fortune bless you! may the middle distance　　135
　　　　Of your young life be pleasant as the foreground –
　　　　The joyous foreground! and, when you have reached it,
　　　　May that which now is the far-off horizon
　　　　(But which will then become the middle distance),

152 *a reverie*: A fit of abstracted musing, a day-dream.

158 *Helen of Troy*: In Greek legend, the daughter of Zeus and Leda, and wife of Menelaus, king of Sparta, whose elopement with Paris brought about the siege and destruction of Troy. The exploits of Helen had been made the subject of a comic opera by Jacques Offenbach, *La Belle Hélène*, first performed in 1865.

163 *the lucid lake of liquid love*: A splendid piece of Gilbertian alliteration to rank with 'To sit in solemn silence in a dull, dark dock' in *The Mikado* and 'jerry-jailing, or jailing in joke' in *The Yeomen of the Guard*.

	In fruitful promise be exceeded only	140
	By that which will have opened, in the meantime,	
	Into a new and glorious horizon!	
Sir M.	Dear Sir, that is an excellent example	
	Of an old school of stately compliment	
	To which I have, through life, been much addicted.	145
	Will you obleege me with a copy of it,	
	In clerkly manuscript, that I myself	
	May use it on appropriate occasions?	
Dr D.	Sir, you shall have a fairly-written copy	
	Ere Sol has sunk into his western slumbers!	150

(*Exit* Dr Daly.)

Sir M. (*to* Alexis, *who is in a reverie*). Come, come, my son – your *fiancée* will be here in five minutes. Rouse yourself to receive her.

Alexis. Oh, rapture!

Sir M. Yes, you are a fortunate young fellow, and I will not disguise 155 from you that this union with the House of Sangazure realizes my fondest wishes. Aline is rich, and she comes of a sufficiently old family, for she is the seven thousand and thirty-seventh in direct descent from Helen of Troy. True, there was a blot on the escutcheon of that lady – that affair with Paris – but where is the family, other than my own, in which there is no flaw? You 160 are a lucky fellow, sir – a very lucky fellow!

Alexis. Father, I am welling over with limpid joy! No sicklying taint of sorrow overlies the lucid lake of liquid love, upon which, hand in hand, Aline and I are to float into eternity!

Sir M. Alexis, I desire that of your love for this young lady you do not 165 speak so openly. You are always singing ballads in praise of her beauty, and you expect the very menials who wait behind your chair, to chorus your ecstasies. It is not delicate.

Alexis. Father, a man who loves as I love –

Sir M. Pooh pooh, sir! fifty years ago I madly loved your future 170 mother-in-law, the Lady Sangazure, and I have reason to believe that she returned my love. But were we guilty of the indelicacy of publicly rushing into each other's arms, exclaiming –

'Oh, my adored one!' 'Beloved boy!'
'Ecstatic rapture!' 'Unmingled joy!' 175

which seems to be the modern fashion of love-making? No! it was 'Madam, I trust you are in the enjoyment of good health' – 'Sir, you are vastly polite, I protest I am mighty well' – and so forth. Much more delicate – much more respectful. But see – Aline approaches – let us retire, that she may compose herself for the interesting ceremony in which she is to play so important a part. 180

(*Exeunt* Sir Marmaduke *and* Alexis.)

196–215 *Oh, happy young heart*
This was one of four songs to be encored on the first night of *The Sorcerer*. The others were Sir Marmaduke and Lady Sangazure's duet 'Welcome joy, adieu to sadness', John Wellington Wells's introductory patter song, and the Act II quintet 'I rejoice that it's decided'.

216 *Enter Lady Sangazure*: Lady Sangazure, it may interest readers to know, is the only principal part in the Savoy Operas (other than *Trial by Jury*, where there is, of course, no dialogue) which has no spoken words at all.

(*Enter* ALINE, *on terrace, preceded by Chorus of Women.*)

CHORUS OF WOMEN.

With heart and with voice
　Let us welcome this mating:
To the youth of her choice,　　　　　　　　185
　With a heart palpitating,
　　Comes the lovely Aline!

May their love never cloy!
　May their bliss be unbounded!
With a halo of joy　　　　　　　　　　190
　May their lives be surrounded!
　　Heaven bless our Aline!

RECITATIVE – ALINE.

My kindly friends, I thank you for this greeting,
And as you wish me every earthly joy,
I trust your wishes may have quick fulfilment!　　195

ARIA – ALINE.

Oh, happy young heart!
　Comes thy young lord a-wooing
With joy in his eyes,
　And pride in his breast –
Make much of thy prize,　　　　　　　200
　For he is the best
That ever came a-suing.
　Yet – yet we must part,
　　　　　Young heart!
　Yet – yet we must part!　　　　　　205

Oh, merry young heart,
　Bright are the days of thy wooing!
But happier far
　The days untried –
No sorrow can mar,　　　　　　　　210
　When Love has tied
The knot there's no undoing.
　Then, never to part,
　　　　　Young heart!
　Then, never to part!　　　　　　　215

(*Enter* LADY SANGAZURE.)

217–20 *My child, I join in these congratulations*

As originally conceived by Gilbert, there was a duet for Aline and her mother and then a full-scale aria for the latter between this recitative and the chorus of men which now follows it. The licence copy sent to the Lord Chamberlain prints this duet as following immediately after the recitative:

DUET - ALINE AND LADY S.

ALINE.	Oh, why art thou sad, my mother?
	All nature is smiling now.
	In this village there's not another
	As solemn and glum as thou!
	It is idle attempt to smother
	Sad thoughts that wring thy brow!
	How can I console my mother?
	Oh answer me quickly – how?
CHORUS.	How can she console her mother?
	Oh answer her quickly – how?
LADY S.	My daughter, be blithe and merry
	Nor think of your sad mamma;
	My grief I will strive to bury
	And join in the gay ha! ha!
	My sorrows are selfish very
	And clash with the loud huzzah!
	They sadden the hey down derry
	And temper the tra! la! la!
CHORUS.	Her grief it is certain very
	Does temper the tra! la! la!

The above duet, which is similar in metre and rhythm to a song, 'Come, bumpers – aye, ever so many', written for Act II of *The Grand Duke* but also cut, was never performed. However, the solo for Lady Sangazure which followed it in the licence copy was also printed in the first published edition of the libretto and was probably sung at early performances. Here it is:

BALLAD - LADY SANGAZURE.

In days gone by, these eyes were bright,
  This bosom fair, these cheeks were rosy,
This faded brow was snowy white,
  These lips were fresh as new-plucked posy;
My girlish love he never guessed,
  Until the day when we were parted;
I treasured it within my heart,
  And lived alone and broken-hearted.

These cheeks are wan with age and care,
  These weary eyes have done their duty,
As white as falling snow my hair,
  And faded all my girlish beauty.
I see my every charm depart;
  But Memory's chain I cannot sever,
For ah, within my poor old heart
  The fire of love burns bright as ever!

235–86 *Welcome joy, adieu to sadness*

The *Observer* review of the first night of *The Sorcerer* commented: 'The duet sung by Sir Marmaduke and Lady Sangazure in Act I is a masterpiece of construction. The Baronet sings to the accompaniment of a gavotte, and suddenly bursts forth into a rapid semi-quaver passage, expressive of his admiration of the lady. She follows his example, and while one sings a slow movement the other sings the *presto* movement alternately.'

RECITATIVE – LADY S.

My child, I join in these congratulations:
Heed not the tear that dims this aged eye!
Old memories crowd around me. Though I sorrow,
'Tis for myself, Aline, and not for thee!　　　　　　220

(*Enter* ALEXIS, *preceded by Chorus of Men.*)

CHORUS OF MEN.

With heart and with voice
　　Let us welcome this mating;
To the maid of his choice,
　　With a heart palpitating,　　　　　　225
　　　　Comes Alexis the brave!

(SIR MARMADUKE *enters.* LADY SANGAZURE *and he exhibit signs of strong emotion at the sight of each other, which they endeavour to repress.* ALEXIS *and* ALINE *rush into each other's arms.*)

RECITATIVE.

ALEXIS.　Oh, my adored one!　　　　　　230
ALINE.　　　　Beloved boy!
ALEXIS.　Ecstatic rapture!
ALINE.　　　　Unmingled joy!

　　　　　　　　　(*They retire up.*)

DUET – SIR MARMADUKE *and* LADY SANGAZURE.

SIR M. (*with stately courtesy*).

　　Welcome joy, adieu to sadness!　　　　　　235
　　　　As Aurora gilds the day,
　　So those eyes, twin orbs of gladness,
　　　　Chase the clouds of care away.
　　Irresistible incentive
　　　　Bids me humbly kiss your hand;　　　　　　240
　　I'm your servant most attentive –
　　　　Most attentive to command!

(*Aside with frantic vehemence*)

　　Wild with adoration!
　　Mad with fascination!　　　　　　245

236 *Aurora*: The rising light of morning, or dawn. The Roman goddess Aurora set out with her rosy fingers before the sun to proclaim the coming of each new day.

251 *apostrophe like this*: An apostrophe is an exclamatory address in the course of a public speech or a poem to a particular person or object. In *The Mikado* (Act I, line 543) Ko-Ko accuses Pish-Tush of interrupting an apostrophe to matrimony.

263 *more truly knightly*: The first-edition libretto has 'true and knightly' here, as does the current Macmillan edition of the Savoy Operas. The licence copy, however, has 'truly knightly', as does the vocal score and other current editions of the libretto.

To indulge my lamentation
  No occasion do I miss!
Goaded to distraction
By maddening inaction,
I find some satisfaction   250
  In apostrophe like this:
  'Sangazure immortal,
    Sangazure divine,
  Welcome to my portal,
    Angel, oh, be mine!'   255

(Aloud with much ceremony)

Irresistible incentive
  Bids me humbly kiss your hand;
I'm your servant most attentive –
  Most attentive to command!   260

LADY S.   Sir, I thank you most politely
  For your graceful courtesee;
Compliment more truly knightly
  Never yet was paid to me!
Chivalry is an ingredient   265
  Sadly lacking in our land –
Sir, I am your most obedient,
  Most obedient to command!

(Aside with great vehemence)

Wild with adoration!   270
Mad with fascination!
To indulge my lamentation
  No occasion do I miss!
Goaded to distraction
By maddening inaction,   275
I find some satisfaction
  In apostrophe like this:
  'Marmaduke immortal,
    Marmaduke divine,
  Take me to thy portal,   280
    Loved one, oh, be mine!'

(Aloud with much ceremony)

Chivalry is an ingredient
  Sadly lacking in our land;

287 *the Notary has entered*: The notary is an ancient legal office whose chief function is to draw up, attest and certify deeds and documents. A great many of these functions are now performed by solicitors, and it is likely that the notary employed to draw up the marriage contract between Alexis and Aline came from this branch of the legal profession. In the first-edition libretto, however, the Notary is at this point referred to as the Counsel, and in the licence copy as an equity draftsman, which would suggest that he is a barrister. The business of the signing of the marriage contract is a take-off of similar scenes in grand opera, as for example in the Second Act of Rossini's *The Barber of Seville*, where a notary presides over the marriage of Rosina and Count Almaviva.

296 *I deliver it*: In early editions of the libretto, and still in the Macmillan edition, the chorus 'See they sign, without a quiver, it' precedes the solo lines for Alexis and Aline.

311 *At last we are alone*: The passage of dialogue which begins here has very close similarities with Gilbert's earlier story, 'An Elixir of Love', on which *The Sorcerer* was based. The central character in the story, it may be recalled, was the curate of Ploverleigh, the Revd Stanley Gay, who was engaged to Jessie Lightly, the only daughter of Sir Caractacus Lightly, a wealthy baronet who had a large house near the village.

> Mr Gay was an aesthetic Leveller. He held that as Love is the great bond of union between man and woman, no arbitrary outside obstacle should be allowed to interfere with its progress. He did not desire to abolish Rank, but he *did* desire that a mere difference in rank should not be an obstacle in the way of making two young people happy. . .
> Stanley Gay and Jessie had for many months given themselves up to the conviction that it was their duty to do all in their power to bring their fellow men and women together in holy matrimony, without regard to distinctions of age or rank. Stanley gave lectures on the subject at mechanics' institutes, and the mechanics were unanimous in their approval of his views. He preached his doctrine in workhouses, in beer-shops, and in lunatic asylums, and his listeners supported him with enthusiasm. He addressed navvies at the roadside on the humanizing advantages that would accrue to them if they married refined and wealthy ladies of rank, and not a navvy dissented. In short, he felt more and more convinced every day that he had at last discovered the true secret of human happiness. Still he had a formidable battle to fight with class prejudice, and he and Jessie pondered gravely on the difficulties that were before them, and on the best means of overcoming them.
> 'It's no use disguising the fact, Jessie,' said Mr Gay, 'that the Countesses won't like it.' And little Jessie gave a sigh, and owned that she expected some difficulty with the Countesses. 'We must look these things in the face, Jessie, it won't do to ignore them. We have convinced the humble mechanics and artisans, but the aristocracy hold aloof.'
> 'The working man is the true Intelligence after all,' said Jessie.
> 'He is a noble creature when he is quite sober,' said Gay. 'God bless him.'

    Sir, I am your most obedient, 285
    Most obedient to command!

(During this the NOTARY *has entered, with marriage contract.)*

RECITATIVE – NOTARY.

    All is prepared for sealing and for signing,
    The contract has been drafted as agreed;
CHORUS.   All is prepared, etc. 290

    Approach the table, oh, ye lovers pining,
    With hand and seal now execute the deed!
CHORUS.   Approach the table, etc.

*(*ALEXIS *and* ALINE *advance and sign,* ALEXIS *supported by*
SIR MARMADUKE, ALINE *by her Mother.)* 295

ALEXIS.   I deliver it – I deliver it
                  As my Act and Deed!

ALINE.   I deliver it – I deliver it
                  As my Act and Deed!

CHORUS.

    See they sign, without a quiver, it – 300
      Then to seal proceed.
    They deliver it – they deliver it
      As their Act and Deed!

    With heart and with voice
      Let us welcome this mating; 305
    Leave them here to rejoice,
      With true love palpitating,
        Alexis the brave,
        And the lovely Aline!

            (Exeunt all but ALEXIS *and* ALINE.*)* 310

ALEXIS. At last we are alone! My darling, you are now irrevocably betrothed to me. Are you not very, very happy?

ALINE. Oh, Alexis, can you doubt it? Do I not love you beyond all on earth, and am I not beloved in return? Is not true love, faithfully given and faithfully returned, the source of every earthly joy? 315

340–55 *Love feeds on many kinds of food, I know*
Alexis' ballad was written at the last moment. It is not included in the licence copy sent to the Lord Chamberlain shortly before the first night. There Alexis goes straight from 'He is a noble creature when he is quite sober' (line 336) to 'But I am going to take a desperate step' (line 357).

341, 343 *some for duty . . . youth and beauty*: One of two instances in *The Sorcerer* of Gilbert's favourite rhyming combination (see the note to *Trial by Jury*, lines 209, 211). The other is in Sir Marmaduke's verse in the Act II quintet:

> No high-born exacting beauty,
> Blazing like a jewelled sun –
> But a wife who'll do her duty,
> As that duty should be done!

ALEXIS. Of that there can be no doubt. Oh, that the world could be persuaded of the truth of that maxim! Oh, that the world would break down the artificial barriers of rank, wealth, education, age, beauty, habits, taste, and temper, and recognize the glorious principle, that in marriage alone is to be found the panacea for every ill! 320

ALINE. Continue to preach that sweet doctrine, and you will succeed, oh, evangel of true happiness!

ALEXIS. I hope so, but as yet the cause progresses but slowly. Still I have made some converts to the principle, that men and women should be coupled in matrimony without distinction of rank. I have lectured on the 325 subject at Mechanics' Institutes, and the mechanics were unanimous in favour of my views. I have preached in workhouses, beershops, and Lunatic Asylums, and I have been received with enthusiasm. I have addressed navvies on the advantages that would accrue to them if they married wealthy ladies of rank, and not a navvy dissented! 330

ALINE. Noble fellows! And yet there are those who hold that the uneducated classes are not open to argument! And what do the countesses say?

ALEXIS. Why, at present, it can't be denied, the aristocracy hold aloof.

ALINE. Ah, the working man is the true Intelligence after all! 335

ALEXIS. He is a noble creature when he is quite sober. Yes, Aline, true happiness comes of true love, and true love should be independent of external influences. It should live upon itself and by itself – in itself love should live for love alone!

BALLAD – ALEXIS.

Love feeds on many kinds of food, I know, 340
    Some love for rank, and some for duty:
Some give their hearts away for empty show,
    And others love for youth and beauty.
To love for money all the world is prone:
    Some love themselves, and live all lonely: 345
Give me the love that loves for love alone –
    I love that love – I love it only!

What man for any other joy can thirst,
    Whose loving wife adores him duly?
Want, misery, and care may do their worst, 350
    If loving woman loves you truly.
A lover's thoughts are ever with his own –
    None truly loved is ever lonely:
Give me the love that loves for love alone –
    I love that love – I love it only! 355

359 *St Mary Axe*: The street, which is pronounced, as it is later spelt in John Wellington Wells's patter song, 'Simmery Axe', runs between Leadenhall Street and Houndsditch in the City of London. In 'An Elixir of Love' Stanley Gay and Jessie Lightly got their magic potion from the firm of Baylis and Culpepper, magicians, in St Martin's Lane.

362–3 *within twelve hours*: Gilbert originally decided that Wells's love philtre should take effect within half an hour. In early editions of the libretto, and in early productions, the time supposed to elapse between Acts I and II was just half an hour. It was later changed to twelve hours. The current Macmillan edition still has 'half an hour' here.

366 *useful thing in a house*: The licence copy and first edition at this point have the additional line for Aline: 'Quite indispensable in the present state of Thames water'. Evidently the river had been cleaned up by the time of the opera's 1884 revival, as the phrase was dropped then.

369–70 *I said a philtre*: This exchange, which anticipates the famous 'orphan'/'often' misunderstanding in *The Pirates of Penzance* (Act I, lines 526–46), was originally longer. After Alexis' line 'I said a philtre', Aline continued: 'So did I, dear. *I* said a filter.' Alexis then responded: 'No dear, you said a filter. I don't mean a filter – I mean a philtre, – ph, you know.' Aline then came in with her line 'You dont mean a love potion?'

381 *Hercules*: In Greek mythology Hercules is, of course, the hero of superhuman strength who was rewarded by Zeus for his twelve great labours with the post of porter in heaven. He is always represented as brawny, muscular and of huge proportions. His namesake in *The Sorcerer* is tiny and weedy. The part is normally played by a small boy. Sir Henry Lytton, who was later to become principal comedian in the D'Oyly Carte Company, made his Gilbert and Sullivan debut in the part in a provincial company in the 1880s.

382 *Enter a Page from tent*: An un-dated D'Oyly Carte Company prompt-book has the following stage direction at this point: 'Enter Page with a pot of jam which he is trying to conceal by holding it to his left side. There is jam on his mouth and as he goes off he helps himself to more in view of the audience.'

ALINE. Oh, Alexis, those are noble principles!

ALEXIS. Yes, Aline, and I am going to take a desperate step in support of them. Have you ever heard of the firm of J. W. Wells & Co., the old-established Family Sorcerers in St Mary Axe?

ALINE. I have seen their advertisement. 360

ALEXIS. They have invented a philtre, which, if report may be believed, is simply infallible. I intend to distribute it through the village, and within twelve hours of my doing so there will not be an adult in the place who will not have learnt the secret of pure and lasting happiness. What do you say to that? 365

ALINE. Well, dear, of course a filter is a very useful thing in a house; but still I don't quite see that it is the sort of thing that places its possessor on the very pinnacle of earthly joy.

ALEXIS. Aline, you misunderstand me. I didn't say a filter – I said a philtre. 370

ALINE (*alarmed*). You don't mean a love-potion?

ALEXIS. On the contrary – I *do* mean a love-potion.

ALINE. Oh, Alexis! I don't think it would be right. I don't indeed. And then – a real magician! Oh, it would be downright wicked.

ALEXIS. Aline, is it, or is it not, a laudable object to steep the whole 375 village up to its lips in love, and to couple them in matrimony without distinction of age, rank, or fortune?

ALINE. Unquestionably, but –

ALEXIS. Then unpleasant as it must be to have recourse to supernatural aid, I must nevertheless pocket my aversion, in deference to the great and 380 good end I have in view. (*Calling*) Hercules.

(*Enter a Page from tent.*)

PAGE. Yes, sir.

ALEXIS. Is Mr Wells there?

PAGE. He's in the tent, sir – refreshing. 385

ALEXIS. Ask him to be so good as to step this way.

PAGE. Yes, sir. (*Exit Page.*)

ALINE. Oh, but, Alexis! A real Sorcerer! Oh, I shall be frightened to death!

ALEXIS. I trust my Aline will not yield to fear while the strong right 390 arm of her Alexis is here to protect her.

ALINE. It's nonsense, dear, to talk of your protecting me with your strong right arm, in face of the fact that this Family Sorcerer could change me into a guinea-pig before you could turn round.

ALEXIS. He *could* change you into a guinea-pig, no doubt, but it is most 395 unlikely that he would take such a liberty. It's a most respectable firm, and I am sure he would never be guilty of so untradesmanlike an act.

398 *Enter Mr Wells*: The D'Oyly Carte stage direction at this point reads: 'Wells affects to
be finishing a meal and cannot speak until he empties his mouth. Business of taking
off his gloves and blowing them out.'

John Wellington Wells is one of the great comic roles in the Savoy Operas and can
be played in a number of different ways. George Grossmith appeared in frock coat and
top hat. In Michael Heyland's D'Oyly Carte production, however, Wells was played
as a sharp East End 'spiv' dressed in frock coat and stylish grey bowler hat.

401 *Yes, sir, we practise Necromancy in all its branches*: For this passage of dialogue Gilbert
borrowed from his earlier story. In 'An Elixir of Love' he had written:

> The firm of Baylis and Culpepper stood at the very head of the London family magicians
> . . . They had a special reputation for a class of serviceable family nativity . . . the
> establishment at St Martin's Lane was also a 'Noted House for Amulets,' and if you wanted
> a neat, well-finished divining-rod, I don't know any place to which I would sooner
> recommend you. Their curses at a shilling per dozen were the cheapest things in the trade,
> and they sold thousands of them in the course of the year. Their blessings – also very cheap
> indeed, and quite effective – were not much asked for. 'We always keep a few on hand as
> curiosities and for completeness, but we don't sell two in the twelvemonth,' said Mr Baylis.
> 'A gentleman bought one last week to send to his mother-in-law, but it turned out that he
> was afflicted in the head, and the persons who had charge of him declined to pay for it, and
> it's been returned to us. But the sale of penny curses, especially on Saturday nights, is
> tremendous. We can't turn 'em out fast enough.'

403 *cast . . . a nativity*: Draw up a horoscope based on the subject's date and time of birth.

404 *Abudah chests*: Abudah was a merchant in Baghdad, haunted every night by an old hag
who appeared from a little box in his chamber and told him to seek out the talisman
of Oromanes. The story of Abudah was included in *Tales of the Genii*, a collection of
pseudo-Persian fairy tales by James Ridley.

408 *a rise in Unified*: A rise in the value of Government stock. In the first-night version
Wells spoke of 'a rise in Turkish stock', a topical reference at a time when Turkey was
borrowing heavily from Western Europe.

415–93 *My name is John Wellington Wells*

This is perhaps the greatest tongue-twister in the entire patter-song repertoire. John
Reed, the D'Oyly Carte principal comedian from 1959 to 1979, described it in an
interview with the *Washington Post* in 1978 as 'a killer. Just a list of words. Now that
is difficult. Nothing leads you to the next one. You could put them in any shape or
form if you lost the rhythm'.

When Sullivan was auditioning George Grossmith, he sang through this number
and then turned to the potential new recruit. 'You can do that?' he asked him.
Grossmith nodded and replied, 'Yes, I think I can do that'. 'Very well,' said Sullivan,
'if you can do that, you can do the rest'.

421 *melt a rich uncle in wax*: This is, of course, a reference to the old superstition that by
melting down a wax model, you could hasten someone's death.

423 *Djinn*: In Arabian mythology a spirit of supernatural powers. The word is more
commonly found as 'genie'.

424 *Number seventy, Simmery Axe*: A long correspondence filled the pages of the Gilbert and
Sullivan Society's journal some years ago as to whether such an address did, in fact,
exist. It seems that there was a 70 St Mary Axe, but the building which had that
number was recently demolished.

425 *a first-rate assortment*: In the first edition of the libretto, in the current Macmillan
edition, and in the Oxford University Press World's Classics edition of the Savoy
Operas, this phrase appears as 'a first-class assortment'. 'First-rate', however, appears
in the licence copy, the vocal score and other recent editions of the libretto and was
sung in D'Oyly Carte performances.

431 *We're keeping a very small prophet*: In early editions this line began 'We keep an
extremely small prophet'.

(*Enter* Mr Wells *from tent.*)

Mr W. Good day, sir. (Aline *much terrified*.)
Alexis. Good day – I believe you are a Sorcerer.   400
Mr W. Yes, sir, we practise Necromancy in all its branches. We've a choice assortment of wishing-caps, divining-rods, amulets, charms, and counter-charms. We can cast you a nativity at a low figure, and we have a horoscope at three-and-six that we can guarantee. Our Abudah chests, each containing a patent Hag who comes out and prophesies disasters, with   405
spring complete, are strongly recommended. Our Aladdin lamps are very chaste, and our Prophetic Tablets, foretelling everything – from a change of Ministry down to a rise in Unified – are much enquired for. Our penny Curse – one of the cheapest things in the trade – is considered infallible. We have some very superior Blessings, too, but they're very little asked for. We've   410
only sold one since Christmas – to a gentleman who bought it to send to his mother-in-law – but it turned out that he was afflicted in the head, and it's been returned on our hands. But our sale of penny Curses, especially on Saturday nights, is tremendous. We can't turn 'em out fast enough.

SONG – Mr Wells.

My name is John Wellington Wells,   415
I'm a dealer in magic and spells,
       In blessings and curses
       And ever-filled purses,
In prophecies, witches, and knells.

If you want a proud foe to 'make tracks' –   420
If you'd melt a rich uncle in wax –
       You've but to look in
       On our resident Djinn,
Number seventy, Simmery Axe!

We've a first-rate assortment of magic;   425
    And for raising a posthumous shade
With effects that are comic or tragic,
    There's no cheaper house in the trade.
Love-philtre – we've quantities of it;
    And for knowledge if any one burns,   430
We're keeping a very small prophet, a prophet
    Who brings us unbounded returns:

       For he can prophesy
       With a wink *of* his eye,

441 *He has answers oracular*: In early editions of the libretto, and in the current Macmillan
version, lines 441–4 appear in the following order:

> Mirrors so magical,
> Tetrapods tragical,
> Bogies spectacular,
> Answers oracular,

Both the Macmillan and World's Classics editions print the word 'With' before 'mirrors
so magical'. No doubt these lines were rearranged to make them easier to sing – it
makes no difference to the sense in which order they come.

443 *Tetrapods*: Verses of four metrical feet, commonly used by Greek tragedians.

455–6 *hosts/Of ghosts*: Shades (pardon the pun) of *Ruddigore*! There, of course, we get plenty
of gaunt and grisly spectres, though Gilbert resists the temptation to repeat the
rhymes he has used in this song. In Sir Roderic Murgatroyd's song 'When the night
wind howls', 'shrouds' are rhymed with 'clouds', not 'crowds' as here, and 'ghost'
with 'toast' rather than 'host'.

Peep with security   435
Into futurity,
Sum up your history,
Clear up a mystery,
Humour proclivity
For a nativity – for a nativity;   440
He has answers oracular,
Bogies spectacular,
Tetrapods tragical,
Mirrors so magical,
Facts astronomical,   445
Solemn or comical,
And, if you want it, he
Makes a reduction on taking a quantity!

      Oh!
If any one anything lacks,   450
He'll find it all ready in stacks,
    If he'll only look in
    On the resident Djinn,
Number seventy, Simmery Axe!

He can raise you hosts   455
        Of ghosts,
And that without reflectors;
  And creepy things
        With wings,
And gaunt and grisly spectres.   460
  He can fill you crowds
        Of shrouds,
And horrify you vastly;
  He can rack your brains
        With chains,   465
And gibberings grim and ghastly!

Then, if you plan it, he
Changes organity,
With an urbanity,
Full of Satanity,   470
Vexes humanity
With an inanity
Fatal to vanity –
Driving your foes to the verge of insanity!

477 *'Lectro-biology*: Electro-biology was an original branch of the study of electricity which dealt with electrical phenomena in living organisms. By the middle of the nineteenth century the phrase had come to be used for a form of hypnosis practised by popular entertainers and based on the so-called principles of animal magnetism.

478 *nosology*: The study of the classification of diseases. An even more extensive list of -ologies, which includes both 'lectro-biology' and nosology, appears in Gilbert's Bab Ballad 'The Student':

> I ask an ap-
> Is it zo-
> Is it conch-
> Is it ge-
> 'Lectro-bi-
> Meteor-   } ology?
> Is it nos-
> Or etym-
> P'raps it's myth-
> Is it the-
> Palaeont-
> Or archae-

495 *a Patent Oxy-Hydrogen Love-at-first-sight Philtre*: This was also the leading article of Messrs Baylis and Culpepper in 'An Elixir of Love'. They sold it at 1s. 1½d. and 2s. 3d., and demand for it was strong enough to keep the firm going, had all its other products ceased selling.

507 *In buying a quantity*: This passage was taken almost word for word from Gilbert's earlier story, where Mr Culpepper tells Stanley Gay and Jessie Lightly: 'In purchasing a large quantity, sir, we would strongly advise you taking it in the wood, and drawing it off as you happen to want it. We have it in four-and-a-half and nine-gallon casks, and we deduct ten per cent for cash payments.'

511–12 *the Army and Navy Stores*: A leading London department store, situated in Victoria Street between Westminster Abbey and Victoria Station. Lines 511–13 were not in the first edition of the libretto and were added by Gilbert at the time of the 1884 revival, possibly in response to an ad-lib 'gag' by one of the company. In the original libretto, after 'prompt cash' Aline had the line 'Oh, Alexis, surely you don't want to lay any down!'

514–15 *Go and fetch the tea-pot*: In 'An Elixir of Love' Stanley Gay used a rather more potent medium than tea in which to mix his love potion and distribute it to his 140 parishioners. He invented a somewhat implausible story that a widowed aunt who lived in Montilla had been compelled to take a large quantity of sherry from a bankrupt wine merchant in payment for a year's rent of her second-floor flat. Gay claimed that he had undertaken to sell the sherry in Ploverleigh and so he announced that he was distributing sample bottles (into which, of course, he had poured the potion) to all the villagers.

Barring tautology,   475
In demonology,
'Lectro-biology,
Mystic nosology,
Spirit philology,
High-class astrology,   480
Such is his knowledge, he
Isn't the man to require an apology!

Oh!
My name is John Wellington Wells,
I'm a dealer in magic and spells,   485
    In blessings and curses
    And ever-filled purses,
In prophecies, witches, and knells.

And if any one anything lacks,
He'll find it all ready in stacks,   490
    If he'll only look in
    On the resident Djinn,
Number seventy, Simmery Axe!

ALEXIS. I have sent for you to consult you on a very important matter. I
believe you advertise a Patent Oxy-Hydrogen Love-at-first-sight Philtre?   495
    MR W. Sir, it is our leading article. (*Producing a phial.*)
    ALEXIS. Now I want to know if you can confidently guarantee it as
possessing all the qualities you claim for it in your advertisment?
    MR W. Sir, we are not in the habit of puffing our goods. Ours is an old-
established house with a large family connection, and every assurance held   500
out in the advertisement is fully realized. (*Hurt.*)
    ALINE (*aside*). Oh, Alexis, don't offend him! He'll change us into
something dreadful – I know he will!
    ALEXIS. I am anxious from purely philanthropical motives to distribute
this philtre, secretly, among the inhabitants of this village. I shall of course   505
require a quantity. How do you sell it?
    MR W. In buying a quantity, sir, we should strongly advise your taking
it in the wood, and drawing it off as you happen to want it. We have it in
four-and-a-half and nine gallon casks – also in pipes and hogsheads for
laying down, and we deduct 10 per cent for prompt cash.   510
    ALEXIS. I should mention that I am a Member of the Army and Navy
Stores.
    MR W. In that case we deduct 25 per cent.
    ALEXIS. Aline, the villagers will assemble to carouse in a few minutes. Go
and fetch the tea-pot.   515

537–93 *Sprites of earth and air*

The incantation scene in *The Sorcerer* is a satire on the scene in Weber's opera *Der Freischütz* in which Max, a young huntsman, meets Caspar, the servant of the Devil, in the Wolf's Glen at midnight to witness the forging of seven magic bullets by Zamiel, a demon.

ALINE. But, Alexis –

ALEXIS. My dear, you must obey me, if you please. Go and fetch the tea-pot.

ALINE (*going*). I'm sure Dr Daly would disapprove of it!

(*Exit* ALINE.)   520

ALEXIS. And how soon does it take effect?

MR W. In twelve hours. Whoever drinks of it loses consciousness for that period, and on waking falls in love, as a matter of course, with the first lady he meets who has also tasted it, and his affection is at once returned. One trial will prove the fact.   525

(*Enter* ALINE *with large tea-pot.*)

ALEXIS. Good: then, Mr Wells, I shall feel obliged if you will at once pour as much philtre into this tea-pot as will suffice to affect the whole village.

ALINE. But bless me, Alexis, many of the villagers are married people!   530

MR W. Madam, this philtre is compounded on the strictest principles. On married people it has no effect whatever. But are you quite sure that you have nerve enough to carry you through the fearful ordeal?

ALEXIS. In the good cause I fear nothing.

MR W. Very good, then, we will proceed at once to the Incantation.   535

(*The stage grows dark.*)

INCANTATION.

MR W.	Sprites of earth and air –	
	Fiends of flame and fire –	
	Demon souls,	
	Come here in shoals,	540
	This dreadful deed inspire!	
	Appear, appear, appear.	
MALE VOICES.	Good master, we are here!	
MR W.	Noisome hags of night –	
	Imps of deadly shade –	545
	Pallid ghosts,	
	Arise in hosts,	
	And lend me all your aid.	
	Appear, appear, appear!	
FEMALE VOICES.	Good master, we are here!	550
ALEXIS (*aside*).	Hark, hark, they assemble,	
	These fiends of the night!	
ALINE (*aside*).	Oh, Alexis, I tremble,	
	Seek safety in flight!	

579 *pouring phial into tea-pot – flash*: This is the only real bit of pyrotechnics in the Savoy
Operas and is something of a stage manager's nightmare. For Michael Heyland's
D'Oyly Carte production a special tea-pot was constructed with a false bottom
concealing batteries and a fuse which triggered off a charge of flash powder. Wells
operated the device by flicking a switch on the tea-pot handle. He wore a witch's
pointed hat which was also wired up with a charge. Peter Riley can only recall one
near-disaster in all his time as stage manager when the hat caught fire and had to be
speedily removed by a stage-hand from the head of the oblivious J. W. Wells.

On the first night, Grossmith delighted the Opéra Comique audience during this
scene by shuffling round the stage clutching his tea-pot and imitating the hissing
funnel of a steam train. This 'locomotive gag', or 'tea-pot dance', as it came to be
known, had never been rehearsed and was one of the very few unauthorized bits of
business which Grossmith introduced into his stage performances in the Savoy
Operas. Gilbert readily approved it.

ARIA – ALINE.

Let us fly to a far-off land,   555
  Where peace and plenty dwell –
Where the sigh of the silver strand
  Is echoed in every shell.
To the joy that land will give,
  On the wings of Love we'll fly;   560
In innocence there to live –
  In innocence there to die!

CHORUS OF SPIRITS.

  Too late – too late,
    It may not be!
  That happy fate   565
    Is not for thee!

ALEXIS, ALINE, *and* MR WELLS.

  Too late – too late,
    That may not be!
  That happy fate
    Is not for { me!   570
                { thee!

MR WELLS.

Now, shrivelled hags, with poison bags,
  Discharge your loathsome loads!
Spit flame and fire, unholy choir!
  Belch forth your venom, toads!
Ye demons fell, with yelp and yell,   575
  Shed curses far afield –
Ye fiends of night, your filthy blight
  In noisome plenty yield!

MR WELLS (*pouring phial into tea-pot – flash*).
                  Number One!
CHORUS.   It is done!   580
MR W. (*same business*).   Number Two! (*flash*).
CHORUS.   One too few!
MR W. (*same business*).   Number Three! (*flash*).
CHORUS.   Set us free!
                Set us free – our work is done.   585
                  Ha! ha! ha!
                Set us free – our course is run!
                  Ha! ha! ha!

594 *Mr Wells beckons villagers*: The original stage direction in the first libretto continued at this point: '*Enter villagers and all the* dramatis personæ, *dancing joyously.* SIR MARMADUKE *enters with* LADY SANGAZURE. VICAR *enters, absorbed in thought. He is followed by* CONSTANCE. COUNSEL *enters, followed by* MRS PARTLET. MRS PARTLET & MR WELLS *distribute tea cups'*.

604 *Sally Lunn*: A plain, light tea-cake, which was usually split, toasted and served with jam. It was named after an eighteenth-century street vendor in Bath. The Sally Lunn makes two appearances in Gilbert's *Bab Ballads*. In 'Pantomimic Presentiments' it is referred to as 'the fine old crusted Sally', while the hero of 'Jester James' breakfasts off 'rolls and Sally Lunns'.

608 *Be happy all*: In the licence copy this is 'Be seated all'.

612–45 *TEA-CUP BRINDISI*
Brindisi is an Italian word for a toast, or health, drunk at some special occasion. It is used in this context to mean a drinking song, of the kind almost invariably found in Italian grand operas. The special feature of this particular toast, of course, is that it is entirely non-alcoholic. In calling it the 'Tea-Cup Brindisi', Gilbert may well have been having a quiet dig at the Victorian temperance movement with its rousing choruses extolling the virtues of tea and water. There is a brindisi of a more conventional kind in the original version of Act II of *The Grand Duke*, where the drink is champagne to celebrate the wedding of the Baroness von Krakenfeldt and the comedian Ludwig:

> So bumpers – aye, ever so many –
> And then, if you will, many more!
> This wine doesn't cost us a penny.
> Though it's Pommery, seventy-four!

ALINE *and* ALEXIS (*aside*).

Let us fly to a far-off land,
   Where peace and plenty dwell –   590
Where the sigh of the silver strand
   Is echoed in every shell.

CHORUS OF FIENDS.

Ha! ha! ha! ha! ha! ha! ha! ha! ha! ha!

(*Stage grows light.* MR WELLS *beckons villagers. Enter villagers and all the*
dramatis personæ, dancing joyously. MRS PARTLET *and* MR WELLS *then*   595
distribute tea-cups.)

CHORUS.

Now to the banquet we press;
   Now for the eggs and the ham;
Now for the mustard and cress,
   Now for the strawberry jam!   600
Now for the tea of our host,
   Now for the rollicking bun,
Now for the muffin and toast,
   And now for the gay Sally Lunn!

WOMEN.   The eggs and the ham, and the strawberry jam!   605
MEN.   The rollicking bun, and the gay Sally Lunn!
   The rollicking, rollicking bun!

RECITATIVE – SIR MARMADUKE.

Be happy all – the feast is spread before ye;
   Fear nothing, but enjoy yourselves, I pray!
Eat, aye, and drink – be merry, I implore ye,   610
   For once let thoughtless Folly rule the day.

TEA-CUP BRINDISI, 1st Verse – SIR M.

Eat, drink, and be gay,
   Banish all worry and sorrow,
Laugh gaily to-day,
   Weep, if you're sorry, to-morrow!   615
Come, pass the cup round –
   I will go bail for the liquor;
It's strong, I'll be bound,
   For it was brewed by the vicar!

621 *a jorum of tea*: Like *brindisi*, jorums are more usually associated with alcoholic liquor. They are large bowls of the kind used for serving punch or fruit cups. The name is thought to derive from King Joram who is described in the Bible (2 Samuel 8.10) as bringing 'vessels of silver, and vessels of gold, and vessels of brass'.

623 *A pretty stiff jorum of tea*: The first-edition libretto has the following stage direction at this point: 'DR DALY *places tea pot on tray held by* CONSTANCE. *He covers it with the cosy. She takes tray into the house.*'

CHORUS.

None so knowing as he   620
At brewing a jorum of tea,
  Ha! ha!
A pretty stiff jorum of tea.

TRIO – MR WELLS, ALINE, *and* ALEXIS (*aside*).

See – see – they drink –
  All thought unheeding,   625
The tea-cups clink,
  They are exceeding!
Their hearts will melt
  In half-an-hour –
Then will be felt   630
  The potion's power!

(*During this verse* CONSTANCE *has brought a small tea-pot, kettle, caddy, and
cosy to* DR DALY. *He makes tea scientifically.*)

BRINDISI, 2nd Verse – DR DALY (*with the tea-pot*).

Pain, trouble, and care,
  Misery, heart-ache, and worry,   635
Quick, out of your lair!
  Get you all gone in a hurry!
Toil, sorrow, and plot,
  Fly away quicker and quicker –
Three spoons to the pot –   640
  That is the brew of your vicar!

CHORUS.

None so cunning as he
At brewing a jorum of tea,
  Ha! ha!
A pretty stiff jorum of tea!   645

ENSEMBLE – ALEXIS *and* ALINE (*aside*).

Oh love, true love – unworldly, abiding!
  Source of all pleasure – true fountain of joy, –
Oh love, true love – divinely confiding,
  Exquisite treasure that knows no alloy!

663 *The company will draw*: In early editions this line was 'Society will draw'.

664 *Those who have partaken of the philtre*: In the first edition of the libretto this stage direction read: '*Those who have partaken of the philtre struggle against its effects, and resume the Brindisi with a violent effort.*' There then followed a reprise of the first verse of the Tea-Cup Brindisi. This was sung during the initial run at the Opéra Comique but cut for the 1884 revival at the Savoy, when the present ending to Act I, with the company falling insensible on the stage, was substituted.

Oh love, true love, rich harvest of gladness,   650
   Peace-bearing tillage – great garner of bliss, –
Oh love, true love, look down on our sadness –
   Dwell in this village – oh, hear us in this!

(It becomes evident by the strange conduct of the characters that the charm is working.
All rub their eyes, and stagger about the stage as if under the influence of a narcotic.)   655

TUTTI *(aside).*
Oh, marvellous illusion!
  Oh, terrible surprise!
What is this strange confusion
  That veils my aching eyes?
I must regain my senses,
  Restoring Reason's law,
Or fearful inferences
  The company will draw!

ALEXIS, MR WELLS, *and* ALINE *(aside).*
A marvellous illusion!
  A terrible surprise
Excites a strange confusion
  Within their aching eyes –
They must regain their senses,   660
  Restoring Reason's law,
Or fearful inferences
  The company will draw!

(Those who have partaken of the philtre struggle in vain against its effects, and, at the
end of the chorus, fall insensible on the stage.)   665

END OF ACT I

1–4 *Scene*: As originally conceived and performed, Act II of *The Sorcerer* was set in the village of Ploverleigh, with the action taking place half an hour after Act I, and with the villagers entering to sing an opening chorus. The licence copy and first published libretto had the following description of the scene: '*Market Place in the village. In centre a market cross or drinking fountain. Enter* PEASANTS *dancing, coupled two and two: an old man with a young girl, then an old woman with a young man, then other ill-assorted couples.*'

3–4 *a dark lantern*: A lantern with a sliding shutter of a kind often used by burglars. It is one of the implements which Samuel distributes to his fellow pirates before their attack on Tremorden Castle in Act II of *The Pirates of Penzance*.

5–30 '*Tis twelve, I think*
   In the first version of *The Sorcerer*, performed in 1877–8, there was no trio for Alexis, Aline and Mr Wells at the beginning of Act II. Nor did the villagers have their chorus 'Why, where be oi, and what be oi a doin''. Instead there was this much shorter opening chorus, which led straight on to Constance's aria 'Dear friends, take pity on my lot':

OPENING CHORUS.

Happy are we in our loving frivolity,
Happy and jolly as people of quality;
Love is the source of all joy to humanity,
Money, position, and rank are a vanity;
Year after year we've been waiting and tarrying,
Without ever dreaming of loving and marrying.
Though we've been hitherto deaf, dumb, and blind to it,
It's pleasant enough when you've made up your mind to it.

   When the opera was revived in 1884, this chorus was cut and the trio and chorus which now form lines 5–58 were added.

17 *A Baronet and K.C.B.*: Baronets, in whose ranks according to the list of *Dramatis personæ* we should number Sir Marmaduke Pointdextre, are members of the lowest hereditary titled order, which was instituted by James I in the early seventeenth century. The Murgatroyds in *Ruddigore* are baronets, and bad baronets at that. Indeed, in the opinion of Rose Maybud, 'All baronets are bad'. Obtaining baronetcies for M.P.s is one of the many tasks that the Duke and Duchess of Plaza-Toro will happily perform for the appropriate fee (*The Gondoliers*, Act II, line 610).
   K.C.B. stands for Knight Commander of the Bath. This is the second class of the Order of the Bath, the first being Grand Cross of the Bath (G.C.B.) and the third Companion of the Bath (C.B.). There are two other K.C.B.s in the Savoy Operas: Sir Joseph Porter in *H.M.S. Pinafore* and Captain Sir Edward Corcoran in *Utopia Limited*. Neither of them is a baronet, however. As both a baronet and a K.C.B., Sir Marmaduke has the right to be called 'Sir' twice over, as it were.

18 *A Doctor of Divinity*: The holder of an advanced degree in theology. It would be comparatively rare for an ordinary country parson to be a doctor of divinity, but Gilbert's village priests are obviously a scholarly lot. According to the pirates of Penzance (*Pirates*, Act I, line 432), another such well-qualified divine lives in the vicinity of their remote seaside lair.

19 *that respectable Q.C.*: As we have already noted (Act I, line 287), a notary is nearly always a solicitor, and it is highly unlikely that a barrister would officiate at the signing of a marriage contract. A solicitor, however, cannot be a Q.C. The initials stand for Queen's Counsel and apply to those senior barristers appointed by the Crown on the nomination of the Lord Chancellor and often known as 'silks' because of their gowns. In the first edition of the libretto, it may be remembered, the Notary was referred to in Act I as the Counsel and could therefore be a Q.C.

ACT II

SCENE. – *Exterior of* SIR MARMADUKE'S *mansion by moonlight. All the peasantry are discovered asleep on the ground, as at the end of Act I. Enter* MR WELLS, *on tiptoe, followed by* ALEXIS *and* ALINE. MR WELLS *carries a dark lantern.*

> TRIO – ALEXIS, ALINE, *and* MR WELLS.
>
> 'Tis twelve, I think,   5
>   And at this mystic hour
> The magic drink
>   Should manifest its power.
> Oh, slumbering forms,
>   How little have ye guessed   10
> The fire that warms
>   Each apathetic breast!

ALEXIS.   But stay, my father is not here!

ALINE.   And pray where is my mother dear?

MR WELLS.   I did not think it meet to see   15
            A dame of lengthy pedigree,
            A Baronet and K.C.B.,
            A Doctor of Divinity,
            And that respectable Q.C.,
            All fast asleep, al-fresco-ly,   20
            And so I had them carried home
            And put to bed respectably!
            I trust my conduct earns your approbation.

ALEXIS.   Sir, you have acted with discrimination,
            And shown more delicate appreciation   25
            Than we expect in persons of your station.

49 *Eh, but oi du loike you*: This rough approximation of a West Country accent is the only hint we are given by Gilbert as to the part of the country in which *The Sorcerer* is set. In his original story 'An Elixir of Love', however, he tells us that Ploverleigh is 'a picturesque little village in Dorsetshire, ten miles from anywhere'. We may reasonably surmise then that we are in Thomas Hardy country, and judging by the thickness of the accents in this chorus, not far from the Devon border.

MR WELLS. But soft – they waken, one by one –
               The spell has worked – the deed is done!
               I would suggest that we retire
               While Love, the Housemaid, lights her kitchen fire!   30

(*Exeunt* MR WELLS, ALEXIS, *and* ALINE, *on tiptoe, as the
villagers stretch their arms, yawn, rub their eyes, and sit up.*)

MEN.   Why, where be oi, and what be oi a doin',
               A sleepin' out, just when the dews du rise?
GIRLS.   Why, that's the very way your health to ruin,   35
               And don't seem quite respectable likewise!
MEN (*staring at girls*).   Eh, that's you!
                      Only think o' that now!
GIRLS (*coyly*).   What may you be at, now?
                      Tell me, du!   40
MEN (*admiringly*).   Eh, what a nose,
                      And eh, what eyes, miss!
                    Lips like a rose,
                      And cheeks likewise, miss!
GIRLS (*coyly*).   Oi tell you true,   45
                      Which I've never done, sir,
                    Oi like you
                      As I never loiked none, sir!
ALL.   Eh, but oi du loike you!

MEN.   If you'll marry me, I'll dig for you and
                      rake for you!   50
GIRLS.   If you'll marry me, I'll scrub for you and
                      bake for you!
MEN.   If you'll marry me, all others I'll forsake
                      for you!
ALL.   All this will I du, if you'll marry me!

GIRLS.   If you'll marry me, I'll cook for you and
                      brew for you!
MEN.   If you'll marry me, I've guineas not a few
                      for you!   55
GIRLS.   If you'll marry me, I'll take you in and du
                      for you!
ALL.   All this will I du, if you'll marry me!
                  Eh, but oi du loike you!

64 *reverend rector*: Dr Daly has already informed us (Act I, line 641) that he is Vicar of Ploverleigh, and that is, indeed, how he appears in the list of *Dramatis personæ*. Now Constance tells us that he is a rector. There is a technical difference between these two clerical titles: rectors were originally those who received the tithes in a parish and vicars those who did the duty of a parish for the owner or owners of the tithes. Strictly speaking, a parish priest is generally either a vicar or a rector, not both.

77 *You very plain old man*: In early performances, the chorus's lines preceded the Notary's and took the form:

> You very, very plain old man,
> She loves, she loves you madly!

The current Macmillan edition of the Savoy Operas still has this original version.

84 *sixty-seven nearly*: At sixty-six, the Notary shares with Scaphio in *Utopia Limited* the distinction of having the oldest declared age in the Savoy Operas. Iolanthe, who boasts a couple of centuries or so, is, of course, much older, but then she is a fairy.

95 *You very plain old man*: Here again, in early libretti and in the current Macmillan version, the chorus preceded the Notary with these lines:

> You're still everything that girls detest,
> But still she loves you dearly!

COUNTRY DANCE.

(*At end of dance, enter* CONSTANCE *in tears, leading*
NOTARY, *who carries an ear-trumpet*.)   60

ARIA – CONSTANCE.

Dear friends, take pity on my lot,
 My cup is not of nectar!
I long have loved – as who would not? –
 Our kind and reverend rector.
Long years ago my love began   65
 So sweetly – yet so sadly –
But when I saw this plain old man,
Away my old affection ran –
 I found I loved him madly.
  Oh!   70

(*To* NOTARY.)   You very, very plain old man,
 I love, I love you madly!
You very plain old man,
 I love you madly!

NOTARY.   I am a very deaf old man,   75
 And hear you very badly!

CHORUS.   You very plain old man,
 She loves you madly!

CONSTANCE.   I know not why I love him so;
 It is enchantment, surely!   80
He's dry and snuffy, deaf and slow,
 Ill-tempered, weak, and poorly!
He's ugly, and absurdly dressed,
 And sixty-seven nearly,
He's everything that I detest,   85
But if the truth must be confessed,
 I love him very dearly!
  Oh!

(*To* NOTARY.)   You're everything that I detest,
 But still I love you dearly!   90
You're all that I detest,
 I love you dearly!

NOTARY.   I caught that line, but for the rest
 I did not hear it clearly!

CHORUS.   You very plain old man,   95
 She loves you dearly!

111 *An anxious care*: Early editions of the libretto, the licence copy, the Oxford University
Press World's Classics edition and the current Macmillan edition all have 'A sorrow
rare' instead of 'An anxious care', which is found in the vocal score and modern libretti
and is generally sung.

(*During this verse* ALINE *and* ALEXIS *have entered at back unobserved.*)

ALINE *and* ALEXIS.

ALEXIS.   Oh joy! oh joy!
           The charm works well,
              And all are now united.   100
ALINE.   The blind young boy
           Obeys the spell,
              Their troth they all have plighted!

ENSEMBLE.

ALINE *and* ALEXIS.	CONSTANCE.	NOTARY.	
Oh joy! oh joy!	Oh, bitter joy!	Oh joy! oh joy!	
The charm works well,	No words can tell	No words can tell	105
And all are now	How my poor heart	My state of mind	
united!	is blighted!	delighted.	
The blind young boy	They'll soon employ	They'll soon employ	
Obeys the spell,	A marriage bell,	A marriage bell,	
Their troth they all	To say that we're	To say that we're	
have plighted.	united.	united.	
True happiness	I do confess	True happiness	110
Reigns everywhere,	An anxious care	Reigns everywhere,	
And dwells with both	My humbled spirit	And dwells with both	
the sexes,	vexes,	the sexes,	
And all will bless	And none will bless	And all will bless	
The thoughtful care	Example rare	Example rare	
Of their beloved	Of their beloved	Of their beloved	
Alexis!	Alexis!	Alexis.	115

(*All, except* ALEXIS *and* ALINE, *exeunt lovingly.*)

ALINE. How joyful they all seem in their new-found happiness! The whole village has paired off in the happiest manner. And yet not a match has been made that the hollow world would not consider ill-advised!

ALEXIS. But we are wiser – far wiser – than the world. Observe the good that will become of these ill-assorted unions. The miserly wife will check the reckless expenditure of her too frivolous consort, the wealthy husband will shower innumerable bonnets on his penniless bride, and the young and lively spouse will cheer the declining days of her aged partner with comic songs unceasing! 120 ... 125

ALINE. What a delightful prospect for him!

ALEXIS. But one thing remains to be done, that my happiness may be complete. We must drink the philtre ourselves, that I may be assured of your love for ever and ever.

ALINE. Oh, Alexis, do you doubt me? Is it necessary that such love as ours should be secured by artificial means? Oh, no, no, no! 130

135 *never, never change*: In Gilbert's original version of *The Sorcerer* this line was the cue for a ballad in which Aline swore her love for Alexis and asked him to have faith in her. The song, which appeared in the licence copy, went as follows:

BALLAD – ALINE.

Have faith in me – thou art my day –
    I turn to thee for love and light –
Take that life-giving love away
    And leave me in eternal night!
Thou art the hill – and I the dale –
    Thou art the sea and I the shell –
Thou art the wind and I the sail –
    Thou art the spring and I the well!
Without that spring no well would be,
    Have faith in me – have faith in me!

Have faith in me – the ripening corn
    Is faithful to the autumn sun!
Thou art the god of my young morn,
    My harvest god – oh doubting one!
Thou art the day and I the hour –
    Thou art the idol – I the throng –
Thou art the tree and I the flower –
    Thou art the singer – I the song.
Oh let the song be sung by thee –
    Have faith in me – have faith in me!

(*At the end of the ballad,* ALEXIS *rises and embraces* ALINE. *Enter* DR DALY.)

Before the first night and the publication of the libretto, Gilbert cut out this song and substituted Alexis' ballad 'Thou hast the power thy vaunted love'. He later reused many of the images from the abandoned song in the duet 'None shall part us' in *Iolanthe* (Act I, lines 229–44).

ALEXIS. My dear Aline, time works terrible changes, and I want to place
our love beyond the chance of change.

ALINE. Alexis, it is already far beyond that chance. Have faith in me, for   135
my love can never, never change!

ALEXIS. Then you absolutely refuse?

ALINE. I do. If you cannot trust me, you have no right to love me – no
right to be loved *by* me.

ALEXIS. Enough, Aline, I shall know how to interpret this refusal.

BALLAD – ALEXIS.

    Thou hast the power thy vaunted love   140
    To sanctify, all doubt above,
        Despite the gathering shade:
    To make that love of thine so sure
    That, come what may, it must endure
        Till time itself shall fade.   145
        Thy love is but a flower
        That fades within the hour!
        If such thy love, oh, shame!
        Call it by other name –
          It is not love!   150

    Thine is the power and thine alone,
    To place me on so proud a throne
        That kings might envy me!
    A priceless throne of love untold,
    More rare than orient pearl and gold.   155
        But no! No, thou wouldst be free!
        Such love is like the ray
        That dies within the day:
        If such thy love, oh, shame!
        Call it by other name –   160
          It is not love!

(*Enter* DR DALY.)

DR D. (*musing*). It is singular – it is very singular. It has overthrown all my
calculations. It is distinctly opposed to the doctrine of averages. I cannot
understand it.   165

ALINE. Dear Dr Daly, what has puzzled you?

DR D. My dear, this village has not hitherto been addicted to marrying
and giving in marriage. Hitherto the youths of this village have not been
enterprising, and the maidens have been distinctly coy. Judge then of my

188–9 *you will, I am sure, be pleased to hear*: The passage of dialogue which begins here has very close similarities with a conversation in 'An Elixir of Love' between Jessie and her father, who has been given some of Mr Gay's sherry by Zorah Clarke, the curate's old housekeeper and cook. Sir Caractacus speaks first:

'You will, I trust, be pleased to hear that my declining years are not unlikely to be solaced by the companionship of a good, virtuous, and companionable woman.'

'My dear papa,' said Jessie, 'do you really mean that – that you are likely to be married?'

'Indeed, Jessie, I think it is more than probable! You know you are going to leave me very soon, and my dear little nurse must be replaced, or what will become of me?'

Jessie's eyes filled with tears – but they were tears of joy.

'I cannot tell you, papa – dear, dear, papa – how happy you have made me.'

'And you will, I am sure, accept your new mamma with every feeling of respect and affection.'

'Any wife of yours is a mamma of mine,' said Jessie.

'My darling! Yes, Jessie, before very long I hope to lead to the altar a bride who will love and honour me as I deserve. She is no light and giddy girl, Jessie. She is a woman of sober age and staid demeanour, yet easy and comfortable in her ways. I am going to marry Mr Gay's cook, Zorah.'

'Zorah,' cried Jessie, 'dear, dear old Zorah! Oh, indeed, I am very, very glad and happy!'

'Bless you, my child,' said the Baronet. 'I knew my pet would not blame her poor old father for acting on the impulse of a heart that has never misled him. Yes, I think – nay, I am sure – that I have taken a wise and prudent step. Zorah is not what the world calls beautiful.'

'Zorah is very good, and very clean and honest, and quite, quite sober in her habits,' said Jessie warmly, 'and that is worth more – far more than beauty, dear papa. Beauty will fade and perish, but personal cleanliness is practically undying. It can be renewed whenever it discovers symptoms of decay. Oh, I am sure you will be happy!' And Jessie hurried off to tell Stanley Gay how nobly the potion had done its work.

surprise when I tell you that the whole village came to me in a body just 170
now, and implored me to join them in matrimony with as little delay as
possible. Even your excellent father has hinted to me that before very long
it is not unlikely that he also may change his condition.

ALINE. Oh, Alexis – do you hear that? Are you not delighted?

ALEXIS. Yes. I confess that a union between your mother and my 175
father would be a happy circumstance indeed. (*Crossing to* DR DALY.) My
dear sir – the news that you bring us is very gratifying.

DR D. Yes – still, in my eyes, it has its melancholy side. This universal
marrying recalls the happy days – now, alas, gone for ever – when I myself
might have – but tush! I am puling. I am too old to marry – and yet, within 180
the last half-hour, I have greatly yearned for companionship. I never
remarked it before, but the young maidens of this village are very comely. So
likewise are the middle-aged. Also the elderly. All are comely – and (*with a
deep sigh*) all are engaged!

ALINE. Here comes your father. 185

(*Enter* SIR MARMADUKE *with* MRS PARTLET, *arm-in-arm*.)

ALINE *and* ALEXIS (*aside*). Mrs Partlet!

SIR M. Dr Daly, give me joy. Alexis, my dear boy, you will, I am sure, be
pleased to hear that my declining days are not unlikely to be solaced by the
companionship of this good, virtuous, and amiable woman. 190

ALEXIS (*rather taken aback*). My dear father, this is not altogether what I
expected. I am certainly taken somewhat by surprise. Still it can hardly be
necessary to assure you that any wife of yours is a mother of mine. (*Aside to*
ALINE.) It is not quite what I could have wished.

MRS P. (*crossing to* ALEXIS). Oh, sir, I entreat your forgiveness. I am 195
aware that socially I am not heverythink that could be desired, nor am I
blessed with an abundance of worldly goods, but I can at least confer on your
estimable father the great and priceless dowry of a true, tender, and lovin'
'art!

ALEXIS (*coldly*). I do not question it. After all, a faithful love is the true 200
source of every earthly joy.

SIR M. I knew that my boy would not blame his poor father for acting on
the impulse of a heart that has never yet misled him. Zorah is not perhaps
what the world calls beautiful –

DR D. Still she is comely – distinctly comely. (*Sighs.*) 205

ALINE. Zorah is very good, and very clean, and honest, and quite, quite
sober in her habits: and that is worth far more than beauty, dear Sir
Marmaduke.

DR D. Yes; beauty will fade and perish, but personal cleanliness is
practically undying, for it can be renewed whenever it discovers symptoms 210
of decay. My dear Sir Marmaduke, I heartily congratulate you. (*Sighs.*)

212–38 *I rejoice that it's decided*
The first-night critics were unanimous in their praise of this number. The *Era* described it as 'the gem of the opera. It is written with delightful fluency and grace, is admirably harmonized, and the melody is fresh as the May dew.' The *Observer* commented: 'It is simply delicious and will be hailed with delight wherever piquant melody and exquisite counterpoint are appreciated.'

236 *No one's left to marry me*: In 'An Elixir of Love' the only person who finds himself unbetrothed in Ploverleigh is the Bishop who happens unexpectedly to visit the village:

> The good old Bishop had drunk freely of the philtre, but there was no one left to love him. It was pitiable to see the poor love-lorn prelate as he wandered disconsolately through the smiling meadows of Ploverleigh, pouring out the accents of his love to an incorporeal abstraction.

The Bishop, like Dr Daly, is destined not to remain single for long, however. Jessie cannot resist the temptation of trying the elixir, and he is the first person whom she meets after drinking it. The Bishop makes amends to the Revd Stanley Gay for taking his sweetheart by giving him the living of the neighbouring parish of Crawleigh, 'worth £1,800 per annum – the duty is extremely light, and the local society is unexceptional'. Gay is left as the only bachelor in Ploverleigh, and he marries off everyone else before taking up his new incumbency. The Bishop and Jessie live happily ever after at the Palace.

QUINTET.

ALEXIS, ALINE, SIR MARMADUKE, ZORAH, *and* DR DALY.

ALEXIS.

I rejoice that it's decided,
   Happy now will be his life,
For my father is provided
   With a true and tender wife.   215

ENSEMBLE.

She will tend him, nurse him, mend him,
   Air his linen, dry his tears;
Bless the thoughtful fates that send him
   Such a wife to soothe his years!

ALINE.

No young giddy thoughtless maiden,   220
   Full of graces, airs, and jeers –
But a sober widow, laden
   With the weight of fifty years!

SIR M.

No high-born exacting beauty,
   Blazing like a jewelled sun –   225
But a wife who'll do her duty,
   As that duty should be done!

ENSEMBLE.   She will tend him, etc.

MRS P.

I'm no saucy minx and giddy –
   Hussies such as them abound –   230
But a clean and tidy widdy
   Well be-known for miles around!

DR D.

All the village now have mated,
   All are happy as can be –
I to live alone am fated: 235
   No one's left to marry me!

241 *Enter Mr Wells*: In early productions, when this act was set in the market place of
Ploverleigh, this stage direction was: 'MR WELLS who has overheard part of the
quintet, and who has remained concealed behind the market cross, comes down as
they go off.'

259 *Why do you gaze at me*: Early editions of the libretto and both the Oxford University
Press and Macmillan versions have 'Why do you glare at one' here. 'Gaze at me'
occurs in the vocal score and modern libretti and is usually sung now.

ENSEMBLE.   No one's left to marry him!
           She will tend him, etc.

(*Exeunt* SIR MARMADUKE, MRS PARTLET, *and* ALINE, *with* ALEXIS.
      DR DALY *looks after them sentimentally, then exits with a sigh.*)   240

(*Enter* MR WELLS.)

RECITATIVE – MR WELLS.

    Oh, I have wrought much evil with my spells!
      And ill I can't undo!
    This is too bad of you, J. W. Wells –
      What wrong have they done you?   245

    And see – another love-lorn lady comes –
      Alas, poor stricken dame!
    A gentle pensiveness her life benumbs –
      And mine, alone, the blame!

(LADY SANGAZURE *enters. She is very melancholy.*)   250

LADY S.   Alas! ah me! and well-a-day!
           I sigh for love, and well I may,
           For I am very old and grey.
              But stay!

(*Sees* MR WELLS, *and becomes fascinated by him.*)   255

RECITATIVE.

LADY S.   What is this fairy form I see before me?
MR W.   Oh, horrible! – she's going to adore me!
           This last catastrophe is overpowering!
LADY S.   Why do you gaze at me with visage lowering?
           For pity's sake recoil not thus from me!   260
MR W.   My lady, leave me – this can never be!

DUET – LADY SANGAZURE *and* MR WELLS.

MR W.   Hate me! I drop my H's – have through life!
LADY S.   Love me! I'll drop them too!
MR W.   Hate me! I always eat peas with a knife!
LADY S.   Love me! I'll eat like you!   265

266 *One Tree Hill*: Harry Benford's *Gilbert and Sullivan Lexicon* lists no fewer than seven possible contenders for this reference. Perhaps the most likely, although it was closed down five years before *The Sorcerer* opened, was an amusement at Greenwich Fair. There were also One Tree Hills in the London suburbs of Blackheath, Hornsey, Honor Oak and New Cross and further out in the Laindon Hills in Essex and near Sevenoaks in Kent.

268 *Rosherville*: A pleasure garden, with a zoo, amusements and theatrical entertainments, which was established in the late 1830s in disused chalk quarries near Gravesend in Kent. It was particularly popular with working-class Londoners. In early libretti, and in the current Macmillan edition, lines 266 and 268 are transposed.

270 *my prejudices I'll for ever drop*: In early editions of the libretto this phrase was 'My prejudices I will drop'.

Gilbert originally intended Wells's duet with Lady Sangazure to be followed by a second incantation scene, in which Wells appeals to his demonic master Ahrimanes to be released from his sorcerer's vows. This lengthy scene, which is similar to the prologue of Heinrich Marschner's opera *The Vampire*, occurs in the licence copy, where it follows after Lady Sangazure's exit (line 303). The first recitative survived, in a rewritten form, into the first production but was cut in the 1884 revival. The rest was never performed and was probably never set to music by Sullivan.

RECITATIVE – Mr Wells.

Oh hideous doom – to scatter desolation,
And cause unhappiness on every hand!
To foster misalliance through the nation
And breed unequal matches in the land!
By nature I am mild, humane and tender,
It racks my soul such fearful sights to see!
I can no longer bear it! I will render
My fearful gift to him who gave it me!

INCANTATION.

Spirits short and spirits long –
Spirits weak and spirits strong –
Spirits slow and spirits fleet –
Spirits mixed and spirits neat –
Spirits dark and spirits fair –
Listen to my heart-felt prayer.

(The stage has grown dark – a gauze descends – imps appear.)

Chorus of Spirits.	We hear the spells
	    J. W. Wells!
	What terrors trouble you,
	    J. W. W.?
	Ha! ha! Ha! ha!
	Some terrors trouble him
	    J. W. Double him!
	Ha! ha! Ha! ha!

(The market cross opens and Ahrimanes is seen through transparency.)

Ahr.	Presumptuous wretch – what favours do you seek? You called me – I am here! What would you? Speak!
Mr W.	Ahrimanes – mighty master – Hear me – hear me now!
Chorus.	Hear him – hear him now!
Mr W.	Avert this terrible disaster – Free me from my vow!

Mr W.	Hate me! I often roll down One Tree Hill!
Lady S.	Love me! I'll meet you there!
Mr W.	Hate me! I spend the day at Rosherville!
Lady S.	Love me! that joy I'll share!

Lady S.	Love me! my prejudices I'll for ever drop!	270
Mr W.	Hate me! that's not enough!	
Lady S.	Love me! I'll come and help you in the shop!	
Mr W.	Hate me! the life is rough!	
Lady S.	Love me! my grammar I will all forswear!	
Mr W.	Hate me! abjure my lot!	275
Lady S.	Love me! I'll stick sunflowers in my hair!	
Mr W.	Hate me! they'll suit you not!	

RECITATIVE – Mr Wells.

At what I am going to say be not enraged –
I may not love you – for I am engaged!

Lady S. (*horrified*).	Engaged!	280
Mr W.	Engaged!	

To a maiden fair,
With bright brown hair,
   And a sweet and simple smile.
Who waits for me   285
By the sounding sea,
   On a South Pacific isle.

Mr W. (*aside*).	A lie!	No maiden waits me there!	
Lady S. (*mournfully*).		She has bright brown hair;	
Mr W. (*aside*).	A lie!	No maiden smiles on me!	290
Lady S. (*mournfully*).		By the sounding sea!	
Ensemble.		The sounding sea.	

ENSEMBLE.

Lady Sangazure	Mr Wells.	
Oh, agony, rage, despair!	Oh, agony, rage, despair!	
The maiden has bright brown hair,	Oh, where will this end – oh, where?	
And mine is as white as snow!	I should like very much to know!	295
False man, it will be your fault,	It will certainly be my fault,	
If I go to my family vault,	If she goes to her family vault,	
And bury my life-long woe!	To bury her life-long woe!	

Both.   The family vault – the family vault.

It will certainly be $\left\{ \begin{matrix} \text{your} \\ \text{my} \end{matrix} \right\}$ fault,   300

If $\left\{ \begin{matrix} \text{I go} \\ \text{she goes} \end{matrix} \right\}$ to $\left\{ \begin{matrix} \text{my} \\ \text{her} \end{matrix} \right\}$ family vault.

To bury $\left\{ \begin{matrix} \text{my} \\ \text{her} \end{matrix} \right\}$ life-long woe!

CHORUS.　　　　Free him from his vow!
　　　　　　　　Hear him, hear him now!
　　　　　　　　Ha! ha! Ha! ha! Ha! ha! Ha! ha!

SOLO – AHRIMANES.

If thou, audacious elf, will yield
　　Alexis to my grasp
And let his doom be signed and sealed
　　In Death's unpleasant clasp –
Or if thou wilt consent, thyself,
　　To come below with me,
I'll grant thy wish, presumptuous elf!
　　I want, or him, or thee!

CHORUS.　　　　Be dutiful, and obey.
　　　　　　　　Give us – give us our prey!
AHR.　　　　　　Or thou – or he
　　　　　　　　Which shall it be?
CHORUS.　　　　Or thou – or he
　　　　　　　　Which shall it be?
MR W.　　　　　Or I – or he –
　　　　　　　　Which shall it be?
CHORUS.　　　　Ha! ha! Ha! ha! Ha! ha! Ha! ha!
MR W.　　　　　Oh master, pity show!
CHORUS.　　　　No! No!
MR W.　　　　　To meet your views I'll try –
　　　　　　　　If one of us must go below –
CHORUS.　　　　Ho! Ho!
MR W.　　　　　I'd rather he than I!
AHR.　　　　　　Much rather?
MR W.　　　　　Much rather!
AHR.　　　　　　Greatly prefer it?
MR W.　　　　　Greatly prefer it!
CHORUS.　　　　Ha! ha! Ha! ha! Ha! ha! Ha! ha!
AHR.　　　　　　Good – be it so.
　　　　　　　　When he will go
　　　　　　　　With me below,
　　　　　　　　Just let me know.
　　　　　　　　Ring out his knell
　　　　　　　　And I will quell
　　　　　　　　The fatal spell
　　　　　　　　Till then – farewell!　　　　　　　*(He disappears.)*
CHORUS.　　　　Farewell! Farewell! Farewell!
　　　　　　　　Ha! ha! Ha! ha! Ha! ha! Ha! ha!

(The stage gains light as MR WELLS *makes off horror-stricken. Enter* ALINE.*)*

304 *Enter Aline*: In the licence copy and the first edition of the libretto, Aline has the following passage of dialogue after her entrance:

> This was to have been the happiest day of my life – but I am very far from happy! Alexis insists that I shall taste the philtre and when I try to persuade him that to do so would be an insult to my pure and lasting love, he tells me that I object because I do not desire that my love for him shall be eternal. Well (*sighing and producing a phial*), I can at least prove to him that, in that, he is unjust.

The first-edition libretto then continues with the recitative 'Alexis! Doubt me not, my loved one'. However, the licence copy goes straight into Aline's ballad, which is given an additional verse before the one now sung ('The fearful deed is done'):

(*Exit* LADY SANGAZURE, *in great anguish, accompanied by* MR WELLS.)

(*Enter* ALINE.)

RECITATIVE – ALINE.

Alexis! Doubt me not, my loved one! See,   305
Thine uttered will is sovereign law to me!
All fear – all thought of ill I cast away!
It is my darling's will, and I obey!

> (*She drinks the philtre.*)

The fearful deed is done,   310
   My love is near!
I go to meet my own
   In trembling fear!
If o'er us aught of ill
   Should cast a shade,   315
It was my darling's will,
   And I obeyed!

(*As* ALINE *is going off, she meets* DR DALY, *entering pensively. He is playing on
a flageolet. Under the influence of the spell she at once becomes strangely fascinated
by him, and exhibits every symptom of being hopelessly in love with him.*)   320

SONG – DR DALY.

Oh, my voice is sad and low
And with timid step I go –
For with load of love o'erladen
I enquire of every maiden,
'Will you wed me, little lady?'   325
Will you share my cottage shady?'
  Little lady answers 'No! No! No!
  Thank you for your kindly proffer –
  Good your heart, and full your coffer;
  Yet I must decline your offer –   330
    I'm engaged to So-and-so!' (*flageolet solo*)
      So-and-so! So-and-so!   ,,   ,,
      So-and-so! So-and-so!   ,,   ,,
    'I'm engaged to So-and-so!'
What a rogue young hearts to pillage!   335
What a worker on Love's tillage!
Every maiden in the village

No need, no need, my own,
   This spell to try.
My love is thine alone –
   For aye – for aye!
But every thought of ill
   I cast away –
It is my darling's will,
   And I obey!   (*She drinks.*)

331 *flageolet solo*: Dr Daly is not the only character in the Savoy Operas to accompany himself on the flageolet. Strephon and Phyllis are also supposed to play the small flute-like instrument at their entrances in Act I of *Iolanthe*. For the initial run of *The Sorcerer* Rutland Barrington learned how to play the flageolet and actually accompanied himself in this song. By the time of the 1884 revival, however, he had lost the knack and since then the accompaniment has generally been played from the orchestra pit. James Walker, musical director of the D'Oyly Carte Opera Company from 1968 to 1971, tried vainly to persuade Kenneth Sandford to emulate Barrington's early achievement.

354 *Rejoice with me*: In the first run of *The Sorcerer* Dr Daly and Aline ended their ensemble by singing these lines together instead of the present 'Rejoice with me':

Ye birds, and brooks, and fruitful trees,
With choral joy delight the breeze –
Rejoice, rejoice with me!

363 *Alexis, don't do that – you must not*: This line recalls the conversation in 'An Elixir of Love' between Stanley Gay and Jessie Lightly after the latter has taken the elixir and fallen in love with the Bishop:

'Why, Jessie – my own little love,' exclaimed Stanley. 'What in the world is the matter?'
And he put his arms fondly round her waist, and endeavoured to raise her face to his.
'Oh, no – no – Stanley – don't – you musn't – indeed, indeed, you musn't.'
'Why, my pet, what can you mean?'
'Oh, Stanley, Stanley – you will never, never forgive me.'
'Nonsense, child,' said he. 'My dear little Jessie is incapable of an act which is beyond the pale of forgiveness.' And he gently kissed her forehead.
'Stanley, you musn't do it – indeed you musn't.'

Is engaged to So-and-so! (*flageolet solo*)
So-and-so! So-and-so!   ,,   ,,
So-and-so! So-and-so!   ,,   ,,   340
All engaged to So-and-so!

(*At the end of the song* Dr Daly *sees* Aline, *and, under the
influence of the potion, falls in love with her.*)

ENSEMBLE – Aline *and* Dr Daly.

Oh, joyous boon! oh, mad delight;
Oh, sun and moon! oh, day and night!   345
  Rejoice, rejoice with me!
Proclaim our joy, ye birds above –
Ye brooklets, murmur forth our love,
  In choral ecstasy:

Dr D.	Oh, joyous boon!
Aline.	Oh, mad delight!
Dr D.	Oh, sun and moon!
Aline.	Oh, day and night!
Both.	Rejoice with me,
	Rejoice with me,
	Rejoice, rejoice with me!

Dr D. line = 350, Rejoice with me = 355 positioned at right margin.

(*Enter* Alexis.)

Alexis (*with rapture*). Aline, my only love, my happiness!
  The philtre – you have tasted it?
Aline (*with confusion*). Yes! Yes!   360
Alexis. Oh, joy, mine, mine for ever, and for aye!
                                      (*Embraces her.*)
Aline. Alexis, don't do that – you must not!
      (Dr Daly *interposes between them.*)
Alexis (*amazed*). Why?   365

DUET – Aline *and* Dr Daly.

Aline.
    Alas! that lovers thus should meet:
      Oh, pity, pity me!
    Oh, charge me not with cold deceit;
      Oh, pity, pity me!
    You bade me drink – with trembling awe   370
    I drank, and, by the potion's law,
    I loved the very first I saw!
      Oh, pity, pity me!

Dr D.	My dear young friend, consolèd be –	
	We pity, pity you.	375
	In this I'm not an agent free –	
	We pity, pity you.	
	Some most extraordinary spell	
	O'er us has cast its magic fell –	
	The consequence I need not tell.	380
	We pity, pity you.	

ENSEMBLE.

Alexis (*alone*).

Some most extraordinary spell

All.

O'er $\left\{ \begin{array}{c} \text{us} \\ \text{them} \end{array} \right\}$ has cast its magic fell –

Alexis (*furiously*).

False one, begone – I spurn thee,
To thy new lover turn thee!   385
Thy perfidy all men shall know.

Aline (*wildly*).   I could not help it!

Alexis (*calling off*).   Come one, come all!

Dr D.   We could not help it!

Alexis (*calling off*).   Obey my call!   390

Aline (*wildly*).   I could not help it!

Alexis (*calling off*).   Come hither, run!

Dr D.   We could not help it!

Alexis (*calling off*).   Come, every one!

(*Enter all the characters except* Lady Sangazure *and* Mr Wells.)   395

Chorus.

Oh, what is the matter, and what is the clatter?
He's glowering at her, and threatens a blow!
Oh, why does he batter the girl he did flatter?
And why does the latter recoil from him so?

RECITATIVE – Alexis.

Prepare for sad surprises –   400
My love Aline despises!
No thought of sorrow shames her –
Another lover claims her!
Be his, false girl, for better or for worse –
But, ere you leave me, may a lover's curse –   405

410–11 *Colonial Bishopric*: Colonial bishops figure in three of Gilbert's *Bab Ballads*. The Bishop of the balmy isle of Rum-Ti-Foo, who is the subject of two ballads, is a good example of the species:

> His people – twenty-three in sum –
> They played the eloquent tum-tum,
> And lived on scalps served up in rum –
>   The only sauce they knew.
>
>   . . .
>
> He only, of the reverend pack
> Who minister to Christians black,
> Brought any useful knowledge back
>   To his Colonial fold.
>
>   . . .
>
> He carried Art, he often said,
> To places where that timid maid
> (Save by Colonial Bishops' aid)
>   Could never hope to roam.

418 *Ahrimanes*: In Zoroastrian (Persian) theology, the personification of evil. He is the same figure as Oromanes mentioned in the story of Abudah's chest (see the note to Act I, line 404). This reference would, of course, be very much clearer if Gilbert had retained the Second Act incantation scene in which Ahrimanes actually appeared and demanded either Wells's or Alexis' death as the price of lifting the spell.

433 *Die thou*: This and the next line were originally given to Lady Sangazure rather than Dr Daly.

437 *popular opinion*: At some stage this phrase was changed to 'public execration'. Both the licence copy and first-edition libretto have 'popular opinion' as now, but the current Macmillan edition has 'public execration'. A libretto dated 1923 in the D'Oyly Carte archives has 'public execration' printed, with 'opinion' written in. It is generally sung now in its original form.

Dr D. (*coming forward*). Hold! Be just. This poor child drank the philtre at your instance. She hurried off to meet you – but, most unhappily, she met me instead. As you had administered the potion to both of us, the result was inevitable. But fear nothing from me – I will be no man's rival. I shall quit the country at once – and bury my sorrow in the congenial gloom of a Colonial   410
Bishopric.

ALEXIS. My excellent old friend! (*Taking his hand – then turning to* MR WELLS, *who has entered with* LADY SANGAZURE.) Oh, Mr Wells, what, what is to be done?

MR W. I do not know – and yet – there is one means by which this   415
spell may be removed.

ALEXIS. Name it – oh, name it!

MR W. Or you or I must yield up his life to Ahrimanes. I would rather it were you. I should have no hesitation in sacrificing my own life to spare yours, but we take stock next week, and it would not be fair on the Co.   420

ALEXIS. True. Well, I am ready!

ALINE. No, no – Alexis – it must not be! Mr Wells, if he must die that all may be restored to their old loves, what is to become of me? I should be left out in the cold, with no love to be restored to!

MR W. True – I did not think of that. (*To the others*.) My friends, I   425
appeal to you, and I will leave the decision in your hands.

FINALE.

MR W.	Or I or he
	Must die!
	Which shall it be?
	Reply! 430
SIR M.	Die thou!
	Thou art the cause of all offending!
DR D.	Die thou!
	Yield thou to this decree unbending!
ALL.	Die thou! Die thou! Die thou! 435
MR W.	So be it! I submit! My fate is sealed.
	To popular opinion thus I yield!
	(*Falls on trap.*)
	Be happy all – leave me to my despair –
	I go – it matters not with whom – or where! 440

(*Gong.*)

(*All quit their present partners, and rejoin their old lovers.* SIR MARMADUKE *leaves* MRS PARTLET, *and goes to* LADY SANGAZURE. ALINE *leaves* DR DALY, *and goes to* ALEXIS. DR DALY *leaves* ALINE, *and goes to* CONSTANCE. NOTARY *leaves* CONSTANCE, *and goes to* MRS PARTLET.   445
All the CHORUS *make a corresponding change.*)

465–6 *Mr Wells sinks through trap*: *The Sorcerer* is the only one of the Savoy Operas which requires a trap-door for its proper production. The Second Act of *Ruddigore* originally required one for the reappearance of Sir Roderic Murgatroyd, but that particular scene was cut out immediately after the first night. A trap-door is sometimes used for *Iolanthe's* ascent from the stream in Act I of *Iolanthe*, but the scene does not demand one.

Not all modern theatres have trap-doors in the stage, and for their 1971 production the D'Oyly Carte Company found it necessary to build the trap into their scenery. A sliding door was put into the veranda of Sir Marmaduke's mansion. As this was only three feet off the level of the stage, John Wellington Wells had to roll over quickly after making his jump into the underworld. A stage-hand crouched by the trap ready to trigger the flash mechanism in the tea-pot (see the note to Act I, line 579) to produce the desired effect after his descent.

As George Grossmith sank slowly through the trap in the first run of *The Sorcerer* he carefully wound his watch, buttoned his gloves and brushed his hat. Michael Heyland continued this business in his production and also had Wells throwing his hat and a shower of business cards into the air at the re-ascent of the final curtain.

In his autobiography, *The Secrets of a Savoyard*, Sir Henry Lytton tells of an embarrassing incident which once occurred when he was playing Wells and making his final descent: 'One night the trap, having dropped a foot or so, refused to move any further, and there was I, enveloped in smoke and brimstone, poised between earth and elsewhere. So all I could do was to jump back on to the boards, make a grimace at the refractory trapdoor, and go off by the ordinary exit. "Hell's full!" shouted an irreverent voice from the gods.'

ALL.

GENTLEMEN.	Oh, my adored one!
LADIES.	Beloved boy!
GENTLEMEN.	Ecstatic rapture!
LADIES.	Unmingled joy!

450

(*They embrace.*)

SIR M.   Come to my mansion, all of you! At least
We'll crown our rapture with another feast!

ENSEMBLE.

SIR MARMADUKE, LADY SANGAZURE, ALEXIS, *and* ALINE.

Now to the banquet we press –
  Now for the eggs and the ham –
Now for the mustard and cress –
  Now for the strawberry jam!

455

DR DALY, CONSTANCE, NOTARY, *and* MRS PARTLET.

Now for the tea of our host –
  Now for the rollicking bun –
Now for the muffin and toast –
  And now for the gay Sally Lunn!
Now for the muffin and toast –
  And now for the gay Sally Lunn!

460

CHORUS.   The eggs and the ham, etc.

(*General Dance. During the symphony* MR WELLS *sinks
through trap amid red fire.*)

465

CURTAIN

PATIENCE

OR

BUNTHORNE'S BRIDE

DRAMATIS PERSONÆ

COLONEL CALVERLEY
MAJOR MURGATROYD   } (*Officers of Dragoon Guards*)
LIEUT. THE DUKE OF DUNSTABLE
REGINALD BUNTHORNE (*a Fleshly Poet*)
ARCHIBALD GROSVENOR (*an Idyllic Poet*)
MR BUNTHORNE'S SOLICITOR
THE LADY ANGELA
THE LADY SAPHIR
THE LADY ELLA   } (*Rapturous Maidens*)
THE LADY JANE
PATIENCE (*a Dairy Maid*)

Chorus of Rapturous Maidens and Officers of Dragoon Guards.

ACT I. – Exterior of Castle Bunthorne.
ACT II. – A Glade.

122

PATIENCE

There is more direct contemporary satire in *Patience* than in any other Savoy Opera. Its target was the aesthetic movement, which flourished in Britain between 1870 and the mid 1880s and introduced the new religion of beauty as a reaction against the ugliness of the Victorian age.

In some ways this strictly contemporary theme makes *Patience* the most dated of all Gilbert and Sullivan's works. Yet modern audiences have little trouble in either enjoying or understanding it. This is no doubt partly because most of us have some impression of the style and mannerisms of the leading figures of the aesthetic movement. Few people nowadays may read Algernon Swinburne's poems or gaze on James Whistler's paintings, but most are at least aware of Oscar Wilde and the Pre-Raphaelites. But there is also another reason why *Patience* is not as dated as it might seem. It is essentially a satire on the affectation and excesses which can accompany artistic movements and cultural fads and of which we have certainly not been free in the latter part of the twentieth century.

Certainly the aesthetic movement was more affected than most and lent itself naturally to ridicule and satire. In 1877 the art world had been torn asunder by a libel action brought by Whistler, the high priest of the aesthetic style in painting, against the critic John Ruskin, who had described one of his paintings, exhibited at the newly opened Grosvenor Gallery, as 'flinging a pot of paint in the public's face'. The subsequent court case, which was finally resolved with Whistler being awarded damages of a penny, produced a string of witnesses arguing the merits of primary colours, Japanese art and harmony of form before a bemused British judge and jury. It may also have given Gilbert the initial idea for a work based on the intense rivalry and jealousy which evidently existed among those who worshipped purity and beauty.

The following year London had its first sight of the figure who was to personify more than anyone else the excesses of aestheticism. Oscar Wilde arrived from Oxford clutching his sacred lily, enthusing about blue and white china and the paintings of the Pre-Raphaelites and describing Henry Irving's legs as 'distinctly precious'.

It was not long before the satirists got to work on this rich material. In 1878 George du Maurier, the leading *Punch* cartoonist, started caricaturing the Pre-Raphaelites and their followers. Four West End plays produced between December 1877 and February 1881 burlesqued the aesthetic movement. The most successful was *The Colonel* by F. C. Burnand (who was, incidentally, Sullivan's librettist for *Cox and Box*), which opened just two months before *Patience*. To make clear that no plagiarism was involved, Richard D'Oyly Carte printed a note in the programme of Gilbert and Sullivan's new opera indicating that it had been completed before Burnand's work was performed.

Gilbert had, in fact, taken rather longer than usual over the libretto of *Patience*, because he had twice changed its basic subject matter. He started out intending to make it a satire on the aesthetic movement but then decided that he could have more fun by poking fun at the prevailing Anglo-Catholic or Tractarian movement in the Church of England, which, with its stress on rituals, vestments and 'bells and smells', was not altogether dissimilar from the style and attitudes of the Pre-Raphaelites.

Gilbert set to work on this new clerical version in the summer of 1880, basing his plot on one of his *Bab Ballads*, 'The Rival Curates', which told of how two clergymen vied with each other in mildness and insipidity until one of them was persuaded to dance, smoke, play croquet and generally adopt a more jocular approach to life. For the opera, he planned to follow the same theme, adding a female chorus of devoted parishioners of the Revd Lawn Tennison, and a male chorus of soldiers whose no-nonsense manliness would contrast with the rather effete ways of the two central characters.

In a letter to Sullivan in November 1880, however, Gilbert announced that he had changed his mind: 'I mistrust the clerical element. I feel hampered by the restrictions which the nature of the subject places upon my freedom of action, and I want to revert to my old idea.' So the rival curates became rival aesthetes once again and the ladies their devoted admirers. The soldiers remained to play much the same role as before.

Patience opened at the Opéra Comique on 23 April 1881 and was an instant success. No fewer than eight of the numbers received an encore on the first night, including Sullivan's haunting madrigal 'I hear the soft note' and the tender duet 'Prithee, pretty maiden'. Altogether, the music for *Patience* shows a greater maturity and originality than that of the earlier Gilbert and Sullivan operas. There are fewer recitatives and solo arias imitative of the grand opera tradition and more duets, trios and other concerted pieces.

On 10 October *Patience* transferred to the brand-new Savoy Theatre which Richard D'Oyly Carte had just built on the south side of the Strand. The theatre was the first in Britain to be lit by electric light. Shortly before the curtain went up for the first time Carte appeared on stage to assure a slightly apprehensive audience that there was no danger in this novel method of illumination. To prove its safety, indeed, he broke an electric lamp without causing a fire. 'A few minutes after Mr Carte had disappeared', the *Orchestra and the Choir* magazine reported, 'the 38 incandescent lamps placed around the dress circle, upper circle and gallery were set in action, the gas was at once extinguished, and a blaze of illumination proclaimed "the light of the future" .'

Patience originally ran for 578 performances, one of the longest first runs of all the Savoy Operas. It is, I think, fair to say that it has not been quite so popular with modern audiences. It is, perhaps, something of an acquired taste. Dame Bridget D'Oyly Carte has told me that it never went down very well in places like Sunderland or Blackpool, although it was always popular in Oxford. A new production designed by Peter Goffin in 1957 was in the D'Oyly Carte repertoire until the 1978–79 season.

In 1969 *Patience* became the third Gilbert and Sullivan opera to be performed by the Sadler's Wells Opera Company, later the English National Opera, at the London Coliseum. John Cox, the producer, was at first tempted to update it by satirizing the 1960s cult of 'flower power' and turning Bunthorne and Grosvenor into hippies, but he resisted the idea, deciding that the theme of 'the military against the beautiful people' was still essentially relevant. The production went to Vienna in 1975 and was revived in London in 1979.

Although originally intended as a piece of ridicule, *Patience* in fact had the overall effect of greatly publicizing and even enhancing the reputation of the aesthetic movement. Several of its leading members delighted in the new fame which the opera gave them. When George Grossmith wrote to James Whistler for permission to reproduce the artist's distinctive lock of white hair in his make-up for Bunthorne, back came the reply: 'Je te savois – mais je ne te savois pas plus brave que moy' – which is roughly translated: 'I knew you, but I did not know you were better than me.'

Oscar Wilde also found new fame as a result of the success of *Patience*. Shortly after the opera had opened in the United States, he was sent across the Atlantic by D'Oyly Carte on a lecture tour, to be, in the words of Max Beerbohm, 'a sandwich board for *Patience*'. Wilde was carefully scheduled to appear in each city just as the opera was about to open there. In Omaha, the local paper reported, 'He wore the suit of black velvet with knee breeches which has been his usual dress in this country. His hair fell about his shoulders in heavy masses, his dreamy, poetic face grew animated, and his large dark eyes lighted up as he entered upon his subject.' A most intense young man, indeed. The mid-Westerners must have wondered just who was imitating whom between the fleshly poet Bunthorne and the fleshly poet Wilde.

1–4 *Scene*: Early libretti included the direction that the entrance to Castle Bunthorne was by a draw-bridge over a moat. A note appended to an early edition of the libretto pointed out that 'the aesthetic dresses are designed by the author'. At one stage Gilbert had toyed with the idea of getting Du Maurier, the *Punch* cartoonist, to design them.

It was originally intended that Lady Jane should be on stage as the curtain rose on Act I. The licence copy contains the following direction: 'JANE, *a gaunt, formidable, portentous, black-haired, heavy-browed aesthete, sits gloomily apart with her back to audience, wrapt in grief.'*

It is interesting to compare the present scene for Act I with the scene Gilbert envisaged when he was intending the opera to be about two rival clergymen (henceforth this will be referred to as the clerical version). The notes for this earlier version survive in the British Library and contain the following description of the opening scene: 'Exterior of country vicarage. Ladies discovered seated on lawn in despairing attitudes, headed by Angela, Ella and Saphir. They are waiting to congratulate the Revd Lawn Tennison on his birthday, and to give him slippers, comforters, braces etc. which they are working upon.'

5–10 *Twenty love-sick maidens we*
The opening phrase of this song is identical with that of 'Hark, those chimes so sweetly sounding', one of the numbers in William Vincent Wallace's opera *Maritana*, written in 1845 and very popular with the Victorians.

Frederic Lloyd, general manager of the D'Oyly Carte Opera Company from 1951 to 1980, was once threatened with prosecution under the Trades Descriptions Act for not fielding a twenty-strong ladies' chorus in performances of *Patience*. He replied that there was nothing in their song to say that all twenty of the love-sick maidens had to be on stage at the same time.

11 *Love feeds on hope*: This line was originally sung as 'Love feeds on love'.

ACT I

SCENE. – *Exterior of Castle Bunthorne. Young maidens dressed in æsthetic draperies are grouped about the stage. They play on lutes, mandolins, etc., as they sing, and all are in the last stage of despair.* ANGELA, ELLA, *and* SAPHIR *lead them.*

CHORUS.

Twenty love-sick maidens we,   5
   Love-sick all against our will.
Twenty years hence we shall be
   Twenty love-sick maidens still.
Twenty love-sick maidens we,
And we die for love of thee.   10

SOLO – ANGELA.

Love feeds on hope, they say, or love will die –
ALL.   Ah, miserie!
Yet my love lives, although no hope have I!
ALL.   Ah, miserie!
Alas, poor heart, go hide thyself away –   15
To weeping concords tune thy roundelay!
                   Ah, miserie!

CHORUS.

All our love is all for one,
   Yet that love he heedeth not,
He is coy and cares for none,   20
   Sad and sorry is our lot!
            Ah, miserie!

23–30 *Go, breaking heart*
Lady Ella's solo is one of the few songs which survived unchanged Gilbert's transition from a clerical to an aesthetic theme. In the former version, it followed a slightly different opening chorus:

> Twenty love-sick maidens we,
>   Sitting by a running rill.
> Twenty years hence we shall be
> Twenty love-sick maidens still.
>   Ah, miserie!
>
> All our love is love for one,
>   Yet that love he prizes not,
> He is coy and cares for none,
>   Sad and sorry is our lot!
>   Ah, miserie!

37 *cynosure*: A centre of attraction. The word comes originally from a Greek phrase meaning dog's tail which was applied to the constellation Ursa Minor, better known as the Pole Star, used by mariners for guiding their ships and a focal point in the heavens.

43 *Happy receipts*: This phrase does not occur in the first edition of the libretto and was introduced by Gilbert for the 1900 revival, probably incorporating an ad-lib made by the cast of the original production.

44 *Fools*: In his manuscript notes on the Savoy Operas J. M. Gordon, who joined the D'Oyly Carte Company in 1883 to play the role of the Colonel in *Patience* and finally retired in 1939 after twenty-nine years as stage manager, made the following observations about the character of Lady Jane and the way that this and her next line should be delivered:

> Lady Jane, an elderly lady who is nearly 'left on the shelf', is a really pathetic figure, not a burlesque of womanhood, but one who begins to see 'her beauty disappear' and hope of marriage fading away. Her first entrance, and first words 'Fools! Fools and blind!' should not be shouted like a bully. She has just made a discovery that may affect them all!

49 *Patience, the village milkmaid*: In Gilbert's earlier clerical version of the opera, Patience was cast as the village schoolmistress, who alone of all the maidens in the parish remained insensible to the charms of the Revd Lawn Tennison.

55 *'twill quickly wear away*: In early libretti, and in the current Macmillan edition of the Savoy Operas, this appears as ''twill quickly pass away'.

59 *Patience appears*: The costume worn by Miss Leonora Braham, who created the role of Patience, would have been instantly recognizable to the first-night audience at the Opéra Comique. It was a copy of the dress worn by the milkmaid in Sir Luke Fildes's painting *'Where are you going to, my pretty maid?'*, reproductions of which hung on many Victorian parlour walls.

SOLO – ELLA.

Go, breaking heart,
  Go, dream of love requited;
Go, foolish heart,   25
  Go, dream of lovers plighted;
Go, madcap heart,
  Go, dream of never waking;
And in thy dream
  Forget that thou art breaking!   30

CHORUS.   Ah, miserie!
ELLA.   Forget that thou art breaking!
CHORUS.   Twenty love-sick maidens, etc.

ANG. There is a strange magic in this love of ours! Rivals as we all are in
the affections of our Reginald, the very hopelessness of our love is a bond   35
that binds us to one another!

SAPH. Jealousy is merged in misery. While he, the very cynosure of our
eyes and hearts, remains icy insensible – what have we to strive for?

ELLA. The love of maidens is, to him, as interesting as the taxes!

SAPH. Would that it were! He pays his taxes.   40

ANG. And cherishes the receipts!

(*Enter* LADY JANE.)

SAPH. Happy receipts!

JANE (*suddenly*). Fools!

ANG. I beg your pardon?   45

JANE. Fools and blind! The man loves – wildly loves!

ANG. But whom? None of us!

JANE. No, none of us. His weird fancy has lighted, for the nonce, on
Patience, the village milkmaid!

SAPH. On Patience? Oh, it cannot be!   50

JANE. Bah! But yesterday I caught him in her dairy, eating fresh butter
with a tablespoon. To-day he is not well!

SAPH. But Patience boasts that she has never loved – that love is, to her,
a sealed book! Oh, he cannot be serious!

JANE. 'Tis but a fleeting fancy – 'twill quickly wear away. (*Aside.*) Oh,   55
Reginald, if you but knew what a wealth of golden love is waiting for you,
stored up in this rugged old bosom of mine, the milkmaid's triumph would
be short indeed!

(PATIENCE *appears on an eminence. She looks down
with pity on the despondent Maidens.*)   60

61–4 *Still brooding on their mad infatuation*
In the clerical version of *Patience*, this recitative was replaced by the following passage:

RECITATIVE.

ANG.	See – hither comes the village schoolmistress,
	Poor Patience – who alone of all womankind
	Remains insensate to his calm attractions!
SAPH.	Unhappy girl – her heart has ne'er known love –
ELLA.	Benighted creature!
ANG.	Miserable maid!

(PATIENCE *appears.*)

PA.	Your pardon, ladies. I intrude upon you. (*Going.*)
ANG.	Come hither, Patience – tell us, is it true
	That you have never loved?
PA.	Most true indeed.
SOPRANOS.	Most marvellous!
CONTRALTOS.	And most deplorable!

Patience's song, 'I cannot tell what this love may be', then followed, as now, after which the Revd Lawn Tennison entered, preceded by a sexton and a beadle whose duties were to keep off the ladies, and followed by 'two grim and portentous middle-aged females dressed in heavy black – Sister Jane and Sister Ann'.

RECITATIVE – PATIENCE.

Still brooding on their mad infatuation!
 I thank thee, Love, thou comest not to me!
Far happier I, free from thy ministration,
 Than dukes or duchesses who love can be!

SAPH. *(looking up)*. 'Tis Patience – happy girl! Loved by a Poet!		65
PA.	Your pardon, ladies. I intrude upon you. *(Going.)*	
ANG.	Nay, pretty child, come hither. Is it true	
	That you have never loved?	
PA.	Most true indeed.	
SOPRANOS. Most marvellous!		70
CONTRALTOS.	And most deplorable!	

SONG – PATIENCE.

I cannot tell what this love may be
That cometh to all, but not to me.
It cannot be kind as they'd imply,
Or why do these ladies sigh?   75
It cannot be joy and rapture deep,
Or why do these gentle ladies weep?
It cannot be blissful as 'tis said,
Or why are their eyes so wondrous red?
 Though everywhere true love I see   80
 A-coming to all, but not to me,
 I cannot tell what this love may be!
  For I am blithe and I am gay,
  While they sit sighing night and day.
  Think of the gulf 'twixt them and me,   85
  'Fal la la la!' – and 'Miserie!'

CHORUS.   Yes, she is blithe, etc.

PA.   If love is a thorn, they show no wit
Who foolishly hug and foster it.
If love is a weed, how simple they   90
Who gather it, day by day!
If love is a nettle that makes you smart,
Then why do you wear it next your heart?
And if it be none of these, say I,
Ah, why do you sit and sob and sigh?   95
  Though everywhere, etc.

CHORUS.   For she is blithe, etc.

106 *The 35th Dragoon Guards*: Military characters appear in nine of the thirteen Savoy Operas. In addition to the Dragoon Guards in *Patience*, there are the marines in *H.M.S. Pinafore*, the First Life Guards in *Utopia Limited*, the chorus of bucks and blades in *Ruddigore*, who were originally dressed as officers of the twenty leading cavalry and infantry regiments of the British Army, the soldiers in *Princess Ida*, and, of course, the Yeomen of the Guard. Then there is Alexis, the Grenadier Guards officer, in *The Sorcerer*, Major-General Stanley in *The Pirates of Penzance* and Private Willis, also of the Grenadier Guards, in *Iolanthe*.

Gilbert himself had a fondness for the Army (see the note to lines 338–69) and he was writing at a time of great militarism and jingoism in Britain. The Afghan and Zulu wars were just over when *Patience* was first performed, and British occupation of Egypt was about to begin.

In his earlier clerical version of *Patience* Gilbert had made his soldiers the 21st Hussars. It is not clear why, other than to rhyme them with 'tunes', he changed them for the aesthetic version to Dragoons. These were mounted infantrymen who took their name from their weapons, carbines called dragons because they spouted fire like the fabulous beasts. As opposed to light cavalry regiments, dragoons were traditionally 'heavies', i.e. burly men who carried fairly heavy weapons.

121–8 *The soldiers of our Queen*
Listening to this splendidly catchy oom-pah-pah tune, it is not difficult to detect the influence on Sullivan of his upbringing in a household where military music must often have been heard. His father was bandmaster at the Royal Military College, Sandhurst, and later a professor at the Army's School of Music at Kneller Hall.

The clerical version contained a two-verse chorus in which the 21st Hussars introduced themselves:

> The twenty-first hussars,
>   Are linked in friendly tether;
> Upon the field of Mars
>   They fight the foe together.
> There every mother's son
>   Prepared to fight and fall is;
> The enemy of one
>   The enemy of all is!
>
> United as a clan
>   We have arranged between us
> To introduce this plan
>   Within the courts of Venus:
> With one emotion stirred
>   Beneath our belts of leather,
> The Colonel gives the word
>   And all propose together!

130–73 *If you want a receipt for that popular mystery*
A song which probably requires more annotation than any other in the entire Gilbert and Sullivan repertoire. Here goes, but first this is how it began when Gilbert was thinking in terms of Hussars rather than Dragoons:

> If you want a receipt of that popular mystery,
>   Known to the world as a British Hussar,
> Take all the remarkable people in history,
>   Choose the best points from each eminent star.

ANG. Ah, Patience, if you have never loved, you have never known true happiness! *(All sigh.)*

PA. But the truly happy always seem to have so much on their minds. 100
The truly happy never seem quite well.

JANE. There is a transcendentality of delirium – an acute accentuation of supremest ecstasy – which the earthy might easily mistake for indigestion. But it is *not* indigestion – it is æsthetic transfiguration! *(To the others.)* Enough of babble. Come! 105

PA. But stay, I have some news for you. The 35th Dragoon Guards have halted in the village, and are even now on their way to this very spot.

ANG. The 35th Dragoon Guards!

SAPH. They are fleshly men, of full habit!

ELLA. We care nothing for Dragoon Guards! 110

PA. But, bless me, you were all engaged to them a year ago!

SAPH. A year ago!

ANG. My poor child, you don't understand these things. A year ago they were very well in our eyes, but since then our tastes have been etherealized, our perceptions exalted. *(To others.)* Come, it is time to lift up 115
our voices in morning carol to our Reginald. Let us to his door.

(The Maidens go off, two and two, into the Castle, singing refrain of 'Twenty love-sick maidens we', and accompanying themselves on harps and mandolins. PATIENCE watches them in surprise, as she climbs the rock by which she entered.)

(March. Enter Officers of Dragoon Guards, led by MAJOR.) 120

CHORUS OF DRAGOONS.

The soldiers of our Queen
  Are linked in friendly tether;
Upon the battle scene
  They fight the foe together.
There every mother's son 125
  Prepared to fight and fall is;
The enemy of one
  The enemy of all is!

(Enter COLONEL.)

SONG – COLONEL.

If you want a receipt for that popular mystery, 130
  Known to the world as a Heavy Dragoon,
Take all the remarkable people in history,
  Rattle them off to a popular tune.

134 *Victory*: Nelson's flagship at the battle of Trafalgar, which provided the model for H.M.S. *Pinafore*.

135 *Bismarck*: The German Chancellor from 1871 to 1890.

136 *Fielding*: Opinions differ as to which Fielding Gilbert has in mind here, but it is probably either Henry, the author of *Tom Jones*, or his half-brother, Sir John, a magistrate who tried to ban performances of *The Beggar's Opera*.

137 *Paget*: Sir Joseph Paget (1814–99), an eminent surgeon and pathologist. Trepanning is a surgical operation on the skull.

138 *Jullien*: Louis Antoine Jullien (1812–60), a French-born conductor who organized concerts and operatic performances at the Drury Lane Theatre in London. In his *Songs of a Savoyard* Gilbert rewrote this line: 'The grace of Mozart, that unparalleled musico'.

139 *Macaulay*: Thomas Babington Macaulay (1800–1859), the Whig historian and politician.

140 *Boucicault*: Dion Boucicault (1822–90), an Irish actor and playwright.

141 *Bishop of Sodor and Man*: The diocese of Sodor and Man is one of the oldest in Britain, having been founded in 447. It now covers only the Isle of Man but it originally also included the Western Isles off Scotland.

142 *D'Orsay*: Count Alfred D'Orsay was an early nineteenth-century Parisian dandy.

144 *Victor Emmanuel*: Victor Emmanuel II (1820–78), King of Italy from 1861 to his death. *Peveril*: Sir Geoffrey Peveril, an old Cavalier who lived in the Peak District of Derbyshire, is the hero of Sir Walter Scott's novel *Peveril of the Peak*.

145 *Thomas Aquinas*: Italian theologian and philosopher (1227–74), was canonized in 1323. *Doctor Sacheverell*: Ecclesiastic and politician (1672–1724), impeached before the House of Lords for preaching against the principles of the 1688 Revolution.

146 *Tupper*: Martin Tupper (1810–89), a popular Victorian author whose most famous work was *Proverbial Philosophy*.

147 *Anthony Trollope*: I know that Trollope, along with Dickens, Thackeray, Tennyson and Defoe, does not need to be explained to a literate and cultured readership, but I cannot resist drawing your attention to the curious coincidence that he died on the last night of the original run of *Patience*, 22 November 1882.
Mr Guizot: François Guizot (1787–1874), French politician and historian.

158 *Lord Waterford*: Henry Beresford, 3rd Marquis of Waterford (1811–59), a well-known practical joker who was killed while hunting.

159 *Roderick*: There are two contenders for this reference: Roderick Dhu, a Scottish outlaw leader defeated by the Saxons who figures in Scott's narrative poem *The Lady of the Lake*, and Roderick, the last Gothic king of Spain, whose overthrow by the Moors is the subject of Scott's poem *The Vision of Don Roderick* and of Southey's *Roderick, the last of the Goths*. Either character would seem to fit.

160 *Paddington Pollaky*: Ignatius Paul Pollaky, a well-known Victorian detective who was based at Paddington Police Station.

161 *Odalisque*: a female member of a harem.

163 *Sir Garnet*: Sir Garnet Wolseley (1833–1913), the Victorian swashbuckling military commander and imperial adventurer who was the model for the modern Major-General in *The Pirates of Penzance*. For the 1900 revival of *Patience* Gilbert altered this line to 'Skill of Lord Roberts', a topical tribute to one of the heroes of the Boer War, and in 1907 he changed it to 'Skill of Lord Wolseley'.

164 *the Stranger*: A tragedy by Benjamin Thompson based on a German story about a Count who leaves his wife and roams the world known only as 'The Stranger'. It was first performed in London in 1798 and often revived.

165 *Manfred*: Once again there are two possibilities here, either the hero of Byron's play *Manfred*, who sells himself to the Devil and lives in solitude in the Alps, or the King of Naples and Sicily who died at the battle of Benevento in 1266.

166 *Beadle of Burlington*: This is almost certainly a reference to the world's smallest police force, the three beadles who patrol the Burlington Arcade just off Piccadilly in the heart of London. They were set up in 1819 to make sure that no one whistled,

The pluck of Lord Nelson on board of the *Victory* –
Genius of Bismarck devising a plan –   135
The humour of Fielding (which sounds contradictory) –
  Coolness of Paget about to trepan –
The science of Jullien, the eminent musico –
  Wit of Macaulay, who wrote of Queen Anne –
The pathos of Paddy, as rendered by Boucicault –   140
  Style of the Bishop of Sodor and Man –
The dash of a D'Orsay, divested of quackery –
Narrative powers of Dickens and Thackeray –
Victor Emmanuel – peak-haunting Peveril –
Thomas Aquinas, and Doctor Sacheverell –   145
  Tupper and Tennyson – Daniel Defoe –
  Anthony Trollope and Mr Guizot! Ah!
    Take of these elements all that is fusible,
    Melt them all down in a pipkin or crucible,
    Set them to simmer and take off the scum,   150
    And a Heavy Dragoon is the residuum!

CHORUS.   Yes! yes! yes! yes!
               A Heavy Dragoon is the residuum!

COL.   If you want a receipt for this soldier-like paragon,
          Get at the wealth of the Czar (if you can) –   155
        The family pride of a Spaniard from Aragon –
          Force of Mephisto pronouncing a ban –
        A smack of Lord Waterford, reckless and rollicky –
          Swagger of Roderick, heading his clan –
        The keen penetration of Paddington Pollaky –   160
          Grace of an Odalisque on a divan –
        The genius strategic of Cæsar or Hannibal –
        Skill of Sir Garnet in thrashing a cannibal –
        Flavour of Hamlet – the Stranger, a touch of him –
        Little of Manfred (but not very much of him) –   165
          Beadle of Burlington – Richardson's show –
          Mr Micawber and Madame Tussaud! Ah!
            Take of these elements all that is fusible,
            Melt them all down in a pipkin or crucible,
            Set them to simmer and take off the scum,   170
            And a Heavy Dragoon is the residuum!

CHORUS.   Yes! yes! yes! yes!
               A Heavy Dragoon is the residuum!

hummed or otherwise disturbed the decorum of the fashionable shopping precinct. A year or two ago the beadles managed to stave off a move to replace their £380 top-hats with economy models costing only £170. American Savoyards have an alternative explanation that this line refers to Erasmus F. Beadle of Burlington, New Jersey, the inventor of the 'dime novel'.

Richardson's show: A travelling show which included melodrama, pantomime, comic songs and incidental music and was a major attraction at Victorian fairs. John Richardson, the founder, died in a workhouse in 1837 at the age of seventy.

167 *Mr Micawber*: Wilkins Micawber is one of the main characters in Dickens's *David Copperfield*.

Madame Tussaud: The waxwork modeller who came to England from France in 1802 also gets a mention in the Mikado's list of punishments that fit the crime (*The Mikado*, Act II, line 354).

I cannot conclude the notes on this song without remarking that Dr Cyril Alington, headmaster of Eton from 1917 to 1933, produced a fine parody which began 'If you want a receipt to construct Aristophanes'. Sadly lack of space prevents me from reproducing it in full.

182 *are you fond of toffee*: In the first American edition of *Patience*, published in 1881 by J. M. Stoddart & Co. and apparently authorized by Gilbert and Sullivan, the word 'candy' is substituted for 'toffee' throughout this exchange.

204 *here I am*: At this point Gilbert originally intended the Duke to have a solo. It is printed in the licence copy, and is bound in at the back of the autograph score, having been torn out of its original position. The song was given its première in a production at Banbury Grammar School in 1967 and subsequently performed by Colin Wright at a D'Oyly Carte last night, although the tune had to be guessed, as the melodic line had disappeared and only the accompaniment was extant. The song goes as follows:

DUKE.	Though men of rank may useless seem,
	    They do good in their generation,
	 They make the wealthy upstart teem
	    With Christian love and self-negation;
	 The bitterest tongue that ever lashed
	    Man's folly, drops with milk and honey,
	 While Scandal hides her head abashed,
	    Brought face to face with Rank and Money!

DRAGOONS.	Yes, Scandal hides her head, etc.
DUKE.	Society forgets her laws, And Prudery her affectation, While Mrs Grundy pleads our cause, And talks 'wild oats' and toleration: Archbishops wink at what they'd think A downright crime is common shoddy, Although Archbishops shouldn't wink At anything – or anybody!
DRAGOONS.	A good Archbishop shouldn't wink At anything – or anybody!

COL. Well, here we are once more on the scene of our former triumphs. But where's the Duke? 175

(*Enter* DUKE , *listlessly, and in low spirits.*)

DUKE. Here I am! (*Sighs.*)
COL. Come, cheer up, don't give way!
DUKE. Oh, for that, I'm as cheerful as a poor devil can be expected to be who has the misfortune to be a duke, with a thousand a day! 180
MAJ. Humph! Most men would envy you!
DUKE. Envy *me*? Tell me, Major, are you fond of toffee?
MAJ. Very!
COL. We are all fond of toffee.
ALL. We are! 185
DUKE. Yes, and toffee in moderation is a capital thing. But to *live* on toffee – toffee for breakfast, toffee for dinner, toffee for tea – to have it supposed that you care for nothing *but* toffee, and that you would consider yourself insulted if anything but toffee were offered to you – how would you like *that*? 190
COL. I can quite believe that, under those circumstances, even toffee would become monotonous.
DUKE. For 'toffee' read flattery, adulation, and abject deference, carried to such a pitch that I began, at last, to think that man was born bent at an angle of forty-five degrees! Great Heavens, what is there to adulate in me! 195
Am I particularly intelligent, or remarkably studious, or excruciatingly witty, or unusually accomplished, or exceptionally virtuous?
COL. You're about as commonplace a young man as ever I saw.
ALL. You are!
DUKE. Exactly! That's it exactly! That describes me to a T! Thank you 200
all very much! Well, I couldn't stand it any longer, so I joined this second-class cavalry regiment. In the Army, thought I, I shall be occasionally snubbed, perhaps even bullied, who knows? The thought was rapture, and here I am.
COL. (*looking off*). Yes, and here are the ladies! 205
DUKE. But who is the gentleman with the long hair?
COL. I don't know.
DUKE. He seems popular!
COL. He *does* seem popular!

(BUNTHORNE *enters, followed by Maidens, two and two, singing and playing* 210
on harps as before. He is composing a poem, and quite absorbed. He sees no one, but
walks across the stage, followed by Maidens. They take no notice of Dragoons – to the
surprise and indignation of those Officers.)

214–19 *In a doleful train*
As originally written, this song began:

> In a melancholy train
> Two and two we walk all day –
> Pity those who love in vain!
> None so sorrowful as they. . .

220-30 *Now is not this ridiculous*
The manuscript of Gilbert's clerical version of *Patience* contains the following numbers at this point:

CHORUS OF SOLDIERS.

> Now is not this ridiculous and is not this preposterous
> And is it not too suicidal enough to urge a man?
> Instead of rushing eagerly to cherish us and foster us
> They all prefer this excellent but very prosy clergyman.
> Instead of slyly peering at us,
> Casting looks endearing at us,
> Flushing at us – blushing at us – flirting with a fan;
> They're actually sneering at us – fleering at us – jeering at us!
> Pretty sort of treatment for a military man!
> They're actually sneering at us – fleering at us – jeering at us!
> Pretty sort of treatment for a military man!

CHORUS OF MAIDENS.

> In a melancholy train
> Two and two we walk all day –
> Pity those who love in vain!
> None so sorrowful as they,
> Who can only sigh and say
> Woe is me: alack-a-day!

1ST LADY.

> Gentle vicar, hear our prayer –
> Twenty love-sick maidens we,
> Young and pretty, dark and fair,
> [*The next four lines are illegible*]

MR L. TENNISON

> Though my book I seem to scan
> Like a serious clergyman
> Who despises female clay,
> I hear plainly all they say,
> Twenty love-sick maidens they!

BEADLE *and* SEXTON.
(*to Officers*)

> He hears plainly all they say,
> Twenty love-sick maidens they!

OFFICERS (*to each other*).

> He hears plainly, etc.

2ND LADY.

> Though so excellently wise
> For a moment mortal be,
> Deign to raise thy gentle eyes
> From thy dry theology –
> Twenty love-sick maidens see –
> Each is kneeling on her knee!

CHORUS OF MAIDENS.

> Twenty love-sick maidens see,
> Each is kneeling on her knee!

OFFICERS.

> Twenty love-sick maidens, etc.

CHORUS OF LADIES.

In a doleful train
   Two and two we walk all day –   215
For we love in vain!
   None so sorrowful as they
      Who can only sigh and say,
      Woe is me, alackaday!

CHORUS OF DRAGOONS.

Now is not this ridiculous – and is not this preposterous?   220
   A thorough-paced absurdity – explain it if you can.
Instead of rushing eagerly to cherish us and foster us,
   They all prefer this melancholy literary man.
        Instead of slyly peering at us,
          Casting looks endearing at us,   225
   Blushing at us, flushing at us – flirting with a fan;
   They're actually sneering at us, fleering at us, jeering at us!
      Pretty sort of treatment for a military man!
      They're actually sneering at us, fleering at us, jeering at us!
      Pretty sort of treatment for a military man!   230

ANG.   Mystic poet, hear our prayer,
            Twenty love-sick maidens we –
          Young and wealthy, dark and fair –
            All of county family.
              And we die for love of thee –   235
            Twenty love-sick maidens we!

CHORUS OF LADIES.   Yes, we die for love of thee –
            Twenty love-sick maidens we!

BUN. (*aside – slyly*).   Though my book I seem to scan
            In a rapt ecstatic way,   240
          Like a literary man
            Who despises female clay,
          I hear plainly all they say,
          Twenty love-sick maidens they!

OFFICERS (*to each other*).   He hears plainly, etc.   245

SAPH.   Though so excellently wise,
           For a moment mortal be,

MR L. TENNISON.	Though as I remarked before 　　Anyone convinced would be, That a work of musty lore 　　Is monopolizing me, Round the corner I can see 　　Each is down upon her knee.
BEADLE *and* SEXTON.	Round the corner he can see, etc.
OFFICERS.	Round the corner he can see, etc.

260 *Now is not this ridiculous*: This ensemble provides a striking example of a musical effect which Sullivan claimed to have invented, the setting of two apparently incompatible choruses in counterpoint to each other. A similar effect is produced in *The Pirates of Penzance*, Act II, line 119.

268 *Good old Bunthorne*: In early editions of the libretto this line was 'Bravo, Bunthorne'.
269 *I droop despairingly*: In an early edition this was 'I despair droopingly'.

Deign to raise thy purple eyes
  From thy heart-drawn poesy.
Twenty love-sick maidens see –   250
Each is kneeling on her knee!   *(All kneel.)*

CHORUS OF LADIES.   Twenty love-sick, etc.

BUN. *(aside).*   Though, as I remarked before,
          Any one convinced would be
      That some transcendental lore   255
          Is monopolizing me,
      Round the corner I can see
      Each is kneeling on her knee!

OFFICERS *(to each other).*   Round the corner, etc.

ENSEMBLE.

OFFICERS.	LADIES.	
Now is not this ridiculous, etc.	In a doleful train, etc.	260

COL. Angela! what is the meaning of this?
ANG. Oh, sir, leave us; our minds are but ill-tuned to light love-talk.
MAJ. But what in the world has come over you all?
JANE. Bunthorne! *He* has come over us. He has come among us, and he
has idealized us.   265
DUKE. Has he succeeded in idealizing *you*?
JANE. He has!
DUKE. Good old Bunthorne!
JANE. My eyes are open; I droop despairingly; I am soulfully intense; I am
limp and I cling!   .   270

(During this BUNTHORNE *is seen in all the agonies of composition. The Maidens
are watching him intently as he writhes. At last he hits on the word he wants and
writes it down. A general sense of relief.)*

BUN. Finished! At last! Finished!

(He staggers, overcome with the mental strain, into arms of COLONEL.*)*   275

COL. Are you better now?
BUN. Yes – oh, it's you – I am better now. The poem is finished, and my
soul had gone out into it. That was all. It was nothing worth mentioning,
it occurs three times a day. *(Sees* PATIENCE, *who has entered during this
scene.)* Ah, Patience! Dear Patience! *(Holds her hand; she seems frightened.)*   280

287 *a . . . fleshly thing*: Something carnal or sensual. In describing Bunthorne as a fleshly poet, Gilbert was not just referring to his size but was establishing him as a true member of the Pre-Raphaelite Brotherhood. In 1871 the poet Robert Buchanan created a sensation in the literary world by publishing a violent attack on the works of Algernon Swinburne, William Morris, Dante Gabriel Rossetti and their followers under the title 'The Fleshly School of Poetry'. The Pre-Raphaelites were furious and vigorously counter-attacked.

292 *think of faint lilies*: Bunthorne has a thing about lilies – he mentions them twice in his patter song ('A languid love for lilies does *not* blight me' and 'If you walk down Piccadilly with a poppy or a lily in your mediæval hand'). They were very much associated with the Pre-Raphaelites, for whom they were a symbol of both purity and beauty. They figure as such in Dante Gabriel Rossetti's painting *The Blessed Damozel*. Oscar Wilde had a particular passion for the flower, and in Max Beerbohm's famous cartoon, *Rossetti's name is heard in America*, he is depicted clasping an enormous and distinctly faint lily in his left hand.

297 *amaranthine asphodel*: More lilies. 'Amaranthine' means everlasting and was applied by the ancient Greeks particularly to flowers that never fade. The asphodel is a member of the lily family, associated with death and the underworld in Greek mythology. The word daffodil is a corruption of 'asphodel'. So this expression could be rendered into plain, modern English as 'fadeless daffodil'. Like the allusion above to faint lilies, this reference provides important ammunition for those who maintain that Bunthorne is based on Oscar Wilde. The reporter from the *Sporting Times* described Wilde's presence at the first night of *Patience* in these words: 'There with the sacred daffodil . . . stood the exponent of uncut hair'.

300 *calomel*: Mercurous chloride, used medicinally as a laxative.

302 *colocynth*: Another strong purgative, derived from the pulp of a bitter apple or gourd-like fruit.

303 *aloe*: I cannot do better than quote the *Oxford English Dictionary*'s definition: 'A nauseous bitter purgative, procured from the inspissated juice of the plant'. The aloe plant itself is a shrub found mostly in South Africa. The purgative drug is extracted from its leaves.

ANG. Will it please you read it to us, sir?
SAPH. This we supplicate. (*All kneel.*)
BUN. Shall I?
ALL THE DRAGOONS. No!
BUN. (*annoyed – to* PATIENCE). I will read it if *you* bid me!   285
PA. (*much frightened*). You can if you like!
BUN. It is a wild, weird, fleshly thing; yet very tender, very yearning, very precious. It is called, 'Oh, Hollow! Hollow! Hollow!'
PA. Is it a hunting song?
BUN. A hunting song? No, it is *not* a hunting song. It is the wail of the   290
poet's heart on discovering that everything is commonplace. To understand it, cling passionately to one another and think of faint lilies. (*They do so as he recites*) –

'OH, HOLLOW! HOLLOW! HOLLOW!'

What time the poet hath hymned   295
The writhing maid, lithe-limbed,
   Quivering on amaranthine asphodel,
How can he paint her woes,
Knowing, as well he knows,
   That all can be set right with calomel?   300

When from the poet's plinth
The amorous colocynth
   Yearns for the aloe, faint with rapturous thrills,
How can he hymn their throes
Knowing, as well he knows,   305
   That they are only uncompounded pills?

Is it, and can it be,
Nature hath this decree,
   Nothing poetic in the world shall dwell?
Or that in all her works   310
Something poetic lurks,
   Even in colocynth and calomel?
            I cannot tell.

(*Exit* BUNTHORNE.)

ANG. How purely fragrant!   315
SAPH. How earnestly precious!
PA. Well, it seems to me to be nonsense.
SAPH. Nonsense, yes, perhaps – but oh, what precious nonsense!
COL. This is all very well, but you seem to forget that you are engaged to us.   320

321 *Empyrean*: Celestial, pertaining to the highest heaven or the abode of God and the angels. At the beginning of Act II of *Princess Ida* the girl graduates sing that they have already taken several easy flights

> Towards the empyrean heights
> Of every kind of lore.

Della Cruscan: The Accademia della Crusca was an institute founded in Florence in the sixteenth century and dedicated to purifying the Italian language. The name was adopted in the late eighteenth century by a group of English poets who were noted for their affected sentimentality.

322 *Early English*: The style of architecture which succeeded the Norman, characterized by pointed arches and lancet windows. It was much favoured by Victorian medievalists and Pre-Raphaelites.

324 *Primary colours*: In general, the Pre-Raphaelites scorned bold, primary colours and preferred to paint in more sombre or pastel shades like the cobwebby grey velvet, with the bloom like cold gravy, so beloved by Lady Jane.

324–5 *Oh, South Kensington*: South Kensington, with its famous School of Design and its recently established museums, was one of the cultural centres of London in the 1880s and a fashionable haunt of artists and Bohemians. Gilbert himself lived in the area, although he would hardly have counted himself among the aesthetic brotherhood.

331 *something Japanese*: A reminder of that penchant for Japanese *objets d'art* among the English upper classes in the 1880s which was to be one of the inspirations for *The Mikado*.

336 *A uniform*: In his earlier clerical version, where Gilbert had already used the phrase about 'the field of Mars' and 'the courts of Venus' in his opening chorus for the soldiers, he rendered this line: 'A uniform that is accustomed to carry everything before it'.

338–69 *When I first put this uniform on*
Gilbert wrote this song from the heart. He himself could not resist the lure of the uniform. As a young man he wanted very much to go into the Royal Artillery. However, the ending of the Crimean War in 1856 when he was just twenty meant that no more officers were required in the regular Army. He consoled himself by joining the militia and was for twenty years an officer in the Royal Aberdeenshire Highlanders, later the 3rd Battalion of the Gordon Highlanders. He retired with the honorary rank of major in 1883. Sixteen years later, at the age of sixty-three, he volunteered for service in the South African War against the Boers.

346 *Hessians*: High boots with tassels, originally worn by the cavalry in the German state of Hesse and later copied by other European armies.

348 *A fact that I counted upon*: In the earlier clerical version this line was 'Like Elkington's window I shone'. Elkington's was a Birmingham firm which in 1840 patented the technique of electroplating silver and was famous for its fine displays of silver-plate.

352 *occurred to me*: Early editions of the libretto and the current Macmillan edition add an extra syllable to this line by ending it 'occurred to me, too'.

SAPH. It can never be. You are not Empyrean. You are not Della Cruscan. You are not even Early English. Oh, be Early English ere it is too late! (*Officers look at each other in astonishment.*)

JANE (*looking at uniform*). Red and Yellow! Primary colours! Oh, South Kensington! 325

DUKE. We didn't design our uniforms, but we don't see how they could be improved.

JANE. No, you wouldn't. Still, there *is* a cobwebby grey velvet, with a tender bloom like cold gravy, which, made Florentine fourteenth-century, trimmed with Venetian leather and Spanish altar lace, and surmounted with 330 something Japanese – it matters not what – would at least be Early English! Come, maidens.

(*Exeunt Maidens, two and two, singing refrain of 'Twenty love-sick maidens we'.*
The Officers watch them off in astonishment.)

DUKE. Gentlemen, this is an insult to the British uniform — 335
COL. A uniform that has been as successful in the courts of Venus as on the field of Mars!

SONG – COLONEL.

When I first put this uniform on,
I said, as I looked in the glass,
'It's one to a million 340
That any civilian
My figure and form will surpass.
Gold lace has a charm for the fair,
And I've plenty of that, and to spare,
While a lover's professions, 345
When uttered in Hessians,
Are eloquent everywhere!'
A fact that I counted upon,
When I first put this uniform on!

CHORUS OF DRAGOONS.

By a simple coincidence, few 350
Could ever have counted upon,
The same thing occurred to me,
When I first put this uniform on!

COL.   I said, when I first put it on,
'It is plain to the veriest dunce 355

361 *But the peripatetics*: 'Peripatetics' is the term given to the philosophy of Aristotle, who used to walk about as he taught his followers. In the clerical version this and the next line had an ecclesiastical flavour:

> The glitter ecstatic
> Of cope and dalmatic . . .

370 *The Dragoons go off angrily*: In the licence copy, the maidens remain on stage for the singing of 'When I first put this uniform on', and this stage direction reads: '*Dragoons go off angrily, left. The ladies go off two and two, right, looking back from time to time sorrowfully at Bunthorne. They sing refrain of "In a melancholy train".* PATIENCE *goes with them.*'

373–96 *Am I alone*

With Bunthorne on the verge of his famous confessional patter song, this is, perhaps, a good point at which to consider the nature of his character.

J. M. Gordon, who in his fifty-six years with the D'Oyly Carte Company had more time than most to reflect on the characters in the operas, summed up Bunthorne thus: 'He is not a young man, but middle-aged, and can be classed as one of the "New Rich", a definite humbug! His aestheticism is to get admiration.'

Several different candidates have been put forward over the years as the most likely model for Bunthorne. The first-night reviewer for *The Times* was convinced that the fleshly poet was based on Algernon Swinburne, the distinctly affected and languid poet who had led the Pre-Raphaelites' counter-attack against Robert Buchanan's criticism of their work in 'The Fleshly School of Poetry'. In support of this thesis, an American scholar, John Bush Jones, has pointed out (in an essay in *W. S. Gilbert: A Century of Scholarship and Commentary*, New York, 1970) that the metres of Bunthorne's two poems, 'Oh, Hollow! Hollow! Hollow!' and 'Heart Foam', are similar to those used by Swinburne, as are the structure and use of words.

Sir Henry Lytton, who played the part many times between 1908 and 1930, was, however, equally emphatic that Bunthorne was modelled on the artist James Whistler, whose libel action against Ruskin almost certainly helped to inspire Gilbert's parody of the jealousy of the artistic world. Many others have seen Bunthorne as essentially a caricature of Oscar Wilde, famous for his worship of lilies, blue-and-white china and things Japanese. It was, indeed, Wilde whom D'Oyly Carte sent to the U.S.A. to publicize *Patience*, but against his claim to be regarded as the main model for Bunthorne must be set the fact that, unlike both Swinburne and Whistler, he was still very little known in 1881. His first volume of poems, for example, did not appear until three months after the opera was first performed.

The truth is almost certainly that Gilbert had no single model for the part but drew on the distinctive characteristics and mannerisms of several of the leading aesthetes of the time. When George Grossmith first appeared on stage in the role of Bunthorne he had the white lock of hair and eyeglass which were Whistler's hallmarks, a velvet coat of the kind worn by Walter Crane, the designer and engraver, and the velvet breeches associated with Wilde. Audrey Williamson has also spotted traces of Edward Burne-Jones and Dante Gabriel Rossetti in Bunthorne's make-up. Perhaps we should simply conclude that he is a kind of all-purpose super-aesthetical Pre-Raphaelite figure.

That every beauty
Will feel it her duty
To yield to its glamour at once.
They will see that I'm freely gold-laced
In a uniform handsome and chaste' –   360
  But the peripatetics
  Of long-haired æsthetics
Are very much more to their taste –
  Which I never counted upon,
  When I first put this uniform on!   365

CHORUS.   By a simple coincidence, few
    Could ever have reckoned upon,
  I didn't anticipate that,
    When I first put this uniform on!
               (*The Dragoons go off angrily.*) 370

(*Enter* BUNTHORNE, *who changes his manner and
becomes intensely melodramatic.*)

RECITATIVE AND SONG – BUNTHORNE.

  Am I alone,
    And unobserved? I am!
  Then let me own   375
    I'm an æsthetic sham!
  This air severe
    Is but a mere
        Veneer!
  This cynic smile   380
    Is but a wile
        Of guile!
  This costume chaste
    Is but good taste
        Misplaced!   385
    Let me confess!
A languid love for lilies does *not* blight me!
Lank limbs and haggard cheeks do *not* delight me!
  I do *not* care for dirty greens
    By any means.   390

  I do *not* long for all one sees
    That's Japanese.
  I am *not* fond of uttering platitudes
    In stained-glass attitudes.

397 *If you're anxious for to shine*: In an early prompt-book in the D'Oyly Carte archives, almost certainly prepared for the 1907 revival of *Patience*, the word 'anxious' has been altered in Gilbert's handwriting to 'eager'. The song appears to have been sung in this latter form in early D'Oyly Carte productions, but 'eager' does not appear in any printed copies of the libretto.

406 *the reign of good Queen Anne*: 1702–14, in case you like to know these things.

408 *the Empress Josephine*: Marie Josèphe Rose Tascher de la Pagerie, to give her her full name, was born in 1763 and married Napoleon Bonaparte in 1796. During her husband's consulate and empire, she held a brilliant court and helped to confirm the reputation of Paris as the artistic capital of the world.

414 *à la Plato*: Platonic love is a condition of friendship and affection in which sexuality plays no part. The Greek philosopher originally applied the concept to Socrates' love for young men, which, he maintained, was entirely pure, though not quite as pure, perhaps, as an attachment to a potato or French bean.

416 *with a poppy or a lily in your mediæval hand*: A very Wildean touch (see the note to line 292 above). The poppy was another flower much favoured by the Pre-Raphaelites. It appears prominently in Rossetti's famous painting *Beata Beatrix*.

In short, my mediævalism's affectation,   395
Born of a morbid love of admiration!

SONG.

If you're anxious for to shine in the high æsthetic line as a man of culture rare,
You must get up all the germs of the transcendental terms, and plant them everywhere.
You must lie upon the daisies and discourse in novel phrases of your complicated state of mind,
The meaning doesn't matter if it's only idle chatter of a transcendental kind.   400
            And every one will say,
            As you walk your mystic way,
'If this young man expresses himself in terms too deep for *me*,
Why, what a very singularly deep young man this deep young man must be!'

Be eloquent in praise of the very dull old days which have long since passed away,   405
And convince 'em, if you can, that the reign of good Queen Anne was Culture's palmiest day.
Of course you will pooh-pooh whatever's fresh and new, and declare it's crude and mean,
For Art stopped short in the cultivated court of the Empress Josephine.
            And every one will say,
            As you walk your mystic way,   410
'If that's not good enough for him which is good enough for *me*,
Why, what a very cultivated kind of youth this kind of youth must be!'

Then a sentimental passion of a vegetable fashion must excite your languid spleen,
An attachment *à la* Plato for a bashful young potato, or a not-too-French French bean!
Though the Philistines may jostle, you will rank as an apostle in the high æsthetic band,   415
If you walk down Piccadilly with a poppy or a lily in your mediæval hand.
            And every one will say,
            As you walk your flowery way,
'If he's content with a vegetable love which would certainly not suit *me*,
Why, what a most particularly pure young man this pure young man must be!'   420

(*At the end of his song* PATIENCE *enters. He sees her.*)

BUN. Ah! Patience, come hither. I am pleased with thee. The bitter-

425 *No, thanks, I have dined*: This line does not occur in the first-edition libretto and was probably an ad-lib made in early performances and later incorporated into the libretto.

443 *Elysian Fields*: The abode of the blessed in Greek mythology, and therefore the happy land. They turn up again in *Ruddigore* (Act I, line 706).

450–51 *If you are fond of touch-and-go jocularity*: Another probable ad-lib which was not in the first-edition libretto.

463 *Aceldama*: A field of blood, or scene of great slaughter. Aceldama was originally the potter's field near Jerusalem which was purchased with the money Judas had taken for betraying Christ (Matthew 27. 7–8). A correspondent to the *Gilbert and Sullivan Journal* in 1926 suggested that this line might provide the sole example in the Savoy Operas of a metrical error on the part of Gilbert. The name Aceldama should properly be pronounced 'Akel'dama' (with the accent on the 'kel'), but this would not scan properly and the word is always incorrectly pronounced with a soft 'c' and the accent on '*dama*'.

hearted one, who finds all else hollow, is pleased with thee. For you are not hollow. *Are* you?

PA. No, thanks, I have dined; but – I beg your pardon – I interrupt you.   425

BUN. Life is made up of interruptions. The tortured soul, yearning for solitude, writhes under them. Oh, but my heart is a-weary! Oh, I am a cursed thing! Don't go.

PA. Really, I'm very sorry —

BUN. Tell me, girl, do you ever yearn?   430

PA. (*misunderstanding him*). I earn my living.

BUN. (*impatiently*). No, no! Do you know what it is to be heart-hungry? Do you know what it is to yearn for the Indefinable, and yet to be brought face to face, daily, with the Multiplication Table? Do you know what it is to seek oceans and to find puddles? – to long for whirlwinds and yet to have to   435 do the best you can with the bellows? That's my case. Oh, I am a cursed thing! Don't go.

PA. If you please, I don't understand you – you frighten me!

BUN. Don't be frightened – it's only poetry.

PA. Well, if that's poetry, I don't like poetry.   440

BUN. (*eagerly*). Don't you? (*Aside.*) Can I trust her? (*Aloud.*) Patience, you don't like poetry – well, between you and me, *I* don't like poetry. It's hollow, unsubstantial – unsatisfactory. What's the use of yearning for Elysian Fields when you know you can't get 'em, and would only let 'em out on building leases if you had 'em?   445

PA. Sir, I —

BUN. Patience, I have long loved you. Let me tell you a secret. I am not as bilious as I look. If you like, I will cut my hair. There is more innocent fun within me than a casual spectator would imagine. You have never seen me frolicsome. Be a good girl – a very good girl – and one day you shall. If you   450 are fond of touch-and-go jocularity – this is the shop for it.

PA. Sir, I will speak plainly. In the matter of love I am untaught. I have never loved but my great-aunt. But I am quite certain that, under any circumstances, I couldn't possibly love *you*.

BUN. Oh, you think not?   455

PA. I'm quite sure of it. Quite sure. Quite.

BUN. Very good. Life is henceforth a blank. I don't care what becomes of me. I have only to ask that you will not abuse my confidence; though *you* despise me, I am extremely popular with the other young ladies.

PA. I only ask that you will leave me and never renew the subject.   460

BUN. Certainly. Broken-hearted and desolate, I go. (*Recites.*)

    'Oh, to be wafted away
        From this black Aceldama of sorrow,
    Where the dust of an earthy to-day
        Is the earth of a dusty to-morrow!'   465

477–8 *the abstraction of refinement*: In the first-night libretto, the dialogue continued at this point:

> ANG. [*continuing*] . . . the idealization of utter unselfishness.
> PA. Love is?
> ANG. Yes.
> PA. Dear me. Go on.
> ANG. True love refines, purifies, elevates, exalts, and chastens. It is the one romantic feature in this chaos of materialism; it is the one unselfish emotion in this whirlpool of grasping greed!

497–519 *Long years ago*
There was originally a second verse to this song, cut soon after the opening night:

PA.
> Time fled, and one unhappy day –
>   The first I'd ever known –
> They took my little friend away,
>   And left me weeping all alone!
> Ah, how I sobbed, and how I cried,
> Then I fell ill and nearly died,
> And even now I weep apace
> When I recall that baby face!
>   We had one hope – one heart – one will –
>   One life, in one employ;
>   And though it's not material, still
>   He was a little *boy*!

ANG.
> Ah, old, old tale of Cupid's touch, etc.

PA.
> Pray don't misconstrue what I say, etc.

ANG.
> No doubt, yet spite of all your pains, etc.

PA.
> Ah, yes, in spite of all my pains, etc.

It is a little thing of my own. I call it 'Heart Foam'. I shall not publish it. Farewell! Patience, Patience, farewell!

(*Exit* BUNTHORNE.)

PA. What on earth does it all mean? Why does he love me? Why does he expect me to love him? He's not a relation! It frightens me! 470

(*Enter* ANGELA.)

ANG. Why, Patience, what is the matter?

PA. Lady Angela, tell me two things. Firstly, what on earth is this love that upsets everybody; and, secondly, how is it to be distinguished from insanity? 475

ANG. Poor blind child! Oh, forgive her, Eros! Why, love is of all passions the most essential! It is the embodiment of purity, the abstraction of refinement! It is the one unselfish emotion in this whirlpool of grasping greed!

PA. Oh, dear, oh! (*Beginning to cry.*) 480

ANG. Why are you crying?

PA. To think that I have lived all these years without having experienced this ennobling and unselfish passion! Why, what a wicked girl I must be! For it *is* unselfish, isn't it?

ANG. Absolutely! Love that is tainted with selfishness is no love. Oh, 485 try, try to love! It really isn't difficult if you give your whole mind to it.

PA. I'll set about it at once. I won't go to bed until I'm head over ears in love with somebody.

ANG. Noble girl! But is it possible that you have never loved anybody?

PA. Yes, one. 490

ANG. Ah! Whom?

PA. My great-aunt —

ANG. Great-aunts don't count.

PA. Then there's nobody. At least – no, nobody. Not since I was a baby. But *that* doesn't count, I suppose. 495

ANG. I don't know. Tell me about it.

DUET – PATIENCE *and* ANGELA.

Long years ago – fourteen, maybe –
    When but a tiny babe of four,
Another baby played with me,
    My elder by a year or more; 500
A little child of beauty rare,
With marvellous eyes and wondrous hair,
Who, in my child-eyes, seemed to me
All that a little child should be!
    Ah, how we loved, that child and I! 505
    How pure our baby joy!

520 *It's perfectly dreadful*: This line originally began: 'It's perfectly appalling to think of the dreadful state'.

523 *Enter Grosvenor*: The character of the idyllic poet and arch-rival to Bunthorne is well summed-up by J. M. Gordon: 'Grosvenor is quite sincere and although undoubtedly vain and conceited, he embraced aestheticism because he thought he had a mission to keep beautiful'. Many Gilbert and Sullivan scholars have seen Oscar Wilde as the main model for Grosvenor, but in his essay 'In Search of Archibald Grosvenor: A New Look at Gilbert's *Patience*', John Bush Jones convincingly advances the claims of William Morris, the poet, designer and pioneer socialist, and Coventry Patmore, the Pre-Raphaelite Roman Catholic poet (see the notes to line 575 and Act II, lines 60–61).

524–51 *Prithee, pretty maiden*
This delightful duet was sung by Derek Oldham and Sylvia Cecil at a party in the White House, Washington, before the presidential inauguration of Franklin D. Roosevelt, a keen Gilbert and Sullivan enthusiast.

540 *I'm a man of propertee*: This admission and the subsequent comment 'Money, I despise it' are cited by John Bush Jones in support of his thesis that Grosvenor is at least partly based on William Morris. Without his own comfortable middle-class upbringing, and the £900 annual income which he inherited at the age of twenty-one, it is doubtful if Morris could ever have embarked on the 'holy warfare' against the forces of capitalism which occupied most of his life.

How true our love – and, by the by,
  He was a little boy!

ANG.
    Ah, old, old tale of Cupid's touch!
    I thought as much – I thought as much!   510
    He *was* a little boy!

PA. (*shocked*).
    Pray don't misconstrue what I say –
    Remember, pray – remember, pray,
    He was a *little* boy!

ANG.
    No doubt! Yet, spite of all your pains,   515
    The interesting fact remains –
    He was a little *boy*!

ENSEMBLE. { Ah, yes, in / No doubt! Yet, } spite of all { my / your } pains, etc.

    (*Exit* ANGELA.)

PA. It's perfectly dreadful to think of the appalling state I must be in! I   520
had no idea that love was a duty. No wonder they all look so unhappy! Upon
my word, I hardly like to associate with myself. I don't think I'm respectable.
I'll go at once and fall in love with — (*Enter* GROSVENOR.) A stranger!

DUET – PATIENCE *and* GROSVENOR.

GROS.
    Prithee, pretty maiden – prithee, tell me true,
    (Hey, but I'm doleful, willow willow waly!)   525
    Have you e'er a lover a-dangling after you?
        Hey willow waly O!
        I would fain discover
        If you have a lover?
        Hey willow waly O!   530

PA.
    Gentle sir, my heart is frolicsome and free –
    (Hey, but he's doleful, willow willow waly!)
    Nobody I care for comes a-courting me –
        Hey willow waly O!
        Nobody I care for   535
        Comes a-courting – therefore,
        Hey willow waly O!

GROS.
    Prithee, pretty maiden, will you marry me?
    (Hey, but I'm hopeful, willow willow waly!)
    I may say, at once, I'm a man of propertee –   540
        Hey willow waly O!
        Money, I despise it;

556 *your Archibald*: Gilbert at first gave Grosvenor the Christian name Algernon, but changed it to Archibald when it was pointed out that a member of the Duke of Westminster's family had the name Algernon Grosvenor. 'Algernon' appears throughout in the licence copy, and it survived in one or two places in the first edition (see the note to line 608).

557 *Chronos*: The Greek word for time, which has given us such terms as chronicle and chronological.

561 *I am much taller and much stouter*: Gilbert originally wrote this line: 'I am much taller and a little stouter than I was'. He apparently altered it to suit the dimensions of the artist playing Grosvenor at a revival.

569–70 *to be madly loved at first sight*: As performed on the first night, the dialogue continued at this point:

> GROS. [*continuing*] . . . by every woman who sets eyes on me!
> PA. Horrible indeed!
> GROS. Ah, Patience, you may thank your stars that you are not cursed with the fatal gift of beauty. It has been my bane through life!
> PA. But why do you make yourself so picturesque, etc.

572 *to escape this persecution*: At this point in an early proof copy is added in red ink: 'A pasteboard nose would do it'.

575 *I am a trustee for Beauty*: John Bush Jones cites this line and Grosvenor's subsequent remark 'I am the Apostle of Simplicity' as further evidence that he is based on William Morris, who was well known for his strong views that objects should be both beautiful and simple.

579 *for I am infallible*: The use of the word 'infallible', which does not appear in the licence copy, may possibly be a survival from Gilbert's earlier clerical version of *Patience*. The phrase 'Apostle of Simplicity' is, perhaps, also more appropriate to a clergyman than a poet.

Many people prize it,
Hey willow waly O!

PA.   Gentle sir, although to marry I design –   545
           (Hey, but he's hopeful, willow willow waly!)
           As yet I do not know you, and so I must decline.
           Hey willow waly O!
           To other maidens go you –
           As yet I do not know you,   550
BOTH.   Hey willow waly O!

GROS. Patience! Can it be that you don't recognize me?

PA. Recognize you? No, indeed I don't!

GROS. Have fifteen years so greatly changed me?

PA. Fifteen years? What do you mean?   555

GROS. Have you forgotten the friend of your youth, your Archibald? – your little playfellow? Oh, Chronos, Chronos, this is too bad of you!

PA. Archibald! Is it possible? Why, let me look! It is! It is! It must be! Oh, how happy I am! I thought we should never meet again! And how you've grown!   560

GROS. Yes, Patience, I am much taller and much stouter than I was.

PA. And how you've improved!

GROS. Yes, Patience, I am very beautiful! (*Sighs.*)

PA. But surely *that* doesn't make you unhappy?

GROS. Yes, Patience. Gifted as I am with a beauty which probably has   565 not its rival on earth, I am, nevertheless, utterly and completely miserable.

PA. Oh – but why?

GROS. My child-love for you has never faded. Conceive, then, the horror of my situation when I tell you that it is my hideous destiny to be madly loved at first sight by every woman I come across!   570

PA. But why do you make yourself so picturesque? Why not disguise yourself, disfigure yourself, anything to escape this persecution?

GROS. No, Patience, that may not be. These gifts – irksome as they are – were given to me for the enjoyment and delectation of my fellow-creatures. I am a trustee for Beauty, and it is my duty to see that the conditions of my   575 trust are faithfully discharged.

PA. And you, too, are a Poet?

GROS. Yes, I am the Apostle of Simplicity. I am called 'Archibald the All-Right' – for I am infallible!

PA. And is it possible that you condescend to love such a girl as I?   580

GROS. Yes, Patience, is it not strange? I have loved you with a Florentine fourteenth-century frenzy for full fifteen years!

PA. Oh, marvellous! I have hitherto been deaf to the voice of love. I seem now to know what love is! It has been revealed to me – it is Archibald Grosvenor!   585

587 *We will never, never part*: In the first edition, Patience had a longer line at this point: 'The purifying gift – the ennobling influence has descended upon me, and I am inconceivably happy! We will never, never part!'

598 *To monopolize those features*: Another line which was originally longer. As first performed, it ran: 'To monopolize those features on which all women love to linger; to keep to myself those attributes which were designed for the enjoyment and delectation of my fellow creatures? It would be unpardonable!'

608 *Farewell, Archibald*: This line was not changed from 'Farewell, Algernon' until the fifth edition of the libretto was published in the early 1910s.

616–22 *Though to marry you would very selfish be*

The licence copy has a new duet for Patience and Grosvenor here instead of the reprise of 'Prithee, pretty maiden' which they now sing:

PA.
Love me with a love enduring –
  You have my complete permission –
Think of everything alluring
  In my girlish disposition.
I shall sneer, but you must flatter –
I shall scoff, but that don't matter –
  Let no slight your passion tame –
  Go on loving just the same!

ENSEMBLE.
Ah, true love, celestial vision,
  How unselfish is your aim –
Though { I treat him / she treats him } with derision,
He will / I shall } love { me / her } just the same!

GROS.
Though I burn with hopeless passion,
  Don't surrender, I implore you –
Though I perish, Romeo fashion,
  Keep your duty well before you!
Act the cold imperious beauty –
  Keep me off – it is your duty –
Cover me with scorn and shame –
I shall love you just the same!

ENSEMBLE.
Ah, true love, celestial vision, etc.

The above number was cut out before rehearsals began. At rehearsal, however, Gilbert and Sullivan realized that at the end of their passage of dialogue Patience and Grosvenor were left on stage with no reason to get off and make way for the finale. The coda of 'Prithee, pretty maiden' was introduced so that they could sing themselves off the stage. It does not appear in early American libretti nor in the 1881 or 1900 editions of the vocal score.

GROS. Yes, Patience, it is!

PA. (*as in a trance*). We will never, never part!

GROS. We will live and die together!

PA. I swear it!

GROS. We both swear it!   590

PA. (*recoiling from him*). But – oh, horror!

GROS. What's the matter?

PA. Why, you are perfection! A source of endless ecstasy to all who know you!

GROS. I know I am. Well?   595

PA. Then, bless my heart, there can be nothing unselfish in loving *you*!

GROS. Merciful powers! I never thought of that!

PA. To monopolize those features on which all women love to linger! It would be unpardonable!

GROS. Why, so it would! Oh, fatal perfection, again you interpose   600
between me and my happiness!

PA. Oh, if you were but a thought less beautiful than you are!

GROS. Would that I were; but candour compels me to admit that I'm not!

PA. Our duty is clear; we must part, and for ever!   605

GROS. Oh, misery! And yet I cannot question the propriety of your decision. Farewell, Patience!

PA. Farewell, Archibald! But stay!

GROS. Yes, Patience?

PA. Although I may not love *you* – for you are perfection – there is   610
nothing to prevent your loving *me*. I am plain, homely, unattractive!

GROS. Why, that's true!

PA. The love of such a man as you for such a girl as I must be unselfish!

GROS. Unselfishness itself!   615

DUET – PATIENCE *and* GROSVENOR.

PA.	Though to marry you would very selfish be –
GROS.	Hey, but I'm doleful – willow willow waly!
PA.	You may, all the same, continue loving me –
GROS.	Hey willow waly O!
BOTH.	All the world ignoring, 620

You'll ⎫
       ⎬ go on adoring –
I'll ⎭

Hey willow waly O!

(*At the end, exeunt despairingly, in opposite directions.*)

630 *Pandæan pleasure*: Pan, the Greek god who presided over shepherds and their flocks, delighted in rural music and was often portrayed playing his row of pipes. The word Pandaean was used in the nineteenth century to describe those who played the pipes of Pan.

631 *Daphnephoric*: In Greek mythology Daphne, the daughter of a river-god, was turned into a bay tree to avoid the amorous advances of Apollo.

FINALE – ACT I.

(Enter BUNTHORNE, *crowned with roses and hung about with garlands, and looking very miserable. He is led by* ANGELA *and* SAPHIR *(each of whom holds* 625
an end of the rose-garland by which he is bound), and accompanied by procession of Maidens. They are dancing classically, and playing on cymbals, double pipes, and other archaic instruments.)

CHORUS.

Let the merry cymbals sound,
  Gaily pipe Pandæan pleasure, 630
With a Daphnephoric bound
  Tread a gay but classic measure,
  Tread a gay but classic measure.
Every heart with hope is beating,
For at this exciting meeting 635
  Fickle Fortune will decide
  Who shall be our Bunthorne's bride!

(Enter Dragoons, led by COLONEL, MAJOR, *and* DUKE.
They are surprised at proceedings.)

CHORUS OF DRAGOONS.

Now tell us, we pray you, 640
Why thus they array you –
Oh, poet, how say you –
  What is it you've done?

DUKE.   Of rite sacrificial,
By sentence judicial, 645
This seems the initial,
  Then why don't you run?

COL.   They cannot have led you
To hang or behead you,
Nor may they *all* wed you, 650
  Unfortunate one!

CHORUS OF DRAGOONS.

Then tell us, we pray you,
Why thus they array you –
Oh, poet, how say you –
  What is it you've done? 655

(Enter SOLICITOR.*)*

658 *my solicitor*: Mr Bunthorne's solicitor must surely have the doubtful distinction of appearing for the shortest time on stage of any principal in the Savoy Operas. The Midshipman in *H.M.S. Pinafore* is another non-speaking role listed in the *Dramatis personæ*, but he is on stage for much of the First Act. Hercules, the page who appears in Act I of *The Sorcerer*, has an even briefer moment of glory, but his name does not appear in the *Dramatis personæ* and so, strictly speaking, he is not a principal as the Solicitor is.

659 *a deserving charity*: Bunthorne's raffling of himself in aid of a deserving charity has certain similarities with another famous scene in operetta, when Danilo, the hero of Franz Lehár's *The Merry Widow* (1905), offers his dance with Anna Glawari to any of her many admirers for 10,000 francs, the proceeds to be devoted to missions overseas.

677–90 *Your maiden hearts, ah, do not steel*
This splendid number, in which the soldiers show their emotions in perfect unison at the Duke's command, recalls two earlier verses with a similar theme, one by Gilbert and another by the mid-Victorian humorous dramatist James Robinson Planché.

Planché's play *The Fair One with the Golden Locks* (1843) has the following scene, on which Gilbert may perhaps, either consciously or unconsciously, have drawn:

GRAND CHAMBERLAIN.
> Yes, noble friends, the news is sad as may be,
> Our mighty king is crying like a baby.
> His nerves have had the cruellest of shocks –
> Rejected by the Fair with Golden Locks,
> He comes: prepare to show your loyal griefs,
> If not by tears, at least by handkerchiefs,
> Let every soldier draw out his bandanna
> And bear't before him in a decent manner.

CAPTAIN OF THE GUARD.
> Draw kerchiefs! (*Soldiers do so.*)
> Present kerchiefs! (*They hold them to their eyes.*)
> Steady there!
> Eyes wet, long faces! Smile men, if you dare.
> (*Enter King and ministers.*)
> Recover kerchiefs!
> (*Soldiers return handkerchiefs to their pockets.*)

In his own Bab Ballad 'The Scornful Colonel', Gilbert portrayed an officer who gave his men six hours a day of sneering drill:

> Now by your right, prepare to 'Whish'!
> Come, all at once and smartly, 'Pish'!
> Prepare to 'Bah'! By sections, 'Phew'!
> Good, at three hundred yards, 'Pooh-Pooh'!

RECITATIVE – Bunthorne.

Heart-broken at my Patience's barbarity,
  By the advice of my solicitor (*introducing his Solicitor*),
In aid – in aid of a deserving charity,
  I've put myself up to be raffled for!   660

MAIDENS.   By the advice of his solicitor
      He's put himself up to be raffled for!

DRAGOONS.   Oh, horror! urged by his solicitor,
      He's put himself up to be raffled for!

MAIDENS.   Oh, heaven's blessing on his solicitor!   665

DRAGOONS.   A hideous curse on his solicitor!

(*The* SOLICITOR, *horrified at the Dragoons' curse, rushes off.*)

COL.   Stay, we implore you,
      Before our hopes are blighted;
      You see before you   670
      The men to whom you're plighted!

CHORUS OF DRAGOONS.

Stay, we implore you,
For we adore you;
To us you're plighted
To be united –   675
      Stay, we implore you!

SOLO – DUKE.

Your maiden hearts, ah, do not steel
To pity's eloquent appeal,
Such conduct British soldiers feel.
(*Aside to Dragoons.*)   Sigh, sigh, all sigh!   680
          (*They all sigh.*)
To foeman's steel we rarely see
A British soldier bend the knee,
Yet, one and all, they kneel to ye –
(*Aside to Dragoons.*)   Kneel, kneel, all kneel!   685
          (*They all kneel.*)

689 *A tear-drop dews each martial eye*: The same imagery occurs in the opening chorus to Act II of *The Pirates of Penzance* when General Stanley's daughters call on him to dry the tear 'That dews that martial cheek'.

700 *blue-and-white . . . pottery*: Blue-and-white oriental ceramics were much in vogue in the late 1870s and early 1880s, particularly among followers of the aesthetic cult. Bunthorne later describes himself as 'A blue-and-white young man' (Act II, line 497). In her Act II aria in *H.M.S. Pinafore* Josephine sings of the 'Rare "blue and white"' in her father's luxurious home.

709 *There's fish in the sea*: This line is based on the old English saying 'There's as good fish in the sea as ever came out of it', meaning that you shouldn't be disheartened if you have lost the chance of something good, because you'll soon get another. The saying is also paraphrased in the finales to Acts I and II of *The Mikado* in the line: 'There's lots of good fish in the sea'.

Our soldiers very seldom cry,
And yet – I need not tell you why –
A tear-drop dews each martial eye!

(*Aside to Dragoons.*)   Weep, weep, all weep!   690

                             (*They all weep.*)

ENSEMBLE.

Our soldiers very seldom cry,
And yet { they / we } need not tell { us / you } why –
A tear-drop dews each martial eye!
Weep, weep, all weep!   695

BUNTHORNE (*who has been impatient during this appeal*).

Come, walk up, and purchase with avidity,
Overcome your diffidence and natural timidity,
Tickets for the raffle should be purchased with rapidity,
    Put in half a guinea and a husband you may gain –
Such a judge of blue-and-white and other kinds of pottery –   700
From early Oriental down to modern terra-cotta-ry –
Put in half a guinea – you may draw him in a lottery –
    Such an opportunity may not occur again.

CHORUS. Such a judge of blue-and-white, etc.

(*Maidens crowd up to purchase tickets; during this Dragoons dance*   705
    in single file round stage, to express their indifference.)

DRAGOONS.   We've been thrown over, we're aware
                  But we don't care – but we don't care!
                  There's fish in the sea, no doubt of it,
                  As good as ever came out of it,   710
                  And some day we shall get our share,
                  So we don't care – so we don't care!

(*During this the Maidens have been buying tickets. At last* JANE *presents*
    herself. BUNTHORNE *looks at her with aversion.*)

RECITATIVE.

BUN.   And are *you* going a ticket for to buy?   715
JANE (*surprised*). Most certainly I am; why shouldn't I?

719 *Maidens blindfold themselves*: This is not the only occasion in the Savoy Operas when characters are blindfolded on stage. In Act I of *The Gondoliers* Marco and Giuseppe Palmieri have handkerchiefs tied over their eyes before selecting the girls they will marry.

727 *Jane puts hand in bag*: The first-edition libretto has a slightly different stage direction at this point: 'JANE *draws a paper, and is about to open it, when* PATIENCE *enters.* PATIENCE *snatches paper from* JANE *and tears it up.*'

739 *If you, with one so lowly, still*: In the licence copy the Dragoons and Bunthorne are given this and the next three lines to repeat before all sing 'Oh, shameless one!'

BUN. (*aside*).　　　　Oh, Fortune, this is hard! (*Aloud.*) Blindfold your eyes;
　　　　　　　　　　Two minutes will decide who wins the prize!
　　　　　　　　　　(*Maidens blindfold themselves.*)

CHORUS OF MAIDENS.

Oh, Fortune, to my aching heart be kind!　　　　　　　　　　　720
Like us, thou art blindfolded, but not blind! (*Each uncovers one eye.*)
Just raise your bandage, thus, that you may see,
And give the prize, and give the prize to me! (*They cover their eyes again.*)
BUN. Come, Lady Jane, I pray you draw the first!
JANE (*joyfully*). He loves me best!　　　　　　　　　　　　725
BUN. (*aside*).　　　　I want to know the worst!

(JANE *puts hand in bag to draw ticket.* PATIENCE *enters and
prevents her doing so.*)

PA. Hold! Stay your hand!
ALL (*uncovering their eyes*). What means this interference?　　　730
　　Of this bold girl I pray you make a clearance!
JANE. Away with you, away with you, and to your milk-pails go!
BUN. (*suddenly*). She wants a ticket! Take a dozen!
PA.　　　　　　　　　　　　　　　　　　　No!

SOLO – PATIENCE (*kneeling to* BUNTHORNE).

　　　　Ah! If there be pardon in your breast　　　　　735
　　　　　For this poor penitent,
　　　　Who, with remorseful thought opprest,
　　　　　Sincerely doth repent;
　　　　If you, with one so lowly, still
　　　　　Desire to be allied,　　　　　　　　740
　　　　Then you may take me, if you will,
　　　　　For I will be your bride!

ALL.　　　　　Oh, shameless one!
　　　　　　Oh, bold-faced thing!
　　　　　Away you run,　　　　　　　745
　　　　　　Go, take you wing,
　　　　　You shameless one!
　　　　　　You bold-faced thing!

BUN.　　　How strong is love! For many and many a week
　　　　She's loved me fondly and has feared to speak,
　　　　But Nature, for restraint too mighty far,　　　750
　　　　Has burst the bonds of Art – and here we are!

770 *Exactly so*: In the licence copy this last 'Exactly so!' is given to the Dragoons, who then continue:

> It's very clear the maiden who
> Devotes herself to loving you
> Is prompted by no selfish view –

BUN. (*meekly*).   Exactly so!

The Dragoons now dance round the stage and then repeat their chorus 'We've been thrown over, we're aware'. After this, the licence copy has a solo for the Colonel, sung as an aside to the audience:

> Oh, do not suppose that a Heavy Dragoon
>   Can throw off a blighted affection so soon!
> Don't judge by our actions or words, we beseech,
>   For our hearts are as soft as an over-ripe peach,
> And though we assume an indifferent air,
>   'Tis but to conceal our enduring despair;
> If you knew what we suffer, you wouldn't impugn
> That pink of perfection – a Heavy Dragoon!

SAPH.   Are you resolved, etc.

777–84 *I hear the soft note*

François Cellier, who conducted the first run of *Patience*, wrote that this was easily the best number in the opera:

> Here the composer gives a remarkable exhibition of his genius for adapting music to the occasion. Moreover, it is a striking instance of Gilbert's appreciation of his colleague's music. In order to give the best effect to the sestette, it was sung by principals and chorus without the slightest movement or action on the stage. In other words, precisely as it might be rendered on a concert platform, except that Gilbert took special pains as regards the picturesque and most effective grouping of the company.

Although described as a sestet, 'I hear the soft note' can equally be described as a madrigal (see the note to *Ruddigore*, Act I, lines 870–903).

783–4 *And never, oh never . . . old, old love again*: The tune to which these lines are sung bears a striking resemblance to the last four bars of the Victorian hymn tune *Pilgrims*, composed by Henry Smart for R. W. Faber's hymn 'Hark! hark, my soul! angelic songs are swelling .

PA.   No, Mr Bunthorne, no – you're wrong again;
                  Permit me – I'll endeavour to explain!

SONG – PATIENCE.

PA.	True love must single-hearted be –	755
BUN.	Exactly so!	
PA.	From every selfish fancy free –	
BUN.	Exactly so!	
PA.	No idle thought of gain or joy	
	A maiden's fancy should employ –	760
	True love must be without alloy.	
ALL.	Exactly so!	

PA.	Imposture to contempt must lead –	
COL.	Exactly so!	
PA.	Blind vanity's dissension's seed –	765
MAJ.	Exactly so!	
PA.	It follows, then, a maiden who	
	Devotes herself to loving you (*indicating*	
	BUNTHORNE)	
	Is prompted by no selfish view –	
ALL.	Exactly so!	770

SAPH.   Are you resolved to wed this shameless one?
ANG.   Is there no chance for any other?
BUN. (*decisively*). None! (*Embraces* PATIENCE.)
                      (*Exeunt* PATIENCE *and* BUNTHORNE.)

  (ANGELA, SAPHIR, *and* ELLA *take* COLONEL, DUKE, *and* MAJOR   775
  down, while Maidens gaze fondly at other Officers.)

SESTET.

I hear the soft note of the echoing voice
    Of an old, old love, long dead –
It whispers my sorrowing heart 'rejoice' –
    For the last sad tear is shed –   780
The pain that is all but a pleasure will change
    For the pleasure that's all but pain,
And never, oh never, our hearts will range
    From that old, old love again!
             (*Maidens embrace Officers.*)   785

CHORUS.   Yes, the pain that is all, etc. (*Embrace.*)

807–15 *ENSEMBLE*

As printed in the first edition of the libretto, each of the verses in the ensemble which ends Act I has another four lines. The original full version is as follows:

MAIDENS.

Oh, list while we a love confess
That words imperfectly express,
Those shell-like ears, ah, do not close
To blighted love's distracting woes!
Nor be distressed, nor scandalized
If what we do is ill-advised,
Or we shall seek within the tomb
Relief from our appalling doom!

PATIENCE.

List, Reginald, while I confess
A love that's all unselfishness;
That it's unselfish, goodness knows,
You won't dispute it, I suppose.
For you are hideous – undersized,
And everything that I've despised,
And I shall love you, I presume,
Until I sink into the tomb!

GROSVENOR.

Again my cursed comeliness
Spreads hopeless anguish and distress;
Thine ears, oh, Fortune, do not close
To my intolerable woes.
Let me be hideous, undersized,
Contemned, degraded, loathed, despised,
Or bid me seek within the tomb
Relief from my detested doom!

BUNTHORNE.

My jealousy I can't express,
Their love they openly confess,
His shell-like ear he does not close
To their recital of their woes –
I'm more than angry and surprised,
I'm pained, and shocked, and scandalized,
But he shall meet a hideous doom
Prepared for him by – I know whom!

In his *First Night Gilbert and Sullivan*, Reginald Allen states that the last four lines of these verses were sung on the first night and were not, in fact, deleted from the libretto until the fifth edition. However, a note by Rupert D'Oyly Carte in the D'Oyly Carte archives says that the additional lines were never set to music by Sullivan and presumably, therefore, never sung.

(*Enter* PATIENCE *and* BUNTHORNE.)

(*As the Dragoons and Maidens are embracing, enter* GROSVENOR, *reading. He takes no notice of them, but comes slowly down, still reading. The Maidens are all strangely fascinated by him, and gradually withdraw from Dragoons.*)   790

ANG.   But who is this, whose god-like grace
              Proclaims he comes of noble race?
              And who is this, whose manly face
              Bears sorrow's interesting trace?

ENSEMBLE – TUTTI.

Yes, who is this, etc.   795

GROS.   I am a broken-hearted troubadour,
          Whose mind's æsthetic and whose tastes are pure!
ANG.   Æsthetic! He is æsthetic!
GROS.   Yes, yes – I am æsthetic
                   And poetic!   800
ALL THE LADIES. Then, we love you!

(*The Maidens leave Dragoons and group, kneeling, around* GROSVENOR.
Fury of BUNTHORNE, *who recognizes a rival.*)

DRAGOONS. They love him! Horror!
BUN. *and* PA. They love him! Horror!   805
GROS. They love me! Horror! Horror! Horror!

ENSEMBLE – TUTTI.

MAIDENS.
Oh, list while we a love confess
That words imperfectly express.
Those shell-like ears, ah, do not
close
To blighted love's distracting
woes!

GROSVENOR.
Again my cursed comeliness
Spreads hopeless anguish and
distress!
Thine ears, oh Fortune, do not
close
To my intolerable woes.   810

PATIENCE.
List, Reginald, while I confess
A love that's all unselfishness;
That it's unselfish, goodness
knows,
You won't dispute it, I suppose?

BUNTHORNE.
My jealousy I can't express,
Their love they openly confess;
His shell-like ears he does not
close
To their recital of their woes.

DRAGOONS.
Now is not this ridiculous, etc.   815

END OF ACT I

1–3 *Scene*: The direction in the first-night libretto for the Act II stage setting read: '*A glade. In the centre a small sheet of water*'. The licence copy further stipulated that there should be both a tree stump and a rock on stage. At the first performances at the Opéra Comique, there was a lake, but this proved impossible to construct on the stage of the Savoy Theatre, with the result that when *Patience* moved there, a significant alteration had to be made to one of the scenes in the Second Act (see the first note to line 409).

Both the licence copy and the first American libretto have Lady Jane leaning on a double bass rather than a cello, but the latter instrument was specified in the first British edition and has generally been used in productions here. In the 1969 Sadler's Wells Opera Company production Heather Begg played a real double-bass herself, but when Gillian Knight took over the part she did not do so. The D'Oyly Carte Company latterly used a 'prop' cello painted entirely white, on which Lady Jane vigorously scraped away while the real music came from the orchestra pit. This scene may well have been intended as a skit on the common custom in early Italian opera for contraltos to be accompanied by the cello or double bass.

8 *they are decaying*: A note by Rupert D'Oyly Carte on a libretto, probably made in the 1930s, states: 'Instead of "decaying", "deteriorating" has been used, decaying being thought too strong.'

16 *lip-salve*: Ointment for the lips.

pearly grey: Face powder. In Gilbert's Bab Ballad 'King Borria Bungalee Boo', the African warriors endeavoured to make themselves fair by applying 'a crimson and pearly-white dye'.

18–33 *Silvered is the raven hair*

Gilbert intended this to be a humorous song, poking fun in a rather ungallant way at the waning attractions of ageing women, very much in the spirit of 'There is beauty in the bellow of the blast' (*The Mikado*, Act II, lines 759–806). However, Sullivan provided a particularly soulful and haunting tune which gives a much sadder and more pathetic flavour to the words than the librettist probably originally intended.

Seeing the suitability of Sullivan's tune for a poignant parlour ballad, the music publishers Chappells commissioned the poet Hugh Conway to provide new lyrics. In this revised form, the song was a popular Victorian fireside favourite:

> In the twilight of our love,
>   In the darkness falling fast;
> Broken by no gleam above;
>   What must be our thoughts the last,
> Silent ere we say farewell,
>   Pausing ere we turn to part,
> Whilst one wish we dare not tell,
>   Echoes yet from heart to heart
> Saddest of all sad regret,
>   'Would we two had never met'.

ACT II

SCENE. – *A glade.* JANE *is discovered leaning on a violoncello, upon which she presently accompanies herself. Chorus of Maidens are heard singing in the distance.*

JANE. The fickle crew have deserted Reginald and sworn allegiance to his rival, and all, forsooth, because he has glanced with passing favour on a 5 puling milkmaid! Fools! of that fancy he will soon weary – and then I, who alone am faithful to him, shall reap my reward. But do not dally too long, Reginald, for my charms are ripe, Reginald, and already they are decaying. Better secure me ere I have gone too far!

RECITATIVE – JANE.

Sad is that woman's lot who, year by year, 10
Sees, one by one, her beauties disappear,
When Time, grown weary of her heart-drawn sighs,
Impatiently begins to 'dim her eyes'!
Compelled, at last, in life's uncertain gloamings,
To wreathe her wrinkled brow with well-saved 'combings', 15
Reduced, with rouge, lip-salve, and pearly grey,
To 'make up' for lost time as best she may!

SONG – JANE.

Silvered is the raven hair,
　　Spreading is the parting straight,
Mottled the complexion fair, 20
　　Halting is the youthful gait,
Hollow is the laughter free,
　　Spectacled the limpid eye –
Little will be left of me
　　In the coming by and by! 25

28 *severely laced*: This phrase was originally written and sung as 'securely laced'.

60–61 *a decalet – a pure and simple thing*: A decalet is a poetic stanza of ten lines. In his essay mentioned earlier (see the notes to Act I, lines 373–96 and 523), John Bush Jones cites Grosvenor's two poems as evidence that Gilbert based his character on Coventry Patmore, whose early poems were about simple domestic subjects. It might be added that the *Cautionary Tales* which Hilaire Belloc published in 1907 also bear more than a passing resemblance to Grosvenor's poems.

Fading is the taper waist,
  Shapeless grows the shapely limb,
And although severely laced,
  Spreading is the figure trim!
Stouter than I used to be,   30
  Still more corpulent grow I –
There will be too much of me
  In the coming by and by!

(*Exit* JANE.)

(*Enter* GROSVENOR, *followed by Maidens, two and two, each playing on an*   35
archaic instrument, as in Act I. He is reading abstractedly, as BUNTHORNE *did in*
Act I, and pays no attention to them.)

CHORUS OF MAIDENS.

Turn, oh, turn in this direction,
  Shed, oh, shed a gentle smile,
With a glance of sad perfection   40
  Our poor fainting hearts beguile!
On such eyes as maidens cherish
  Let thy fond adorers gaze,
Or incontinently perish
  In their all-consuming rays!   45

(*He sits – they group around him.*)

GROS. (*aside*). The old, old tale. How rapturously these maidens love me,
and how hopelessly! Oh, Patience, Patience, with the love of thee in
my heart, what have I for these poor mad maidens but an unvalued pity?
Alas, they will die of hopeless love for me, as I shall die of hopeless love for   50
thee!

ANG. Sir, will it please you read to us?

GROS. (*sighing*). Yes, child, if you will. What shall I read?

ANG. One of your own poems.

GROS. One of my own poems? Better not, my child. *They* will not cure   55
thee of thy love.

ELLA. Mr Bunthorne used to read us a poem of his own every day.

SAPH. And, to do him justice, he read them extremely well.

GROS. Oh, did he so? Well, who am I that I should take upon myself
to withhold my gifts from you? What am I but a trustee? Here is a decalet –   60
a pure and simple thing, a very daisy – a babe might understand it. To
appreciate it, it is not necessary to think of anything at all.

ANG. Let us think of nothing at all!

64–73, *Gentle Jane . . . Teasing Tom*: Gilbert wrote both these poems for his earlier clerical

79–88 version of *Patience*, where they were given to the Revd Lawn Tennison to declaim. In that version, each of the poems had a refrain for the chorus at the end:

> Oh may we all endeavour to gain
> The happy rewards of Gentle Jane!

and

> Oh may we all take warning from
> The wicked career of Teasing Tom!

'Teasing Tom' has echoes of one of Gilbert's *Bab Ballads*, 'Gentle Archibald', which tells of a little boy prone to equally unpleasant acts:

> He boiled his little sister JANE;
> He painted blue his aged mother;
> Sat down upon his little brother;
> Tripped up his cousins with his hoop;
> Put pussy in his father's soup;
> Placed beetles in his uncle's shoe;
> Cut a policeman right in two;
> Spread devastation round, and, ah,
> He red-hot-pokered his papa!

In early performances, Saphir had the following line after Grosvenor had finished his poems and before Angela came in with 'Marked you how grandly . . .': 'How simple, how earnest – how true'.

92 *Oh, sir, you are indeed a true poet*: In the first edition of the libretto Ella did not say anything at this point but had a longer version of the later line now given to Saphir: 'Oh, sir, do not send us from you, for our love leaps to our lips, and our hearts go out to you.'

94 *Ladies, I am sorry*: As originally performed, Grosvenor's lines at this point went: 'Ladies, I am sorry to distress you, but you have been following me about ever since Monday, and this is Saturday. I should like the usual half-holiday, and if you will kindly allow me to close early today, I shall take it as a personal favour'. By the late 1870s the Saturday half-holiday, which had originally been a privilege largely restricted to those working in the textile trade, had become general for most working people.

GROSVENOR *recites.*

Gentle Jane was as good as gold,
She always did as she was told; 65
She never spoke when her mouth was full,
Or caught bluebottles their legs to pull,
Or spilt plum jam on her nice new frock,
Or put white mice in the eight-day clock,
Or vivisected her last new doll, 70
Or fostered a passion for alcohol.
And when she grew up she was given in marriage
To a first-class earl who keeps his carriage!

GROS. I believe I am right in saying that there is not one word in that
decalet which is calculated to bring the blush of shame to the cheek of 75
modesty.
ANG. Not one; it is purity itself.
GROS. Here's another.

Teasing Tom was a very bad boy,
A great big squirt was his favourite toy; 80
He put live shrimps in his father's boots,
And sewed up the sleeves of his Sunday suits;
He punched his poor little sisters' heads,
And cayenne-peppered their four-post beds,
He plastered their hair with cobbler's wax, 85
And dropped hot halfpennies down their backs.
The consequence was he was lost totally,
And married a girl in the *corps de bally!*

ANG. Marked you how grandly – how relentlessly – the damning
catalogue of crime strode on, till Retribution, like a poisèd hawk, came 90
swooping down upon the Wrong-Doer? Oh, it was terrible!
ELLA. Oh, sir, you are indeed a true poet, for you touch our hearts, and
they go out to you!
GROS. (*aside*). This is simply cloying. (*Aloud.*) Ladies, I am sorry to
appear ungallant, but this is Saturday, and you have been following me 95
about ever since Monday. I should like the usual half-holiday. I shall take it
as a personal favour if you will kindly allow me to close early to-day.
SAPH. Oh, sir, do not send us from you!
GROS. Poor, poor girls! It is best to speak plainly. I know that I am
loved by you, but I never can love you in return, for my heart is fixed 100
elsewhere! Remember the fable of the Magnet and the Churn!

105–38 *A magnet hung in a hardware shop*

This song is associated with an embarrassing incident which occurred on the first night of *Patience* at the Savoy Theatre. Rutland Barrington, who created the part of Archibald Grosvenor, recalls in his memoirs:

> When I took my seat on a rustic tree-trunk preparatory to singing 'The Magnet and the Churn', I heard an ominous kind of r-r-r-i-p-p and immediately felt conscious of a horrible draught on my right leg. My beautiful knee breeches had gone crack. It was an awful moment. Had they but been made of red velvet it would not have mattered so much, for I felt I was blushing all over and it might have escaped notice, though some of the aesthetic maidens were already choking with laughter.

'The Magnet and the Churn' was parodied in *The Poet and the Puppets*, a burlesque about Oscar Wilde by Charles Brookfield which was first produced in London in 1892, just after Wilde's first play, *Lady Windermere's Fan*, had opened in the West End:

> A poet lived in a handsome style,
> His books had sold and he'd made his pile.
> His articles, stories and lectures too
> Had brought success, as ev'rbody knew.
> But the poet was tired of writing tales
> Of curious women and singular males,
> So, soon as he'd finished his Dorian Gray,
> He set to work on a four-act play.
> A four-act play, a four-act play.
> A most aesthetic, very magnetic fancy, let us say.
> He filled his purse by writing verse,
> So why not a four-act play?

139 *They go off in low spirits*: The stage direction in the licence copy at this point reads: 'They go off as in Act I singing "In a melancholy train", and gazing back at him from time to time'.

ANG. (*wildly*). But we don't know the fable of the Magnet and the Churn.

GROS. Don't you? Then I will sing it to you.

SONG – GROSVENOR.

A magnet hung in a hardware shop,	105
And all around was a loving crop	
Of scissors and needles, nails and knives,	
Offering love for all their lives;	
But for iron the magnet felt no whim,	
Though he charmed iron, it charmed not him;	110
From needles and nails and knives he'd turn,	
For he'd set his love on a Silver Churn!	

ALL.   A Silver Churn?
GROS.   A Silver Churn!

His most æsthetic,	115
Very magnetic	
Fancy took this turn –	
'If I can wheedle	
A knife or a needle,	
Why not a Silver Churn?'	120

CHORUS.   His most æsthetic, etc.

GROS. And Iron and Steel expressed surprise,	
The needles opened their well-drilled eyes,	
The penknives felt 'shut up', no doubt,	
The scissors declared themselves 'cut out',	125
The kettles they boiled with rage, 'tis said,	
While every nail went off its head,	
And hither and thither began to roam,	
Till a hammer came up – and drove them home.	

ALL.   It drove them home?   130
GROS.   It drove them home!

While this magnetic,	
Peripatetic	
Lover he lived to learn,	
By no endeavour	135
Can magnet ever	
Attract a Silver Churn!	

ALL.   While this magnetic, etc.

(*They go off in low spirits, gazing back at him from time to time.*)

152 *Madly, hopelessly, despairingly*: Grosvenor's words foreshadow the response of Rose
   Maybud to Sir Ruthven's question whether she loves him: 'Madly, passionately'
   (*Ruddigore*, Act II, lines 589, 592 and 595).

GROS. At last they are gone! What is this mysterious fascination that I   140
seem to exercise over all I come across? A curse on my fatal beauty, for I am
sick of conquests!

(PATIENCE *appears.*)

PA. Archibald!
GROS. (*turns and sees her*). Patience!   145
PA. I have escaped with difficulty from my Reginald. I wanted to see you
so much that I might ask you if you still love me as fondly as ever?
GROS. Love you? If the devotion of a lifetime — (*Seizes her hand.*)
PA. (*indignantly*). Hold! Unhand me, or I scream! (*He releases her.*) If you
are a gentleman, pray remember that I am another's! (*Very tenderly.*) But you   150
do love me, don't you?
GROS. Madly, hopelessly, despairingly!
PA. That's right! I never can be yours; but that's right!
GROS. And you love this Bunthorne?
PA. With a heart-whole ecstasy that withers, and scorches, and burns,   155
and stings! (*Sadly.*) It is my duty.
GROS. Admirable girl! But you are not happy with him?
PA. Happy? I am miserable beyond description!
GROS. That's right! I never can be yours; but that's right!
PA. But go now. I see dear Reginald approaching. Farewell, dear   160
Archibald; I cannot tell you how happy it has made me to know that you still
love me.
GROS. Ah, if I only dared — (*Advances towards her.*)
PA. Sir! this language to one who is promised to another! (*Tenderly.*) Oh,
Archibald, think of me sometimes, for my heart is breaking! He is so   165
unkind to me, and you would be so loving!
GROS. Loving! (*Advances towards her.*)
PA. Advance one step, and as I am a good and pure woman, I scream!
(*Tenderly.*) Farewell, Archibald! (*Sternly.*) Stop there! (*Tenderly.*) Think of me
sometimes! (*Angrily.*) Advance at your peril! Once more, adieu!   170

(GROSVENOR *sighs, gazes sorrowfully at her, sighs deeply,*
and exits. She bursts into tears.)

(*Enter* BUNTHORNE, *followed by* JANE. *He is moody and preoccupied.*)

JANE *sings.*

In a doleful train,
    One and one I walk all day;   175
For I love in vain –
    None so sorrowful as they

185 *Don't you interfere*: Echoes of yet another Savoy Opera here, this time the exchange between Cousin Hebe and Sir Joseph Porter originally intended for Act II of *H.M.S. Pinafore* but cut out before the first performance (see the note to *H.M.S. Pinafore*, Act II, line 428).

204 *Oh, can't you, though*: This and the next line for Bunthorne were not in the first-edition libretto and were inserted in an early prompt copy, apparently to incorporate an ad-lib gag which Gilbert approved.

Who can only sigh and say,
Woe is me, alackaday!
Woe is me, alackaday, and woe! 180

BUN. (*seeing* PATIENCE). Crying, eh? What are you crying about?
PA. I've only been thinking how dearly I love you!
BUN. Love me! Bah!
JANE. Love him! Bah!
BUN. (*to* JANE). Don't you interfere. 185
JANE. He always crushes me!
PA. (*going to him*). What is the matter, dear Reginald? If you have any sorrow, tell it to me, that I may share it with you. (*Sighing.*) It is my duty!
BUN. (*snappishly*). Whom were you talking with just now?
PA. With dear Archibald. 190
BUN. (*furiously*). With dear Archibald! Upon my honour, this is too much!
JANE. A great deal too much!
BUN. (*angrily to* JANE). Do be quiet!
JANE. Crushed again! 195
PA. I think he is the noblest, purest, and most perfect being I have ever met. But I don't love him. It is true that he is devotedly attached to me, but indeed I don't love *him*. Whenever he grows affectionate, I scream. It is my duty! (*Sighing.*)
BUN. I dare say! 200
JANE. So do I! *I* dare say!
PA. Why, how could I love him and love you too? You can't love two people at once!
BUN. Oh, can't you, though!
PA. No, you can't; I only wish you could. 205
BUN. I don't believe you know what love is!
PA. (*sighing*). Yes, I do. There was a happy time when I didn't, but a bitter experience has taught me.

(*Exeunt* BUNTHORNE *and* JANE.)

BALLAD – PATIENCE.

Love is a plaintive song, 210
  Sung by a suffering maid,
Telling a tale of wrong,
  Telling of hope betrayed;
Tuned to each changing note,
  Sorry when *he* is sad, 215
Blind to his every mote,
  Merry when he is glad!

236 *smug-faced idiot*: Originally this was 'idyllic idiot'.

238 *Too mild*: This is another of the lines cited by John Bush Jones in his argument that Gilbert had Coventry Patmore at least partially in mind when he created the character of Grosvenor. Patmore was frequently criticized for his excessive mildness and 'insipid amiability'. But this line could also be a hangover from the clerical version of *Patience*, where the two clergymen vie with each other in their mildness in the manner of the rival curates in Gilbert's earlier Bab Ballad.

254–89 *So go to him and say to him, with compliment ironical*
The *Illustrated London News* reported that on the opening night this number had the unique distinction of receiving a triple encore. It has been a particular favourite with audiences ever since.

Love that no wrong can cure,
Love that is always new,
That is the love that's pure,   220
That is the love that's true!

Rendering good for ill,
Smiling at every frown,
Yielding your own self-will,
Laughing your tear-drops down;   225
Never a selfish whim,
Trouble, or pain to stir;
Everything for him,
Nothing at all for her!
Love that will aye endure,   230
Though the rewards be few,
That is the love that's pure,
That is the love that's true!

(*At the end of ballad exit* PATIENCE, *weeping.*)

(*Enter* BUNTHORNE *and* JANE.)   235

BUN. Everything has gone wrong with me since that smug-faced idiot came here. Before that I was admired – I may say, loved.

JANE. Too mild – adored!

BUN. Do let a poet soliloquize! The damozels used to follow me wherever I went; now they all follow him!   240

JANE. Not all! *I* am still faithful to you.

BUN. Yes, and a pretty damozel *you* are!

JANE. No, not pretty. Massive. Cheer up! I will never leave you, I swear it!

BUN. Oh, thank you! I know what it is; it's his confounded mildness.   245 They find me too highly spiced, if you please! And no doubt I *am* highly spiced.

JANE. Not for my taste!

BUN. (*savagely*). No, but I am for theirs. But I will show the world I can be as mild as he. If they want insipidity, they shall have it. I'll meet this   250 fellow on his own ground and beat him on it.

JANE. You shall. And I will help you.

BUN. You will? Jane, there's a good deal of good in you, after all!

DUET – BUNTHORNE *and* JANE.

JANE.   So go to him and say to him, with compliment ironical –

258 *Your style is much too sanctified*: This line looks distinctly as though it has been left over from the clerical version, being much more appropriate to clergymen than aesthetic poets. However, there is no trace of it in the manuscript of Gilbert's earlier version which survives in the British Library.

280 *quiddity*: The *Oxford English Dictionary* defines a quiddity as 'a captious nicety in argument, a quirk or quibble'. The word derives from the Latin word *quid* and originally meant the real nature of things. It is all very philosophical – better, surely, to be like Ruth and the Pirate King in *The Pirates of Penzance* and just concentrate on quips and quibbles.

290 *Exeunt Jane and Bunthorne together*: For a long time in D'Oyly Carte productions Lady Jane at this point picked up Bunthorne in her arms and carried him off the stage. In his autobiography, *The Secrets of a Savoyard*, Sir Henry Lytton recalls being dropped with a terrible crash by Miss Bertha Lewis, the company's leading contralto for twenty years until her untimely death following a car accident in 1931. Lytton writes: 'In the shelter of the wings I remonstrated with her, pointing out that this was a distinct departure from what Gilbert intended. All the sympathy I got was, "Well, I've dropped you only twice in eight years".'

BUN.	Sing 'Hey to you – Good day to you' – And that's what I shall say!	255
JANE.	'Your style is much too sanctified – your cut is too canonical' –	
BUN.	Sing 'Bah to you – Ha! ha! to you' – And that's what I shall say!	260
JANE.	'I was the beau ideal of the morbid young æsthetical – To doubt my inspiration was regarded as heretical – Until you cut me out with your placidity emetical.' –	
BUN.	Sing 'Booh to you – Pooh, pooh to you' – And that's what I shall say!	265
BOTH.	Sing 'Hey to you – good day to you' – Sing 'Bah to you – ha! ha! to you' – Sing 'Booh to you – pooh, pooh to you' –	270

And that's what $\begin{Bmatrix} \text{you should} \\ \text{I shall} \end{Bmatrix}$ say!

BUN. JANE.	I'll tell him that unless he will consent to be more jocular – Sing 'Booh to you – Pooh, pooh to you' – And that's what you should say!	275
BUN. JANE.	To cut his curly hair, and stick an eyeglass in his ocular – Sing 'Bah to you – Ha! ha! to you' – And that's what you should say!	
BUN.	To stuff his conversation full of quibble and of quiddity – To dine on chops and roly-poly pudding with avidity – He'd better clear away with all convenient rapidity.	280
JANE.	Sing 'Hey to you – Good day to you' – And that's what you should say!	285
BOTH.	Sing 'Booh to you – pooh, pooh to you' – Sing 'Bah to you – ha! ha! to you' – Sing 'Hey to you – good day to you' –	

And that's what $\begin{Bmatrix} \text{you should} \\ \text{I shall} \end{Bmatrix}$ say!

(*Exeunt* JANE *and* BUNTHORNE *together.*)   290

296–315 *It's clear that mediæval art alone retains its zest*

The transformation of the soldiers into aesthetes was always conceived by Gilbert as one of the show-stopping scenes in *Patience*. In the letter he sent to Sullivan announcing that he had decided to abandon the idea of basing the plot around clergymen and to return instead to his original idea of a skit on the Pre-Raphaelites, he wrote: 'The Hussars will become aesthetic young men (abandoning their profession for the purpose) – in this latter capacity they will carry lilies in their hands, wear long hair, and stand in stained glass attitudes'.

There is a celebrated photograph taken in 1881 of the original Duke, Colonel and Major (Durward Lely, Richard Temple and Frank Thornton) with droopy moustaches, striking stained glass attitudes and clad in velvet floppy hats and suits. I have reproduced it in my book *William Morris and His World* (1978). The *Daily News* first-night reviewer commented that the three officers appeared 'looking like figures cut out of a Pre-Raphaelite picture and vivified. The constrained attitudes, distorted positions, and grotesque gestures of the three, and the quaint music which they sing, produced a richly humorous effect'.

In the licence copy, this song had only one verse, going straight from 'angular and flat' (line 302) to 'To cultivate the trim' (line 313). The American scholar Jane Steadman has pointed out in her essay 'The Genesis of *Patience*' (in *W. S. Gilbert: A Century of Scholarship and Commentary*, New York, 1970) that in its original form the song could apply equally well to the Victorian High Church movement as to the Pre-Raphaelites. It is true that a predilection for medievalism and Early English architecture was common to both these groups. However, this song does not appear in Gilbert's manuscript for the clerical version of the opera, and there is no particular reason to think that he originally conceived it as a number in which the soldiers would assume the somewhat affected manners and attitudes of the Tractarians in the Church of England.

(*Enter* DUKE, COLONEL, *and* MAJOR. *They have abandoned their uniforms, and are dressed and made up in imitation of Æsthetics. They have long hair, and other outward signs of attachment to the brotherhood. As they sing they walk in stiff, constrained, and angular attitudes – a grotesque exaggeration of the attitudes adopted by* BUNTHORNE *and the Maidens in Act I.*)   295

TRIO – DUKE, COLONEL, *and* MAJOR.

It's clear that mediæval art alone retains its zest,
To charm and please its devotees we've done our little best.
We're not quite sure if all we do has the Early English ring;
But, as far as we can judge, it's something like this sort of thing:
      You hold yourself like this (*attitude*),   300
      You hold yourself like that (*attitude*),
By hook and crook you try to look both angular and flat (*attitude*).
      We venture to expect
      That what we recollect,
Though but a part of true High Art, will have its due effect.   305

If this is not exactly right, we hope you won't upbraid;
You can't get high Æsthetic tastes, like trousers, ready made.
True views on Mediævalism Time alone will bring,
But, as far as we can judge, it's something like this sort of thing:
      You hold yourself like this (*attitude*),   310
      You hold yourself like that (*attitude*),
By hook and crook you try to look both angular and flat (*attitude*).
      To cultivate the trim
      Rigidity of limb,
You ought to get a Marionette, and form your style on him (*attitude*).   315

COL. (*attitude*). Yes, it's quite clear that our only chance of making a lasting impression on these young ladies is to become as æsthetic as they are.

MAJ. (*attitude*). No doubt. The only question is how far we've succeeded in doing so. I don't know why, but I've an idea that this is not quite right.   320

DUKE. (*attitude*). I don't like it. I never did. I don't see what it means. I do it, but I don't like it.

COL. My good friend, the question is not whether we like it, but whether they do. They understand these things – we don't. Now I shouldn't be surprised if this is effective enough – at a distance.   325

MAJ. I can't help thinking we're a little stiff at it. It would be extremely awkward if we were to be 'struck' so!

COL. I don't think we shall be struck so. Perhaps we're a little awkward at first – but everything must have a beginning. Oh, here they come! 'Tention!   330

333 *the Inner Brotherhood*: This phrase removes any possible doubt about who it is that the soldiers are trying to imitate; it was the term which the Pre-Raphaelites applied to themselves. The Pre-Raphaelite Brotherhood was set up in 1848 by William Holman Hunt, John Everett Millais, Dante Gabriel Rossetti and four friends. They chose the word 'Brotherhood' because of its medieval associations and its aura of secrecy.

336 *How Botticellian! How Fra Angelican*: The guiding principle which gave the Pre-Raphaelites their name was, of course, their desire to return to the pure principles of medieval art before they had begun to be corrupted by the academic and classical approach of Renaissance artists like Raphael (1483-1520). Fra Angelico (1400-1455) and Botticelli (1445-1510) were early Renaissance Florentine artists whose work was admired by the Pre-Raphaelites.

341 *jolly utter*: The aesthetic movement developed its own rather over-blown vocabulary in which such words as 'supreme', 'utter', 'consummate', 'precious' and 'intense' figured prominently. In this line Gilbert creates a splendidly discordant effect by pairing the ultra-philistine 'jolly' with the super-aesthetic 'utter'.

356 *By sections of threes – Rapture*: This echoes the command of the Scornful Colonel in Gilbert's Bab Ballad of that name: 'By sections, "Phew"!' (see the note to lines 677–90 in Act I).

363 *hooking you*: In early performances the Colonel's speech was followed by a further passage of essentially superfluous dialogue before the singing of the quintet. Part of this is still printed in the current Macmillan edition:

DUKE. Won't it be rather awkward?

COL. Awkward, not at all. Observe, suppose you choose Angela, I take Saphir, Major takes nobody. Suppose you choose Saphir, Major takes Angela, I take nobody. Suppose you choose neither, I take Angela, Major takes Saphir. Clear as day!

ANG. Capital!

SAPH. The very thing!

(*They strike fresh attitudes, as* ANGELA *and* SAPHIR *enter.*)

ANG. (*seeing them*). Oh, Saphir – see – see! The immortal fire has descended on them, and they are of the Inner Brotherhood – perceptively intense and consummately utter. (*The Officers have some difficulty in maintaining their constrained attitudes.*) 335

SAPH. (*in admiration*). How Botticellian! How Fra Angelican! Oh, Art, we thank thee for this boon!

COL. (*apologetically*). I'm afraid we're not quite right.

ANG. Not supremely, perhaps, but oh, so all-but! (*To* SAPHIR.) Oh, Saphir, are they not quite too all-but? 340

SAPH. They are indeed jolly utter!

MAJ. (*in agony*). I wonder what the Inner Brotherhood usually recommend for cramp?

COL. Ladies, we will not deceive you. We are doing this at some personal inconvenience with a view of expressing the extremity of our devotion to 345
you. We trust that it is not without its effect.

ANG. We will not deny that we are much moved by this proof of your attachment.

SAPH. Yes, your conversion to the principles of Æsthetic Art in its highest development has touched us deeply. 350

ANG. And if Mr Grosvenor should remain obdurate –

SAPH. Which we have every reason to believe he will –

MAJ. (*aside, in agony*). I wish they'd make haste.

ANG. We are not prepared to say that our yearning hearts will not go out to you. 355

COL. (*as giving a word of command*). By sections of threes – Rapture! (*All strike a fresh attitude, expressive of æsthetic rapture.*)

SAPH. Oh, it's extremely good – for beginners it's admirable.

MAJ. The only question is, who will take who?

COL. Oh, the Duke chooses first, as a matter of course. 360

DUKE. Oh, I couldn't think of it – you are really too good!

COL. Nothing of the kind. You are a great matrimonial fish, and it's only fair that each of these ladies should have a chance of hooking you.

QUINTET.

DUKE, COLONEL, MAJOR, ANGELA, *and* SAPHIR.

DUKE (*taking* SAPHIR).

If Saphir I choose to marry,
I shall be fixed up for life; 365

Then the Colonel need not tarry,
　Angela can be his wife.
　　　　　　　(*Handing* ANGELA *to* COLONEL.)

(DUKE *dances with* SAPHIR, COLONEL *with* ANGELA,
　　　MAJOR *dances alone*.)　　　　　　　　　370

MAJOR (*dancing alone*).

In that case unprecedented,
　Single I shall live and die –
I shall have to be contented
　With their heartfelt sympathy!

ALL (*dancing as before*).

He will have to be contented　　　　　　　375
　With our heartfelt sympathy!

DUKE (*taking* ANGELA).

If on Angy I determine,
　At my wedding she'll appear
Decked in diamond and ermine,
　Major then can take Saphir!　　　　　　　380
　　　　　　　(*Handing* SAPHIR *to* MAJOR.)

(DUKE *dances with* ANGELA, MAJOR *with* SAPHIR,
　　　COLONEL *dances alone*.)

COLONEL (*dancing*).

In that case unprecedented,
　Single I shall live and die –　　　　　　385
I shall have to be contented
　With their heartfelt sympathy!

ALL (*dancing as before*).

He will have to be contented
　With our heartfelt sympathy!

DUKE (*taking both* ANGELA *and* SAPHIR).

After some debate internal,　　　　　　　390

409 *Looking at his reflection in hand-mirror*: As originally performed at the Opéra Comique, Bunthorne at this point gazed into a lake on the stage. The stage direction in the first-edition libretto reads: *'Reclining on bank of lake, and looking at his reflection in the water'*. It was not practicable to re-create the lake on the stage of the new Savoy Theatre and when the opera moved there, the business with the hand-mirror was substituted. It has continued ever since.

Narcissus: One with excessive self-admiration. In Greek mythology Narcissus was a beautiful youth who saw his reflection in a fountain and thought that it must be the presiding nymph of the place. He jumped in to reach it and drowned.

410 *Enter Bunthorne, moodily*: The direction in the licence copy for this entrance gives the additional information that *'His hair now resembles Grosvenor's – that is to say it is lank instead of being bushy; and he has shaved his moustache'*.

413 *Ah, Bunthorne*: As originally performed, this exchange went as follows:

> GROS. Ah, Bunthorne! come here – look! Is it not beautiful?
> (BUN. *also reclines behind lake, so that the actions of both are reflected in the water*.)
> BUN. (*looking in lake*). Which?
> GROS. Mine.
> BUN. Bah! I am in no mood for trifling.

If on neither I decide,
Saphir then can take the Colonel,
                      (*Handing* SAPHIR *to* COLONEL.)
Angy be the Major's bride!
                      (*Handing* ANGELA *to* MAJOR.)   395

(COLONEL *dances with* SAPHIR, MAJOR *with* ANGELA,
     DUKE *dances alone.*)

DUKE (*dancing*).
In that case unprecedented,
Single I must live and die –
I shall have to be contented   400
With their heartfelt sympathy!

ALL (*dancing as before*).

He will have to be contented
With our heartfelt sympathy.

(*At the end*, DUKE, COLONEL, *and* MAJOR, *and two girls*
                      dance off arm-in-arm.)   405

(*Enter* GROSVENOR.)

GROS. It is very pleasant to be alone. It is pleasant to be able to gaze at
leisure upon those features which all others may gaze upon at their good
will! (*Looking at his reflection in hand-mirror.*) Ah, I am a very Narcissus!

(*Enter* BUNTHORNE, *moodily.*)   410

BUN. It's no use; I can't live without admiration. Since Grosvenor came
here, insipidity has been at a premium. Ah, he is there!
GROS. Ah, Bunthorne! come here – look! Very graceful, isn't it!
BUN. (*taking hand-mirror*). Allow me; I haven't seen it. Yes, it is graceful.
GROS. (*re-taking hand-mirror*). Oh, good gracious! not that – this —   415
BUN. You don't mean that! Bah! I am in no mood for trifling.
GROS. And what is amiss?
BUN. Ever since you came here, you have entirely monopolized the
attentions of the young ladies. I don't like it, sir!
GROS. My dear sir, how can I help it? They are the plague of my life. My   420
dear Mr Bunthorne, with your personal disadvantages, you can have no idea
of the inconvenience of being madly loved, at first sight, by every woman
you meet.

434–5 *have a back parting*: This is not in the original libretto and was almost certainly an ad-lib incorporated with Gilbert's approval into later editions. The whole idea of a back parting would have struck the Pre-Raphaelites as appallingly philistine and prosaic. If they parted their hair at all, it was generally in the middle. On the D'Oyly Carte recording of *Patience*, produced by Decca in 1961, Grosvenor interjects 'Beg pardon' at the words 'back parting' and Bunthorne repeats them.

439 *I am a man with a mission*: Originally Grosvenor had a longer speech at this point: 'I am a man with a mission. I am here to preach, in my own person, the Principles of Perfection. I am, as it were, a Banquet of Beauty upon which all who will may feast. It is most unpleasant to be a Banquet, but I must not shirk my responsibilities.'

BUN. Sir, until you came here I was adored!

GROS. Exactly – until I came here. That's my grievance. I cut everybody   425
out! I assure you, if you could only suggest some means whereby,
consistently with my duty to society, I could escape these inconvenient
attentions, you would earn my everlasting gratitude.

BUN. I will do so at once. However popular it may be with the world at
large, your personal appearance is highly objectionable to *me*.   430

GROS. It is? (*Shaking his hand.*) Oh, thank you! thank you! How can I
express my gratitude?

BUN. By making a complete change at once. Your conversation must
henceforth be perfectly matter-of-fact. You must cut your hair, and have a
back parting. In appearance and costume you must be absolutely   435
commonplace.

GROS. (*decidedly*). No. Pardon me, that's impossible.

BUN. Take care! When I am thwarted I am very terrible.

GROS. I can't help that. I am a man with a mission. And that mission
must be fulfilled.   440

BUN. I don't think you quite appreciate the consequences of thwarting
me.

GROS. I don't care what they are.

BUN. Suppose – I won't go so far as to say that I will do it – but suppose
for one moment I were to curse you? (GROSVENOR *quails.*) Ah! Very well.   445
Take care.

GROS. But surely you would never do that? (*In great alarm.*)

BUN. I don't know. It would be an extreme measure, no doubt. Still —

GROS. (*wildly*). But you would not do it – I am sure you would not.
(*Throwing himself at* BUNTHORNE's *knees, and clinging to him.*) Oh, reflect,   450
reflect! You had a mother once.

BUN. Never!

GROS. Then you had an aunt! (BUNTHORNE *affected.*) Ah! I see you had!
By the memory of that aunt, I implore you to pause ere you resort to this last
fearful expedient. Oh, Mr Bunthorne, reflect, reflect! (*Weeping.*)   455

BUN. (*aside, after a struggle with himself*). I must not allow myself to be
unmanned! (*Aloud.*) It is useless. Consent at once, or may a nephew's
curse —

GROS. Hold! Are you absolutely resolved?

BUN. Absolutely.   460

GROS. Will nothing shake you?

BUN. Nothing. I am adamant.

GROS. Very good. (*Rising.*) Then I yield.

BUN. Ha! You swear it?

GROS. I do, cheerfully. I have long wished for a reasonable pretext for   465
such a change as you suggest. It has come at last. I do it on compulsion!

BUN. Victory! I triumph!

478 *A most intense young man*: In early libretti, Bunthorne sang lines 478–81 as a solo before they were repeated by both men singing together. Similarly, Grosvenor first sang lines 492–5 on his own.

486 *black-and-tan*: A breed of small terrier dog.

488 *Monday Pops*: Forerunners of the modern Promenade Concerts, the Monday Pops were weekly concerts of classical music organized by the music publishers Chappells. They began in 1859 in the St James's Hall and in 1901 transferred to the Queen's Hall. They are mentioned by the Mikado as a suitable punishment for the music-hall singer (*The Mikado*, Act II, line 376).

494 *jolly Bank-holiday*: A highly topical reference when *Patience* was written. Two measures successfully piloted through Parliament in 1871 and 1875 by the Liberal M.P. Sir John Lubbock had established Boxing Day, Easter Monday, Whit Monday and the first Monday in August as bank (i.e. public) holidays.

497 *A blue-and-white young man*: See the note to line 700 in Act I.

498 *Francesca di Rimini*: Francesca da Rimini was the daughter of a thirteenth-century Lord of Ravenna who was killed by her husband for being the secret lover of his brother. The story was immortalized in Dante's *Inferno*.

500 *Chancery Lane*: The street which goes through the heart of legal London, joining Gray's Inn to the north with Fleet Street (the Law Courts and the Middle and Inner Temples) to the south and Lincoln's Inn halfway down. Strephon speaks in Act I of *Iolanthe* of being led there, singing, by a servile usher.

501 *Somerset House*: A large and imposing building constructed in 1776 on the site of Protector Somerset's town house between the Strand and the Thames. In its time, it has housed many Government departments, including the Navy Office, the Board of Inland Revenue and the Registrar of Births, Marriages and Deaths.

503 *Threepenny-bus*: The first buses to run in London charged fares of sixpence to a shilling depending on the distance. However, competition between rival companies was so intense that the fares came down to a uniform threepence. For the 1900 revival of *Patience*, Gilbert changed the phrase to 'twopenny tube'. The Central London Underground Railway, which had opened that year, charged a uniform fare of twopence on its journeys between Shepherd's Bush and Bank stations. Since the turn of the century there has been no attempt to up-date this line to match rising prices – which is, perhaps, just as well: Grosvenor would have had great difficulty in keeping abreast of the recent tussle over London's bus and tube fares between the Greater London Council and the law lords. How Gilbert would have loved it, though!

DUET – BUNTHORNE *and* GROSVENOR.

BUN.
When I go out of door,
Of damozels a score
   (All sighing and burning,
   And clinging and yearning)   470
Will follow me as before.
I shall, with cultured taste,
Distinguish gems from paste,
   And 'High diddle diddle'   475
   Will rank as an idyll,
If I pronounce it chaste!

BOTH.
   A most intense young man,
   A soulful-eyed young man,
An ultra-poetical, super-æsthetical,   480
   Out-of-the-way young man!

GROS.
Conceive me, if you can,
An every-day young man:
   A commonplace type,
   With a stick and a pipe,   485
And a half-bred black-and-tan;
   Who thinks suburban 'hops'
   More fun than 'Monday Pops',
Who's fond of his dinner,
And doesn't get thinner   490
   On bottled beer and chops.

BOTH.
   A commonplace young man,
   A matter-of-fact young man,
A steady and stolid-y, jolly Bank-holiday
   Every-day young man!   495

BUN.
   A Japanese young man,
   A blue-and-white young man,
Francesca di Rimini, miminy, piminy,
   Je-ne-sais-quoi young man!

GROS.
   A Chancery Lane young man,   500
   A Somerset House young man,
A very delectable, highly respectable,
   Threepenny-bus young man!

506 *greenery-yallery*: Green and yellow were much favoured by the Pre-Raphaelite painters. The rhythm and sound of this line bear a striking resemblance to a refrain from one of Gilbert's *Bab Ballads*, 'Down to the Derby':

> Palery alery, smokery, jokery, rambling,
> scrambling, crash along, dash along –
> Down to the Derby as all of us go.

Grosvenor Gallery: Founded by Sir Coutts Lindsay in New Bond Street in 1877, the Grosvenor Gallery was much patronized by the Pre-Raphaelites and came to rival the Royal Academy as the leading arbiter of artistic taste in Britain. Whistler's painting *Nocturne in Black and Gold*, which provoked Ruskin's damning comment mentioned in the introduction, was one of the gallery's first exhibits.

508 *Sewell & Cross*: A high-class drapers and costumiers in Soho. It also gets a mention in *Princess Ida* (Act II, line 132).

509 *Howell & James*: Another fashionable Victorian drapery store in Regent Street.

510 *What's the next article*: This derives from the favourite phrase of the eager young salesman behind the counter: 'What's the next article I can show you?'

511 *Waterloo House*: Waterloo House was a large and imposing Regency building which formerly stood in Cockspur Street, just off Trafalgar Square, and which was for some time occupied by yet another leading drapery firm, Halling, Pearce and Stone. The firm later merged with the department store Swan and Edgar.

521 *Reginald! Dancing*: In the first-edition libretto this line continued: 'And – what in the world have you done to yourself?'

BUN.	A pallid and thin young man,
	A haggard and lank young man,
	A greenery-yallery, Grosvenor Gallery,
	Foot-in-the-grave young man!

505

GROS.	A Sewell & Cross young man,
	A Howell & James young man,
	A pushing young particle – 'What's the next article?' –
	Waterloo House young man!

510

ENSEMBLE.

BUN.	GROS.
Conceive me, if you can,	Conceive me, if you can,
A crotchety, cracked young man,	A matter-of-fact young man,
An ultra-poetical, super-æsthetical,	An alphabetical, arithmetical,
Out-of-the-way young man!	Every-day young man!

515

(*At the end,* GROSVENOR *dances off.* BUNTHORNE *remains.*)

BUN. It is all right! I have committed my last act of ill-nature, and henceforth I'm a changed character. (*Dances about stage, humming refrain of last air.*)

(*Enter* PATIENCE. *She gazes in astonishment at him.*)

520

PA. Reginald! Dancing! And – what in the world is the matter with you?
BUN. Patience, I'm a changed man. Hitherto I've been gloomy, moody, fitful – uncertain in temper and selfish in disposition –
PA. You have, indeed! (*Sighing.*)

525

BUN. All that is changed. I have reformed. I have modelled myself upon Mr Grosvenor. Henceforth I am mildly cheerful. My conversation will blend amusement with instruction. I shall still be æsthetic; but my æstheticism will be of the most pastoral kind.
PA. Oh, Reginald! Is all this true?

530

BUN. Quite true. Observe how amiable I am. (*Assuming a fixed smile.*)
PA. But, Reginald, how long will this last?
BUN. With occasional intervals for rest and refreshment, as long as I do.
PA. Oh, Reginald, I'm so happy! (*In his arms.*) Oh, dear, dear Reginald, I cannot express the joy I feel at this change. It will no longer be a duty to love you, but a pleasure – a rapture – an ecstasy!

535

BUN. My darling!
PA. But – oh, horror! (*Recoiling from him.*)

547 *But, stop a bit*: As originally performed, there was a longer passage of dialogue at this
point than now survives:

> BUN. But –
> PA. It is useless, Reginald. When you were objectionable I could love you
> conscientiously, but now that you are endowed with every quality that can make a woman
> happy, it would be the height of selfishness even to think of such a thing.
> BUN. But stop a bit, I don't want to reform – I'll relapse – I'll be as I was.
> PA. No; love should purify – it should never debase. Farewell, Reginald – think of me
> sometimes as one who did her duty to you at all cost – at all sacrifice.
> BUN. But I assure you, I – interrupted.

550–51 *suit of dittoes*: A suit made of the same material throughout, so that the jacket,
waistcoat and trousers all match. In D'Oyly Carte productions the new-look Grosvenor
appeared in a suit of extremely loud checks.

551 *a pot hat*: A small round hat not unlike a bowler.

557 *Swears & Wells*: A famous firm of furriers and costumiers which originally traded from
Regent Street and later moved to Oxford Street. Its shop there has since been taken
over by Cheap Jacks, selling jeans.

558 *Madame Louise*: A fashionable Regent Street milliners.

This chorus was originally written to be sung in the following way:

> GROS. I'm a Waterloo House young man,
> GIRLS. We're Swears and Wells young girls,
> GROS. I'm a Sewell & Cross young man,
> GIRLS. We're Madame Louise young girls

ENSEMBLE.

GROS.	GIRLS.
A steady and stolidy, jolly Bank-holiday	We're prettily pattering, cheerily chattering,
Every-day young man!	Every-day young girls!

566 *I can't help it*: In delivering this and his subsequent lines, Grosvenor exchanges his
affected aesthetic tones for a strong Cockney accent. Captain Corcoran undergoes a
similar vocal metamorphosis at the end of Act II of *H.M.S. Pinafore*.

567 *never set eyes on you again*: In the 1961 D'Oyly Carte recording Grosvenor interjects here
'Oh, I say'.

BUN. What's the matter?

PA. Is it quite certain that you have absolutely reformed – that you are   540
henceforth a perfect being – utterly free from defect of any kind?

BUN. It is quite certain. I have sworn it.

PA. Then I never can be yours!

BUN. Why not?

PA. Love, to be pure, must be absolutely unselfish, and there can be   545
nothing unselfish in loving so perfect a being as you have now become!

BUN. But, stop a bit! I don't want to change – I'll relapse – I'll be as I was
– interrupted!

(*Enter* GROSVENOR, *followed by all the 'every-day young girls', who are followed
by Chorus of Dragoons. He has had his hair cut, and is dressed in an ordinary suit*   550
*of dittoes and a pot hat. They all dance cheerfully round the stage in marked contrast
to their former languor.*)

CHORUS – GROSVENOR *and* GIRLS.

GROSVENOR.

I'm a Waterloo House young man,
A Sewell & Cross young man,
A steady and stolid-y, jolly Bank-holiday,   555
Every-day young man!

GIRLS.

We're Swears & Wells young girls,
We're Madame Louise young girls,
We're prettily pattering, cheerily chattering,
Every-day young girls!   560

BUN. Angela – Ella – Saphir – what – what does this mean?

ANG. It means that Archibald the All-Right cannot be all-wrong; and if the
All-Right chooses to discard æstheticism, it proves that æstheticism ought to
be discarded.

PA. Oh, Archibald! Archibald! I'm shocked – surprised – horrified!   565

GROS. I can't help it. I'm not a free agent. I do it on compulsion.

PA. This is terrible. Go! I shall never set eyes on you again. But – oh,
joy!

GROS. What is the matter?

PA. Is it quite, quite certain that you will always be a commonplace   570
young man?

GROS. Always – I've sworn it.

578 *Crushed again*: This line is not in the licence copy. Instead Bunthorne says 'Oh mercy! I'm lost! lost! lost!'

587 *Ladies, the Duke has at length determined to select a bride*: Gilbert originally intended both the Colonel and the Duke to express their sentiments in song before the finale. The licence-copy version, which was probably never set to music, of this passage, following the flourish and the entrance of the three officers, is as follows:

RECITATIVE – DUKE.
Ladies, I've great and glorious news for you,
His grace the Duke, whose social position
Is rivalled only by his wealth stupendous,
To choose a bride from you has just decided!

ALL.   Oh rapture!

SOLO – DUKE.
I have a goodly prize to give away,
Which I must do without more hesitation;
You are all beautiful as a summer's day,
For all I feel an equal admiration;
I'd share it with you all right willingly,
If that could be arranged with due propriety,
But that, I need not say, can scarcely be,
Until we have recognized society.
I have resolved – for men of high degree
Should show the way in self-denying actions –
To give it to that maid who seems to be
Most wanting in material attractions!
Jane!

JANE (*leaving* BUNTHORNE'S *arms*). Duke! (JANE *and* DUKE *embrace.* BUN. *is utterly miserable*).

(JANE *pairs off with* DUKE, ANG. *with* COL., SAPH. *with* MAJOR, ELLA *with* CAPT. *Each girl takes a Dragoon.* PATIENCE *of course, has paired with* GROSVENOR.)

There is a blank after the title 'FINALE' in the licence copy.

PA. Why, then, there's nothing to prevent my loving you with all the fervour at my command!

GROS. Why, that's true. 575

PA. My Archibald!

GROS. My Patience! (*They embrace.*)

BUN. Crushed again!

(*Enter* JANE.)

JANE. (*who is still æsthetic*). Cheer up! I am still here. I have never left you, 580 and I never will!

BUN. Thank you, Jane. After all, there is no denying it, you're a fine figure of a woman!

JANE. My Reginald!

BUN. My Jane! 585

(*Flourish. Enter* COLONEL, DUKE, *and* MAJOR.)

COL. Ladies, the Duke has at length determined to select a bride! (*General excitement.*)

DUKE. I have a great gift to bestow. Approach, such of you as are truly lovely. (*All come forward, bashfully, except* JANE *and* PATIENCE.) In personal 590 appearance you have all that is necessary to make a woman happy. In common fairness, I think I ought to choose the only one among you who has the misfortune to be distinctly plain. (*Girls retire disappointed.*) Jane!

JANE (*leaving* BUNTHORNE'S *arms*). Duke! (JANE *and* DUKE *embrace.* BUNTHORNE *is utterly disgusted.*) 595

BUN. Crushed again!

FINALE.

DUKE.
    After much debate internal,
      I on Lady Jane decide,
    Saphir now may take the Colonel,
      Angy be the Major's bride! 600

(SAPHIR *pairs off with* COLONEL, ANGELA *with* MAJOR, ELLA *with* SOLICITOR.)

BUN.
    In that case unprecedented,
      Single I must live and die –
    I shall have to be contented
      With a tulip or li*ly*! 605

(*Takes a lily from button-hole and gazes affectionately at it.*)

ALL.

     He will have to be contented
      With a tulip or li*l*y!

     Greatly pleased with one another,   610
      To get married we decide.
     Each of us will wed the other,
      Nobody be Bunthorne's Bride!

     DANCE.

        CURTAIN

PRINCESS IDA

OR

CASTLE ADAMANT

DRAMATIS PERSONÆ

KING HILDEBRAND
HILARION (*his Son*)
CYRIL ⎫
FLORIAN ⎬ (*Hilarion's Friends*)
KING GAMA
ARAC ⎫
GURON ⎬ (*his Sons*)
SCYNTHIUS ⎭
PRINCESS IDA (*Gama's Daughter*)
LADY BLANCHE (*Professor of Abstract Science*)
LADY PSYCHE (*Professor of Humanities*)
MELISSA (*Lady Blanche's Daughter*)
SACHARISSA ⎫
CHLOE ⎬ (*Girl Graduates*)
ADA ⎭

Soldiers, Courtiers, 'Girl Graduates', 'Daughters of the Plough', etc.

ACT I. – Pavilion in King Hildebrand's Palace.
ACT II. – Gardens of Castle Adamant.
ACT III. – Courtyard of Castle Adamant.

PRINCESS IDA

Princess Ida is the only Savoy Opera to have three acts and to be written in
blank verse. Gilbert lifted nearly all of the dialogue from his earlier play, *The
Princess*, which had been performed at the Olympic Theatre in 1870. That
play was itself based on Alfred, Lord Tennyson's long poem *The Princess*,
which had first appeared in 1847. The new opera was accordingly billed as
'A Respectful Operatic Per-Version of Tennyson's "Princess".'

In both his play and his opera libretto, Gilbert closely followed the details
of the Poet Laureate's story. It tells of a prince who had been betrothed in
childhood to Princess Ida, daughter of the neighbouring King Gama.
Becoming a devotee of women's rights, however, the princess has abjured
men and set up an all-female university. The prince and two companions
gain entrance to the university disguised as girl students, but their true
identity is discovered by the two tutors, Lady Psyche and Lady Blanche, and
eventually by the princess herself. A battle ensues between the forces of the
prince's father and those of King Gama, led by his mighty son Arac. There
is much bloodshed and the university is turned into a hospital. Womanly
pity eventually leads Princess Ida to accept her betrothal to the prince, and
so all ends happily.

With such an epic theme as his basis, Gilbert was not able in *Princess Ida*
to create his usual mixture of mistaken identities, magic potions and sharp
satirical digs at contemporary figures. It is true that he was able to poke some
gentle fun at the movement for women's education, which had gained
momentum in the 1870s with the founding of Girton and Newnham colleges
at Cambridge and Somerville and Lady Margaret Hall at Oxford. But,
although *Princess Ida* is not devoid of patter songs and humorous moments,
it is a much more serious work than any of the Savoy Operas which preceded
it.

As such, it must have come as something of a relief to Sullivan, who was
becoming increasingly impatient with Gilbert's topsy-turvy plots. The two
men had fallen out in the summer of 1883 over the theme for their next joint
work, with the composer firmly resisting the librettist's proposals for another
opera based on his favourite idea of a magic lozenge. Sullivan had been

knighted in May of that year and felt himself now to be above the role of mere tune-smith to his dominant partner. It was probably only because of the relative seriousness of the *Princess Ida* libretto that he agreed to participate. In the event, he produced a delightful score which is closer to grand opera in its harmonies and ensembles than any of his earlier works.

The opera opened at the Savoy Theatre on 5 January 1884. Sullivan was only just able to conduct the first performance. A combination of fatigue, strain and a recurrence of a chronic kidney complaint had reduced him to a state of near collapse, and he was not expected to be present at the first night. Indeed, D'Oyly Carte had printed in the programme that François Cellier would conduct. However, by injecting himself with large quantities of morphine and taking copious cups of black coffee, Sullivan was able to get up from his sick bed and stagger to the theatre.

Sullivan did not take his place at the conductor's rostrum until nearly half an hour after the performance was due to start and, with unduly long intervals for scene changes between the acts, he did not finally lay down his baton until nearly midnight. He collapsed just after taking his bow with Gilbert. In his diary, however, he noted that the evening had been a 'brilliant success'.

Certainly the first-night audience seems to have enjoyed the new work. Gilbert was sitting quietly in the green room reading the paper during the last act when the Frenchman whom he had commissioned to design the silver-gilt armour for Gama's three sons burst in shouting excitedly: '*Mais savez-vous, monsieur, que vous avez là un succès solide?*' The librettist, slightly taken aback by this display of Gallic temperament, replied that it seemed to be going quite well. '*Mais vous êtes si calme!*' was the astonished Frenchman's response. 'I suppose he expected to see me kissing all the carpenters,' Gilbert later remarked.

In retrospect, Gilbert was right to be cautious. The critics were by no means as enthusiastic about *Princess Ida* as the first-night audience had been, and its initial run of 246 performances was one of the shortest of all the Savoy Operas. Three weeks after the opening, Sullivan told Gilbert that he would not work on any more comic operas, and it looked as though their collaboration was at an end.

Its length and its subject matter, so closely tied to the work of a now largely unread poet, have meant that *Princess Ida* has not fared particularly well in the twentieth century. It was not revived in London until 1919 and was always one of the least frequently performed works in the D'Oyly Carte repertoire. A new production directed by Robert Gibson and designed by James Wade was introduced in 1954 to replace one the costumes and scenery for which had been destroyed in the war. This version, which with its fantastic Gothic designs succeeded in capturing the dream-like quality of Tennyson's original poem, received its final British performance at Sadler's

Wells Theatre on 4 January 1978 and its last-ever performance at the National Arts Centre, Ottawa, Canada, on 4 August 1978.

It would be a great pity if *Princess Ida* were to fade away into oblivion now that the D'Oyly Carte Company is no more. Although it lacks the rich characterization and enduring humour of most of the other Savoy Operas, it contains some of the finest music which Sullivan ever wrote, ranging from the poignant delicacy of 'The World is but a broken toy' and the 'Expressive glances' trio to the Handelian martial splendour of 'This helmet, I suppose'. Nor, one might add, is the theme of the opera completely irrelevant in an age which has seen the rise of women's lib.

Whatever its ultimate fate, though, *Princess Ida* has at least had one moment of glory and earned itself a small footnote in the history of Britain in the twentieth century. Before Neville Chamberlain's historic statement of 3 September 1939 announcing a state of war between Britain and Germany, the B.B.C. broadcast a recorded selection of music from the opera. According to the recollection of one of those who heard it, the music was faded out just after the words 'Order comes to fight, ha! ha! / Order is obeyed' (Act I, lines 200–201).

1–3 *Scene*: In the first edition of the libretto, this act was described as a prologue, the present Act II as Act I, and Act III as Act II.

13 *Prince Hilarion*: In Tennyson's *The Princess* neither the prince betrothed as a child to Princess Ida nor his father is named. Gilbert gave them the names Hilarion and Hildebrand for his play and retained them for the opera.

16 *Ida*: Princess Ida, on the other hand, was given her name by Tennyson rather than Gilbert. Ida was a mountain in Phrygia near Troy from whose summit, according to ancient Greek legend, the gods watched the Trojan War. There was another Mount Ida in Crete, where Zeus was said to have been brought up.

ACT I

SCENE. – *Pavilion attached to* KING HILDEBRAND'S *Palace. Soldiers and Courtiers discovered looking out through opera-glasses, telescopes, etc.,* FLORIAN *leading.*

CHORUS.

Search throughout the panorama
For a sign of royal Gama,   5
   Who to-day should cross the water
   With his fascinating daughter –
    Ida is her name.

Some misfortune evidently
Has detained them – consequently   10
   Search throughout the panorama
   For the daughter of King Gama,
    Prince Hilarion's flame!

SOLO.

FLOR. Will Prince Hilarion's hopes be sadly blighted?
ALL.   Who can tell? Who can tell?   15
FLOR. Will Ida break the vows that she has plighted?
ALL.   Who can tell? Who can tell?
FLOR. Will she back out, and say she did not mean them?
ALL.   Who can tell?
FLOR. If so, there'll be the deuce to pay between them!   20

ALL.   No, no – we'll not despair, we'll not despair,
         For Gama would not dare
         To make a deadly foe
         Of Hildebrand, and so,
          Search throughout, etc.   25

(*Enter* KING HILDEBRAND, *with* CYRIL.)

27 *See you no sign of Gama*: The blank verse in which all the dialogue of *Princess Ida* is written is made up of heroic metres, i.e. lines of ten syllables. For the most part Gilbert lifted it directly from his earlier play *The Princess*.

39 *As though Dame Nature*: For his new 1954 D'Oyly Carte production Robert Gibson proposed several cuts in dialogue to speed up the action of the opera. Among them were this and the succeeding line, line 46, and lines 51–2.

46 *His 'sting' is present*: Until now, the dialogue of *Princess Ida* has exactly followed that of Gilbert's *The Princess*; this is the first line that is different. In *The Princess* Hilarion continues after 'his sting lay in his tongue':

> His bitter insolence still rankles here
> Although a score of years have come and gone.
> His sting is present – though his tongue is past.
> His outer man, gnarled, knotted, as it was,
> Seemed to his cruel and tyrannical within
> Hyperion to a Saturday Review.

CYR.   Oh bear with him. He is an old man.
Old men are fretful – peevish – as we know –
A worm will sometimes turn. So will the milk
Of human kindness, if it's kept too long.

FLOR.   But stay, my liege, o'er yonder mountain's brow, etc.

57 *en cavalier*: Like a knight.

62 *For Gama place the richest robes*: This whole passage (lines 62–70) was another cut proposed by Robert Gibson. He no doubt felt that it was superfluous, since Hildebrand's subsequent song makes exactly the same point. However, he reckoned without the combined forces of the D'Oyly Carte artistes and fans, who objected to what they regarded as the mutilation of Gilbert's words. Several of the cuts which Gibson tried to introduce in 1954 were ignored, and gradually more and more of the original dialogue was restored.

HILD. See you no sign of Gama?

FLOR.   None, my liege!

HILD. It's very odd indeed. If Gama fail

To put in an appearance at our Court   30

Before the sun has set in yonder west,

And fail to bring the Princess Ida here

To whom our son Hilarion was betrothed

At the extremely early age of one,

There's war between King Gama and ourselves!   35

(*Aside to* CYRIL.) Oh, Cyril, how I dread this interview!

It's twenty years since he and I have met.

He was a twisted monster – all awry –

As though Dame Nature, angry with her work,

Had crumpled it in fitful petulance!   40

CYR. But, sir, a twisted and ungainly trunk

Often bears goodly fruit. Perhaps he was

A kind, well-spoken gentleman?

HILD.   Oh, no!

For, adder-like, his sting lay in his tongue.   45

(His 'sting' is present, though his 'stung' is past.)

FLOR. (*looking through glass*). But stay, my liege; o'er yonder mountain's brow

Comes a small body, bearing Gama's arms;

And now I look more closely at it, sir,

I see attached to it King Gama's legs;   50

From which I gather this corollary

That that small body must be Gama's own!

HILD. Ha! Is the Princess with him?

FLOR.   Well, my liege,

Unless her highness is full six feet high,   55

And wears mustachios too – and smokes cigars –

And rides *en cavalier* in coat of steel –

I do not think she is.

HILD.   One never knows.

She's a strange girl, I've heard, and does odd things! 60

Come, bustle there!

For Gama place the richest robes we own –

For Gama place the coarsest prison dress –

For Gama let our best spare bed be aired –

For Gama let our deepest dungeon yawn –   65

For Gama lay the costliest banquet out –

For Gama place cold water and dry bread!

For as King Gama brings the Princess here,

Or brings her not, so shall King Gama have

Much more than everything – much less than nothing! 70

94 *quarter-day*: Quarter-days are not quite as sure as this chorus makes them seem. It all depends on whether you go for the new style – in which case they fall on 25 March, 24 June, 29 September and 25 December – or the old – where they occur on 6 April, 6 July, 11 October and 6 January. In Scotland, needless to say, things are different, and the quarter-days fall on 2 February, 15 May, 1 August and 11 November.

SONG – HILDEBRAND *and* CHORUS.

HILD. Now hearken to my strict command
On every hand, on every hand –

CHORUS.

To your command,
On every hand,
We dutifully bow!   75

HILD. If Gama bring the Princess here,
Give him good cheer, give him good cheer.

CHORUS.

If she come here
We'll give him a cheer,
And we will show you how.   80
Hip, hip, hurrah! hip, hip, hurrah!
Hip, hip, hurrah! hurrah! hurrah!
We'll shout and sing
Long live the King,
And his daughter, too, I trow!   85
Then shout ha! ha! hip, hip, hurrah!
Hip, hip, hip, hip, hurrah!
For the fair Princess and her good papa,
Hurrah! hurrah!

HILD. But if he fails to keep his troth,   90
Upon our oath, we'll trounce them both!

CHORUS.

He'll trounce them both,
Upon his oath,
As sure as quarter-day!

HILD. We'll shut him up in a dungeon cell,   95
And toll his knell on a funeral bell.

CHORUS.

From dungeon cell,
His funeral knell
Shall strike him with dismay!

115–30 *Ida was a twelvemonth old*

In making Princess Ida only one at the time of her betrothal, Gilbert departed from Tennyson's original. Here is the relevant passage from the Poet Laureate's *Princess*, in which, incidentally, the prince is the story-teller:

> Now it chanced that I had been,
> While life was yet in bud and blade, betroth'd
> To one, a neighbouring Princess: she to me
> Was proxy wedded with a bootless calf
> At eight years old; and still from time to time
> Came murmurs of her beauty from the South.

Ida and Hilarion are not the only characters in the Savoy Operas betrothed at a very early age. Luiz and Casilda in *The Gondoliers* shared the same happy experience. The situation of Patience and Archibald Grosvenor in *Patience* is, of course, similar but not identical: they were only ever childhood friends and were never engaged.

133 *King Gama is in sight*: This and the next two lines depart slightly from the text of Gilbert's earlier play, which at this point has the lines:

HILD.	My son, King Gama's host is now in sight –
	Prepare to meet the fascinating bride
	To whom you were betrothed so long ago.
	Why, how you sigh!
HIL.	My liege, I'm much afraid
	The Princess Ida has not come with him.
	I've heard she has forsworn the world, etc.

In Tennyson's poem, it is Gama who tells the prince and his companions of his daughter's renunciation of the world of men:

> At last she begg'd a boon,
> A certain summer-palace which I have
> Hard by your father's frontier: I said no,
> Yet being an easy man, gave it: and there,
> All wild to found a University
> For maidens, on the spur she fled; and more
> We know not, – only this: they see no men.

Hip, hip, hurrah! hip, hip, hurrah!   100
Hip, hip, hurrah! hurrah! hurrah!
  As up we string
  The faithless King,
  In the old familiar way!
We'll shout ha! ha! hip, hip, hurrah!   105
Hip, hip, hip, hip, hurrah!
As we make an end of her false papa,
  Hurrah! hurrah!

           (*Exeunt all.*)

   (*Enter* HILARION.)   110

RECITATIVE – HILARION.

To-day we meet, my baby bride and I –
 But ah, my hopes are balanced by my fears!
What transmutations have been conjured by
 The silent alchemy of twenty years!

BALLAD – HILARION.

Ida was a twelvemonth old,   115
 Twenty years ago!
I was twice her age, I'm told,
 Twenty years ago!
Husband twice as old as wife
Argues ill for married life,   120
Baleful prophecies were rife,
 Twenty years ago!

Still, I was a tiny prince
 Twenty years ago.
She has gained upon me, since   125
 Twenty years ago.
Though she's twenty-one, it's true,
I am barely twenty-two –
False and foolish prophets you,
 Twenty years ago!   130

   (*Enter* HILDEBRAND.)

HIL. Well, father, is there news for me at last?
HILD. King Gama is in sight, but much I fear
   With no Princess!

146 *I think I see her now*: Hilarion's exchange with his father recalls a passage from Shakespeare's *Hamlet*, Act I, Scene 2:

HAMLET.	. . . methinks I see my father.
HORATIO.	Where, my lord?
HAMLET.	In my mind's eye, Horatio.

150 *How exquisite she looked*: Much of this passage (lines 150–51, 153–4 and 157–9) was included in Robert Gibson's original list of cuts for the 1954 revival. The *Gilbert and Sullivan Journal*, which had led a campaign against the cuts, delightedly reported in its January 1955 issue, however, that all but two of the lines (153–4) had been restored.

164 *From the distant panorama*: The first American edition of the *Princess Ida* libretto has a longer version of this chorus, the first four lines of which, followed by 'Ida is her name', as in the opening chorus, are also in the licence copy and first British libretto:

> From the distant panorama
> Come the sons of royal Gama.
> Who, today, should cross the water
> With his fascinating daughter –
> Should she not refuse.
>
> They are heralds evidently,
> And are sacred consequently,
> Let us hail sons of Gama,
> Who from yonder panorama
> Come to bring us news!

169 *Enter Arac, Guron, and Scynthius*: Only Arac is mentioned by name in Tennyson's *Princess*, although it is revealed there that he has two brothers who are twins.

Sullivan provided some splendid clodhopping staccato chords for the entrance of the three brothers. An early D'Oyly Carte prompt-book contains a detailed direction as to how they were to be used to best effect: 'The three enter, great swords held in right hand only and sloping down over right shoulder – start on last 8 bars of the 2/4, take 7 steps to centre and front, then through symphony in 3/2 take 12 steps to front (3 steps to a bar), and bring swords down point to ground on 13th beat'.

HIL.   Alas, my liege, I've heard   135
That Princess Ida has forsworn the world,
And, with a band of women, shut herself
Within a lonely country house, and there
Devotes herself to stern philosophies!

HILD.   Then I should say the loss of such a wife   140
Is one to which a reasonable man
Would easily be reconciled.

HIL.   Oh, no!
Or I am not a reasonable man.
She *is* my wife – has been for twenty years!   145
(*Holding glass*). I think I see her now.

HILD.   Ha! let me look!
HIL.   In my mind's eye, I mean – a blushing bride,
All bib and tucker, frill and furbelow!
How exquisite she looked as she was borne,   150
Recumbent, in her foster-mother's arms!
How the bride wept – nor would be comforted
Until the hireling mother-for-the-nonce
Administered refreshment in the vestry.
And I remember feeling much annoyed   155
That she should weep at marrying with me.
But then I thought, 'These brides are all alike.
You cry at marrying me? How much more cause
You'd have to cry if it were broken off!'
These were my thoughts; I kept them to myself,   160
For at that age I had not learnt to speak.

(*Exeunt* HILDEBRAND *and* HILARION.)

(*Enter Courtiers.*)

CHORUS.

From the distant panorama
Come the sons of royal Gama.   165
They are heralds evidently,
And are sacred consequently,
Sons of Gama, hail! oh, hail!

(*Enter* ARAC, GURON, *and* SCYNTHIUS.)

170–202 *We are warriors three*

This trio was much appreciated by several first-night reviewers. The *Sunday Times* commented:

> It begins with a pure bit of Handel, the deep voice or voices running in strict counterpart against the unison of the lower strings; the effect of this is exceedingly droll, and it is still more so later on when the brass come in with their soft chords, and the flutes with their delicate embroidery. .

The *Saturday Review* was equally enthusiastic:

> There is a distinct drollery in the accompaniment to the song and trio for Arac and his brethren, 'We are warriors three'. Bass chords support the first verse, brass boldly aids the assertion 'On the whole we are not intelligent'; and the delight of the warriors in their own trade of fighting is emphasized by rapid and elaborate passages for the flute.

201 *Order is obeyed*: These were almost certainly the last words to be heard on the B.B.C. Home Service on the morning of 3 September 1939 before Neville Chamberlain's announcement that Britain was at war with Germany (see the introduction).

SONG – ARAC.

We are warriors three,   170
  Sons of Gama, Rex.
Like most sons are we,
  Masculine in sex.

ALL THREE.   Yes, yes, yes,
                Masculine in sex.   175

ARAC.   Politics we bar,
              They are not our bent;
            On the whole we are
              Not intelligent.

ALL THREE.   No, no, no,   180
                Not intelligent.

ARAC.   But with doughty heart,
              And with trusty blade
            We can play our part –
              Fighting is our trade.   185

ALL THREE.   Yes, yes, yes,
                Fighting is our trade.

ALL THREE.   Bold, and fierce, and strong, ha! ha!
              For a war we burn,
            With its right or wrong, ha! ha!   190
              We have no concern.
            Order comes to fight, ha! ha!
              Order is obeyed,
            We are men of might, ha! ha!
              Fighting is our trade.   195
                Yes, yes, yes,
            Fighting is our trade, ha! ha!

CHORUS.

They are men of might, ha! ha!
Fighting is their trade.
Order comes to fight, ha! ha!   200
Order is obeyed,
      Fighting is their trade!

(*Enter* KING GAMA.)

204–30 *If you give me your attention, I will tell you what I am*
And if you give me yours, I will tell you something more about Gama. Gilbert based his character fairly closely on Tennyson's original, as described in *The Princess*:

> His name was Gama; crack'd and small his voice,
> But bland the smile that like a wrinkling wind
> On glassy water drove his cheeks in lines;
> A little dry old man, without a star,
> Not like a king.

In one important respect, Gilbert added his own element to the character of Gama built up by the Poet Laureate. Tennyson never specifically mentions that the king is a hunchback. In the Gilbertian version he is, of course, 'a twisted monster all awry', or, as the *Morning Post* first-night reviewer described him, 'a compound of Louis XVI, Dick Deadeye and Richard III'.

Gama has always been played by D'Oyly Carte comedians as a particularly ugly and grotesque figure. It took Sir Henry Lytton more than an hour to apply the make-up needed to turn his normally cheerful countenance into something suitably 'grim and ghastly'.

George Grossmith, who created the role of Gama, was at first slightly worried that this introductory patter song might have been directed at himself. Gilbert assured him that far from this being the case: 'I meant it for myself. I thought it my duty to live up to my own reputation'.

231 *He can't think why*: This chorus was omitted from early libretti, though not from the vocal score.

233 *So this is Castle Hildebrand*: Gama's visit to Hildebrand's court is another departure from Tennyson's story. In the original *Princess*, Hilarion, Florian and Cyril go to Gama's court, where they find out from him about Ida's university.

SONG – GAMA.

If you give me your attention, I will tell you what I am:
I'm a genuine philanthropist – all other kinds are sham.   205
Each little fault of temper and each social defect
In my erring fellow-creatures I endeavour to correct.
To all their little weaknesses I open people's eyes;
And little plans to snub the self-sufficient I devise;
I love my fellow-creatures – I do all the good I can –   210
Yet everybody says I'm such a disagreeable man!
    And I can't think why!

To compliments inflated I've a withering reply;
And vanity I always do my best to mortify;
A charitable action I can skilfully dissect;   215
And interested motives I'm delighted to detect;
I know everybody's income and what everybody earns;
And I carefully compare it with the income-tax returns;
But to benefit humanity however much I plan,
Yet everybody says I'm such a disagreeable man!   220
    And I can't think why!

I'm sure I'm no ascetic; I'm as pleasant as can be;
You'll always find me ready with a crushing repartee,
I've an irritating chuckle, I've a celebrated sneer,
I've an entertaining snigger, I've a fascinating leer.   225
To everybody's prejudice I know a thing or two;
I can tell a woman's age in half a minute – and I do.
But although I try to make myself as pleasant as I can,
Yet everybody says I am a disagreeable man!
    And I can't think why!   230

CHORUS.   He can't think why!

(*Enter* HILDEBRAND, HILARION, CYRIL, *and* FLORIAN.)

GAMA.   So this is Castle Hildebrand? Well, well!
    Dame Rumour whispered that the place was grand;
    She told me that your taste was exquisite,   235
    Superb, unparalleled!
HILD. (*gratified*).   Oh, really, King!
GAMA.   But she's a liar! Why, how old you've grown!
    Is this Hilarion? Why, you've changed too –
    You were a singularly handsome child!   240

255–6 *am I not the worst/Of Nature's blunders*: Gama's deliberate tactic of playing up his physical ugliness and unpleasantness recalls Dick Deadeye's remarks in Act I of *H.M.S. Pinafore*:

> DICK. I'm ugly too, ain't I?
> BUTTERCUP. You are certainly plain.
> DICK. And I'm three-cornered too, ain't I?
> BUTTERCUP. You are rather triangular.

(*To* FLOR.) Are you a courtier? Come, then, ply your trade,
    Tell me some lies. How do you like your King?
    Vile rumour says he's all but imbecile.
    Now, that's not true?
FLOR.   My lord, we love our King.   245
    His wise remarks are valued by his court
    As precious stones.
GAMA.   And for the self-same cause,
    Like precious stones, his sensible remarks
    Derive their value from their scarcity!   250
    Come now, be honest, tell the truth for once!
    Tell it of me. Come, come, I'll harm you not.
    This leg is crooked – this foot is ill-designed –
    This shoulder wears a hump! Come, out with it!
    Look, here's my face! Now, am I not the worst 255
    Of Nature's blunders?
CYR.   Nature never errs.
    To those who know the workings of your mind,
    Your face and figure, sir, suggest a book
    Appropriately bound.   260
GAMA (*enraged*).   Why, harkye, sir,
    How dare you bandy words with me?
CYR.   No need
    To bandy aught that appertains to you.
GAMA (*furiously*). Do you permit this, King?   265
HILD.   We are in doubt
    Whether to treat you as an honoured guest,
    Or as a traitor knave who plights his word
    And breaks it.
GAMA (*quickly*).   If the casting vote's with me, 270
    I give it for the former!
HILD.   We shall see.
    By the terms of our contract, signed and sealed,
    You're bound to bring the Princess here to-day:
    Why is she not with you?   275
GAMA.   Answer me this:
    What think you of a wealthy purse-proud man,
    Who, when he calls upon a starving friend,
    Pulls out his gold and flourishes his notes,
    And flashes diamonds in the pauper's eyes? 280
    What name have you for such an one?
HILD.   A snob.
GAMA. Just so. The girl has beauty, virtue, wit,
    Grace, humour, wisdom, charity, and pluck.

295 *a woman's University*: In setting up her all-female college, Princess Ida was following a distinguished group of pioneers. The first women's college in the vicinity of Cambridge had been founded in 1869 by Miss Anne Clough. Originally sited at Hitchin, it moved to the village of Girton, two miles north-west of Cambridge, in 1873. Two years later the combined efforts of Mrs Josephine Butler, Professor Henry Sidgwick, John Stuart Mill and Professor Henry Fawcett established Newnham College. Oxford followed suit in 1879 with the setting up of Somerville College and Lady Margaret Hall.

296 *a hundred girls*: In Gilbert's play *The Princess* the size of Ida's university is given as 500 girls. Presumably the figure was scaled down for the opera so that the dozen D'Oyly Carte chorus girls would not seem too disproportionately small a sample of the total student body.

301 *With all my heart, if she's the prettiest*: This is the first point in *Princess Ida* where Gilbert adds new dialogue that he had not already used in *The Princess*. Part of the passage between lines 301 and 320 was specially written for the opera, although the remarks about Dr Watts's hymns and the accomplished hen who crows were in the earlier play, where they were given to Gobbo, the old porter at the university who is the only character from Gilbert's *The Princess* not to appear in *Princess Ida*.

307 *safety matches*: Gama's reference to safety matches, like his subsequent remark about Dr Watts, is, of course, an anachronism. The manufacture of the first safety match, which could be ignited only by being struck against a specially prepared surface on the side of the box, took place in 1855.

309 *So you've no chance*: In Gilbert's play this line is the cue for a speech by Hilarion which anticipates some of the metaphors used in the song 'Expressive glances':

> We'll try, at all events.
> Cyril and Florian here will go with me
> And we will storm them ere the week is out!
> With sighs we'll charge our mines and countermines
> Dance steps shall be our scaling-ladders, with
> Those croquet mallets for our battering rams.
> Fair flowers shall bear the only blades we wield
> Our eyes shall be our very deadliest darts
> And bon-bon crackers our artillery!

315 *Dr Watts*: Isaac Watts (1674–1748) was a Nonconformist minister who wrote some of the greatest hymns in the English language including 'O God Our Help in Ages Past' and 'When I survey the Wondrous Cross'.

321–38 *Perhaps if you address the lady*
This is one of only four duets in the Savoy Operas for the principal comedian and baritone characters, the George Grossmith and Rutland Barrington roles, as they have been dubbed. The others are 'When I go out of door' for Bunthorne and Grosvenor in *Patience*, 'Hereupon we're both agreed' for Jack Point and Wilfred Shadbolt in *The Yeomen of the Guard* and 'Big bombs, small bombs, great guns and little ones' for Rudolph and Ludwig in *The Grand Duke*.

<table>
<tr><td></td><td>Would it be kindly, think you, to parade</td><td>285</td></tr>
<tr><td></td><td>These brilliant qualities before *your* eyes?</td><td></td></tr>
<tr><td></td><td>Oh, no, King Hildebrand, I am no snob!</td><td></td></tr>
<tr><td>HILD.</td><td>(*furiously*). Stop that tongue,</td><td></td></tr>
<tr><td></td><td>Or you shall lose the monkey head that holds it!</td><td></td></tr>
<tr><td>GAMA.</td><td>Bravo! your King deprives me of my head,</td><td>290</td></tr>
<tr><td></td><td>That he and I may meet on equal terms!</td><td></td></tr>
<tr><td>HILD.</td><td>Where is she now?</td><td></td></tr>
<tr><td>GAMA.</td><td>In Castle Adamant,</td><td></td></tr>
<tr><td></td><td>One of my many country houses. There</td><td></td></tr>
<tr><td></td><td>She rules a woman's University,</td><td>295</td></tr>
<tr><td></td><td>With full a hundred girls, who learn of her.</td><td></td></tr>
<tr><td>CYR.</td><td>A hundred girls! A hundred ecstasies!</td><td></td></tr>
<tr><td>GAMA.</td><td>But no mere girls, my good young gentleman;</td><td></td></tr>
<tr><td></td><td>With all the college learning that you boast,</td><td></td></tr>
<tr><td></td><td>The youngest there will prove a match for *you*.</td><td>300</td></tr>
<tr><td>CYR.</td><td>With all my heart, if she's the prettiest!</td><td></td></tr>
<tr><td>(*To* FLOR.)</td><td>Fancy, a hundred matches – all alight! –</td><td></td></tr>
<tr><td></td><td>That's if I strike them as I hope to do!</td><td></td></tr>
<tr><td>GAMA.</td><td>Despair your hope; their hearts are dead to men.</td><td></td></tr>
<tr><td></td><td>He who desires to gain their favour must</td><td>305</td></tr>
<tr><td></td><td>Be qualified to strike their teeming brains,</td><td></td></tr>
<tr><td></td><td>And not their hearts. They're safety matches, sir,</td><td></td></tr>
<tr><td></td><td>And they light only on the knowledge box –</td><td></td></tr>
<tr><td></td><td>So *you've* no chance!</td><td></td></tr>
<tr><td>FLOR.</td><td>Are there no males whatever in those walls?</td><td>310</td></tr>
<tr><td>GAMA.</td><td>None, gentlemen, excepting letter mails –</td><td></td></tr>
<tr><td></td><td>And they are driven (as males often are</td><td></td></tr>
<tr><td></td><td>In other large communities) by women.</td><td></td></tr>
<tr><td></td><td>Why, bless my heart, she's so particular</td><td></td></tr>
<tr><td></td><td>She'll scarcely suffer Dr Watts's hymns –</td><td>315</td></tr>
<tr><td></td><td>And all the animals she owns are 'hers'!</td><td></td></tr>
<tr><td></td><td>The ladies rise at cockcrow every morn –</td><td></td></tr>
<tr><td>CYR.</td><td>Ah, then they have male poultry?</td><td></td></tr>
<tr><td>GAMA.</td><td>Not at all,</td><td></td></tr>
<tr><td>(*Confidentially*.)</td><td>The crowing's done by an accomplished hen!</td><td>320</td></tr>
</table>

DUET – GAMA *and* HILDEBRAND.

<table>
<tr><td>GAMA.</td><td>Perhaps if you address the lady</td><td></td></tr>
<tr><td></td><td>Most politely, most politely –</td><td></td></tr>
<tr><td></td><td>Flatter and impress the lady,</td><td></td></tr>
<tr><td></td><td>Most politely, most politely –</td><td></td></tr>
<tr><td></td><td>Humbly beg and humbly sue –</td><td>325</td></tr>
</table>

347 *Sillery*: A very high-class sparkling wine, produced in and around the village of Sillery in Champagne.

353 *triolet*: A stanza of eight lines, constructed on two rhymes, in which the first line is repeated as the fourth and seventh, and the second as the eighth. 'Expressive glances' is not, therefore, strictly speaking a triolet at all.

	She may deign to look on you,	
	But your doing you must do	
	Most politely, most politely, most politely!	
CHORUS.	Humbly beg and humbly sue, etc.	
HILD.	Go you, and inform the lady,	330
	Most politely, most politely,	
	If she don't, we'll storm the lady	
	Most politely, most politely!	
(*To* GAMA.)	You'll remain as hostage here;	
	Should Hilarion disappear,	335
	We will hang you, never fear,	
	Most politely, most politely, most politely!	
CHORUS.	You'll remain as hostage here, etc.	

(GAMA, ARAC, GURON, *and* SCYNTHIUS *are marched off in custody,*
                                        HILDEBRAND *following.*)   340

RECITATIVE – HILARION.

Come, Cyril, Florian, our course is plain,
   To-morrow morn fair Ida we'll engage;
But we will use no force her love to gain,
   Nature has armed us for the war we wage!

TRIO – HILARION, CYRIL, *and* FLORIAN.

HIL.	Expressive glances	345
	Shall be our lances,	
	And pops of Sillery	
	Our light artillery.	
	We'll storm their bowers	
	With scented showers	350
	Of fairest flowers	
	That we can buy!	
CHORUS.	Oh, dainty triolet!	
	Oh, fragrant violet!	
	Oh, gentle heigho-let	355
	(Or little sigh).	
	On sweet urbanity,	
	Though mere inanity	
	To touch their vanity	
	We will rely!	360

383 *This seems unnecessarily severe*: The part of King Gama is smaller than most of Gilbert and Sullivan's comic roles. He does not appear at all in the long Second Act, and apart from these two lines here, his singing is confined to the two patter songs in Acts I and III and his Act I duet with Hildebrand. George Grossmith became extremely irritated at having to sit through long rehearsals, and he eventually asked Sullivan with some exasperation: 'Could you tell me, Sir Arthur, what the words "This seems unnecessarily severe" have reference to?' The composer replied 'Because you are to be detained in prison, of course.' 'Thank you,' Grossmith responded. 'I thought they had reference to my having been detained here three hours a day for the past fortnight to sing them.' Sullivan took the hint and excused Grossmith from the remaining rehearsals.

393 *the rum-tum-tum*: This tongue-twisting chorus appears with more booms and less tum-tums in the first-edition libretto:

> Boom! boom! boom! boom!
> Rum-tummy-tummy-tum!
> Boom! boom!

CYR.
When day is fading,
With serenading
  And such frivolity
  We'll prove our quality.
A sweet profusion 365
Of soft allusion
This bold intrusion
  Shall justify.

CHORUS.
      Oh, dainty triolet, etc.

FLOR.
We'll charm their senses 370
With verbal fences,
  With ballads amatory
  And declamatory.
Little heeding
Their pretty pleading, 375
Our love exceeding
  We'll justify!

CHORUS.
      Oh, dainty triolet, etc.

(*Re-enter* GAMA, ARAC, GURON, *and* SCYNTHIUS *heavily ironed,*
    followed by HILDEBRAND.) 380

RECITATIVE.

GAMA.   Must we, till then, in prison cell be thrust?
HILD.   You must!
GAMA.   This seems unnecessarily severe!
ARAC, GURON, *and* SCYNTHIUS.   Hear, hear!

TRIO – ARAC, GURON, *and* SCYNTHIUS.

For a month to dwell 385
In a dungeon cell;
  Growing thin and wizen
  In a solitary prison,
Is a poor look-out
For a soldier stout, 390
  Who is longing for the rattle
  Of a complicated battle –
For the rum-tum-tum
Of the military drum,
  And the guns that go boom! boom! 395

406–7 *Yes, the fascinating rattle*: This and the next line do not appear in the first-edition libretto, and are not in the current Macmillan edition.

417 *Gama, Arac, Guron, and Scynthius are marched off*: In a letter which he sent to Sullivan on 22 September 1883 together with the completed manuscript of Act I Gilbert wrote:

> Don't you think the Act might end with 'Oh dainty triolet, etc'. followed by the departure of the princes, Arac, Guron and Scynthius breaking from their captors to rush after Hilarion, Cyril and Florian – to be recaptured at once, as the Act drop falls, this business to be without words, and done to symphony? It would make a good picture, I think.

This proposal was not taken up. Instead in D'Oyly Carte productions the act ended with Gama making a return entrance and shaking his fist at Hildebrand to make a picture as the curtain fell.

ALL.   The rum-tum-tum
      Of the military drum, etc.

HILD.   When Hilarion's bride
      Has at length complied
        With the just conditions   400
        Of our requisitions,
      You may go in haste
      And indulge your taste
        For the fascinating rattle
        Of a complicated battle –   405
        Yes, the fascinating rattle
        Of a complicated battle.
      For the rum-tum-tum
      Of the military drum,
        And the guns that go boom! boom! 410

ALL.   For the rum-tum-tum
      Of the military drum, etc.

ALL.   But till that time $\left\{ \begin{array}{l} \text{we'll} \\ \text{you'll} \end{array} \right\}$ here remain,

      And bail $\left\{ \begin{array}{l} \text{they} \\ \text{we} \end{array} \right\}$ will not entertain,

      Should she $\left\{ \begin{array}{l} \text{his} \\ \text{our} \end{array} \right\}$ mandate disobey,   415

      $\left. \begin{array}{l} \text{Our} \\ \text{Your} \end{array} \right\}$ lives the penalty will pay!

(GAMA, ARAC, GURON, *and* SCYNTHIUS *are marched off.*)

END OF ACT I

1–3 *Scene*: In order to economize on scene changes, the same set was used for both Acts II and III in the 1954 D'Oyly Carte revival of *Princess Ida*. It depicted the garden courtyard of Castle Adamant, with a moat at the rear.

The first-night reviewer for *The Times* commented on the frivolity of the scene at Castle Adamant compared with the stately atmosphere of Ida's university in Tennyson's poem. He singled out the gowns of the lady students for particular remark: 'They are beautifully designed and grouped together, form a perfect bouquet of harmonious colour; they will, we seriously apprehend, cause a revolution at Newnham and Girton, but they certainly do not suggest the severity of academic discipline.'

4 *empyrean heights*: The highest heaven, the abode of God and the angels. In Act I of *Patience* Saphir, besotted with aestheticism, tells Colonel Calverley scornfully 'You are not Empyrean. You are not Della Cruscan. You are not even Early English.'

14–21 *If you'd climb the Helicon*
The authors whom Lady Psyche lists in this song are all noted for their eroticism or obscenity – a nice little Gilbertian dig at classical education and the difficulties of extending it to the fairer sex. The first-night reviewer for the *Theatre* magazine took exception to Psyche's list, not for its indelicacy but for the liberties it took with classical pronunciation. 'It is surely inelegant', he wrote, 'to coerce *Helicon* into rhyming with *Anacreon*, *Metamorphoses* with *Aristophanes*, and *horresco referens*! *Juvenal* with *all*'.

14 *Helicon*: The home of the Muses, a part of Parnassus which contained the fountains of Aganippe and Hippocrene.

15 *Anacreon*: A Greek lyric poet, born *c*. 570 B.C., who wrote chiefly in praise of women and wine.

16 *Ovid's Metamorphoses*: The *Metamorphoses*, a collection of poems which ran to fifteen books, was one of the longest works of the Latin poet Publius Ovidius Naso (43 B.C. – *c*. A.D. 18). They begin with the change of the universe from chaos to order and end with the transformation of Julius Caesar into a god. Ovid is mentioned in both *Ruddigore* (see the note to Act I, line 401) and *Iolanthe*.

17 *Aristophanes*: The great Greek comic dramatist (*c*. 450–385 B.C.) whose famous croaking chorus from *The Frogs*, you may recall, is known to Major-General Stanley in *The Pirates of Penzance*.

18 *Juvenal*: A Roman satirist (A.D. 60–140) whose work included a strong attack on women.

21 *Bowdlerized*: Cleansed of any passages which might be calculated to bring a blush of shame to a modest maiden's cheek. The term derives from Thomas Bowdler, who in 1818 brought out an edition of Shakespeare from which 'those words are omitted which cannot with propriety be read aloud in a family'.

22 *Ah! we will get them Bowdlerized*: In the licence copy a two-line chorus is printed here:

Yes, we'll do as we're advised,
We will get them Bowdlerized.

ACT II

SCENE. – *Gardens in Castle Adamant. A river runs across the back of the stage, crossed by a rustic bridge. Castle Adamant in the distance. Girl graduates discovered seated at the feet of* LADY PSYCHE.

CHORUS.

Towards the empyrean heights
   Of every kind of lore,
We've taken several easy flights,   5
   And mean to take some more.
In trying to achieve success
   No envy racks our heart,
And all the knowledge we possess,   10
   We mutually impart.

SONG – MELISSA.

Pray, what authors should she read
Who in Classics would succeed?

PSYCHE.

If you'd climb the Helicon,
You should read Anacreon,   15
Ovid's *Metamorphoses*,
Likewise Aristophanes,
And the works of Juvenal:
These are worth attention, all;
But, if you will be advised,   20
You will get them Bowdlerized!

CHORUS.

Ah! we will get them Bowdlerized!

45 *Enter Lady Blanche*: Gilbert retained both the names and the essential characteristics of the two professors in Tennyson's poem. In *The Princess* Lady Psyche was described as both the prettier and the better natured. Blanche is traditionally played as a formidable and extremely crusty battle-axe.

47 *The Princess Ida's list of punishments*: In Gilbert's earlier play *The Princess*, Ida had a rather long list of punishments to mete out. Sacharissa was expelled, as in the opera, for bringing a set of chessmen into the university, Chloe was gated for a week for declining 'that hideous verse *amo*' (to which the girl rejoined 'I really thought she wished all students to decline to love'). Phyllis lost three terms for a sketch of a double perambulator, and Sylvia was rusticated for a month because she had put three rows of lace round her graduate's gown.

SOLO – SACHARISSA.

Pray you, tell us, if you can,
What's the thing that's known as Man?

PSYCHE.

Man will swear and Man will storm –   25
Man is not at all good form –
Man is of no kind of use –
Man's a donkey – Man's a goose –
Man is coarse and Man is plain –
Man is more or less insane –   30
Man's a ribald – Man's a rake,
Man is Nature's sole mistake!

CHORUS.

We'll a memorandum make –
Man is Nature's sole mistake!

And thus to empyrean height   35
　Of every kind of lore,
In search of wisdom's pure delight,
　Ambitiously we soar.
In trying to achieve success
　No envy racks our heart,   40
For all we know and all we guess,
　We mutually impart!
And all the knowledge we possess
　We mutually impart!

(*Enter* LADY BLANCHE. *All stand up demurely.*)   45

BLA.　　Attention, ladies, while I read to you
　　　　The Princess Ida's list of punishments.
　　　　The first is Sacharissa. She's expelled!
ALL.　　Expelled!
BLA.　　　　　Expelled, because although she knew   50
　　　　No man of any kind may pass our walls,
　　　　She dared to bring a set of chessmen here!
SACH. (*crying*).　I meant no harm; they're only men of wood!
BLA.　　They're men with whom you give each other mate,
　　　　And that's enough! The next is Chloe.   55
CHLOE.　　　　　　　　　　　Ah!

61 *Double perambulator*: This curious contraption was to figure again in Gilbert's writings. In his story 'The Fairy's Dilemma', which appeared in the Christmas 1900 number of the *Graphic*, he wrote: 'I see a nursemaid advancing with a double perambulator, and escorted by a trooper of the 2nd Life Guards.'

74 *Enter the Princess*: Here is Tennyson's description of Princess Ida as first seen by Hilarion:

> There at a board by tome and paper sat,
> With two tame leopards couch'd beside her throne,
> All beauty compass'd in a female form,
> The Princess; liker to the inhabitant
> Of some clear planet close upon the Sun
> Than our man's earth; such eyes were in her head,
> And so much grace and power, breathing down
> From over her arch'd brows, with every turn
> Lived through her to the tips of her long hands,
> And to the feet.

79 *Minerva*: A Roman goddess, identified with the Greek Athena, who was patroness of the arts and goddess of memory and warfare.

80–89 *Oh, goddess wise*

As originally sung in early productions, the order of this aria was reversed, with lines 84–7 preceding lines 80–83.

90 *Neophytes*: New converts, novices.

BLA.   Chloe will lose three terms, for yesterday,
            When looking through her drawing-book, I found
            A sketch of a perambulator!
ALL (*horrified*).   Oh!   60
BLA.   *Double* perambulator, shameless girl!
            That's all at present. Now, attention, pray;
            Your Principal the Princess comes to give
            Her usual inaugural address
            To those young ladies who joined yesterday.   65

CHORUS.

            Mighty maiden with a mission,
                Paragon of common sense,
            Running fount of erudition,
                Miracle of eloquence,
                We are blind, and we would see;   70
                We are bound, and would be free;
                We are dumb, and we would talk;
                We are lame, and we would walk.

            (*Enter the* PRINCESS.)

            Mighty maiden with a mission –   75
                Paragon of common sense;
            Running fount of erudition –
                Miracle of eloquence!

PRIN. (*recitative.*)   Minerva! Minerva, oh, hear me!

ARIA.

            Oh, goddess wise   80
                That lovest light,
                Endow with sight
            Their unillumined eyes.
            At this my call,
                A fervent few   85
                Have come to woo
            The rays that from thee fall.
        Let fervent words and fervent thoughts be mine,
        That I may lead them to thy sacred shrine!

            Women of Adamant, fair Neophytes –   90
            Who thirst for such instruction as we give,

92 *while I unfold a parable*: The entire passage of dialogue from here down to 'Logic?' (line 109) was among the cuts made in the 1954 D'Oyly Carte production.

114 *He'd rather pass the day*: This was originally written 'He'd rather spend the day'.

122 *Let red be worn with yellow*: Primary colours! Lady Jane would have a fit! (See *Patience*, Act I, line 324.)

131 *Let Swan secede from Edgar*: Here begins a plug for some of the most fashionable drapery and millinery establishments in late Victorian London. Swan and Edgar, the last to disappear, were first of all in Regent Street and then just off Piccadilly Circus. The first-night review in the *Sportsman* commented that the girl graduates 'were dressed with a quaint richness, suggesting Portia after a visit to Swan and Edgar's.' Gask and Gask in Leicester Square specialized in silks; Sewell and Cross, who also received a mention in *Patience* (Act II, line 508), were in Soho; and Lewis and Allenby were in St George's House, on the corner of Conduit Street and Regent Street. Mention of these largely defunct trade names led to lines 131–2 also being among the proposed cuts in 1954. A note in a D'Oyly Carte prompt copy of *c.* 1955, however, states that 'These cuts in Ida's speech are still liable to change', and it goes on to indicate that at the time of writing only these lines were out, and lines 92–109 mentioned above were in again.

Attend, while I unfold a parable.
The elephant is mightier than Man,
Yet Man subdues him. Why? The elephant
Is elephantine everywhere but here (*tapping her forehead*),　　　　95
And Man, whose brain is to the elephant's
As Woman's brain to Man's – (that's rule of three), –
Conquers the foolish giant of the woods,
As Woman, in her turn, shall conquer Man.
In Mathematics, Woman leads the way:　　　　100
The narrow-minded pedant still believes
That two and two make four! Why, we can prove,
We women – household drudges as we are –
That two and two make five – or three – or seven;
Or five-and-twenty, if the case demands!　　　　105
Diplomacy? The wiliest diplomat
Is absolutely helpless in our hands,
He wheedles monarchs – woman wheedles him!
Logic? Why, tyrant Man himself admits
It's waste of time to argue with a woman!　　　　110
Then we excel in social qualities:
Though Man professes that he holds our sex
In utter scorn, I venture to believe
He'd rather pass the day with one of you,
Than with five hundred of his fellow-men!　　　　115
In all things we excel. Believing this,
A hundred maidens here have sworn to place
Their feet upon his neck. If we succeed,
We'll treat him better than he treated us:
But if we fail, why, then let hope fail too!　　　　120
Let no one care a penny how she looks –
Let red be worn with yellow – blue with green –
Crimson with scarlet – violet with blue!
Let all your things misfit, and you yourselves
At inconvenient moments come undone!　　　　125
Let hair-pins lose their virtue; let the hook
Disdain the fascination of the eye –
The bashful button modestly evade
The soft embraces of the button-hole!
Let old associations all dissolve,　　　　130
Let Swan secede from Edgar – Gask from Gask,
Sewell from Cross – Lewis from Allenby!
In other words – let Chaos come again!
(*Coming down.*) Who lectures in the Hall of Arts to-day?

135 *Abstract Philosophy*: This subject might seem more in Lady Psyche's line. She is, after all, the Professor of Humanities. In Gilbert's earlier play, however, she was the Professor of Experimental Science, contrasting with Lady Blanche's role as Professor of Abstract Science.

147 *The Princess Ida Is our head*: Lady Blanche's feeling that she had been ousted by Lady Psyche in Princess Ida's affections is made much of in Tennyson's poem, where Melissa tells Hilarion and his friends:

> My mother, 'tis her wont from night to night
> To rail at Lady Psyche and her side.
> She says the Princess should have been the Head,
> Herself and Lady Psyche the two arms;
> And so it was agreed when first they came;
> But Lady Psyche was the right hand now,
> And she the left, or not, or seldom used . . .

Tennyson also explains, again through Melissa talking to Hilarion, the story of how Lady Blanche came to be supplanted:

> She had the care of Lady Ida's youth,
> And from the Queen's decease she brought her up
> But when your sister came she won the heart
> Of Ida: they were still together, grew
> (For so they said themselves) inosculated;
> Consonant chords that shiver to one note;
> One mind in all things: yet my mother still
> Affirms your Psyche thieved her theories,
> And angled with them for her pupil's love:
> She calls her plagiarist; I know not what.

164–87 *Come, mighty Must*
This burlesque of the rather over-blown Victorian drawing-room ballad was for a long time cut in D'Oyly Carte productions. A note by Rupert D'Oyly Carte in a prompt copy indicates that it was not sung in 1930, and this cut continued until the war. It was also omitted from the 1954 revival, although it was reintroduced by the company for the 1977–8 season.

BLA.	I, madam, on Abstract Philosophy.	135

BLA. I, madam, on Abstract Philosophy. 135
There I propose considering, at length,
Three points – The Is, the Might Be, and the Must.
Whether the Is, from being actual fact,
Is more important than the vague Might Be,
Or the Might Be, from taking wider scope, 140
Is for that reason greater than the Is:
And lastly, how the Is and Might Be stand
Compared with the inevitable Must!

PRIN. The subject's deep – how do you treat it, pray?

BLA. Madam, I take three possibilities, 145
And strike a balance, then, between the three:
As thus: The Princess Ida Is our head,
The Lady Psyche Might Be, – Lady Blanche,
Neglected Blanche, inevitably Must.
Given these three hypotheses – to find 150
The actual betting against each of them!

PRIN. Your theme's ambitious: pray you, bear in mind
Who highest soar fall farthest. Fare you well,
You and your pupils! Maidens, follow me.

(*Exeunt* PRINCESS *and Maidens singing refrain of chorus, 'And* 155
thus to empyrean heights', etc. Manet LADY BLANCHE.)

BLA. I should command here – I was born to rule,
But do I rule? I don't. Why? I don't know.
I shall some day. Not yet. I bide my time.
I once was Some One – and the Was Will Be. 160
The Present as we speak becomes the Past,
The Past repeats itself, and so is Future!
This sounds involved. It's not. It's right enough.

SONG – LADY BLANCHE.

Come, mighty Must!
  Inevitable Shall! 165
In thee I trust.
  Time weaves my coronal!
Go, mocking Is!
  Go, disappointing Was!
That I am this 170
  Ye are the cursèd cause!
Yet humble second shall be first,
  I ween;

189 *Enter Hilarion, Cyril, and Florian*: The stage direction at this point in an early D'Oyly Carte prompt-book reads: 'Symphony – All heads appear top of wall – then down. Hilarion comes over wall on 12th bar on to rostrum and down steps – looks off right, Cyril on 16th bar follows Hilarion, Florian on 18th bar comes down. Dust clothes with their handkerchiefs.'

191–218 *Gently, gently*

This number was adopted in the 1920s as the theme song of the Oxford University Gilbert and Sullivan Society and sung at the beginning and end of each meeting.

More recently, it was sung with particular aptness on the evening of 23 February 1977 when a bomb scare at Sadler's Wells Theatre brought the curtain down on a D'Oyly Carte production just as the three intrepid chums were about to clamber into view. The audience were forced to spend an hour outside in the street until the theatre was searched and cleared. The first words that they heard from stage when they had finally filed back in again were the moderately reassuring: 'Gently, gently,/Evidently/ We are safe so far'.

211 *throttles*: The human rather than the automobile variety, of course: i.e. the throat.

And dead and buried be the curst
    Has Been!   175

Oh, weak Might Be!
  Oh, May, Might, Could, Would, Should!
How powerless ye
  For evil or for good!
In every sense   180
  Your moods I cheerless call,
Whate'er your tense
  Ye are Imperfect, all!
Ye have deceived the trust I've shown
    In ye!   185
Away! The Mighty Must alone
    Shall be!

                              (*Exit* LADY BLANCHE.)

(*Enter* HILARION, CYRIL, *and* FLORIAN, *climbing over wall, and creeping
   cautiously among the trees and rocks at the back of the stage.*)   190

        TRIO – HILARION, CYRIL, FLORIAN.

        Gently, gently,
        Evidently
          We are safe so far,
        After scaling
        Fence and paling,   195
          Here, at last, we are!

        In this college
        Useful knowledge
          Everywhere one finds,
        And already,   200
        Growing steady,
          We've enlarged our minds.

CYR.   We've learnt that prickly cactus
          Has the power to attract us
                    When we fall.   205
HIL. *and* FLOR.   When we fall!
HIL.   That nothing man unsettles
          Like a bed of stinging nettles,
                    Short or tall.
CYR. *and* FLOR.   Short or tall!   210
FLOR.   That bull-dogs feed on throttles –

227 *they'll set the Thames on fire*: Do something remarkable and exciting. Similar sayings exist in Germany and France, where the respective rivers are the Rhine and the Seine; and the ancient Romans had an expression *Tiberium accendere nequaquam potest* ('It is not at all possible to set light to the Tiber').

231 *Circe*: A sorceress in Greek mythology who lived on the island of Aeaea. When Ulysses landed there, she turned his companions into swine.

234 *trepan*: Ensnare or catch in a trap. The word occurs with a very different meaning in Colonel Calverley's recipe for a Heavy Dragoon in *Patience*, when he sings of the 'Coolness of Paget about to trepan' (Act 1, line 137).

235 *sunbeams from cucumbers*: This curious notion is taken from a passage in *Gulliver's Travels* in which Jonathan Swift recounts that his hero 'had been eight years upon a project for extracting sunbeams out of cucumbers, which were to be put into phials hermetically sealed, and let out to warm the air in raw inclement summers'.

241–4 *These are the phenomena*
In the licence copy and the first edition of the libretto the last two lines of this refrain are printed as:

> Hopes that we shall see
> At this Universitee!

The current Macmillan edition has a slightly different version of these lines:

> Is hoping we shall see
> At her Universitee!

	That we don't like broken bottles	
	On a wall.	
CYR. *and* HIL.	On a wall!	
HIL.	That spring-guns breathe defiance!	215
	And that burglary's a science	
	After all!	
CYR. *and* FLOR.	After all!	

RECITATIVE – FLORIAN.

A Woman's college! maddest folly going!
What can girls learn within its walls worth knowing?   220
I'll lay a crown (the Princess shall decide it)
I'll teach them twice as much in half-an-hour outside it.

HILARION.

Hush, scoffer; ere you sound your puny thunder,
List to their aims, and bow your head in wonder!

They intend to send a wire   225
    To the moon – to the moon;
And they'll set the Thames on fire
    Very soon – very soon;
Then they learn to make silk purses
    With their rigs – with their rigs,   230
From the ears of Lady Circe's
    Piggy-wigs – piggy-wigs.
And weasels at their slumbers
    They trepan – they trepan;
To get sunbeams from *cucumbers*,   235
    They've a plan – they've a plan.
They've a firmly rooted notion
They can cross the Polar Ocean,
And they'll find Perpetual Motion,
    If they can – if they can.   240

ALL. These are the phenomena
      That every pretty domina
          Is hoping at her Universitee
          We shall see!

CYR. As for fashion, they forswear it,   245
          So they say – so they say;
      And the circle – they will square it

251 *And they'll practise what they're preaching*: Until the war this line was sung as 'And the niggers they'll be bleaching'. It was changed for the 1954 revival for the same reason that the word 'nigger' was removed from *The Mikado* in 1948 (see the notes to Act I, line 251, and Act II, line 358, of *The Mikado*).

262–7 *In this college*
This refrain does not appear in the first edition.

268 *So that's the Princess Ida's castle*: For the 1954 revival, in keeping with the new stage setting for Act II, these lines were changed to:

> So this is the Princess Ida's castle! Well,
> They must be lovely girls, indeed, if it requires
> Such walls as these to keep intruders off!

278 *matriculate*: Enrol as students.
Let's try them on: A stage direction in an early D'Oyly Carte prompt copy reads: 'Florian throws Cyril's (robe) to Hilarion, who passes it on to him – then Hilarion's and retains third one. Hilarion gets into his at once. Florian also – makes muff of scarf part. Cyril has difficulty – first getting into sleeves – then buttons up robe inside his legs. Hilarion assists him.'

        Some fine day – some fine day;
      Then the little pigs they're teaching
        For to fly – for to fly;   250
      And they'll practise what they're preaching
        By and by – by and by!
      Each newly-joined aspirant
        To the clan – to the clan –
      Must repudiate the tyrant   255
        Known as Man – known as Man.
      They mock at him and flout him,
      For they do not care about him,
      And they're 'going to do without him'
        If they can – if they can!   260

ALL.   These are the phenomena, etc.

        In this college
        Useful knowledge
        Ev'rywhere one finds,
        And already,   265
        Growing steady,
        We've enlarg'd our minds.

HIL.   So that's the Princess Ida's castle! Well,
      They must be lovely girls, indeed, if it requires
      Such walls as those to keep intruders off!   270
CYR.   To keep men off is only half their charge,
      And that the easier half. I much suspect
      The object of these walls is not so much
      To keep men off as keep the maidens in!
FLOR.   But what are these? (*Examining some Collegiate robes.*)   275
HIL. (*looking at them*). Why, Academic robes,
      Worn by the lady undergraduates
      When they matriculate. Let's try them on. (*They do so.*)
      Why, see, – we're covered to the very toes.
      Three lovely lady undergraduates   280
      Who, weary of the world and all its wooing –
FLOR.   And penitent for deeds there's no undoing –
CYR.   Looked at askance by well-conducted maids –
ALL.   Seek sanctuary in these classic shades!

      TRIO – HILARION, CYRIL, FLORIAN.

HIL.   I am a maiden, cold and stately,   285
        Heartless I, with a face divine.

289 *Haughty, humble, coy, or free*: The same prompt-book has the direction here: 'Actions: "Haughty" – both hands out flat to left. "Humble" – cross hands on breast. "Coy" – left hand under right elbow, right finger to lips, curtsey. "Free" – throw both hands out open.' These actions continued to be used in D'Oyly Carte productions to the end.

310 *We are three students*: Compare Tennyson's original lines:

> Three ladies of the Northern empire pray
> Your Highness would enroll them with your own
> As Lady Psyche's pupils.

What do I want with a heart, innately?
Every heart I meet is mine!

ALL.　　　Haughty, humble, coy, or free,
　　　　　Little care I what maid may be.　　　　　　　　290
　　　　So that a maid is fair to see,
　　　　　Every maid is the maid for me! (*Dance.*)

CYR.　　I am a maiden frank and simple,
　　　　　Brimming with joyous roguery;
　　　　Merriment lurks in every dimple,　　　　　　　　295
　　　　　Nobody breaks more hearts than I!

ALL.　　　Haughty, humble, coy, or free, etc. (*Dance.*)

FLOR.　I am a maiden coyly blushing,
　　　　　Timid am I as a startled hind;
　　　　Every suitor sets me flushing:　　　　　　　　　300
　　　　　I am the maid that wins mankind!

ALL.　　　Haughty, humble, coy, or free, etc.

　　　(*Enter the* PRINCESS *reading. She does not see them.*)

FLOR.　But who comes here? The Princess, as I live!
　　　　What shall we do?　　　　　　　　　　　　　　305
HIL. (*aside*).　　　　　　　　　　Why, we must brave it out!
　　　　(*Aloud*). Madam, accept our humblest reverence.

　　　(*They bow, then, suddenly recollecting themselves, curtsey.*)

PRIN. (*surprised*). We greet you, ladies. What would you with us?
HIL. (*aside*). What shall I say? (*Aloud.*) We are three students, ma'am,　310
　　　　Three well-born maids of liberal estate,
　　　　Who wish to join this University.

　　　(HILARION *and* FLORIAN *curtsey again.* CYRIL *bows extravagantly,*
　　　　then, being recalled to himself by FLORIAN, *curtsies.*)

PRIN.　If, as you say, you wish to join our ranks,　　　　315
　　　　And will subscribe to all our rules, 'tis well.
FLOR.　To all your rules we cheerfully subscribe.
PRIN.　You say you're noblewomen. Well, you'll find
　　　　No sham degrees for noblewomen here.

320 *sizars . . . servitors*: Students who received their board and lodging free in return for performing duties of the kind that would normally be done by servants. They were called sizars at Cambridge and Trinity College, Dublin, and servitors at Oxford. Lines 320–24 were cut in the 1954 production.

322 *tufts*: Gold tassels worn on the caps of peers' sons at Oxford.

328 *will you swear*: In Tennyson's poem, Hilarion and his two friends were required to agree to a slightly different set of rules when they enrolled as students at the princess's university:

> Not for three years to correspond with home;
> Not for three years to cross the liberties;
> Not for three years to speak with any men.

344 *And we have never fished*: Lines 344–52 were cut in the 1954 revival.

	You'll find no sizars here, or servitors,	320
	Or other cruel distinctions, meant to draw	
	A line 'twixt rich and poor: you'll find no tufts	
	To mark nobility, except such tufts	
	As indicate nobility of brain.	
	As for your fellow-students, mark me well:	325
	There are a hundred maids within these walls,	
	All good, all learned, and all beautiful:	
	They are prepared to love you: will you swear	
	To give the fullness of your love to them?	
HIL.	Upon our words and honours, ma'am, we will!	330
PRIN.	But we go further: will you undertake	
	That you will never marry any man?	
FLOR.	Indeed we never will!	
PRIN.	Consider well,	
	You must prefer our maids to all mankind!	335
HIL.	To all mankind we much prefer your maids!	
CYR.	We should be dolts indeed, if we did not,	
	Seeing how fair —	
HIL.	(*aside to* CYRIL). Take care – that's rather strong!	
PRIN.	But have you left no lovers at your home	340
	Who may pursue you here?	
HIL.	No, madam, none.	
	We're homely ladies, as no doubt you see,	
	And we have never fished for lover's love.	
	We smile at girls who deck themselves with gems,	345
	False hair, and meretricious ornament,	
	To chain the fleeting fancy of a man,	
	But do not imitate them. What we have	
	Of hair, is all our own. Our colour, too,	
	Unladylike, but not unwomanly,	350
	Is Nature's handiwork, and man has learnt	
	To reckon Nature an impertinence.	
PRIN.	Well, beauty counts for naught within these walls;	
	If all you say is true, you'll pass with us	
	A happy, happy time!	355
CYR.	If, as you say,	
	A hundred lovely maidens wait within,	
	To welcome us with smiles and open arms,	
	I think there's very little doubt we shall!	

QUARTET – PRINCESS, HILARION, CYRIL, FLORIAN.

PRIN.	The world is but a broken toy,	360

374 *Unreal its loveliest hue*: In the first-edition libretto and vocal score, and therefore possibly in early performances, Hilarion's verse was succeeded by the following ensemble:

PRINCESS.	HILARION, CYRIL *and* FLORIAN.
The world is but a broken toy,	The world is but a broken toy,
Its pleasure hollow – false its joy,	We freely give it up with joy,
Unreal its loveliest hue,	Unreal its loveliest hue,
Alas!	Alas!
Its pains alone are true,	We quite agree with you,
Alas!	Alas!
Its pains alone are true!	We quite agree with you!

Its pleasure hollow – false its joy,
Unreal its loveliest hue,
Alas!
Its pains alone are true,
Alas!   365
Its pains alone are true.

HIL. The world is everything you say,
The world we think has had its day.
Its merriment is slow,
Alas!   370
We've tried it, and we know,
Alas!
We've tried it and we know.

ALL. Unreal its loveliest hue,
Its pains alone are true.   375
Alas!
The world is but a broken toy,
Its pleasure hollow – false its joy,
Unreal its loveliest hue,
Alas!   380
Its pains alone are true,
Alas!
Its pains alone are true!

(*Exit* PRINCESS. *The three gentlemen watch her off.* LADY
PSYCHE *enters, and regards them with amazement.*) 385

HIL. I'faith, the plunge is taken, gentlemen!
For, willy-nilly, we are maidens now,
And maids against our will we must remain!

(*All laugh heartily.*)

PSY. (*aside*). These ladies are unseemly in their mirth. 390

(*The gentlemen see her, and, in confusion, resume
their modest demeanour.*)

FLOR. (*aside*). Here's a catastrophe, Hilarion!
This is my sister! She'll remember me,
Though years have passed since she and I have met! 395
HIL. (*aside to* FLORIAN). Then make a virtue of necessity,
And trust our secret to her gentle care.
FLOR. (*to* PSYCHE, *who has watched* CYRIL *in amazement*). Psyche!
Why, don't you know me? Florian!

411 *Are you that learned little Psyche*: This passage bears a close resemblance to Tennyson's original:

> 'Are you that Psyche,' Florian added; 'she
> With whom I sang about the morning hills,
> Flung ball, flew kite, and raced the purple fly,
> And snared the squirrel of the glen? are you
> That Psyche wont to bind my throbbing brow,
> To smooth my pillow, mix the foaming draught
> Of fever, tell me pleasant tales, and read
> My sickness down to happy dreams? are you
> That brother-sister Psyche, both in one?

421 *Hipparchus*: If the Greek astronomer first determined longitude in 163 B.C., then it was at the extremely early age of minus three, as most sources agree in putting his birth at c. 160 B.C. Hipparchus, who worked at Rhodes, was the world's first systematic astronomer and the inventor of trigonometry.

422 *that small phenomenon*: Shades of the infant phenomenon in Charles Dickens's *Nicholas Nickleby* (1839). Lines 414–23 were also cut in the 1954 D'Oyly Carte revival.

433–66 *A Lady fair, of lineage high*

The tune of this song, which was entitled in the first-edition libretto 'The Ape and the Lady', was thought by some critics to be distinctly derivative. The *Weekly Times* commented on its resemblance to 'The Bailiff's Daughter of Islington', while the *Saturday Review* noted ' "The Ape and the Lady" did duty in *Patience* as "The Magnet and the Churn" '.

Psy. (*amazed*). Why, Florian!   400

Flor.   My sister! (*embraces her*).

Psy.   Oh, my dear!
What are you doing here – and who are these?

Hil. I am that Prince Hilarion to whom
Your Princess is betrothed. I come to claim   405
Her plighted love. Your brother Florian
And Cyril come to see me safely through.

Psy. The Prince Hilarion? Cyril too? How strange!
My earliest playfellows!

Hil.   Why, let me look!   410
Are you that learned little Psyche who
At school alarmed her mates because she called
A buttercup 'ranunculus bulbosus'?

Cyr. Are you indeed that Lady Psyche who
At children's parties drove the conjurer wild,   415
Explaining all his tricks before he did them?

Hil. Are you that learned little Psyche who
At dinner parties, brought in to dessert,
Would tackle visitors with 'You don't know
Who first determined longitude – I do –   420
Hipparchus 'twas – B.C. one sixty-three!'
Are you indeed that small phenomenon?

Psy. That small phenomenon indeed am I!
But, gentlemen, 'tis death to enter here:
We have all promised to renounce mankind!   425

Flor. Renounce mankind? On what ground do you base
This senseless resolution?

Psy.   Senseless? No.
We are all taught, and, being taught, believe
That Man, sprung from an Ape, is Ape at heart.   430

Cyr. That's rather strong.

Psy.   The truth is always strong!

SONG – Lady Psyche.

A Lady fair, of lineage high,
Was loved by an Ape, in the days gone by.
The Maid was radiant as the sun,   435
The Ape was a most unsightly one –
    So it would not do –
    His scheme fell through,
For the Maid, when his love took formal shape,

458 *Darwinian Man*: A nice dig at the theory of evolution, which had been propounded by Charles Darwin in his book *The Origin of Species* in 1859.

464 *While a man, however well-behaved*: The licence copy and first-edition libretto have this version, which was sung in recent D'Oyly Carte productions. The vocal score, Oxford University Press World's Classics edition and Macmillan edition, however, have 'While Darwinian Man, though well-behaved'.

468 *Oh, Lady Psyche*: Here is how Tennyson handled this incident:

> Then Lady Psyche, 'Ah – Melissa – you!
> You heard us?' and Melissa, 'O pardon me
> I heard, I could not help it, did not wish:
> But, dearest Lady, pray you fear me not,
> Nor think I bear that heart within my breast,
> To give three gallant gentlemen to death.'

Expressed such terror   440
At his monstrous error,
That he stammered an apology and made his 'scape,
The picture of a disconcerted Ape.

With a view to rise in the social scale,
He shaved his bristles, and he docked his tail,   445
He grew moustachios, and he took his tub,
And he paid a guinea to a toilet club –
　　But it would not do,
　　The scheme fell through –
For the Maid was Beauty's fairest Queen,   450
　　With golden tresses,
　　Like a real princess's,
While the Ape, despite his razor keen,
Was the apiest Ape that ever was seen!

He bought white ties, and he bought dress suits,   455
He crammed his feet into bright tight boots –
And to start in life on a brand-new plan,
He christened himself Darwinian Man!
　　But it would not do,
　　The scheme fell through –   460
For the Maiden fair, whom the monkey craved,
　　Was a radiant Being,
　　With a brain far-seeing –
While a man, however well-behaved,
At best is only a monkey shaved!   465

ALL.　　While Darwinian Man, etc.

(*During this* MELISSA *has entered unobserved; she looks on in amazement.*)

MEL. (*coming down*). Oh, Lady Psyche!
PSY. (*terrified*).　　　　　　　　　　What! you heard us then?
　　Oh, all is lost!   470
MEL.　　　　　　　　　　Not so! I'll breathe no word!

(*Advancing in astonishment to* FLORIAN.)

How marvellously strange! and are you then
Indeed young men?
FLOR.　　　　　　　　　Well, yes, just now we are –   475
But hope by dint of study to become,
In course of time, young women.
MEL. (*eagerly*).　　　　　　　　　　No, no, no –

491–520 *The woman of the wisest wit*

The first American edition of the libretto has a completely different version of this quintet; it is presumably the original version, which was in the British libretto when it was shipped out to the U.S.A. for rehearsal there. Gilbert subsequently changed the song but was unable to get the new version across the Atlantic in time for it to appear in the first U.S. edition:

QUINTET.

PSYCHE, MELISSA, HILARION, CYRIL, FLORIAN.

PSY.
> If we discharged our duty clear
> We should denounce your presence here,
> What should we do
> We plainly view
> *In speculum veluti.**

HIL.
> If that's the case, don't wait a bit
> But trick it, cheat it, swindle it;
> 'Twere pity great
> To hesitate
> Distinctly 'do' your duty!

ALL.
> Oh duty, when you check our ease,
> Uncertain, coy, and hard to please†
> When you are 'done', as you are now,
> An unimportant person thou.

MEL.
> But if we 'did' our duty thus
> The consequence might fall on us;
> 'Twould give you pain
> To see us slain
> In all your youth and beauty!

CYR.
> If 'doing' it distress you so,
> Dismiss it, sack it, let it go;
> Don't pause a while
> Dispense with it
> In fact, 'discharge' your duty!

ALL.
> Oh duty, when you check our ease,
> Uncertain, coy, and hard to please,
> When you're discharged as you are now
> An unimportant person thou!

* 'As if in a mirror'.
† This line is borrowed from Sir Walter Scott's poem *Marmion*.

Oh, don't do that! Is this indeed a man?
I've often heard of them, but, till to-day,   480
Never set eyes on one. They told me men
Were hideous, idiotic, and deformed!
They're quite as beautiful as women are!
As beautiful, they're infinitely more so!
Their cheeks have not that pulpy softness which   485
One gets so weary of in womankind:
Their features are more marked – and – oh, their chins!
How curious! (*Feeling his chin.*)

FLOR.   I fear it's rather rough.

MEL. (*eagerly*). Oh, don't apologize – I like it so!   490

QUINTET – PSYCHE, MELISSA, HILARION,
           CYRIL, FLORIAN.

PSY.   The woman of the wisest wit
                May sometimes be mistaken, O!
         In Ida's views, I must admit,
                My faith is somewhat shaken, O!

CYR.   On every other point than this   495
                Her learning is untainted, O!
         But Man's a theme with which she is
                Entirely unacquainted, O!
                – acquainted, O!
                – acquainted, O!   500
         Entirely unacquainted, O!

ALL.   Then jump for joy and gaily bound,
         The truth is found – the truth is found!
         Set bells a-ringing through the air –
         Ring here and there and everywhere –   505
         And echo forth the joyous sound,
         The truth is found – the truth is found!

                                             (*Dance.*)

MEL.   My natural instinct teaches me
                (And instinct is important, O!)   510
         You're everything you ought to be,
                And nothing that you oughtn't, O!

HIL.   That fact was seen at once by you
                In casual conversation, O!
         Which is most creditable to   515
                Your powers of observation, O!
                – servation, O!

536 *Two are tenors, one is a baritone*: In the first edition of the libretto this line is 'One is a tenor, two are baritones'. However, it is doubtful if this was ever said, since Hilarion, Cyril and Florian were originally played by Henry Bracy (tenor), Durward Lely (tenor) and Charles Ryley (baritone).

542 *an étui*: A needle-case. In some editions of the libretto, 'cigar case' has been substituted for '*étui*'. The reference to an *étui* containing scissors and needles is a hangover from Gilbert's earlier play. There, in the absence of any singing, Lady Blanche establishes the true sex of Hilarion and his friends when, her suspicions already aroused, she finds that they are unable to carry out a simple test in needlework which she sets them.

– servation, O!
Your powers of observation, O!

ALL.	Then jump for joy, etc.	520

(*Exeunt* PSYCHE, HILARION, CYRIL, *and* FLORIAN. MELISSA *going.*)

(*Enter* LADY BLANCHE.)

BLA.   Melissa!
MEL. (*returning*).   Mother!
BLA.   Here – a word with you.   525
    Those are the three new students?
MEL. (*confused*).   Yes, they are.
    They're charming girls.
BLA.   Particularly so.
    So graceful, and so very womanly!   530
    So skilled in all a girl's accomplishments!
MEL. (*confused*).   Yes – very skilled.
BLA.   They sing so nicely too!
MEL.   They *do* sing nicely!
BLA.   Humph! It's very odd.   535
    Two are tenors, one is a baritone!
MEL. (*much agitated*).   They've all got colds!
BLA.   Colds! Bah! D'ye think I'm blind?
    These 'girls' are men disguised!
MEL.   Oh no – indeed!   540
    You wrong these gentlemen – I mean – why, see,
    Here is an *étui* dropped by one of them (*picking up an étui*)
    Containing scissors, needles, and —
BLA. (*opening it*).   Cigars!
    Why, these *are* men! And you knew this, you minx!   545
MEL.   Oh, spare them – they are gentlemen indeed.
    The Prince Hilarion (married years ago
    To Princess Ida) with two trusted friends!
    Consider, mother, he's her husband now,
    And has been, twenty years! Consider, too,   550
    You're only second here – you should be first.
    Assist the Prince's plan, and when he gains
    The Princess Ida, why, you *will* be first.
    You will design the fashions – think of that –
    And always serve out all the punishments!   555
    The scheme is harmless, mother – wink at it!
BLA. (*aside*).   The prospect's tempting! Well, well, well, I'll try –
    Though I've not winked at anything for years!
    'Tis but one step towards my destiny –
    The mighty Must! the inevitable Shall!   560

561 *Now wouldn't you like to rule the roast*: This phrase is often quoted in the form 'rule the roost' and assumed to derive from a cock keeping his hens in order. In fact this is a modern version of the original saying, which was as Gilbert has it here, and which perhaps referred to the person who supervised the roasting of the family joint of meat in the kitchen. Thomas Heywood's *History of Women* (c. 1630) refers to 'her that ruled the roast in the kitchen'.

577 *Plantagenet*: The name given since the seventeenth century to the British monarchs from Henry II to Richard III, i.e. the descendants of Geoffrey, Count of Anjou. It probably derives from Geoffrey's habit of wearing a sprig of broom (*planta genista*) in his cap.

DUET – MELISSA *and* LADY BLANCHE.

MEL. Now wouldn't you like to rule the roast,
   And guide this University?
BLA.   I must agree
    'Twould pleasant be.
     (Sing hey, a Proper Pride!)   565
MEL. And wouldn't you like to clear the coast
   Of malice and perversity?

BLA.   Without a doubt
    I'll bundle 'em out,
     Sing hey, when I preside!   570
BOTH. Sing hey! Sing, hoity, toity! Sorry for some!

 Sing, marry come up and $\left\{ \begin{array}{c} my \\ her \end{array} \right\}$ day will come!
   Sing, Proper Pride
   Is the horse to ride,
  And Happy-go-lucky, my Lady, O!   575
BLA. For years I've writhed beneath her sneers,
   Although a born Plantagenet!
MEL.   You're much too meek,
    Or you would speak.
     (Sing hey, I'll say no more!)   580
BLA. Her elder I, by several years,
   Although you'd ne'er imagine it.
MEL.   Sing, so I've heard
    But never a word
     Have I e'er believed before!   585
BOTH. Sing hey!, Sing, hoity, toity! Sorry for some!

 Sing, marry come up and $\left\{ \begin{array}{c} my \\ her \end{array} \right\}$ day will come!
   Sing, she shall learn
   That a worm will turn.
  Sing Happy-go-lucky, my Lady, O!   590
       (*Exit* LADY BLANCHE.)
MEL. Saved for a time, at least!

   (*Enter* FLORIAN, *on tiptoe.*)

FLOR. (*whispering*).   Melissa – come!
MEL. Oh, sir! you must away from this at once – 595
  My mother guessed your sex! It was my fault –
  I blushed and stammered so that she exclaimed,
  'Can these be men?' Then, seeing this, 'Why, these —

599–600 *'are men'/Stuck in her throat*: A take-off of the celebrated passage in Shakespeare's *Macbeth*, Act II, Scene 2, when Macbeth is describing to his wife the murder of Duncan:

> But wherefore could not I pronounce 'Amen'?
> I had most need of blessing, and 'Amen'
> Stuck in my throat.

607 *Daughters of the Plough*: These Amazonian beings are described thus in Tennyson's poem:

> Eight daughters of the plough, stronger than men,
> Huge women blowzed with health, and wind, and rain,
> And labour. Each was like a Druid rock.

In Gilbert's play *The Princess*, Hilarion and his companions are told by Gobbo, the porter and only male in Ida's stronghold, that the daughters of the plough were 'rescued in time from perilous husbandry' to do manual work at the university.
bearing luncheon: The stage direction originally read *'bearing luncheon, which they spread on the rocks'*. This is one of two scenes in which meals are taken on stage in the Savoy Operas, not counting the spaghetti consumed by the Duke of Plaza-Toro and his retinue in the 1968 D'Oyly Carte production of *The Gondoliers* (see the note to Act I, line 572). The other is the feast at the end of Act I of *The Sorcerer*.
   Peter Riley, the last general manager of the D'Oyly Carte company, remembers this scene as a prop master's nightmare: 'You never came off the stage with as much prop food as you'd gone on with. The chorus girls used to delight in pulling the heads off the pheasants and legs off the chickens. We eventually tried substituting real biscuits and crisps but the girls ate them before they got on.'
609 *asphodel*: An echo of *Patience* and Bunthorne's 'amaranthine asphodel' (Act I, line 297). Asphodels are lilies; in Greek mythology the everlasting flowers that carpeted the Elysian fields.

631 *to droop and pine and mope*: Just like a love-sick boy. Compare *Trial by Jury*, line 63: 'I used to mope, and sigh, and pant'.

'*Are men*', she would have added, but '*are men*'
Stuck in her throat! She keeps your secret, sir,   600
For reasons of her own – but fly from this
And take me with you – that is – no – not that!

FLOR. I'll go, but not without you! (*Bell.*) Why, what's that?
MEL. The luncheon bell.
FLOR.   I'll wait for luncheon then!   605

(*Enter* HILARION *with* PRINCESS, CYRIL *with* PSYCHE, LADY
BLANCHE *and* LADIES. *Also 'Daughters of the Plough' bearing luncheon.*)

CHORUS.

Merrily ring the luncheon bell!
Here in meadow of asphodel,
Feast we body and mind as well,   610
Merrily ring the luncheon bell!

SOLO – BLANCHE.

Hunger, I beg to state,
Is highly indelicate,
This is a fact profoundly true,
So learn your appetites to subdue.   615

CHORUS.   Yes, yes,
We'll learn our appetites to subdue!

SOLO – CYRIL (*eating*).

Madam, your words so wise,
Nobody should despise,
Cursed with an appetite keen I am   620
And I'll subdue it –
I'll subdue it –
I'll subdue it with cold roast lamb!

CHORUS.   Yes – yes –
We'll subdue it with cold roast lamb!   625

Merrily ring, etc.

PRIN. You say you know the court of Hildebrand?
        There is a Prince there – I forget his name –
HIL. Hilarion?
PRIN.   Exactly – is he well?   630
HIL. If it be well to droop and pine and mope,

637 *booby*: Another throw-back to *Trial by Jury*, where the Judge, it may be remembered, had a brief which he bought from a booby. In this case a booby means a fool or dunce.

671–94 *Would you know the kind of maid*
Cyril's drunken kissing-song has its parallel in Tennyson's poem:

> Cyril, with whom the bell-mouth'd glass had wrought,
> Or master'd by the sense of sport, began
> To troll a careless, careless tavern-catch
> Of Moll and Meg, and strange experiences
> Unmeet for ladies. Florian nodded at him,
> I frowning; Psyche flush'd and wann'd and shook;
> The lilylike Melissa droop'd her brows;
> 'Forbear,' the Princess cried; 'Forbear, Sir' I;
> And heated thro' and thro' with wrath and love,
> I smote him on the breast; he started up;
> There rose a shriek as of a city sack'd;
> Melissa clamour'd 'Flee the death;' 'To horse'
> Said Ida; 'home! to horse' and fled.

To sigh 'Oh, Ida! Ida!' all day long,
'Ida! my love! my life! Oh, come to me!'
If it be well, I say, to do all this,
Then Prince Hilarion is very well.   635

PRIN.   He breathes *our* name? Well, it's a common one!
And is the booby comely?

HIL.   Pretty well.
I've heard it said that if I dressed myself
In Prince Hilarion's clothes (supposing this   640
Consisted with my maiden modesty),
I might be taken for Hilarion's self.
But what is this to you or me, who think
Of all mankind with undisguised contempt?

PRIN.   Contempt? Why, damsel, when I think of man,   645
Contempt is not the word.

CYR. (*getting tipsy*).   I'm sure of that,
Or if it is, it surely should not be!

HIL. (*aside to* CYRIL).   Be quiet, idiot, or they'll find us out.

CYR.   The Prince Hilarion's a goodly lad!   650

PRIN.   *You* know him then?

CYR. (*tipsily*).   I rather think I do!
We are inseparables!

PRIN.   Why, what's this?
You love him then?   655

CYR.   We do indeed – all three!

HIL.   Madam, she jests! (*Aside to* CYRIL.) Remember where you are!

CYR.   Jests? Not at all! Why, bless my heart alive,
You and Hilarion, when at the Court,
Rode the same horse!   660

PRIN. (*horrified*)   Astride?

CYR.   Of course! Why not?
Wore the same clothes – and once or twice, I think,
Got tipsy in the same good company!

PRIN.   Well, these are nice young ladies, on my word! 665

CYR. (*tipsy*).   Don't you remember that old kissing-song
He'd sing to blushing Mistress Lalage,
The hostess of the Pigeons? Thus it ran:

SONG – CYRIL.

(*During symphony* HILARION *and* FLORIAN *try to stop* CYRIL.
He shakes them off angrily.)   670

Would you know the kind of maid

705 *Loses her balance, and falls into the stream*: The incident of Ida's fall into the moat, and her
subsequent rescue by Hilarion, which Gilbert took from Tennyson's original, was,
most unusually for a piece of D'Oyly Carte business, clumsily staged in the first
production of *Princess Ida*. The *Sporting Times* commented: 'The water is so hard and
so near the platform that Miss Braham always remains in sight, and as she jumps in
face foremost the portion of her person that is not usually presented to an audience is
most prominent.' The *Sportsman* was equally unimpressed: 'The plunge and Hilarion's
jump into the water were badly managed and evoked the derisive laughter of "the
gods", the simple facts of the case being that the scene had not been studied from the
theatrical Olympian heights.'

Sets my heart aflame-a?
Eyes must be downcast and staid,
  Cheeks must flush for shame-a!
    She may neither dance nor sing,   675
    But, demure in everything,
    Hang her head in modest way,
    With pouting lips that seem to say,
    'Oh, kiss me, kiss me, kiss me, kiss me,
    Though I die of shame-a!'   680
  Please you, that's the kind of maid
  Sets my heart aflame-a!

When a maid is bold and gay
  With a tongue goes clang-a,
Flaunting it in brave array,   685
  Maiden may go hang-a!
    Sunflower gay and hollyhock
    Never shall my garden stock;
    Mine the blushing rose of May,
    With pouting lips that seem to say,   690
    'Oh, kiss me, kiss me, kiss me, kiss me,
    Though I die of shame-a!'
  Please you, that's the kind of maid
  Sets my heart aflame-a!

PRIN.   Infamous creature, get you hence away!   695

(HILARION, *who has been with difficulty restrained by* FLORIAN *during this song, breaks from him and strikes* CYRIL *furiously on the breast.*)

HIL.   Dog! there is something more to sing about!
CYR. (*sobered*).   Hilarion, are you mad?
PRIN. (*horrified*).   Hilarion? Help!   700
  Why, these are men! Lost! lost! betrayed! undone!
        (*Running on to bridge.*)
  Girls, get you hence! Man-monsters, if you dare
  Approach one step, I — Ah!
        (*Loses her balance, and falls into the stream.*)   705
PSY.   Oh! save her, sir!
BLA.   It's useless, sir, – you'll only catch your death!
        (HILARION *springs in.*)
SACH.   He catches her!
MEL.   And now he lets her go!   710
  Again she's in his grasp —

715 *She's saved*: In the earliest published libretto there was a stage direction here before the finale: '*Hilarion is seen swimming with the Princess in one arm. The Princess and he are brought to land.*'

Psy.   And now she's not.
       He seizes her back hair!
Bla. (*not looking*).   And it comes off!
Psy.   No, no! She's saved! – she's saved! – she's saved! – she's saved!   715

FINALE.

Chorus of Ladies.

    Oh! joy, our chief is saved,
      And by Hilarion's hand;
    The torrent fierce he braved,
      And brought her safe to land!
        For his intrusion we must own   720
        This doughty deed may well atone!

Prin.   Stand forth ye three,
        Whoe'er ye be,
    And hearken to our stern decree!

Hil., Cyr., *and* Flor.   Have mercy, O lady, – disregard your oaths!   725

Prin.   I know not mercy, men in women's clothes!
      The man whose sacrilegious eyes
      Invade our strict seclusion, dies.
      Arrest these coarse intruding spies!

    (*They are arrested by the 'Daughters of the Plough'.*)   730

Flor., Cyr., *and* Ladies. Have mercy, O lady, – disregard your oaths!
Prin.   I know not mercy, men in women's clothes!

    (Cyril *and* Florian *are bound.*)

SONG – Hilarion.

    Whom thou hast chained must wear his chain,
      Thou canst not set him free,   735
    He wrestles with his bonds in vain
      Who lives by loving thee!
    If heart of stone for heart of fire,
      Be all thou hast to give,
    If dead to me my heart's desire,   740
    Why should I wish to live?

742 *Have mercy, O lady*: This interpolation is not found in the first edition of the libretto.

764 *Is battered by them*: The first edition of the libretto has three additional lines for the chorus, to be sung after the yielding of the gate and entrance of the soldiers:

ALL.   Too late – too late!
                                          The castle gate
                                          Is battered by them!

FLOR., CYR., *and* LADIES.   Have mercy, O lady!

> No word of thine – no stern command
>   Can teach my heart to rove,
> Then rather perish by thy hand, 745
>   Than live without thy love!
> A loveless life apart from thee
>   Were hopeless slavery,
> If kindly death will set me free,
>   Why should I fear to die? 750

LADIES.   Have mercy! Have mercy!

> *(He is bound by two of the attendants, and the three*
>   *gentlemen are marched off.)*

> *(Enter* MELISSA.*)*

MEL.   Madam, without the castle walls 755
          An armèd band
        Demand admittance to our halls
          For Hildebrand!

ALL.   Oh, horror!

PRIN.   Deny them! 760
              We will defy them!

ALL.   Too late – too late!
             The castle gate
           Is battered by them!

(The gate yields. SOLDIERS *rush in.* ARAC, GURON, *and* SCYNTHIUS 765
  are with them, but with their hands handcuffed.)

ENSEMBLE.

GIRLS.	MEN.
Rend the air with wailing,	Walls and fences scaling,
Shed the shameful tear!	Promptly we appear;
Walls are unavailing,	Walls are unavailing,
Man has entered here!	We have entered here. 770
Shame and desecration	Female execration
Are his staunch allies,	Stifle if you're wise,
Let your lamentation	Stop your lamentation,
Echo to the skies!	Dry your pretty eyes!

777 *beard a maiden in her lair*: It is normally, of course, lions who are bearded in their lairs, as in the proverb song in *Iolanthe* (Act II, line 384). The expression means defying someone directly and face to face.

(*Enter* HILDEBRAND.)   775

RECITATIVE.

PRIN.   Audacious tyrant, do you dare
           To beard a maiden in her lair?

HILD.   Since you inquire,
             We've no desire
           To beard a maiden here, or anywhere!   780

SOL.   No, no – we've no desire
           To beard a maiden here, or anywhere!
           No, no, no, no.

SOLO – HILDEBRAND.

    Some years ago
    No doubt you know   785
(And if you don't I'll tell you so)
    You gave your troth
    Upon your oath
To Hilarion my son.
    A vow you make   790
    You must not break,
(If you think you may, it's a great mistake),
    For a bride's a bride
    Though the knot were tied
      At the early age of one!   795
        And I'm a peppery kind of King,
        Who's indisposed for parleying
        To fit the wit of a bit of a chit,
        And that's the long and the short of it!

SOL.   For he's a peppery kind of King, etc.   800

    If you decide
    To pocket your pride
And let Hilarion claim his bride,
    Why, well and good,
    It's understood   805
We'll let bygones go by –
    But if you choose
    To sulk in the blues

822–3 *we're taught/To shame it*: The rather fastidious reviewer of *The Theatre* took great exception to this line: 'Death, figuratively speaking, may be braved, defied, scorned, met with courage and the reverse; but it cannot be shamed.'

841 *I rather think I dare*: This line was not in the original libretto.

I'll make the whole of you shake in your shoes.
    I'll storm your walls,   810
    And level your halls,
        In the twinkling of an eye!
            For I'm a peppery Potentate,
            Who's little inclined his claim to bate,
            To fit the wit of a bit of a chit,   815
            And that's the long and the short of it!

SOL.   For he's a peppery Potentate, etc.

TRIO – ARAC, GURON, *and* SCYNTHIUS.

We may remark, though nothing can
            Dismay us,
That if you thwart this gentleman,   820
            He'll slay us.
We don't fear death, of course – we're taught
            To shame it;
But still upon the whole we thought
            We'd name it.   825
(*To each other*.) Yes, yes, yes, better perhaps to name it.
            Our interests we would not press
            With chatter,
Three hulking brothers more or less
            Don't matter;   830
If you'd pooh-pooh this monarch's plan,
            Pooh-pooh it,
But when he says he'll hang a man,
            He'll do it.
(*To each other*.) Yes, yes, yes, devil doubt he'll do it.   835
PRIN. (*Recitative*). Be reassured, nor fear his anger blind,
            His menaces are idle as the wind.
            He dares not kill you – vengeance lurks behind!
AR., GUR., SCYN. *We* rather think he dares, but never mind!
                No, no, no, – never, never mind!   840
HILD.   I rather think I dare, but never, never mind!
            Enough of parley – as a special boon,
            We give you till to-morrow afternoon;
            Release Hilarion, then, and be his bride,
            Or you'll incur the guilt of fratricide!   845

ENSEMBLE.

PRINCESS.

To yield at once to such a foe
With shame were rife;
So quick! away with him, although
He saved my life!
That he is fair, and strong, and
tall,
Is very evident to all,
Yet I will die before I call
Myself his wife!

THE OTHERS.

Oh! yield at once, 'twere better so
Than risk a strife!
And let the Prince Hilarion go –
He saved thy life!
Hilarion's fair, and strong, and
tall –
A worse misfortune might befall –
It's not so dreadful, after all,
To be his wife!   850

SOLO – PRINCESS.

Though I am but a girl,
Defiance thus I hurl,   855
   Our banners all
   On outer wall
We fearlessly unfurl.

ALL.   Though she is but a girl, etc.

PRINCESS.

To yield at once, etc.

THE OTHERS.

Oh! yield at once, etc.   860

(*The* PRINCESS *stands, surrounded by girls kneeling.* HILDEBRAND *and soldiers stand on built rocks at back and sides of stage. Picture.*)

END OF ACT II

1–2 *Scene*: Tennyson gives a vivid description of the courtyard of the university in *The Princess*:

> a court
> Compact of lucid marbles, boss'd with lengths
> Of classic frieze, with ample awnings gay
> Betwixt the pillars, and with great urns of flowers.
> The Muses and the Graces, group'd in threes,
> Enring'd a billowing fountain in the midst; ·
> And here and there on lattice edges lay
> Or book or lute.

3–10 *Death to the invader*

An early D'Oyly Carte prompt-book gives the following directions for this number:

Death to the invader!	*arms up*
Strike a deadly blow,	*blow*
As an old Crusader	*arms up*
Struck his Paynim foe!	*blow*
Let our martial thunder	
Fill his soul with wonder	
Tear his ranks asunder,	*arms open*
Lay the tyrant low!	*point*

6 *Paynim*: Pagan or heathen. The word was originally applied to the Saracens who fought the Crusaders.

ACT III

SCENE. – *Outer Walls and Courtyard of Castle Adamant.* MELISSA, SACHARISSA, *and ladies discovered, armed with battleaxes.*

CHORUS.

Death to the invader!
  Strike a deadly blow,
As an old Crusader
  Struck his Paynim foe!   5
Let our martial thunder
Fill his soul with wonder,
Tear his ranks asunder,
  Lay the tyrant low!   10

SOLO – MELISSA.

Thus our courage, all untarnished
  We're instructed to display:
But to tell the truth unvarnished,
  We are more inclined to say,
'Please you, do not hurt us.'   15

CHORUS.   'Do not hurt us, if it please you!'
MEL.   'Please you let us be.'
CHORUS.   'Let us be – let us be!'
MEL.   'Soldiers disconcert us.'
CHORUS.   'Disconcert us, if it please you!'   20
MEL.   'Frightened maids are we.'
CHORUS.   'Maids are we – maids are we!'

MELISSA.

But 'twould be an error
To confess our terror,

27 *Death to the invader*: In early libretti, the chorus repeated all eight lines of 'Death to the invader' at this point, not just the first four as now.

38 *One moment, ma'am*: The passage from here to line 49 was among the cuts proposed for the 1954 D'Oyly Carte revival, but a *stet* is written against it in the prompt copy, and in the end it was not removed. Other proposed cuts which were implemented include the phrases 'get you hence' (line 68) and 'That in the heat and turmoil of the fight' (line 75), and the passage from 'But, happily' to 'such as soldiers love' (lines 85–8).

25

So, in Ida's name,
Boldly we exclaim:

CHORUS.

Death to the invader!
  Strike a deadly blow,
As an old Crusader
  Struck his Paynim foe!

30

(*Flourish. Enter* PRINCESS, *armed, attended by*
BLANCHE *and* PSYCHE.)

PRIN.   I like your spirit, girls! We have to meet
Stern bearded warriors in fight to-day:
Wear naught but what is necessary to
Preserve your dignity before their eyes,
And give your limbs full play.

35

BLA.   One moment, ma'am,
Here is a paradox we should not pass
Without inquiry. We are prone to say,
'This thing is Needful – that, Superfluous' –
Yet they invariably co-exist!
We find the Needful comprehended in
The circle of the grand Superfluous,
Yet the Superfluous cannot be bought
Unless you're amply furnished with the Needful.
These singular considerations are –

40

45

PRIN.   Superfluous, yet not Needful – so you see
The terms may independently exist.

(*To Ladies.*) Women of Adamant, we have to show
That Woman, educated to the task,
Can meet Man, face to face, on his own ground,
And beat him there. Now let us set to work:
Where is our lady surgeon?

50

SAC.   Madam, here!

55

PRIN.   We shall require your skill to heal the wounds
Of those that fall.

SAC. (*alarmed*).   What, heal the wounded?

PRIN.   Yes!

SAC.   And cut off real live legs and arms?

60

PRIN.   Of course!

SAC.   I wouldn't do it for a thousand pounds!

PRIN.   Why, how is this? Are you faint-hearted, girl?
You've often cut them off in theory!

70 *My fusiliers, advance*: In Gilbert's earlier play, this passage was:

> My Amazons, advance!
> Where are your muskets, pray?

96 *fulminating*: Exploding, from the Latin word *fulminare*, meaning to send forth thunder or lightning.

98 *saltpetre*: A crystalline substance, with the chemical name potassium nitrate, which is the chief constituent of gunpowder.

105 *Exeunt all but Princess*: In early libretti the stage direction here read: 'Exeunt all but Princess, singing refrain of "Death to the Invader" *pianissimo*.'

For a period before the war the D'Oyly Carte company altered the order of the Third Act of *Princess Ida*. Ida's next two lines and her song 'I built upon a rock' were moved from their original position, and introduced instead just before the gates are opened to let in the soldiers (line 234). I cannot discover exactly when this change was made, although it was certainly in operation at the time of the D'Oyly Carte recordings in 1923 and 1930. The 1954 revival restored the original order.

SAC.	In theory I'll cut them off again	65
	With pleasure, and as often as you like,	
	But not in practice.	
PRIN.	Coward! get you hence,	
	I've craft enough for that, and courage too,	
	I'll do your work! My fusiliers, advance!	70
	Why, you are armed with axes! Gilded toys!	
	Where are your rifles, pray?	
CHLOE.	Why, please you, ma'am,	
	We left them in the armoury, for fear	
	That in the heat and turmoil of the fight,	75
	They might go off!	
PRIN.	'They might!' Oh, craven souls!	
	Go off yourselves! Thank heaven, I have a heart	
	That quails not at the thought of meeting men;	
	I will discharge your rifles! Off with you!	80
	Where's my bandmistress?	
ADA.	Please you, ma'am, the band	
	Do not feel well, and can't come out to-day!	
PRIN.	Why, this is flat rebellion! I've no time	
	To talk to them just now. But, happily,	85
	I can play several instruments at once,	
	And I will drown the shrieks of those that fall	
	With trumpet music, such as soldiers love!	
	How stand we with respect to gunpowder?	
	My Lady Psyche – you who superintend	90
	Our lab'ratory – are you well prepared	
	To blow these bearded rascals into shreds?	
PSY.	Why, madam –	
PRIN.	Well?	
PSY.	Let us try gentler means.	95
	We can dispense with fulminating grains	
	While we have eyes with which to flash our rage!	
	We can dispense with villainous saltpetre	
	While we have tongues with which to blow them up!	
	We can dispense, in short, with all the arts	100
	That brutalize the practical polemist!	
PRIN. (*contemptuously*).	I never knew a more dispensing chemist!	
	Away, away – I'll meet these men alone	
	Since all my women have deserted me!	

(Exeunt all but PRINCESS.)   105

PRIN.	So fail my cherished plans – so fails my faith –	
	And with it hope, and all that comes of hope!	

108–35 *I built upon a rock*

This is one of the nearest approximations to a grand-opera aria in the entire Savoy repertoire. It is also strongly suggestive of the sacred oratorio style of which Sullivan was a leading exponent. The critics were generally enthusiastic. *The Times* described it as 'the best musical lyric in the score', the *Daily Telegraph* detected the influence of Schubert, and the *Saturday Review* commented that it appeared as though in this case Sullivan was setting Tennyson rather than Gilbert. The only dissenting note was struck by *Truth*, which suggested that the song might advantageously have been cut: 'It is the right music in the wrong place.'

As originally written, Ida's song was shorter and in a different form from the present version. This is how it appears in the first edition of the libretto:

> I built upon a rock,
>   But ere Destruction's hand
>   Dealt equal lot
>   To Court and cot,
>   My rock had turned to sand!
>   Ah, faithless rock,
>   My simple faith to mock!
>
> I leant upon an oak,
>   But in the hour of need,
>   Alack-a-day,
>   My trusted stay
>   Was but a bruised reed!
>   Ah, trait'rous oak,
>   Thy worthlessness to cloak!
>
> I drew a sword of steel,
>   But when to home and hearth
>   The battle's breath
>   Bore fire and death,
>   My sword was but a lath!
>   Ah, coward steel,
>   That fear can unanneal!

126 *lath*: A thin, narrow piece of wood.

133 *unanneal*: Steel is annealed or toughened by being exposed to continuous and gradually diminishing heat. The word 'unannealed' also appears in *The Pirates of Penzance* (Act II, line 551) but is wrongly used there (see the note).

SONG – PRINCESS.

I built upon a rock,
  But ere Destruction's hand
    Dealt equal lot   110
    To Court and cot,
  My rock had turned to sand!
I leant upon an oak,
  But in the hour of need,
    Alack-a-day,   115
    My trusted stay
  Was but a bruisèd reed!
    Ah, faithless rock,
    My simple faith to mock!
    Ah, trait'rous oak,   120
    Thy worthlessness to cloak.

I drew a sword of steel,
  But when to home and hearth
    The battle's breath
    Bore fire and death,   125
  My sword was but a lath!
I lit a beacon fire,
  But on a stormy day
    Of frost and rime,
    In wintertime,   130
  My fire had died away!
    Ah, coward steel,
    That fear can unanneal!
    Ah, false fire indeed,
    To fail me in my need!   135

(*She sinks on a seat. Enter* CHLOE *and all the ladies.*)

CHLOE.   Madam, your father and your brothers claim
An audience!
PRIN.   What do they do here?
CHLOE.   They come   140
To fight for you!
PRIN.   Admit them!
BLA.   Infamous!
One's brothers, ma'am, are men!
PRIN.   So I have heard. 145
But all my women seem to fail me when

160 *popinjays*: An old name for a parrot, figuratively applied to people to suggest vanity and empty conceit. In 'I have a song to sing, O' in Act I of *The Yeomen of the Guard*, Jack Point sings:

> It's a song of a popinjay, bravely born,
> Who turned up his noble nose with scorn . . .

161 *jack-a-dandy*: Smart, foppish, pert or conceited.

167–8 *I am possessed/By the pale devil of a shaking heart*: This was another of the lines to which *The Theatre* took exception (see the note to Act II, lines 822–3). It commented: 'Confusion of metaphor makes sheer nonsense of this utterance. The frightened monarch might just as plausibly claim to be possessed by the green phantom of a crawling liver.'

180–227 *Whene'er I spoke*
The tune of Gama's patter song was altered by Sullivan only a few days before the first performance, much to the dismay of George Grossmith, who found it very difficult to unlearn the old tune and substitute the new one.

The current Macmillan edition of the Savoy Operas has 'Whene'er I poke' as the first line of the song. This may possibly be a hang-over from an early present-tense version of the song. The licence copy and all editions of the libretto that I have seen have 'Whene'er I spoke', which of course, fits with the past tense of 'smiled' and 'voted'.

I need them most. In this emergency,
Even one's brothers may be turned to use.

(*Enter* GAMA , *quite pale and unnerved.*)

GAMA.   My daughter! 150
PRIN.   Father! thou art free!
GAMA.   Aye, free!
Free as a tethered ass! I come to thee
With words from Hildebrand. Those duly given
I must return to blank captivity. 155
I'm free so far.
PRIN.   Your message.
GAMA.   Hildebrand
Is loth to war with women. Pit my sons,
My three brave sons, against these popinjays, 160
These tufted jack-a-dandy featherheads,
And on the issue let thy hand depend!
PRIN.   Insult on insult's head! Are we a stake
For fighting men? What fiend possesses thee,
That thou hast come with offers such as these 165
From such as he to such an one as I?
GAMA.   I am possessed
By the pale devil of a shaking heart!
My stubborn will is bent. I dare not face
That devilish monarch's black malignity! 170
He tortures me with torments worse than death,
I haven't anything to grumble at!
He finds out what particular meats I love,
And gives me them. The very choicest wines,
The costliest robes – the richest rooms are mine: 175
He suffers none to thwart my simplest plan,
And gives strict orders none should contradict me!
He's made my life a curse! (*weeps*).
PRIN.   My tortured father!

SONG – GAMA.

Whene'er I spoke 180
Sarcastic joke
    Replete with malice spiteful,
This people mild
Politely smiled,
    And voted me delightful! 185

197 *German bands*: Irritating fellow countrymen of the 'mystical Germans/Who preach from ten till four' who so annoyed the Mikado (*The Mikado*, Act II, lines 348–9), German musicians were a common sight on the streets of Victorian London. They tended to wear uniforms and play marches and other stirring oom-pah-pah numbers. A correspondent to the *Gilbert and Sullivan Journal* in the 1930s recalled that they were in the habit of erecting music stands in the street for their performances.

207 *hurdy-gurds*: The hurdy–gurdy was originally a lute-like instrument with strings, sounded by turning a handle. The words later came to be applied to the barrel organs which were so familiar a feature of the street life of Victorian Britain.

211 *I offered gold*: The first American edition of the libretto, which almost certainly contains material originally in the British libretto but later altered (see the note to Act II, lines 491–520), has a different version of this third verse:

> Upon the stage
> Plays, ripe with age,
> And not too much protracted,
> With faultless taste
> Were always placed
> And excellently acted;
> Now when he sees
> Good comedies
> It irritates King Gama,
> With no excuse
> For rank abuse
> Who can enjoy the drama?

Now when a wight
Sits up all night
   Ill-natured jokes devising,
And all his wiles
Are met with smiles,   190
   It's hard, there's no disguising! Ah!

Oh, don't the days seem lank and long
When all goes right and nothing goes wrong,
And isn't your life extremely flat
With nothing whatever to grumble at!   195

CHORUS.   Oh, isn't your life, etc.

     When German bands
     From music stands
   Played Wagner imper*fect*ly –
     I bade them go –   200
     They didn't say no,
   But off they went directly!
     The organ boys
     They stopped their noise
   With readiness surprising,   205
     And grinning herds
     Of hurdy-gurds
   Retired apologizing! Ah!

Oh, don't the days seem lank and long, etc.

CHORUS.   Oh, isn't your life, etc.   210

     I offered gold
     In sums untold
   To all who'd contradict me –
     I said I'd pay
     A pound a day   215
   To anyone who kicked me –
     I bribed with toys
     Great vulgar boys
   To utter something spiteful,
     But, bless you, no!   220
     They *would* be so
   Confoundedly politeful! Ah!

232 *Open the gates*: This and the next line were among the cuts made in 1954.

247 *molly-coddle*: A pampered creature.

In short, these aggravating lads,
They tickle my tastes, they feed my fads,
They give me this and they give me that,   225
And I've nothing whatever to grumble at!

CHORUS.   Oh, isn't your life, etc.

(*He bursts into tears, and falls sobbing on a seat.*)

PRIN.   My poor old father! How he must have suffered!
          Well, well, I yield!   230
GAMA (*hysterically*). She yields! I'm saved, I'm saved!   (*Exit.*)
PRIN.   Open the gates – admit these warriors,
          Then get you all within the castle walls.   (*Exit.*)

(*The gates are opened, and the girls mount the battlements as soldiers
enter. Also* ARAC, GURON, *and* SCYNTHIUS.)   235

CHORUS OF SOLDIERS.

When anger spreads his wing,
    And all seems dark as night for it,
    There's nothing but to fight for it,
But ere you pitch your ring,
    Select a pretty site for it,   240
    (This spot is suited quite for it),
And then you gaily sing,

'Oh, I love the jolly rattle
Of an ordeal by battle,
There's an end of tittle-tattle,   245
    When your enemy is dead.
It's an arrant molly-coddle
Fears a crack upon his noddle
And he's only fit to swaddle
    In a downy feather-bed!' –   250

ENSEMBLE.

GIRLS.	MEN.
For a fight's a kind of thing	Oh, I love the jolly rattle, etc.
That I love to look upon,	
So let us sing,	
Long live the King,	
And his son Hilarion!	

255

256–90 *This helmet, I suppose*

This splendid spoof of Handelian style was originally sung slightly later in Act III, just before the full-scale fight between the forces of Hildebrand and Gama (line 327). In the first edition of the libretto the stage direction and subsequent dialogue which now start at line 292 followed straight on from 'For a fight's a kind of thing'. The current Macmillan edition still has the original placing of 'This helmet, I suppose', although it was certainly changed to its present position before 1930.

The American first edition of the libretto has a different version of the song, with an introductory chorus:

CHORUS.

With hearts resolved and courage grave,
The warriors now begin
May fortune's shield protect the brave,
And may the best men win!

SOLO – Arac.

Where'er we go
To fight the foe
We never throw a chance away,
And at last
We always cast
Each useless circumstance away.
A helmet bright
Is far from light,
Life guardsmen know how true it is.
(*Taking off helmet*).

A bright cuirass
We also class
With useless superfluities (*taking off cuirass*)
All this array
Is in the way
It is, upon my word it is –
For who can fight
When locked up tight
In lobster-like absurdities?

(*By this time they have removed all their armour and wear nothing but a close-fitting shape suit.*)

Though brasses
And tasses
And showy cuirasses
Are all very useful to dazzle the lasses,
He clashes with asses
Who cumbers with masses
Of metal
His fettle,
Tra, la, la, la, la!

The Three.   Yes, yes, yes!
Tra, la, la, la, la!

All.   Yes, yes, yes!
Tra, la, la, la, la!

265 *cuirass*: A piece of armour reaching down to the waist and consisting of a breast-plate and back-plate fastened together. The term cuirass was sometimes also used for the breast-plate alone.

275 *brassets*: Armour for the upper arm, more usually spelt 'brassards' or 'brassarts'.

291 *shape suits*: Tight-fitting pants and pullover tunic.

SONG – ARAC.

This helmet, I suppose,
Was meant to ward off blows,
    It's very hot,
    And weighs a lot,
As many a guardsman knows,   260
So off that helmet goes.

ALL.   Yes, yes, yes,
So off that helmet goes!
               (Giving their helmets to attendants.)

ARAC.   This tight-fitting cuirass   265
Is but a useless mass,
    It's made of steel,
    And weighs a deal,
A man is but an ass
Who fights in a cuirass,   270
So off goes that cuirass.

ALL.   Yes, yes, yes,
So off goes that cuirass!
            (Removing cuirasses.)

ARAC.   These brassets, truth to tell,   275
May look uncommon well,
    But in a fight
    They're much too tight,
They're like a lobster shell!

ALL.   Yes, yes, yes,   280
They're like a lobster shell.
            (Removing their brassets.)

ARAC.   These things I treat the same *(indicating leg pieces)*.
(I quite forget their name)
    They turn one's legs   285
    To cribbage pegs –
Their aid I thus disclaim,
Though I forget their name!

ALL.   Yes, yes, yes,

Their aid $\left\{\begin{array}{c} \text{we} \\ \text{they} \end{array}\right\}$ thus disclaim!   290

(They remove their leg pieces and wear close-fitting shape suits.)

306 *virago*: A man-like or heroic woman; an Amazon.
   termagant: An impudent or quarrelsome woman, a shrew.

(HILARION, FLORIAN, *and* CYRIL *are brought out by the 'Daughters of the Plough'. They are still bound and wear the robes. Enter* GAMA.)

GAMA.	Hilarion! Cyril! Florian! dressed as women!
	Is this indeed Hilarion?
HIL.	Yes, it is!
GAMA.	Why, you look handsome in your women's clothes!
	Stick to 'em! men's attire becomes you not!

(*To* CYRIL *and* FLORIAN.) And you, young ladies, will you please to pray
    King Hildebrand to set me free again?   300
    Hang on his neck and gaze into his eyes,
    He never could resist a pretty face!

HIL.	You dog, you'll find, though I wear woman's garb,
	My sword is long and sharp!
GAMA.	Hush, pretty one!

    Here's a virago! Here's a termagant!
    If length and sharpness go for anything,
    You'll want no sword while you can wag your tongue!

CYR.	What need to waste your words on such as he?
	He's old and crippled.
GAMA.	Aye, but I've three sons,

    Fine fellows, young, and muscular, and brave,
    They're well worth talking to! Come, what d'ye say?

ARAC.	Aye, pretty ones, engage yourselves with us,
	If three rude warriors affright you not!
HIL.	Old as you are, I'd wring your shrivelled neck
	If you were not the Princess Ida's father.
GAMA.	If I were not the Princess Ida's father,

    And so had not her brothers for my sons,
    No doubt you'd wring my neck – in safety too!   320
    Come, come, Hilarion, begin, begin!
    Give them no quarter – they will give you none.
    You've this advantage over warriors
    Who kill their country's enemies for pay, –
    You know what you are fighting for – look there!   325
          (*Pointing to Ladies on the battlements.*)

(*Desperate fight between the three Princes and the three Knights, during which the Ladies on the battlements and the Soldiers on the stage sing the following chorus:*)

        This is our duty plain towards
           Our Princess all immaculate,
        We ought to bless her brothers' swords
           And piously ejaculate:

Line numbers in right margin: 295, 300, 305, 310, 315, 320, 325, 330

333 *Oh, Hungary*: This sudden suggestion that Gama and his sons are from Hungary was not well received by the *Theatre* reviewer:

> Why Hungary, I humbly ask? Up to the moment at which this astounding invocation is pronounced, with scarcely less amazing unanimity, by the rival hosts of Hildebrand and Ida, the author has not even so much as hinted to us that Castle Adamant is situate in the Realm of the Five Rivers. Barely ten minutes before the final fall of the curtain – and for no conceivable reason connected with the story of the play – he informs us that Gama and his sons are Magyars to a man. But stay: can it be that Mr Gilbert confers this nationality upon one of his two Royal Families in order to obtain a rhyme for the word 'ironmongery', which occurs later on in the above-quoted verse? It must be; but I contend that such a *pis-aller* is scarcely worthy of so facile and fertile a rhymster.

The American first edition has a second verse to the soldiers' chorus:

> But if our hearts assert their sway,
>   (And hearts are all fantastical)
> We shall be more disposed to say
>   These words enthusiastical:
>   Hilarion!
>   Hilarion!
> Oh prosper, Prince Hilarion!
>   In mode complete
>   May you defeat
> Each meddlesome Hungarian!

344 *Ladies, my brothers*: This and the next line were among the cuts made in the 1954 production. An early D'Oyly Carte prompt-book has the following stage direction after the words 'Bind up their wounds': 'Sacharissa goes to Arac, Chloe to Scynthius, and Ada to Guron. They place bandages (linen) round their heads as they lie on the ground, the three then rise and stand in places till curtain.'

365 *If you enlist*: This and the following line were cut in the 1954 revival, as was the passage from line 377 to line 382.

Oh, Hungary!
Oh, Hungary!
Oh, doughty sons of Hungary!   335
May all success
Attend and bless
Your warlike ironmongery!
Hilarion! Hilarion! Hilarion!

(*By this time,* ARAC, GURON, *and* SCYNTHIUS *are on the ground, wounded*   340
– HILARION, CYRIL, *and* FLORIAN *stand over them.*)

PRIN. (*entering through gate and followed by Ladies,* HILDEBRAND, *and*
GAMA). Hold! stay your hands! – we yield ourselves to you!
    Ladies, my brothers all lie bleeding there!
    Bind up their wounds – but look the other way.   345
(*Coming down.*) Is this the end? (*bitterly to* LADY BLANCHE). How say
      you, Lady Blanche –
    Can I with dignity my post resign?
    And if I do, will you then take my place?
BLA.   To answer this, it's meet that we consult
    The great Potential Mysteries; I mean   350
    The five Subjunctive Possibilities –
    The May, the Might, the Would, the Could, the Should.
    Can you resign? The prince May claim you; if
    He Might, you Could – and if you Should, I Would!
PRIN.   I thought as much! Then, to my fate I yield –   355
    So ends my cherished scheme! Oh, I had hoped
    To band all women with my maiden throng,
    And make them all abjure tyrannic Man!
HILD.   A noble aim!
PRIN.   You ridicule it now;   360
    But if I carried out this glorious scheme,
    At my exalted name Posterity
    Would bow in gratitude!
HILD.   But pray reflect –
    If you enlist all women in your cause,
    And make them all abjure tyrannic Man,   365
    The obvious question then arises, 'How
    Is this Posterity to be provided?'
PRIN.   I never thought of that! My Lady Blanche,
    How do you solve the riddle?   370
BLA.   Don't ask me –
    Abstract Philosophy won't answer it.
    Take him – he is your Shall. Give in to Fate!

380–81 *Experiments, the proverb says, are made/On humble subjects*: The saying *Fiat experimentum in corpore vile* is said to derive from the experience of the French humorist Muret (1526–85), who, while in a trance, narrowly escaped dissection by experimenting surgeons.

403–6 *We will walk this world . . . I love thee – Come*: This is the only occasion in his 'Respectful Operatic Per-Version' where Gilbert quotes the words of the Poet Laureate. These lines come towards the end of *The Princess*. They are followed there by these concluding lines:

> Yield thyself up: my hopes and thine are one:
> Accomplish thou my manhood and thyself;
> Lay thy sweet hands in mine and trust to me.

407–31 *FINALE*

In his autobiographical notes written *c*. 1939 and reflecting on his long career with the D'Oyly Carte company, J. M. Gordon mentions some inappropriate clowning that went on in the finale of *Princess Ida*: 'Lady Blanche standing legs apart – to support Gama when he leans against her, a distinguished lady of title, and continuing to let him do so and not resenting this indignity. It is not the Savoy tradition of 1884 but vulgarity brought in years ago.'

PRIN. And you desert me. I alone am staunch!

HIL. Madam, you placed your trust in Woman – well, 375
     Woman has failed you utterly – try Man,
     Give him one chance, it's only fair – besides,
     Women are far too precious, too divine,
     To try unproven theories upon.
     Experiments, the proverb says, are made 380
     On humble subjects – try our grosser clay,
     And mould it as you will!

CYR.   Remember, too,
     Dear Madam, if at any time you feel
     A-weary of the Prince, you can return 385
     To Castle Adamant, and rule your girls
     As heretofore, you know.

PRIN.   And shall I find
     The Lady Psyche here?

PSY.   If Cyril, ma'am, 390
     Does not behave himself, I think you will.

PRIN. And you, Melissa, shall I find *you* here?

MEL. Madam, however Florian turns out,
     Unhesitatingly I answer, No!

GAMA. Consider this, my love, if your mamma 395
     Had looked on matters from your point of view
     (I wish she had), why, where would you have been?

BLA. There's an unbounded field of speculation,
     On which I could discourse for hours!

PRIN.   No doubt! 400
     We will not trouble you. Hilarion,
     I have been wrong – I see my error now.
     Take me, Hilarion – 'We will walk this world
     Yoked in all exercise of noble end!
     And so through those dark gates across the wild 405
     That no man knows! Indeed, I love thee – Come!'

FINALE.

PRIN.   With joy abiding,
       Together gliding
         Through life's variety,
          In sweet society,
       And thus enthroning 410
       The love I'm owning,
       On this atoning
         I will rely!

432 *CURTAIN*: A stage direction in an early prompt-book reads: 'For return curtain Hildebrand and Gama are seen grasping each other's hands – the feud is ended.'

CHORUS.   It were profanity   415
                   For poor humanity
                   To treat as vanity
                       The sway of Love.
                   In no locality
                   Or principality   420
                   Is our mortality
                       Its sway above!

HILARION.   When day is fading,
                   With serenading
                       And such frivolity   425
                       Of tender quality –
                   With scented showers
                   Of fairest flowers,
                   The happy hours
                       Will gaily fly!   430

CHORUS.   It were profanity, etc.

CURTAIN

RUDDIGORE

OR

THE WITCH'S CURSE

DRAMATIS PERSONÆ

MORTALS

SIR RUTHVEN MURGATROYD (*disguised as Robin Oakapple, a Young Farmer*)
RICHARD DAUNTLESS (*his Foster-Brother – a Man-o'-war's man*)
SIR DESPARD MURGATROYD, OF RUDDIGORE (*a Wicked Baronet*)
OLD ADAM GOODHEART (*Robin's Faithful Servant*)
ROSE MAYBUD (*a Village Maiden*)
MAD MARGARET
DAME HANNAH (*Rose's Aunt*)
ZORAH }
RUTH } (*Professional Bridesmaids*)

GHOSTS

SIR RUPERT MURGATROYD (*the First Baronet*)
SIR JASPER MURGATROYD (*the Third Baronet*)
SIR LIONEL MURGATROYD (*the Sixth Baronet*)
SIR CONRAD MURGATROYD (*the Twelfth Baronet*)
SIR DESMOND MURGATROYD (*the Sixteenth Baronet*)
SIR GILBERT MURGATROYD (*the Eighteenth Baronet*)
SIR MERVYN MURGATROYD (*the Twentieth Baronet*)
AND
SIR RODERIC MURGATROYD (*the Twenty-first Baronet*)
*Chorus of Officers, Ancestors, Professional Bridesmaids,
and Villagers.*

ACT I. – The Fishing Village of Rederring, in Cornwall.
ACT II. – The Picture Gallery in Ruddigore Castle.
Time – Early in the 19th century.

RUDDIGORE

Ruddigore was the first of Gilbert and Sullivan's works to receive a less than rapturous reception from the first-night audience. Boos and hisses mingled with the applause when the curtain went down on the first performance at the Savoy Theatre on 22 January 1887.

It was, of course, extraordinarily difficult to produce a work that could match the popularity of *The Mikado*, which had been taken off at the Savoy on 19 January after a record run of 672 performances. But it was not just in comparison with their previous work that critics and public alike judged Gilbert and Sullivan's new opera to be something of a flop. There were other more specific weaknesses which they detected in the burlesque of Victorian melodrama about bad baronets and innocent maidens.

The original title of the opera, which was *Ruddygore,* caused considerable offence. It was felt to be decidedly coarse for a work intended for a respectable family audience. Gilbert at first made light of the objections. When a fellow member of his club commented that he saw no difference between *Ruddygore* and *Bloodygore*, the author responded: 'Then I suppose you'll take it that if I say "I admire your ruddy countenance," I mean "I like your bloody cheek."' He impishly suggested to another detractor that the opera should be re-titled 'Kensington Gore, or Not so good as the *Mikado*'. Within a few days, however, he had taken heed of the criticism and changed the title to the less offensive *Ruddigore*.

The construction of the opera also provoked complaint. The First Act, although long (running to eighty-eight minutes, it is, indeed, the longest first act in all the Savoy repertoire), was reasonably well received by audiences and critics alike. The Second Act, however, was thought to drag and to lack any dramatic shape. The scene in which the ghosts step down from their portraits was clumsily managed in early performances, and the later encounter between Dame Hannah and the ghost of Sir Roderic Murgatroyd was generally thought to lack conviction and by some also to lack taste. A second appearance by the ghosts at the end of the act also jarred on many. Gilbert and Sullivan responded by substantially altering the Second Act and reducing its length.

In fact, *Ruddigore* was not in the end the disaster that it threatened to be on the opening night. It ran at the Savoy for a total of 288 performances, more than the first run of *Princess Ida*. Gilbert commented: 'I could do with a few more such failures.' It was not revived until 1920, when it was performed at the King's Theatre, Glasgow, with further substantial cuts made in both the First and Second Acts and with a new overture by Geoffrey Toye to replace Sullivan's original, which contained several tunes which were no longer heard in the opera. This production was extremely popular, and Gilbert's widow considered it much better than her husband's original. The D'Oyly Carte costumes and scenery were destroyed in the war, and in the autumn of 1948 a new production was mounted by Peter Goffin. Rehearsals for this were only just getting under way when Rupert D'Oyly Carte died, and his daughter, Bridget, was suddenly thrown into running the company and seeing the new *Ruddigore* on to the stage. This she did most successfully. It opened in Newcastle in November 1948, was seen in London the following year, and remained in the D'Oyly Carte repertoire until the company's closure.

Although it is not performed as often as other Savoy Operas, it seems unlikely that *Ruddigore* will disappear completely from either the professional or the amateur repertoire. In 1975 it was performed by Kent Opera, and it is still regularly put on by amateur societies and schools. A film for the television and home video market has recently been made which 'stars' Vincent Price as the evil Sir Despard Murgatroyd.

Certainly it would be a great shame if the strains of *Ruddigore* were to be heard no more. Sullivan, who set the songs in intervals from composing his oratorio *The Golden Legend*, based on a poem by Henry Longfellow, produced some memorable music, ranging from the delicate 'If somebody there chanced to be', 'Prithee, pretty maiden' and 'There grew a little flower' to the breezy 'In sailing o'er life's ocean wide' and the frighteningly eerie 'When the night wind howls'. Gilbert's take-off of the black-and-white morality and crude characterization of Victorian melodrama, while perhaps itself a little dated and heavy-handed now, still has an undeniable humour and produces in the figure of Sir Despard Murgatroyd a perfect caricature of the stage villain.

Ruddigore also has an important place in D'Oyly Carte folk history. It was as Sir Ruthven Murgatroyd, alias the poor and blameless peasant Robin Oakapple, that one of the greatest ever Savoyards made his first appearance as a principal with the company. George Grossmith had been taken seriously ill with peritonitis at the end of the first week of the opera's initial run. His understudy, who had only been in the job for a week and who had to go on at a few hours' notice, was a young man who used the stage name H. A. Henri but whose real name was Henry Lytton. He was an enormous success in the role and went on to play all the principal baritone and comic parts in the Savoy Operas. After a brief period away he returned to the company in

1908 and ten years later became the principal comedian. Lytton was knighted in 1930 and retired in 1934, fifty years after he had first joined the D'Oyly Carte Company as a member of the chorus in *Princess Ida*.

1–3 *Scene*: *Ruddigore* is not the only Gilbert and Sullivan opera to be set in Cornwall. So also, of course, is *The Pirates of Penzance*, although, unlike Penzance, Rederring is an entirely fictional location and not to be taken too seriously.

Gilbert seems to have had several changes of mind about the period in which the opera should be set, but eventually he opted for the beginning of the nineteenth century. *The World* noted 'The time is George III' and *The Times* that 'the opening scene represents a fishing village eighty or ninety years ago'.

The set for Act I changed very little in successive D'Oyly Carte productions. The *Sporting Life*'s description of the scene at the first performance could equally well describe the 1948 setting that was in use up to 1982: 'The main part of the village itself straggles away from Rose Maybud's cottage along the cliffs, which, with the porched cottage aforesaid, lock in a picturesque harbour. Some spreading chestnut trees occupy the side of the picture of the scene. The sea opens in the centre.'

4–11 *Fair is Rose as bright May-day*

Although successive editions of the vocal score print the words of this opening chorus as they are given opposite, and that is how it is generally sung, nearly all editions of the libretti add an extra syllable to each line by inserting a 'the' as follows:

> Fair is Rose as the bright May-day;
>   Soft is Rose as the warm west-wind;
> Sweet is Rose as the new-mown hay –
>   Rose is the queen of maiden-kind!

15 *Can't long remain unclaimed*: In a pre-production copy of *Ruddigore* which pre-dates the licence copy and in early published editions of the libretto this line appears as 'Won't very long remain unclaimed', and lines 18–19 appear as:

> And though she's the fairest flower that blows,
>   Nobody yet has married Rose!

In his pre-production copy these lines are altered in Gilbert's handwriting to their present version.

ACT I

Scene. – The fishing village of Rederring (in Cornwall). Rose Maybud's *cottage is seen* L. *Villagers and* Dame Hannah *discovered. Enter Chorus of Bridesmaids. They range themselves in front of* Rose's *cottage.*

Chorus of Bridesmaids.

Fair is Rose as bright May-day;
   Soft is Rose as warm west-wind;   5
Sweet is Rose as new-mown hay –
   Rose is queen of maiden-kind!
     Rose, all glowing
       With virgin blushes, say –
     Is anybody going   10
       To marry you to-day?

SOLO – Zorah.

Every day, as the days roll on,
Bridesmaids' garb we gaily don,
Sure that a maid so fairly famed
Can't long remain unclaimed.   15
Hour by hour and day by day,
Several months have passed away,
Though she's the fairest flower that blows,
No one has married Rose!

Chorus.

Rose, all glowing   20
   With virgin blushes, say –
Is anybody going
   To marry you to-day?

47–8 *one of the bad Baronets of Ruddigore*: Baronets are members of the lowest hereditary titled order in Britain, which was instituted by James I in the early seventeenth century. They are styled 'Sir' and the title is normally shortened to 'Bart' after their names. Apart from *Ruddigore*, which is fairly stuffed with them, the only other Savoy Opera to contain a baronet is *The Sorcerer*, with Sir Marmaduke Pointdextre as an elderly example of the species.

Gilbert was to return to the theme of bad baronets in his story 'The Fairy's Dilemma' which appeared in the Christmas 1900 edition of the *Graphic* magazine. It tells of an apparently wicked baronet, Sir Trevor Mauleverer, who is assisted by the Demon Alcohol to carry off a virtuous young governess to whom he had taken a fancy. In the event, however, Sir Trevor proves to be a good baronet, as the Demon explains to the fairy who tries to help the girl:

> I rashly assumed, as you did, that, being a Baronet, he must be a bad one. Such a name, too – Sir Trevor Mauleverer! There's villainy in every letter of it! But (it's just like my luck) when I appeared to him and offered to help him to carry off Miss Collins, he indignantly rebuked me and gave me this tract! (producing a leaflet headed 'Where the Devil are you Going?') He turns out to be a Nonconformist Baronet of the very strictest principles.

58–103 *Sir Rupert Murgatroyd*
This song evidently caused Gilbert some difficulty. The pre-production libretto referred to above contains three crossings-out and substitutions in his hand, only one of which was incorporated into the final libretto. The word 'ruthlessly' in line 60 is

ZORAH. Hour by hour and day by day,
Months have passed away.　　　　　　　　　　　　　25

CHORUS. Fair is Rose as bright May-day, etc.

(DAME HANNAH *comes down.*)

HANNAH. Nay, gentle maidens, you sing well but vainly, for Rose is still heart-free, and looks but coldly upon her many suitors.

ZORAH. It's very disappointing. Every young man in the village is in　30 love with her, but they are appalled by her beauty and modesty, and won't declare themselves; so, until she makes her own choice, there's no chance for anybody else.

RUTH. This is, perhaps, the only village in the world that possesses an endowed corps of professional bridesmaids who are bound to be on duty　35 every day from ten to four – and it is at least six months since our services were required. The pious charity by which we exist is practically wasted!

ZOR. We shall be disendowed – that will be the end of it! Dame Hannah – you're a nice old person – *you* could marry if you liked. There's old Adam – Robin's faithful servant – he loves you with all the frenzy of a boy　40 of fourteen.

HAN. Nay – that may never be, for I am pledged!

ALL. To whom?

HAN. To an eternal maidenhood! Many years ago I was betrothed to a god-like youth who woo'd me under an assumed name. But on the very day　45 upon which our wedding was to have been celebrated, I discovered that he was no other than Sir Roderic Murgatroyd, one of the bad Baronets of Ruddigore, and the uncle of the man who now bears that title. As a son of that accursed race he was no husband for an honest girl, so, madly as I loved him, I left him then and there. He died but ten years since, but I never saw　50 him again.

ZOR. But why should you not marry a bad Baronet of Ruddigore?

RUTH. All baronets are bad; but was he worse than other baronets?

HAN. My child, he was accursed.

ZOR. But who cursed him? Not you, I trust!　　　　　　　　　　55

HAN. The curse is on all his line and has been, ever since the time of Sir Rupert, the first Baronet. Listen, and you shall hear the legend:

LEGEND – HANNAH.

Sir Rupert Murgatroyd
　　His leisure and his riches
He ruthlessly employed　　　　　　　　　　　　　60
　　In persecuting witches.

crossed out and 'cruelly' inserted instead, the original 'And broil them at the stake' (line 66) is scored out and replaced by the present version, and 'on each withered limb' (line 77) is replaced by 'on each palsied limb'.

The chorus 'This sport he much enjoyed' was dropped from the 1920 revival of *Ruddigore* but reinstated in the 1948 production. The pre-production libretto has the following additional chorus after the third verse (to be sung after line 89), which was, however, dropped before the first performance:

> This doom they can't avoid,
> These lords of Murgatroyd –
>   Both last and first,
>   You're all accurst
> Oh, House of Murgatroyd!

With fear he'd make them quake –
He'd duck them in his lake –
  He'd break their bones
    With sticks and stones,   65
And burn them at the stake!

CHORUS.
    This sport he much enjoyed,
    Did Rupert Murgatroyd –
      No sense of shame
      Or pity came   70
    To Rupert Murgatroyd!

Once, on the village green,
  A palsied hag he roasted,
And what took place, I ween,
  Shook his composure boasted;   75
For, as the torture grim
Seized on each withered limb,
    The writhing dame
    'Mid fire and flame
Yelled forth this curse on him: 80

'Each lord of Ruddigore,
  Despite his best endeavour,
Shall do one crime, or more,
  Once, every day, for ever!
This doom he can't defy,   85
However he may try,
    For should he stay
    His hand, that day
In torture he shall die!'

The prophecy came true: 90
  Each heir who held the title
Had, every day, to do
  Some crime of import vital;
Until, with guilt o'erplied,
'I'll sin no more!' he cried,   95
    And on the day
    He said that say,
In agony he died!

CHORUS.
And thus, with sinning cloyed,
Has died each Murgatroyd,   100

110 *Rowbottom*: The pre-production libretto includes a further item in Rose's list of gifts at this point: 'a pair of spectacles for blind Timothy'. This rather tasteless joke did not find its way into the licence copy or first edition of the libretto.

118–19 *a plated dish-cover*: A dome-shaped, silver plated cover for dishes of hot food.
119 *the workhouse door*: With this heart-tugging description of her origins Rose Maybud establishes herself as a tragic heroine in the best tradition of Victorian melodrama. Workhouses were, of course, institutions established for paupers and vagrants, and it was not uncommon for desperate mothers to dump their babies on the doorstep so that they could be looked after by the parish.
123 *the wife of a Lord Mayor*: This remark caused much amusement at the opening night of *Ruddigore*. In the absence of royalty, the royal box at the Savoy was occupied by the Lord Mayor of London, Sir Richard Hanson, and his wife, who must have been conscious of many heads turning in her direction at this point.

133 *the manners of a Marquis*: Marquis (also spelt 'Marquess') is the second highest title of nobility in Britain ranking immediately below that of duke and above that of earl. It was first conferred on Richard II's favourite, Robert de Vere, who was created Marquess of Dublin in 1385.
133–4 *the morals of a Methodist*: 'Methodist' was, of course, the term applied to John Wesley and his followers who forsook the Church of England in the 1730s and 1740s and formed what they regarded as a simpler and purer church. The Methodists have since been one of the largest Nonconformist denominations in Britain and also one of the biggest churches in the U.S.A. In *The Gondoliers* (Act I, lines 311–12) the Duke of Plaza-Toro relates how the King of Barataria became a Wesleyan Methodist 'of the most bigoted and persecuting type'.

And so shall fall,
Both one and all,
Each coming Murgatroyd!

(*Exeunt Chorus of Bridesmaids.*)

(*Enter* ROSE MAYBUD *from cottage, with small basket on her arm.*)   105

HAN. Whither away, dear Rose? On some errand of charity, as is thy wont?

ROSE. A few gifts, dear aunt, for deserving villagers. Lo, here is some peppermint rock for old gaffer Gadderby, a set of false teeth for pretty little Ruth Rowbottom, and a pound of snuff for the poor orphan girl on the hill.   110

HAN. Ah, Rose, pity that so much goodness should not help to make some gallant youth happy for life! Rose, why dost thou harden that little heart of thine? Is there none hereaway whom thou couldst love?

ROSE. And if there were such an one, verily it would ill become me to tell him so.   115

HAN. Nay, dear one, where true love is, there is little need of prim formality.

ROSE. Hush, dear aunt, for thy words pain me sorely. Hung in a plated dish-cover to the knocker of the workhouse door, with naught that I could call mine own, save a change of baby-linen and a book of etiquette, little   120 wonder if I have always regarded that work as a voice from a parent's tomb. This hallowed volume (*producing a book of etiquette*), composed, if I may believe the title-page, by no less an authority than the wife of a Lord Mayor, has been, through life, my guide and monitor. By its solemn precepts I have learnt to test the moral worth of all who approach me. The man who bites his   125 bread, or eats peas with a knife, I look upon as a lost creature, and he who has not acquired the proper way of entering and leaving a room is the object of my pitying horror. There are those in this village who bite their nails, dear aunt, and nearly all are wont to use their pocket combs in public places. In truth I could pursue this painful theme much further, but behold, I have said   130 enough.

HAN. But is there not one among them who is faultless, in thine eyes? For example – young Robin. He combines the manners of a Marquis with the morals of a Methodist. Couldst thou not love *him*?

ROSE. And even if I could, how should I confess it unto him? For lo, he   135 is shy, and sayeth naught!

BALLAD – ROSE.

If somebody there chanced to be
Who loved me in a manner true,

146, 166 *Ah*: These sustained notes are the cue for a change of key from A minor to A major, which greatly enhances the haunting effect of this waltz song.

My heart would point him out to me,
  And I would point him out to you. 140
(Referring But here it says of those who point,
to book.)   Their manners must be out of joint –
    You *may* not point –
    You *must* not point –
    It's manners out of joint, to point! 145
Ah! Had I the love of such as he,
  Some quiet spot he'd take me to,
Then he could whisper it to me,
  And I could whisper it to you.
(Referring But whispering, I've somewhere met, 150
to book.) Is contrary to etiquette:
    Where can it be? *(Searching book.)*
    Now let me see – *(Finding reference.)*
      Yes, yes!
It's contrary to etiquette! 155

            (Showing it to Dame Hannah.*)*

If any well-bred youth I knew,
  Polite and gentle, neat and trim,
Then I would hint as much to you,
  And you could hint as much to him. 160
(Referring But here it says, in plainest print,
to book.)   'It's most unladylike to hint' –
    You *may* not hint,
    You *must* not hint –
    It says you mustn't hint, in print! 165
Ah! And if I loved him through and through –
  (True love and not a passing whim),
Then I could speak of it to you,
  And you could speak of it to him.
(Referring But here I find it doesn't do 170
to book.) To speak until you're spoken to.
    Where can it be? *(Searching book.)*
    Now let me see – *(Finding reference.)*
      Yes, yes!
'Don't speak until you're spoken to!' 175

            (Exit Dame Hannah.*)*

Rose. Poor aunt! Little did the good soul think, when she breathed the
hallowed name of Robin, that he would do even as well as another. But he
resembleth all the youths in this village, in that he is unduly bashful in my
presence, and lo, it is hard to bring him to the point. But soft, he is here! 180

184 *I wished to say that*: In his biography of George Grossmith, privately published in 1982, Tony Joseph points to the similarity between this passage for Rose and Robin and the opening dialogue of Grossmith's comic piece *Cups and Saucers*, which had been written eleven years earlier than *Ruddigore*:

GENERAL.	How fine it was today.
MRS WORCESTER.	It was.
GENERAL.	It was.
MRS WORCESTER.	Yes, it was. (*Pause*).
GENERAL.	And yesterday was wet.
MRS WORCESTER.	It was.
GENERAL.	It was.
MRS WORCESTER.	Yes, it was.

After this hesitant and bashful start, the relationship between the general and Mrs Worcester blossoms, and in the end, like Robin and Rose Maybud, they marry and live happily ever after.

203-45 *I know a youth who loves a little maid*

This delightful little duet echoes the theme of one of Gilbert's *Bab Ballads*, 'The Modest Couple':

When man and maiden meet, I like to see a drooping eye,
I always droop my own – I am the shyest of the shy.
I'm also fond of bashfulness, and sitting down on thorns,
For modesty's a quality that womankind adorns.

Whenever I am introduced to any pretty maid,
My knees they knock together, just as if I were afraid;
I flutter, and I stammer, and I turn a pleasing red,
For to laugh, and flirt, and ogle I consider most ill-bred.

In his prompt copy, Gilbert wrote the following directions beside this song:

As each sings they regard the other and then look away sheepishly.
Between each verse both take *one* step towards each other.
For the last verse they are back to back.

(ROSE *is about to go when* ROBIN *enters and calls her.*)

ROBIN. Mistress Rose!
ROSE. (*Surprised.*) Master Robin!
ROB. I wished to say that – it is fine.
ROSE. It is passing fine. 185
ROB. But we do want rain.
ROSE. Aye, sorely! Is that all?
ROB. (*Sighing.*) That is all.
ROSE. Good day, Master Robin!
ROB. Good day, Mistress Rose! (*Both going – both stop.*) 190
ROSE. } I crave pardon, I —
ROB. { I beg pardon, I —
ROSE. You were about to say? —
ROB. I would fain consult you —
ROSE. Truly? 195
ROB. It is about a friend.
ROSE. In truth I have a friend myself.
ROB. Indeed? I mean, of course —
ROSE. And I would fain consult you —
ROB. (*Anxiously.*) About him? 200
ROSE. (*Prudishly.*) About her.
ROB. (*Relieved.*) Let us consult one another.

DUET – ROBIN *and* ROSE.

ROB.
I know a youth who loves a little maid –
  (Hey, but his face is a sight for to see!)
Silent is he, for he's modest and afraid – 205
  (Hey, but he's timid as a youth can be!)

ROSE.
I know a maid who loves a gallant youth,
  (Hey, but she sickens as the days go by!)
She cannot tell him all the sad, sad truth –
  (Hey, but I think that little maid will die!) 210

ROB.   Poor little man!

ROSE.   Poor little maid!

ROB.   Poor little man!

ROSE.   Poor little maid!

BOTH.   Now tell me pray, and tell me true, 215

What in the world should the $\begin{cases} \text{young man} \\ \text{maiden} \end{cases}$ do?

221 *She's very thin*: In the pre-production libretto, Gilbert crossed out 'thin' and substituted 'sad'.

233 *I should fan his honest flame*: In the pre-production version, licence copy and first published edition of the libretto this line appeared as 'I would feed his honest flame'.

248 *Enter Old Adam*: Old Adam Goodheart, while a caricature of all faithful retainers, is clearly specifically modelled on Adam, the elderly servant in Shakespeare's *As You Like It*, who is given to such utterances as: 'O my gentle master! O my sweet master!'

ROB.   He cannot eat and he cannot sleep –
    (Hey, but his face is a sight for to see!)
    Daily he goes for to wail – for to weep
    (Hey, but he's wretched as a youth can be!)   220

ROSE.   She's very thin and she's very pale —
    (Hey, but she sickens as the days go by!)
    Daily she goes for to weep – for to wail –
    (Hey, but I think that little maid will die!)

ROB.   Poor little maid!   225

ROSE.   Poor little man!

ROB.   Poor little maid!

ROSE.   Poor little man!

BOTH.   Now tell me pray, and tell me true,
    What in the world should the $\left\{ \begin{array}{c} \text{young man} \\ \text{maiden} \end{array} \right\}$ do?   230

ROSE.   If I were the youth I should offer her my name –
    (Hey, but her face is a sight for to see!)

ROB.   If I were the maid I should fan his honest flame –
    (Hey, but he's bashful as a youth can be!)

ROSE.   If I were the youth I should speak to her to-day –   235
    (Hey, but she sickens as the days go by!)

ROB.   If I were the maid I should meet the lad half way –
    (For I really do believe that timid youth will die!)

ROSE.   Poor little man!

ROB.   Poor little maid!   240

ROSE.   Poor little man!

ROB.   Poor little maid!

BOTH.   I thank you, $\left\{ \begin{array}{c} \text{miss,} \\ \text{sir,} \end{array} \right\}$ for your counsel true;

    I'll tell that $\left\{ \begin{array}{c} \text{youth} \\ \text{maid} \end{array} \right\}$ what $\left\{ \begin{array}{c} \text{he} \\ \text{she} \end{array} \right\}$ ought to do!

                         (*Exit* ROSE.)   245

    ROB. Poor child! I sometimes think that if she wasn't quite so particular I might venture – but no, no – even then I should be unworthy of her!

    (*He sits desponding. Enter* OLD ADAM.)

249 *Sir Ruthven Murgatroyd*: Ruthven (pronounced 'Rivven') is an old Scottish family name which was, indeed, hated. In 1600 the Earl of Gowrie, whose family name was Ruthven, kidnapped James VI of Scotland (later to be James I of England). In retribution, a law was passed banning the name Ruthven for all time. It was later relaxed for one branch of the family. Ruthven was also the name of the central character in Marschner's opera *Der Vampyr* (1828), a vampire held in thrall by an evil master and forced to commit murderous deeds.

254 *Oakapple*: The gall or swelling on oak leaves. Oakapple Day is celebrated in England on 29 May, the birthday of King Charles II, who, after his defeat in the battle of Worcester in the English Civil War, evaded capture by hiding in an oak tree at Boscobel in Shropshire. In the original list of *Dramatis personæ* Robin appears simply as Robin Oakapple, with no mention of being Sir Ruthven Murgatroyd. In most editions of the libretto his name appears as Robin throughout, but in some it is changed in the Second Act to Sir Ruthven.

276 *welkin*: The sky, or firmament.

285 *a Revenue sloop*: A patrol boat engaged on coastal duties to deter smuggling.

286 *Cape Finistere*: The most westerly point in Spain, Cape Finisterre (properly spelt that way and not as in the libretto) juts into the Atlantic about thirty miles west of Santiago.

285–329 *I shipped, d'ye see, in a Revenue sloop*:
This rollicking sea shanty caused considerable offence to the French, who were

ADAM. My kind master is sad! Dear Sir Ruthven Murgatroyd —

ROB. Hush! As you love me, breathe not that hated name. Twenty   250
years ago, in horror at the prospect of inheriting that hideous title, and with
it the ban that compels all who succeed to the baronetcy to commit at least
one deadly crime per day, for life, I fled my home, and concealed myself in
this innocent village under the name of Robin Oakapple. My younger
brother, Despard, believing me to be dead, succeeded to the title and its   255
attendant curse. For twenty years I have been dead and buried. Don't dig me
up now.

ADAM. Dear master, it shall be as you wish, for have I not sworn to obey
you for ever in all things? Yet, as we are here alone, and as I belong to that
particular description of good old man to whom the truth is a refreshing   260
novelty, let me call you by your own right title once more! (ROBIN *assents*.)
Sir Ruthven Murgatroyd! Baronet! Of Ruddigore! Whew! It's like eight hours
at the seaside!

ROB. My poor old friend! Would there were more like you!

ADAM. Would there were indeed! But I bring you good tidings. Your   265
foster-brother, Richard, has returned from sea – his ship the *Tom-Tit* rides
yonder at anchor, and he himself is even now in this very village!

ROB. My beloved foster-brother? No, no – it cannot be!

ADAM. It is even so – and see, he comes this way!

          (*Exeunt together.*)   270

(*Enter Chorus of Bridesmaids.*)

CHORUS.

From the briny sea
    Comes young Richard, all victorious!
Valorous is he –
    His achievements all are glorious!   275
Let the welkin ring
With the news we bring
    Sing it – shout it –
    Tell about it –
    Shout it!   280
Safe and sound returneth he,
All victorious from the sea!

(*Enter* RICHARD. *The girls welcome him as he greets
old acquaintances.*)

BALLAD – RICHARD.

I shipped, d'ye see, in a Revenue sloop,   285
    And, off Cape Finistere,

persuaded by the London correspondent of *Le Figaro* that it mocked them and depicted them as criminal and cowardly. *Figaro* published this translation of the second verse:

> *Notre capitaine est debout et il dit,*
> * Nous n'avons pas à craindre ce navire,*
> * Nous le prendrons si nous voulons,*
> * Il ne saurait combattre,*
> *Ce n'est qu'un sale Monsieur.*
> *Mais attaquer un Français, c'est frapper une fille,*
> * Voilà une besogne honteuse.*
> *Avec tous nos défauts, nous sommes de fiers Bretons;*
> *Eux ne sont que des misérables 'Parlez-vous'.*

The Paris correspondent of the *Daily Telegraph* reported:

> Quite a storm of indignation has been raised here owing to the fact that Mr Gilbert's funny stanzas in *Ruddygore* about the British revenue cutter steering away from the French frigate have been deplorably misunderstood. The two Savoyards, Messrs Gilbert & Sullivan, are calmly invited by one critic to come across the Channel and find out for themselves the difference between a Frenchman and a 'gal'.

The Era commented:

> We can only hope that, in the present electric state of the European atmosphere, a declaration of war between the two countries may not be the ultimate result of the misunderstanding. This would certainly be an excellent advertisement for the latest Savoy opera; but the contrast between means and end, in such a case, would be a little too much like the primitive method of obtaining roast pork in Charles Lamb's Chinamen, who burnt down their huts to cook their dinners.

In the event, war was avoided. Gallic tempers cooled, and perhaps some Frenchman studied the whole song and came to realize that far from being an attack on them it was, in fact, just as much, if not more, a send-up of the British and a satire on their patriotic fervour.

292 *up with her ports*: Open the hinged covers over the gun-ports so that the cannon could be fired.

303 *strike*: Strike her colours and pull down her flag, i.e. surrender.

315 *up with our helm*: Move the tiller so that the bow of the ship is turned away from the wind.
scuds before the breeze: Sail down wind.

A merchantman we see,
A Frenchman, going free,
So we made for the bold Mounseer,
D'ye see?   290
We made for the bold Mounseer.
But she proved to be a Frigate – and she up with her ports,
And fires with a thirty-two!
It come uncommon near,
But we answered with a cheer,   295
Which paralysed the Parley-voo,
D'ye see?
Which paralysed the Parley-voo!

CHORUS. Which paralysed the Parley-voo, etc.

Then our Captain he up and he says, says he,   300
'That chap we need not fear, –
We can take her, if we like,
She is sartin for to strike,
For she's only a darned Mounseer,
D'ye see?   305
She's only a darned Mounseer!
But to fight a French fal-lal – it's like hittin' of a gal –
It's a lubberly thing for to do;
For we, with all our faults,
Why, we're sturdy British salts,   310
While she's only a Parley-voo,
D'ye see?
While she's only a poor Parley-voo!'

CHORUS. While she's only a Parley-voo, etc.

So we up with our helm, and we scuds before the breeze   315
As we gives a compassionating cheer;
Froggee answers with a shout
As he sees us go about,
Which was grateful of the poor Mounseer,
D'ye see?   320
Which was grateful of the poor Mounseer!
And I'll wager in their joy they kissed each other's cheek
(Which is what them furriners do),
And they blessed their lucky stars
We were hardy British tars   325
Who had pity on a poor Parley-voo,

329 *Hornpipe*: The idea of a hornpipe to follow Richard Dauntless's opening song was suggested at an early rehearsal by Durward Lely, who created the role. Gilbert took up the suggestion and asked the tenor if he could dance a hornpipe. Lely replied that he didn't know, as he had never tried, but went off to learn the steps from the ballet master at the Drury Lane Theatre. He later recalled:

> Sullivan wrote a hornpipe – really the old stereotyped sailor's hornpipe musically inverted – and I set to work to learn the ten or twelve steps. It was the success of the opening night. The 'Parlez-voo' went well but the dance that followed brought down the house. I understand that the tenors touring in the provinces cursed me, as they all had to go through the hornpipe whether they could dance or not.

340 *stow my jawin' tackle*: Stop talking.

341 *belay*: Make fast or stop.

'vast heavin': Stop sighing.

341–2 *a-cockbill*: Out of sorts. In nautical terminology the phrase usually refers either to the condition of the anchor when it turns on its side and will not dig into the mud as it should, or to the yards when they are placed at an angle with the deck. Traditionally the foreyard arm was put a-cockbill, and moved from its usual horizontal position, as a sign of sorrow, and particularly when the ship was about to be scrapped.

345 *to'-gall'n'-m'st*: The topgallant-mast is the highest section of the mast above the topsail.

346 *fore-stay*: Rigging which holds the mast in position and prevents it from leaning backwards.

barrowknight: Slang for baronet.

360 *binnacle light*: Compass light.

on a bowline: Close-hauled, i.e. sailing close to the wind.

365 *under my lee*: Sheltered from the wind by me.

365–6 *fish you two together*: Splice or join you.

367–8 *feeling his pulse*: An early D'Oyly Carte prompt-book has the following direction at this point: 'Robin takes watch from his pocket, listens to see that it is going and then looks at watch, holding Richard's hand'.

D'ye see?
Who had pity on a poor Parley-voo!

CHORUS.   Who had pity on a poor Parley-voo, etc. (*Hornpipe.*)

(*Exeunt* CHORUS.)   330

(*Enter* ROBIN.)

ROB. Richard!

RICH. Robin!

ROB. My beloved foster-brother, and very dearest friend, welcome
home again after ten long years at sea! It is such deeds as yours that cause   335
our flag to be loved and dreaded throughout the civilized world!

RICH. Why, lord love ye, Rob, that's but a trifle to what we *have* done in
the way of sparing life! I believe I may say, without exaggeration, that the
marciful little *Tom-Tit* has spared more French frigates than any craft afloat!
But 'taint for a British seaman to brag, so I'll just stow my jawin' tackle and   340
belay. (ROBIN *sighs*.) But 'vast heavin', messmate, what's brought *you* all a-
cockbill?

ROB. Alas, Dick, I love Rose Maybud, and love in vain!

RICH. *You* love in vain? Come, that's too good! Why, you're a fine
strapping muscular young fellow – tall and strong as a to'-gall'n'-m'st – taut   345
as a fore-stay – aye, and a barrowknight to boot, if all had their rights!

ROB. Hush, Richard – not a word about my true rank, which none here
suspect. Yes, I know well enough that few men are better calculated to win
a woman's heart than I. I'm a fine fellow, Dick, and worthy any woman's
love – happy the girl who gets me, say I. But I'm timid, Dick; shy – nervous   350
– modest – retiring – diffident – and I cannot tell her, Dick, I cannot tell her!
Ah, you've no idea what a poor opinion I have of myself, and how little I
deserve it.

RICH. Robin, do you call to mind how, years ago, we swore that, come
what might, we would always act upon our hearts' dictates?   355

ROB. Aye, Dick, and I've always kept that oath. In doubt, difficulty, and
danger I've always asked my heart what I should do, and it has never failed
me.

RICH. Right! Let your heart be your compass, with a clear conscience for
your binnacle light, and you'll sail ten knots on a bowline, clear of shoals,   360
rocks, and quicksands! Well, now, what does my heart say in this here
difficult situation? Why, it says, 'Dick,' it says – (it calls me Dick acos it's
known me from a babby) – 'Dick,' it says, '*you* ain't shy – *you* ain't modest
– speak you up for him as is!' Robin, my lad, just you lay me alongside, and
when she's becalmed under my lee, I'll spin her a yarn that shall sarve to fish   365
you two together for life!

ROB. Will you do this thing for me? Can you, do you think? Yes (*feeling
his pulse*). There's no false modesty about *you*. Your – what I would call

370 *a bos'n's mate*: The assistant to the boatswain (pronounced 'bosun'), the warrant officer in charge of sails, rigging, anchors and cables and responsible for all work carried out on deck. *H.M.S. Pinafore* has a boatswain's mate, Bob Becket, among its crew members.

373–410 *My boy, you may take it from me*
A rather clever parody of this song appeared in the periodical *Jack and Jill* on 12 February 1887, shortly after *Ruddigore* had been altered to meet the complaints of critics and public about the Second Act:

> Dear Ed., – You may take it from me,
> That of all the big blunders accurst,
>   With which a play's saddled
>   And all its points addled,
> A weak second act is the worst.
> Though as brilliant as brilliant can be,
> Be the start of your early romance,
>   You must not be uncertain
>   About your last curtain,
> Or your piece will not have a fair chance.
>
>   If you wish with your play to advance
>   Beyond the so-called op'ras from France,
>   You must heed it and knead it,
>   And carefully 'weed' it,
>   Or really you'd have little chance.
>
> Alas! this, at first, was the case
>   With the startlingly named *Ruddygore*,
>   Tho' in all London City
>   No writer's so witty
>   As Gilbert – he's proved it before.
> The defects of his shady Act Two
>   His denouement so ghastly,
>   Have been raised vastly,
> And now you may reckon 'twill do.
>
>   So *Ruddygore* now will advance,
>   Yea, on to success will it prance,
>   Savoyards then stump it,
>   And blow praise's trumpet,
>   As soon as you all get a chance.

379 *A Crichton of early romance*: James Crichton was a sixteenth-century Scottish scholar and adventurer who earned the nickname 'the Admirable Crichton' for his accomplishments and adventures. In early performances of *Iolanthe* Lord Mountararat had a song, later cut out, which began 'De Belville was regarded as the Crichton of his age' (see the note to *Iolanthe*, Act II, line 216).

401 *Ovid and Horace*: The Latin amatory poet Ovidius Naso turns up also in the Fairy Queen's song 'Oh, foolish fay' in *Iolanthe* (Act II, line 185) and in the Lady Psyche's list of classical authors to be read by young ladies in *Princess Ida* (Act II, line 16). This is the only mention in the Savoy Operas, however, of Horace, the Roman lyric poet who lived from 65 B.C. to A.D. 8 and is remembered chiefly for his odes.

402 *Swinburne and Morris*: A decidedly anachronistic reference if *Ruddigore* is set, as early libretti suggest, in the reign of George III. Neither of these gentlemen was around at that time. Algernon Charles Swinburne, who was born in 1837 and died in 1909, was the languid Pre-Raphaelite poet who probably provided at least one of the models for the character of Bunthorne in *Patience*. William Morris (1834–96) was the shaggy,

bumptious self-assertiveness (I mean the expression in its complimentary
sense) has already made you a bos'n's mate, and it will make an admiral of   370
you in time, if you work it properly, you dear, incompetent old impostor! My
dear fellow, I'd give my right arm for one tenth of your modest assurance!

SONG – Robin.

My boy, you may take it from me,
  That of all the afflictions accurst
    With which a man's saddled   375
    And hampered and addled,
  A diffident nature's the worst.
Though clever as clever can be –
  A Crichton of early romance –
    You must stir it and stump it,   380
    And blow your own trumpet,
  Or, trust me, you haven't a chance!

    If you wish in the world to advance,
    Your merits you're bound to enhance,
      You must stir it and stump it,   385
      And blow your own trumpet,
    Or, trust me, you haven't a chance!

Now take, for example, *my* case:
  I've a bright intellectual brain –
    In all London city   390
    There's no one so witty –
  I've thought so again and again.
I've a highly intelligent face –
  My features cannot be denied –
    But, whatever I try, sir,   395
    I fail in – and why, sir?
  I'm modesty personified!

    If you wish in the world to advance, etc.

As a poet, I'm tender and quaint –
  I've passion and fervour and grace –   400
    From Ovid and Horace
    To Swinburne and Morris,
  They all of them take a back place.
Then I sing and I play and I paint:
  Though none are accomplished as I,   405

rumbustious designer, poet and revolutionary socialist who may conceivably have been in Gilbert's mind when he created the character of Bunthorne's great rival, Archibald Grosvenor. Morris gets another mention, this time for his famous wallpapers, in Rudolph's song 'When you find you're a broken-down critter' in Act I of *The Grand Duke*.

413 *Plead for him*: Gilbert originally intended Rose Maybud to enter at this point. A note in his prompt-book reads: 'Rose enters at "Plead for him". She affects to be interested with the shipping, and is at the top of the steps at "fit to marry Lord Nelson"'.

419–20 *took flat aback*: Stopped dead. The term is used of a square-rigged ship when a change in the direction of the wind causes it to stop moving forward.

426 *Parbuckle*: Raise or lower objects such as casks or guns by means of a sling slipped under them.

435 *never sail under false colours*: The expression 'to sail under false colours', which means to use deception to attain your object, derives from the practice of pirate ships approaching their unsuspecting victims with a false flag at the mast.

To say so were treason:
You ask me the reason?
I'm diffident, modest, and shy!

If you wish in the world to advance, etc.

BOTH. If you wish in the world to advance, etc.   (*Exit* ROBIN.)   410

RICH. (*looking after him*). Ah, it's a thousand pities he's such a poor opinion of himself, for a finer fellow don't walk! Well, I'll do my best for him. 'Plead for him as though it was for your own father' – that's what my heart's a-remarkin' to me just now. But here she comes! Steady! Steady it is! (*Enter* ROSE – *he is much struck by her.*) By the Port Admiral, but she's a tight little   415 craft! Come, come, she's not for you, Dick, and yet – she's fit to marry Lord Nelson! By the Flag of Old England, I can't look at her unmoved.

ROSE. Sir, you are agitated —

RICH. Aye, aye, my lass, well said! I am agitated, true enough! – took flat aback, my girl; but 'tis naught – 'twill pass. (*Aside.*) This here heart of   420 mine's a-dictatin' to me like anythink. Question is, Have I a right to disregard its promptings?

ROSE. Can I do aught to relieve thine anguish, for it seemeth to me that thou art in sore trouble? This apple – (*offering a damaged apple*).

RICH. (*looking at it and returning it*). No, my lass, 'tain't that: I'm – I'm   425 took flat aback – I never see anything like you in all my born days. Parbuckle me, if you ain't the loveliest gal I've ever set eyes on. There – I can't say fairer than that, can I?

ROSE. No. (*Aside.*) The question is, Is it meet that an utter stranger should thus express himself? (*Refers to book.*) Yes – 'Always speak the truth.'   430

RICH. I'd no thoughts of sayin' this here to you on my own account, for, truth to tell, I was chartered by another; but when I see you my heart it up and it says, says it, 'This is the very lass for *you*, Dick' – 'speak up to her, Dick,' it says – (it calls me Dick acos we was at school together) – 'tell her all, Dick,' it says, 'never sail under false colours – it's mean!' *That's* what my   435 heart tells me to say, and in my rough, common-sailor fashion, I've said it, and I'm a-waiting for your reply. I'm a-tremblin', miss. Lookye here – (*holding out his hand*). That's narvousness!

ROSE (*aside*). Now, how should a maiden deal with such an one? (*Consults book.*) 'Keep no one in unnecessary suspense.' (*Aloud.*) Behold, I   440 will not keep you in unnecessary suspense. (*Refers to book.*) 'In accepting an offer of marriage, do so with apparent hesitation.' (*Aloud.*) I take you, but with a certain show of reluctance. (*Refers to book.*) 'Avoid any appearance of eagerness.' (*Aloud.*) Though you will bear in mind that I am far from anxious to do so. (*Refers to book.*) 'A little show of emotion will not be misplaced!'   445 (*Aloud.*) Pardon this tear! (*Wipes her eye.*)

447 *blue-jacket*: Sailor. The name derives from the colour of their jackets.

454–77 *The battle's roar is over*
This duet was dropped in the 1920 revival and in the 1948 production, although it was sung in the 1922 and 1962 D'Oyly Carte recordings. It was reinstated in 1977.

458 *welter*: The rolling, tossing or tumbling of waves.
459 *From war's alarms*: In his pre-production copy, Gilbert crossed out 'war's' and substituted 'waves'', but this alteration was not incorporated in the final libretto.

RICH. Rose, you've made me the happiest blue-jacket in England! I wouldn't change places with the Admiral of the Fleet, no matter who he's a-huggin' of at this present moment! But, axin' your pardon, miss (*wiping his lips with his hand*), might I be permitted to salute the flag I'm a-goin' to sail under? 450

ROSE (*referring to book*). 'An engaged young lady should not permit too many familiarities.' (*Aloud.*) Once! (RICHARD *kisses her.*)

DUET – RICHARD *and* ROSE.

RICH.
The battle's roar is over,
        O my love! 455
Embrace thy tender lover,
        O my love!
    From tempests' welter,
    From war's alarms,
    O give me shelter 460
        Within those arms!
Thy smile alluring,
All heart-ache curing,
Gives peace enduring,
        O my love! 465

ROSE.
If heart both true and tender,
        O my love!
A life-love can engender,
        O my love!
    A truce to sighing 470
    And tears of brine,
    For joy undying
        Shall aye be mine,
BOTH.
And thou and I, love,
Shall live and die, love, 475
Without a sigh, love –
        My own, my love!

(*Enter* ROBIN, *with* CHORUS OF BRIDESMAIDS.)

CHORUS.

If well his suit has sped,
Oh, may they soon be wed! 480
Oh, tell us, tell us, pray,
What doth the maiden say?

485 *Let the nuptial knot*: This and the next three lines do not appear in the first edition of the libretto.

517–18 *for behold*: The Biblical language which Rose is given further confirms the impression of an innocent, virtuous, chaste young maiden, the archetypcal heroine of Victorian melodrama.

In singing are we justified,
　　Hail the Bridegroom – hail the Bride!
　　Let the nuptial knot be tied:　　　　　　　　　　　　485
　　　　In fair phrases
　　　　Hymn their praises,
　　Hail the Bridegroom – hail the Bride?

Rob. Well – what news? Have you spoken to her?
Rich. Aye, my lad, I have – so to speak – spoke her.　　490
Rob. And she refuses?
Rich. Why, no, I can't truly say she do.
Rob. Then she accepts! My darling! (*Embraces her.*)

Bridesmaids.　　Hail the Bridegroom – hail the Bride! etc.

Rose (*aside, referring to her book*). Now, what should a maiden do when　495
she is embraced by the wrong gentleman?
Rich. Belay, my lad, belay. You don't understand.
Rose. Oh, sir, belay, I beseech you!
Rich. You see, it's like this: she accepts – but it's *me*!
Rob. You! (Richard *embraces* Rose.)　　　　　　　　　500

Bridesmaids.　　Hail the Bridegroom – hail the Bride!
　　　　　　　　When the nuptial knot is tied —

Rob. (*interrupting angrily*). Hold your tongues, will you! Now then, what
does this mean?
Rich. My poor lad, my heart grieves for thee, but it's like this: the　505
moment I see her, and just as I was a-goin' to mention your name, my heart
it up and it says, says it – 'Dick, you've fell in love with her yourself,' it says.
'Be honest and sailor-like – don't skulk under false colours – speak up,' it
says, 'take her, you dog, and with her my blessin'!'

Bridesmaids.　　Hail the Bridegroom – hail the Bride! —　　510

Rob. Will you be quiet! Go away! (Chorus *make faces at him and
exeunt.*) Vulgar girls!
Rich. What could I do? I'm bound to obey my heart's dictates.
Rob. Of course – no doubt. It's quite right – I don't mind – that is, not
particularly – only it's – it *is* disappointing, you know.　　　　515
Rose (*to* Robin). Oh, but, sir, I knew not that thou didst seek me in
wedlock, or in very truth I should not have hearkened unto this man, for
behold, he is but a lowly mariner, and very poor withal, whereas thou art a
tiller of the land, and thou hast fat oxen, and many sheep and swine, a
considerable dairy farm and much corn and oil!　　　　　　520

536 *Thankye, Rob*: At this point Gilbert's pre-production prompt copy contains the direction 'Richard dances', followed by this additional line:

> ROB. (*as* RICH. *dances*) There! that's only a bit of it.

This line was used in all D'Oyly Carte productions.

546 *You are, you know you are, you dog*: Gilbert used this same form of words in one of his *Bab Ballads*, 'Babette's Love':

> He called his Bill, who pulled his curl,
>   He said, 'My Bill, I understand
> You've captivated some young gurl
>   On this here French and foreign land.
> Her tender heart your beauties jog –
> They do, you know they do, you dog.

547 *Lothario*: A seducer of women and debauchee. The name derives from a character in Nicholas Rowe's play *The Fair Penitent* (1703). Rowe probably based his Lothario on an earlier character with the same name in Sir William Davenant's play *Cruel Brother* (1630).

548 *turning-in a dead-eye*: A dead-eye is a round block of wood with three holes drilled through it which is used as a block and tackle to apply tension to the sides of the mast. Gilbert used the expression for the surname of the villainous and misshapen sailor in *H.M.S. Pinafore*. To turn in a dead-eye is to wrap rope around it and bind it with lighter cord.

RICH. That's true, my lass, but it's done now, ain't it, Rob?

ROSE. Still it may be that I should not be happy in thy love. I am passing young and little able to judge. Moreover, as to thy character I know naught!

ROB. Nay, Rose, I'll answer for that. Dick has won thy love fairly. 525
Broken-hearted as I am, I'll stand up for Dick through thick and thin!

RICH. (*with emotion*). Thankye, messmate! that's well said. That's spoken honest. Thankye, Rob! (*Grasps his hand.*)

ROSE. Yet methinks I have heard that sailors are but worldly men, and little prone to lead serious and thoughtful lives! 530

ROB. And what then? Admit that Dick is *not* a steady character, and that when he's excited he uses language that would make your hair curl. Grant that – he does. It's the truth, and I'm not going to deny it. But look at his *good* qualities. He's as nimble as a pony, and his hornpipe is the talk of the Fleet! 535

RICH. Thankye, Rob! That's well spoken. Thankye, Rob!

ROSE. But it may be that he drinketh strong waters which do bemuse a man, and make him even as the wild beasts of the desert!

ROB. Well, suppose he does, and I don't say he don't, for rum's his bane, and ever has been. He *does* drink – I won't deny it. But what of that? 540
Look at his arms – tattooed to the shoulder! (RICH. *rolls up his sleeves.*) No, no – I won't hear a word against Dick!

ROSE. But they say that mariners are but rarely true to those whom they profess to love!

ROB. Granted – granted – and I don't say that Dick isn't as bad as any 545
of 'em. (RICH. *chuckles.*) You are, you know you are, you dog! a devil of a fellow – a regular out-and-out Lothario! But what then? You can't have everything, and a better hand at turning-in a dead-eye don't walk a deck! And what an accomplishment *that* is in a family man! No, no – not a word against Dick. I'll stick up for him through thick and thin! 550

RICH. Thankye, Rob, thankye. You're a true friend. I've acted accordin' to my heart's dictates, and such orders as them no man should disobey.

ENSEMBLE – RICHARD, ROBIN, *and* ROSE.

> In sailing o'er life's ocean wide
> Your heart should be your only guide;
> With summer sea and favouring wind, 555
> Yourself in port you'll surely find.

SOLO – RICHARD.

> *My* heart says, 'To this maiden strike –
> She's captured you.

561 *If other man*: This appears erroneously in some editions as 'If other men'.

565 *My heart says, 'You've a prosperous lot'*: The original version of Robin's verse, altered by Gilbert to the present version in his pre-production prompt copy, was:

> My heart says, 'You're a prosperous man,
>   With acres wide;
> You mean to settle all you can
>   Upon your bride.'

589–619 *Cheerily carols the lark*
Mad Margaret's opening recitative, quite unlike anything else in the Savoy Operas in its evocation of distraction and confusion, was parodied in the issue of *Jack and Jill* quoted from above (see the note to lines 373–410):

> Lo! We would make a remark
>   (Hinder us not)
> Re – the latest Gilbertian 'lark'
>   The Savoyards have got.
>   And that lark
>   We'd remark
>   (Keep it dark),
>   At first dragged somewhat.
>
> Humorous, mind, is each speech
> Penned by great G,
> And the songs are the same – all and each
>   Bubble with glee.
>   Yet each speech
>   Seemed to reach
>   To a 'preach'
>   Near the end – d'ye see?

She's just the sort of girl you like –
    You know you do.
If other man her heart should gain,
    I shall resign.'
That's what it says to me quite plain,
    This heart of mine.

560

SOLO – Robin.

My heart says, 'You've a prosperous lot,
    With acres wide;
You mean to settle all you've got
    Upon your bride.'
It don't pretend to shape my acts
    By word or sign;
It merely states these simple facts,
    This heart of mine!

565

570

SOLO – Rose.

Ten minutes since my heart said 'white' –
    It now says 'black'.
It then said 'left' – it now says 'right' –
    Hearts often tack.
I must obey its latest strain –
    You tell me so. (*To* Richard.)
But should it change its mind again,
    I'll let you know.
(*Turning from* Richard *to* Robin, *who embraces her.*)

575

580

ENSEMBLE.

In sailing o'er life's ocean wide
No doubt the heart should be your guide;
But it is awkward when you find
A heart that does not know its mind!

585

(*Exeunt* Robin *with* Rose L., *and* Richard, *weeping*, R.)

(*Enter* Mad Margaret. *She is wildly dressed in picturesque tatters, and is an obvious caricature of theatrical madness.*)

SCENA – Margaret.

Cheerily carols the lark
    Over the cot.

590

607 *Daft Madge*: Amateur and professional performers alike are often uncertain as to exactly how Mad Margaret should be played. Gilbert introduces her with the comment that she is 'an obvious caricature of stage madness', but does this mean she should be played in a wildly histrionic style, with exaggerated ravings and outbursts? Jessie Bond, the mezzo-soprano who created the role, which was her favourite part, emphatically rejected such an interpretation. She wrote in the December 1927 edition of the *Gilbert and Sullivan Journal*:

> Why, oh! why, must she be played like a raving lunatic whose only place should be the asylum? Margaret is not a mad girl really. She is a distraught girl – a genuine creature of pity, possibly – but a wild maniac she most certainly is not on any possible showing.
>
>
> 'Tis only
> That I'm
> Love – lonely!
> That's all.
>
>
> In these few, simple words, which are really the key to the reading of the part, she tells her own story. Love-loneliness – that is her trouble. She is just a sad, solitary figure whose head has been turned crazy, but not demented, by heart-hungry grief. Suggesting her as a wild-eyed, gabbling idiot is not only inartistic, but it shows a woeful mis-reading of the spirit of the part.

620–39 *To a garden full of posies*
This ballad was not originally written for *Ruddigore*. It first appeared in the Christmas 1881 edition of the *Illustrated Sporting and Dramatic News* and was reused by Gilbert six years later for this opera.

628 *Cytherean posies*: In Greek mythology the island of Cythera, off the Peloponnese, was the place where Aphrodite, the goddess of love and sensual beauty, and the equivalent of the Roman Venus, rose from the sea.

Merrily whistles the clerk
  Scratching a blot.
    But the lark
    And the clerk,
    I remark,   595
  Comfort me not!

Over the ripening peach
  Buzzes the bee.
Splash on the billowy beach
  Tumbles the sea.   600
    But the peach
    And the beach
    They are each
  Nothing to me!

    And why?   605
    Who am I?
Daft Madge! Crazy Meg!
Mad Margaret! Poor Peg!
    He! he! he! (*chuckling*).

    Mad, I?   610
      Yes, very!
    But why?
      Mystery!
        Don't call!

No crime –   615
  'Tis only
That I'm
    Love – lonely!
      That's all!

BALLAD.

To a garden full of posies   620
  Cometh one to gather flowers,
  And he wanders through its bowers
Toying with the wanton roses,
  Who, uprising from their beds,
  Hold on high their shameless heads   625
With their pretty lips a-pouting,
Never doubting – never doubting
  That for Cytherean posies
  He would gather aught but roses!

635 *Hope lay nestling*: The pre-production libretto has 'Love lay nestling' here.

666 *an Italian glance*: There is some doubt as to the origins and precise meaning of this phrase. In his *The Gilbert and Sullivan Operas – A Concordance* (New York, 1935) Frederick J. Halton suggested that the expression derived from Machiavelli and denoted cynicism and lack of feeling. The American scholar Jane Steadman gives a different interpretation, however, suggesting that Gilbert had in mind the Gothic villain in Ann Radcliffe's novel *The Italian* (1797).

Gilbert himself gave the following stage direction in his prompt-book for the 'business' of the glance: 'For the Italian glance Margaret folds arms and approaches Rose melodramatically – looks rudely into her face and steps back into attitude'.

In a nest of weeds and nettles 630
   Lay a violet, half-hidden,
   Hoping that his glance unbidden
Yet might fall upon her petals.
   Though she lived alone, apart,
   Hope lay nestling at her heart, 635
But, alas, the cruel awaking
Set her little heart a-breaking,
   For he gathered for his posies
   Only roses – only roses!

                                   (Bursts into tears.) 640

     (Enter ROSE.*)*

ROSE. A maiden, and in tears? Can I do aught to soften thy sorrow? This apple – *(offering apple)*.
MAR. *(Examines it and rejects it.)* No! *(Mysteriously.)* Tell me, are you mad? 645
ROSE. I? No! That is, I think not.
MAR. That's well! Then you don't love Sir Despard Murgatroyd? All mad girls love him. *I* love him. I'm poor Mad Margaret – Crazy Meg – Poor Peg! He! he! he! he! *(chuckling)*.
ROSE. Thou lovest the bad Baronet of Ruddigore? Oh, horrible – too 650 horrible!
MAR. You pity me? Then be my mother! The squirrel had a mother, but she drank and the squirrel fled! Hush! They sing a brave song in our parts – it runs somewhat thus: *(Sings.)*

       'The cat and the dog and the little puppee 655
       Sat down in a – down in a – in a —'

I forget what they sat down in, but so the song goes! Listen – I've come to pinch her!
ROSE. Mercy, whom?
MAR. You mean 'who'. 660
ROSE. Nay! it is the accusative after the verb.
MAR. True. *(Whispers melodramatically.)* I have come to pinch Rose Maybud!
ROSE. *(Aside, alarmed.)* Rose Maybud!
MAR. Aye! I love him – he loved me once. But that's all gone, Fisht! He 665 gave me an Italian glance – thus – *(business)* – and made me his. He will give *her* an Italian glance, and make *her* his. But it shall not be, for I'll stamp on her – stamp on her – stamp on her! Did you ever kill anybody? No? Why not? Listen – I killed a fly this morning! It buzzed, and I wouldn't have it. So it died – pop! So shall she! 670

680 *affidavit*: A statement made in writing, and confirmed on oath, which is intended to be used in court. An affidavit is normally sworn before a Commissioner for Oaths. In *Iolanthe* (Act I, line 458) the Lord Chancellor tells Strephon that 'an affidavit from a thunderstorm' would be acceptable as evidence in his defence that chorused Nature had bid him disobey an order of the Court of Chancery.

684 *They sing choruses in public*: This line never fails to raise an amused titter from audiences. The Savoy Operas are of course stuffed full of people singing choruses in public. They broke new ground in musical theatre in using the chorus to represent real people with a meaningful role in the action rather than just as a passive vehicle for setting the scene or telling a story. Mad they may occasionally feel, but countless members of choirs and amateur operatic societies have cause to thank Gilbert and Sullivan for giving them so many splendid choruses to sing.

688 *Enter Chorus of Bucks and Blades*: In the original production, and in the 1920 revival, the Bucks and Blades (i.e. dashing Regency dandies) made their entrance dressed in the uniforms worn by officers of the twenty cavalry and infantry regiments which made up the British Army in the period of the Napoleonic Wars. For the 1948 production the uniforms were dropped and the male chorus dressed instead in grey top hats and coloured frock coats.

696 *Hearty greeting offer we*: In the first-edition libretto, the bridesmaids had another seven lines, balancing the male chorus:

> Your exceeding
> Easy breeding
> Just the thing our hearts to pillage –
> Cheers us, charms us,
> Quite disarms us:
> Welcome, welcome to our village;
> To our village welcome be.

706 *Elysian*: In Greek mythology, the Elysian Fields were the abode of the blessed. They also crop up in *Patience* (Act I, line 444).

707 *Amaryllis*: A rustic sweetheart. The name occurs in the pastoral poetry of Virgil and Theocritus, and John Milton's poem *Lycidas* contains the famous line: 'To sport with Amaryllis in the shade'.

ROSE. But, behold, *I* am Rose Maybud, and I would fain not die 'pop'.

MAR. You are Rose Maybud?

ROSE. Yes, sweet Rose Maybud!

MAR. Strange! They told me she was beautiful! And *he* loves *you*! No, no! If I thought that, I would treat you as the auctioneer and land-agent treated the lady-bird – I would rend you asunder! 675

ROSE. Nay, be pacified, for behold I am pledged to another, and lo, we are to be wedded this very day!

MAR. Swear me that! Come to a Commissioner and let me have it on affidavit! *I* once made an affidavit – but it died – it died – it died! But see, they come – Sir Despard and his evil crew! Hide, hide – they are all mad – quite mad! 680

ROSE. What makes you think that?

MAR. Hush! They sing choruses in public. That's mad enough, I think! Go – hide away, or they will seize you! Hush! Quite softly – quite, quite softly! 685

(Exeunt together, on tiptoe.)

*(Enter Chorus of Bucks and Blades, heralded by
Chorus of Bridesmaids.)*

CHORUS OF BRIDESMAIDS.

> Welcome, gentry, 690
> For your entry
> Sets our tender hearts a-beating.
> Men of station,
> Admiration
> Prompts this unaffected greeting. 695
> Hearty greeting offer we!

CHORUS OF BUCKS AND BLADES.

> When thoroughly tired
> Of being admired
> By ladies of gentle degree – degree,
> With flattery sated, 700
> High-flown and inflated,
> Away from the city we flee – we flee!

> From charms intramural
> To prettiness rural
> The sudden transition 705
> Is simply Elysian,
> Come, Amaryllis,

708 *Chloe and Phyllis*: Both these names were used for shepherdesses in Greek pastoral poetry and so came to symbolize idyllic rustic maidenhood. Gilbert had used both names for heroines in earlier works: Chloe in *Happy Arcadia* (1872) and Phyllis in *Iolanthe* (1882).

724 *Enter Sir Despard Murgatroyd*: The supreme caricature of the stage villain in Victorian melodrama (the sort of character audiences were expected to hiss every time he came on to the stage), Sir Despard originally made his entrance dressed in the uniform of the Tenth Hussars. In the 1948 revival, however, he was given a suitably melodramatic costume of pillar-box red and billiard-table green, primary colours of a clashing intensity that would have filled Lady Jane with Pre-Raphaelite horror (see *Patience*, Act I, line 324).

732 *why am I husky and hoarse*: The first-night reviewer for *The Times* somewhat unkindly took this line to be an allusion to the vocal qualities of Rutland Barrington, who created the role of Sir Despard. Barrington, who was no opera singer, is said to have had a rather husky delivery, though he was in better voice for the opening of *Ruddigore* than for the first night of *Patience*, when he had had to struggle through the role of Grosvenor while nursing a severe sore throat.

Come, Chloe and Phyllis,
Your slaves, for the moment, are we!

CHORUS OF BRIDESMAIDS.

The sons of the tillage   710
Who dwell in this village
Are people of lowly degree – degree.
Though honest and active,
They're most unattractive,
And awkward as awkward can be – can be.   715
They're clumsy clodhoppers
With axes and choppers,
And shepherds and ploughmen
And drovers and cowmen,
Hedgers and reapers   720
And carters and keepers,
But never a lover for me!

ENSEMBLE.

BRIDESMAIDS.	BUCKS AND BLADES.
So, welcome, gentry, etc.	When thoroughly tired, etc.

(*Enter* SIR DESPARD MURGATROYD.)

SONG AND CHORUS – SIR DESPARD.

SIR D.	Oh, why am I moody and sad?	725
CH.	Can't guess!	
SIR D.	And why am I guiltily mad?	
CH.	Confess!	
SIR D.	Because I am thoroughly bad!	
CH.	Oh yes –	730
SIR D.	You'll see it at once in my face.	
	Oh, why am I husky and hoarse?	
CH.	Ah, why?	
SIR D.	It's the workings of conscience, of course.	
CH.	Fie, fie!	735
SIR D.	And huskiness stands for remorse,	
CH.	Oh my!	
SIR D.	At least it does so in my case!	
SIR D.	When in crime one is fully employed –	
CH.	Like you –	740

767 *All the Girls express their horror of Sir Despard*: Gilbert's own stage direction for the first production at this point reads: 'Sir Despard offers flower to ladies right. They shrink from him as he does so – he stamps – they scream and exit. He does the same business with ladies left and again to ladies up stage right centre. He then stamps upon the flower and strikes attitude of disgust'.

769 *Poor children*: Gilbert originally intended Mad Margaret to enter in the middle of this speech by Sir Despard, and he wrote a substantial passage of dialogue and a duet for them which was cut out before the first performance. It survives in the pre-production libretto, though not in the later licence copy. This is how the scene was originally conceived:

> SIR D. Poor children, how they loathe me – me whose hands are certainly steeped in infamy, but whose heart is as the heart of a little child! Oh Ruthven, my elder brother, if you had not died mysteriously in childhood, you would have been me, I should have been you, and all would have been well!
>
> (*Enter* MARGARET.)
>
> MAR. (*wildly*). Despard. How de do? How de do? How de do?
> SIR D. Margaret Mackintosh? Why do you follow me about everywhere?
> MAR. You are here to carry off Rose Maybud! But, don't do it – don't do it! Better not – better not – he! he! he! (*chuckling*).
> SIR D. My good girl, I don't want Rose Maybud. But what is a poor baronet to do . . .
> [as now].

776 *and built an orphan asylum*: At this point, the original dialogue continued:

> SIR D. Yesterday I fractured a skull and founded a hospital. This morning I robbed a bank and endowed a bishopric. Tomorrow I carry off Rose –
> MAR. (*significantly*). Tomorrow – you – carry off Rose?
> SIR D. Certainly – and build a cathedral.
> MAR. (*with intensity*). If you carry off Rose Maybud, I'll bite you!
> SIR D. Really, Margaret, if a man commit an error – and atone with a cathedral.
> MAR. Not a word. I am desperate.

> DUET – MARGARET, SIR DESPARD *and* CHORUS.
>
> MAR.　　If you attempt to take the girl and carry her off, away –
> SIR D.　　Sing hey, sing ho, and exactly so,
> 　　　　(*to audience*) And it's all for the love of a lad, poor thing.
> MAR.　　Your doom shall be a terrible one, and fill you with dismay.
> SIR D.　　Sing bless my soul, with a poison bowl!
> 　　　　(*to audience*) And it's all for the love of a lad, poor thing.
> MAR.　　A nightly course of apple-pie beds, tin-tacks upon your chair –
> 　　　　And prickly things, with terrible stings, shall tickle you everywhere –
> 　　　　I rather think you'll find your razors rasp you when you shave,
> 　　　　And I'll hurry you, worry you, flurry you, scurry you, into an early grave!
> CHORUS.　And the owl shall smile, and the snail shall sneeze,
> 　　　　And the tadpole kneel on his bended knees;
> 　　　　The slug shall shout, and the crow turn pale,
> 　　　　Before Mad Margaret's curse shall fail!
> SIR D.　　(*aside*) And it's all for the love of a lad, poor thing!
> MAR.　　Your breakfast bread I'll daily spread with mouldy mothery jam!
> SIR D.　　Sing hey the dart in her wounded heart,
> 　　　　(*aside*) And it's all for the love of a lad, poor thing!
> MAR.　　You shall eat French eggs, Australian beef, and American hardboiled ham!
> SIR D.　　Sing hey the lead in her poor thick head,
> 　　　　(*aside*) And it's all for the love of a lad, poor thing!
> MAR.　　If this you do, your sheets I'll strew with Abernethy crumbs,
> 　　　　I'll line your hat with cobbler's wax – your gloves shall split at the thumbs –

SIR D.	Your expression gets warped and destroyed:	
CH.	It do.	
SIR D.	It's a penalty none can avoid;	
CH.	How true!	
SIR D.	I once was a nice-looking youth;	745
	But like stone from a strong catapult –	
CH. (*explaining to each other*).	A trice –	
SIR D.	I rushed at my terrible cult –	
CH. (*explaining to each other*).	That's vice –	
SIR D.	Observe the unpleasant result!	750
CH.	Not nice.	
SIR D.	Indeed I am telling the truth!	

SIR D.	Oh, innocent, happy though poor!	
CH.	That's we –	
SIR D.	If I had been virtuous, I'm sure –	755
CH.	Like me –	
SIR D.	I should be as nice-looking as you're!	
CH.	May be.	
SIR D.	You are very nice-looking indeed!	
	Oh, innocents, listen in time –	760
CH.	We *doe*,	
SIR D.	Avoid an existence of crime –	
CH.	Just so –	
SIR D.	Or you'll be as ugly as I'm –	
CH. (*loudly*).	No! No!	765
SIR D.	And now, if you please, we'll proceed.	

(*All the Girls express their horror of* SIR DESPARD. *As he approaches them they fly from him, terror-stricken, leaving him alone on the stage.*)

SIR D. Poor children, how they loathe me – me whose hands are certainly steeped in infamy, but whose heart is as the heart of a little child! 770 But what *is* a poor baronet to do, when a whole picture gallery of ancestors step down from their frames and threaten him with an excruciating death if he hesitate to commit his daily crime? But ha! ha! I am even with them! (*Mysteriously.*) I get my crime over the first thing in the morning, and then, ha! ha! for the rest of the day I do good – I do good – I do good! (*Melo-* 775 *dramatically.*) Two days since, I stole a child and built an orphan asylum. Yesterday I robbed a bank and endowed a bishopric. To-day I carry off Rose Maybud and atone with a cathedral! This is what it is to be the sport and toy of a Picture Gallery! But I will be bitterly revenged upon them! I will give them all to the Nation, and nobody shall ever look upon their faces again! 780

(*Enter* RICHARD.)

> With damp cigars and flat champagne I'll blight you in your bloom,
> And I'll hurry you, worry you, flurry you, scurry you into an early tomb.

CHORUS. And the cat shall crow, and the gnat shall neigh,
And the toad shall trot, and the bat shall bray,
And the snake shall snore, and the worm shall wail,
Before Mad Margaret's curse shall fail!

SIR D. (*aside*) And it's all for the love of a lad, poor thing!

Sir Despard then continued with his speech 'This is what it is to be the sport and toy of a Picture Gallery' as now.

779–80 *I will give them all to the Nation*: Following the refusal of the Arts Council to give a grant to the D'Oyly Carte Opera Company in 1980, Kenneth Sandford changed this line to 'I will give them all to the Arts Council'. Audiences roared in approval of this sentiment and turned their boos and hisses from Sir Despard to the gentlemen responsible for dispensing public money to the arts, but to no avail. Despite petitions and many entreaties in the press, the Arts Council would not change its mind and, denied any support from public funds, the company which had faithfully performed the works of Gilbert and Sullivan for more than a century was forced to break up in March 1982.

815 *stand off and on*: Vacillate or dither. In nautical terminology, the expression means to tack in and out along the shore.

817 *bring her to*: Stop her advance.

RICH. Ax your honour's pardon, but —

SIR D. Ha! observed! And by a mariner! What would you with me, fellow?

RICH. Your honour, I'm a poor man-o'-war's man, becalmed in the   785
doldrums —

SIR D. I don't know them.

RICH. And I make bold to ax your honour's advice. Does your honour know what it is to have a heart?

SIR D. My honour knows what it is to have a complete apparatus for   790
conducting the circulation of the blood through the veins and arteries of the human body.

RICH. Aye, but has your honour a heart that ups and looks you in the face, and gives you quarter-deck orders that it's life and death to disobey?

SIR D. I have not a heart of that description, but I have a Picture   795
Gallery that presumes to take that liberty.

RICH. Well, your honour, it's like this – Your honour had an elder brother —

SIR D. It had.

RICH. Who should have inherited your title and, with it, its cuss.   800

SIR D. Aye, but he died. Oh, Ruthven! —

RICH. He didn't.

SIR D. He did *not*?

RICH. He didn't. On the contrary, he lives in this here very village, under the name of Robin Oakapple, and he's a-going to marry Rose Maybud   805
this very day.

SIR D. Ruthven alive, and going to marry Rose Maybud! Can this be possible?

RICH. Now the question I was going to ask your honour is – Ought I to tell your honour this?   810

SIR D. I don't know. It's a delicate point. I think you ought. Mind, I'm not sure, but I think so.

RICH. That's what my heart says. It says, 'Dick,' it says (it calls me Dick acos it's entitled to take that liberty), 'that there young gal would recoil from him if she knowed what he really were. Ought you to stand off and on,   815
and let this young gal take this false step and never fire a shot across her bows to bring her to? No,' it says, 'you did *not* ought.' And I won't ought, accordin'.

SIR D. Then you really feel yourself at liberty to tell me that my elder brother lives – that I may charge him with his cruel deceit, and transfer to his   820
shoulders the hideous thraldom under which I have laboured for so many years! Free – free at last! Free to live a blameless life, and to die beloved and regretted by all who knew me!

824–47 *You understand*

This duet must be one of the most tiring of all the Savoy numbers to perform. Richard and Sir Despard traditionally sing it while skipping from one foot to the other and dance round between each verse. At the end there is further 'business', dating back to the first production and recorded in Gilbert's prompt-book, when each waves the other to go off the stage first in an elaborate and seemingly never-ending show of politeness.

DUET – Sir Despard *and* Richard.

Rich.	You understand?	
Sir D.	I think I do;	825
	With vigour unshaken	
	This step shall be taken.	
	It's neatly planned.	
Rich.	I think so too;	
	I'll readily bet it	830
	You'll never regret it!	

Rich.   You understand?
Sir D.   I think I do;   825
          With vigour unshaken
          This step shall be taken.
     It's neatly planned.
Rich.   I think so too;
          I'll readily bet it   830
          You'll never regret it!

Both.   For duty, duty must be done;
     The rule applies to every one,
     And painful though that duty be,
     To shirk the task were fiddle-de-dee!   835

Sir D.   The bridegroom comes –
Rich.   Likewise the bride –
          The maidens are very
          Elated and merry;
     They are her chums.   840
Sir D.   To lash their pride
          Were almost a pity,
          The pretty committee!

Both.   But duty, duty must be done;
     The rule applies to every one,   845
     And painful though that duty be,
     To shirk the task were fiddle-de-dee!

(Exeunt Richard *and* Sir Despard.*)*

(Enter Chorus of Bridesmaids and Bucks.)

Chorus of Bridesmaids.

Hail the bride of seventeen summers: 850
     In fair phrases
     Hymn her praises;
Lift your song on high, all comers.
     She rejoices
     In your voices.   855
Smiling summer beams upon her,
Shedding every blessing on her:
     Maidens greet her –
     Kindly treat her –
You may all be brides some day!   860

866 *True and trusty*: In the first published libretto, the Bucks and Blades were given another five lines to sing so that their chorus was the same length as the girls':

> Happiness untold awaits them
> When the parson consecrates them;
> People near them,
> Loudly cheer them –
> You'll be bridegrooms some fine day.

870–903 *When the buds are blossoming*
This song, which appeared in early libretti as 'Where the buds are blossoming', is one of only two numbers which are described as madrigals in the Savoy Operas. The other is 'Brightly dawns our wedding day' in Act II of *The Mikado*. However, both 'Strange adventure' in Act II of *The Yeomen of the Guard*, which is described as a quartet, and 'I hear the soft note' in Act I of *Patience*, which is described as a sestet, broadly conform to the dictionary definition of a madrigal as a contrapuntal and generally unaccompanied part-song for several voices.

CHORUS OF BUCKS.

Hail the bridegroom who advances,
    Agitated,
    Yet elated.
He's in easy circumstances,
    Young and lusty,   865
    True and trusty.

ALL.   Smiling summer beams upon her, etc.

(*Enter* ROBIN, *attended by* RICHARD *and* OLD ADAM, *meeting* ROSE, *attended by* ZORAH *and* DAME HANNAH. ROSE *and* ROBIN *embrace*.)

MADRIGAL.

ROSE, DAME HANNAH, RICHARD, OLD ADAM *with* CHORUS.

ROSE.   When the buds are blossoming,   870
        Smiling welcome to the spring,
        Lovers choose a wedding day –
        Life is love in merry May!
GIRLS.   Spring is green –
        Summer's rose –   875
QUARTET.   It is sad when summer goes,
        Fa la, la, etc.
MEN.   Autumn's gold –
        Winter's grey –
QUARTET.   Winter still is far away –   880
        Fa la, la, etc.
CHORUS.   Leaves in autumn fade and fall,
        Winter is the end of all.
        Spring and summer teem with glee:
        Spring and summer, then, for me!   885
        Fa la, la, etc.

HANNAH.   In the spring-time seed is sown:
        In the summer grass is mown:
        In the autumn you may reap:
        Winter is the time for sleep.
            890
GIRLS.   Spring is hope –
        Summer's joy –
QUARTET.   Spring and summer never cloy,
        Fa la, la, etc.

906 *my elder brother*: At this point in the original production, Robin interjected 'Ah, lost one!'

909 *O wonder*: This line was not sung in the original production. The earliest pre-production libretto has four lines for the chorus at this point which were cut out before the first night:

> What means this interfering?
> At once be disappearing,
> Or cheer with welcome hearty
> Our Rose's wedding party.

MEN.	Autumn, toil –	895
	Winter, rest –	
QUARTET.	Winter, after all, is best –	
	Fa la, la, etc.	
CHORUS.	Spring and summer pleasure you,	
	Autumn, aye, and winter too –	900
	Every season has its cheer,	
	Life is lovely all the year!	
	Fa la, la, etc.	

GAVOTTE.

(*After Gavotte, enter* SIR DESPARD.)

SIR D.   Hold, bride and bridegroom, ere you wed each other,   905
I claim young Robin as my elder brother!
His rightful title I have long enjoyed:
I claim him as Sir Ruthven Murgatroyd!

CHORUS. O wonder!

ROSE (*wildly*).   Deny the falsehood, Robin, as you should,   910
It is a plot!

ROB.   I would, if conscientiously I could,
But I cannot!

CHORUS. Ah, base one! Ah, base one!

SOLO – ROBIN.

As pure and blameless peasant,   915
I cannot, I regret,
Deny a truth unpleasant,
I am that Baronet!

CHORUS.   He is that Baronet!

But when completely rated   920
Bad Baronet am I,
That I am what he's stated
I'll recklessly deny!

CHORUS.   He'll recklessly deny!

926 *taradiddles*: Lies or fibs. In the finale of Act I of *Iolanthe*, the peers and fairies have considerable fun singing 'Taradiddle, taradiddle, tol loy lay!' to show what they think of each others' stories.

ROB.	When I'm a bad Bart, I will tell taradiddles!	925
CHORUS.	He'll tell taradiddles when he's a bad Bart.	
ROB.	I'll play a bad part on the falsest of fiddles.	
CHORUS.	On very false fiddles he'll play a bad part!	
ROB.	But until that takes place I must be conscientious –	
CHORUS.	He'll be conscientious until that takes place.	930
ROB.	Then adieu with good grace to my morals sententious!	
CHORUS.	To morals sententious adieu with good grace!	

ROB. *and* CHORUS. When $\begin{Bmatrix} \text{I'm} \\ \text{he's} \end{Bmatrix}$ a bad Bart $\begin{Bmatrix} \text{I} \\ \text{he} \end{Bmatrix}$ will tell taradiddles, etc.

ZOR.	Who is the wretch who hath betrayed thee?	
	Let him stand forth!	935
RICH. (*coming forward*).	'Twas I!	
ALL.	Die, traitor!	
RICH.	Hold! my conscience made me!	
	Withhold your wrath!	

SOLO – RICHARD.

Within this breast there beats a heart 940
   Whose voice can't be gainsaid.
It bade me thy true rank impart,
   And I at once obeyed.
I knew 'twould blight thy budding fate –
I knew 'twould cause thee anguish great – 945
But did I therefore hesitate?
   No! I at once obeyed!

ALL.   Acclaim him who, when his true heart
Bade him young Robin's rank impart,
   Immediately obeyed! 950

SOLO – ROSE (*addressing* ROBIN).

Farewell!
Thou hadst my heart –
   'Twas quickly won!
But now we part –
   Thy face I shun! 955
Farewell!
Go bend the knee
   At Vice's shrine,

962 *I am thy bride*: In the first edition of the libretto, the chorus was given a shout of 'hurray' at the end of Rose's solo.

985 *Hail the Bridegroom – hail the Bride*: In the first edition of the libretto this line appeared as 'Let the nuptial knot be tied'.

Of life with me
All hope resign.   960
Farewell! Farewell! Farewell!

(*To* SIR DESPARD.)   Take me – I am thy bride!

BRIDESMAIDS.

Hail the Bridegroom – hail the Bride!
When the nuptial knot is tied;
Every day will bring some joy   965
That can never, never cloy!

(*Enter* MARGARET, *who listens.*)

SIR D.	Excuse me, I'm a virtuous person now –
ROSE.	That's why I wed you!
SIR D.	And I to Margaret must keep my vow! 970
MAR.	Have I misread you?
	Oh, joy! with newly kindled rapture warmed,
	I kneel before you! (*Kneels.*)
SIR D.	I once disliked you; now that I've reformed,
	How I adore you! (*They embrace.*) 975

BRIDESMAIDS.

Hail the Bridegroom – hail the Bride!
When the nuptial knot is tied;
Every day will bring some joy
That can never, never cloy!

ROSE.	Richard, of him I love bereft, 980
	Through thy design,
	Thou art the only one that's left,
	So I am thine! (*They embrace.*)

BRIDESMAIDS.

Hail the Bridegroom – hail the Bride!
Hail the Bridegroom – hail the Bride! 985

DUET – ROSE *and* RICHARD.

Oh, happy the lily
  When kissed by the bee;

1008 *opossum*: A small marsupial mammal of nocturnal habits found in America and Australia. Opossums are distinguished for their versatile big toes, which they use for grasping things. They do indeed live in trees but seem an unlikely species for early nineteenth-century Cornish folk to come across. However, if you try rhyming cats or squirrels with 'come across 'em', you'll see exactly why Gilbert had to go abroad on this particular occasion.

And, sipping tranquilly,
    Quite happy is he;
And happy the filly   990
    That neighs in her pride;
But happier than any,
A pound to a penny,
A lover is, when he
    Embraces his bride!   995

DUET – SIR DESPARD *and* MARGARET.

Oh, happy the flowers
    That blossom in June,
And happy the bowers
    That gain by the boon,
But happier by hours   1000
    The man of descent,
Who, folly regretting,
Is bent on forgetting
His bad baronetting,
    And means to repent!   1005

TRIO – HANNAH, ADAM, *and* ZORAH.

Oh, happy the blossom
    That blooms on the lea,
Likewise the opossum
    That sits on a tree,
But when you come across 'em,   1010
    They cannot compare
With those who are treading
The dance at a wedding,
While people are spreading
    The best of good fare!   1015

SOLO – ROBIN.

Oh, wretched the debtor
    Who's signing a deed!
And wretched the letter
    That no one can read!
But very much better   1020
    Their lot it must be

1027 *DANCE*

In his original prompt-book Gilbert directed 'Robin joins wildly in dance (with Zorah) falling senseless at end'. The first published libretto included the printed direction at the end of Act I '*At the end of the dance* ROBIN *falls senseless on the stage. Picture*'. Although this direction is retained in the current Macmillan edition, it does not appear in most modern versions of the libretto. For the 1920 revival a new direction was substituted: '*Dance is broken up as Robin comes down and all exit in confusion at nearest exits. Girls scream in terror as they rush off right and left*'. The 1948 production broadly followed this formula, with Robin appearing in the same brilliant red and green garb as Sir Despard and cracking his whip menacingly as the curtain fell.

Than that of the person
I'm making this verse on,
Whose head there's a curse on –
 Alluding to me!

1025

ENSEMBLE with CHORUS.

Oh, happy the lily, etc.

DANCE.

END OF ACT I

2 *from the time of James I*: The Murgatroyds must be representatives of one of the oldest baronetcies in England and they must also be among the shortest-lived. The order itself was instituted by James I, who reigned from 1603 to 1625. The action of *Ruddigore* is set early in the nineteenth century, and we are told in the list of *Dramatis personæ* that Sir Roderic was the twenty-first baronet. So the family has got through twenty-one senior members in about 200 years, with each Murgatroyd holding his title for an average of only 9½ years!

4 *Sir Roderic*: In the pre-production libretto Sir Roderic was described in the directions at the beginning of Act II as being 'attired as a Lord Mayor'. In D'Oyly Carte productions he was always portrayed wearing a cloak and tricorn hat.

10 *elision*: The action of dropping a letter or syllable in pronunciation. Its use here suggests that Robin should in the next line pronounce his real name as it is written rather than as 'Rivven'.

12 *valley-de-sham*: A corruption of the French *valet de chambre*, meaning personal manservant.

20 *valley-de-sham*: In the original libretto there were three additional verses to this song:

ROB. My face is the index to my mind,
All venom and spleen and gall – ha! ha!
   Or, properly speaking,
   It soon will be reeking
With venom and spleen and gall – ha! ha!

ADAM. My name from Adam Goodheart you'll find
I've changed to Gideon Crawle – ha! ha!
   For a bad Bart's steward
   Whose heart is much too hard,
Is always Gideon Crawle – ha! ha!

BOTH. How providential when you find
The face an index to the mind,
And evil men compelled to call
Themselves by names like Gideon Crawle!

21 *old Adam*: In keeping with the verses quoted above, throughout the first edition of the libretto Old Adam is always referred to as 'Gideon Crawle' in the Second Act. Gilbert later decided against this change of name and restored 'old Adam'. However, line 308 was overlooked and remained in successive editions of the libretto until 1959 as 'Gideon Crawle, it won't do'.

24–5 *greatest villain unhung*: Gilbert's original dialogue, as contained in the pre-production libretto, continued at this point:

ADAM. [continuing] . . . It's a dreadful position for a good old man.
ROB. Very likely, but don't be gratuitously offensive, Gideon Crawle.
ADAM. Sir, I am the ready instrument of your abominable misdeeds because I have sworn to obey you in all things, but I have *not* sworn to allow deliberate and systematic villainy to pass unreproved. If you insist upon it I will swear that, too, but I have not sworn it yet.
ROB. Come, Gideon, I haven't done anything very bad, so far.
ADAM. No. Owing to a series of evasions which, as a blameless character, I must denounce as contemptible, you have, so far, nothing serious on your conscience. But that can't last, and the sooner you yield to your destiny the better. Now, sir, to business . . . [as now].

ACT II

SCENE. – Picture Gallery in Ruddigore Castle. The walls are covered with full-length portraits of the Baronets of Ruddigore from the time of JAMES I *– the first being that of* SIR RUPERT, *alluded to in the legend; the last, that of the last deceased Baronet,* SIR RODERIC. *Enter* ROBIN *and* ADAM *melodramatically. They are greatly altered in appearance,* ROBIN *wearing the haggard aspect of a* 5
guilty roué; ADAM, *that of the wicked steward to such a man.*

DUET – ROBIN *and* ADAM.

ROB.
I once was as meek as a new-born lamb,
I'm now Sir Murgatroyd – ha! ha!
With greater precision
(Without the elision),
Sir Ruthven Murgatroyd – ha! ha! 10

ADAM.
And I, who was once his *valley-de-sham*,
As steward I'm now employed – ha! ha!
The dickens may take him –
I'll never forsake him!
As steward I'm now employed – ha! ha! 15

BOTH.
How dreadful when an innocent heart
Becomes, perforce, a bad young Bart.,
And still more hard on old Adam,
His former faithful *valley-de-sham*! 20

ROB. This is a painful state of things, old Adam!

ADAM. Painful, indeed! Ah, my poor master, when I swore that, come what would, I would serve you in all things for ever, I little thought to what a pass it would bring me! The confidential adviser to the greatest villain unhung! Now, sir, to business. What crime do you propose to commit to- 25
day?

ROB. How should I know? As my confidential adviser, it's your duty to suggest something.

41 *It would be simply rude*: In the pre-production libretto Adam had a longer speech at this point and the bridesmaids sang a chorus on their entrance as follows:

ADAM. It would be simply rude – nothing more. Now if you were to seize Rose Maybud and confine her in the lowest dungeon beneath the castle moat, that would be disgraceful indeed. But soft – they come!

(ADAM *and* ROBIN *retire up as* CHORUS OF BRIDESMAIDS *enters.*)

CHORUS OF BRIDESMAIDS.

Although in fashion regular
Both Rose and Richard plighted are –
　A picturesque event –
The wedding would be null and void
Unless Sir Ruthven Murgatroyd
　Accorded his consent.
　　Which to refuse
　　He will not choose –
　　Of that we're confident.

And so we come in duty bound,
His views upon the point to sound
　(The usual compliment).
Our landlord he – it would not do
Sir Ruthven's wishes to pooh-pooh;
　Or he might raise our rent –
　　And that would be
　　To you and me
　　Most inconvenient!

(*Enter* RICHARD *and* ROSE.)

CHORUS.　　　　　　Hail the bridegroom – hail the bride!
　　　　　　　　　When the nuptial knot is tied,
　　　　　　　　　Life will be one happy dream,
　　　　　　　　　Joyfulness reign all supreme.

The duet 'Happily coupled are we' followed on immediately after this chorus. In the pre-production copy, all the above is crossed out in Gilbert's hand.

ADAM. Sir, I loathe the life you are leading, but a good old man's oath is paramount, and I obey. Richard Dauntless is here with pretty Rose Maybud, to ask your consent to their marriage. Poison their beer. 30

ROB. No – not that – I know I'm a bad Bart., but I'm not as bad a Bart. as all that.

ADAM. Well, there you are, you see! It's no use my making suggestions if you don't adopt them. 35

ROB. (*melodramatically*). How would it be, do you think, were I to lure him here with cunning wile – bind him with good stout rope to yonder post – and then, by making hideous faces at him, curdle the heart-blood in his arteries, and freeze the very marrow in his bones? How say you, Adam, is not the scheme well planned? 40

ADAM. It would be simply rude – nothing more. But soft – they come!

(ADAM *and* ROBIN *exeunt as* RICHARD *and* ROSE *enter, preceded by Chorus of Bridesmaids.*)

DUET – RICHARD *and* ROSE.

RICH.

Happily coupled are we,
                You see – 45
I am a jolly Jack Tar,
                My star,
        And you are the fairest,
        The richest and rarest
Of innocent lasses you are, 50
                By far –
Of innocent lasses you are!
Fanned by a favouring gale,
                You'll sail
Over life's treacherous sea 55
                With me,
        And as for bad weather,
        We'll brave it together,
And you shall creep under my lee,
                My wee! 60
And you shall creep under my lee!

For you are such a smart little craft –
Such a neat little, sweet little craft,
        Such a bright little, tight little,
        Slight little, light little, 65
Trim little, prim little craft!

CHORUS.

For she is such, etc.

68 *My hopes will be blighted, I fear*: The whole of Rose's verse was cut in the 1920 revival and has only occasionally been heard since in D'Oyly Carte productions. It was not sung on the company's last recording of *Ruddigore* in 1962.

96 *producing a Union Jack*: This is one of two occasions in the Savoy Operas when the stage directions call for a display of the British flag, the other being at the end of Act I of *The Pirates of Penzance*, where Major-General Stanley defiantly waves a Union Jack at the skull and cross-bones of the Pirate King.

Several reviewers felt that the business with the Union Jack did not really come off very well. The *Sunday Express* critic, for example, pointed to the similarity with the scene in *The Pirates* and went on: 'In itself it is not funny, it is not particularly happy as a parody as ridiculing national sentiment'. There was some suggestion, in fact, that in this scene Gilbert was not just ridiculing patriotic sentiment but also making a jibe at the Unionists who opposed Home Rule for Ireland. He himself vehemently denied that any such political satire was intended.

Gilbert's original stage direction for the business with the Union Jack was: 'Richard takes flag from Zorah. Ladies kneel, Rose with arms crossed on breast and seraphic smile. Richard waves flag with left hand through his speech'.

ROSE.   My hopes will be blighted, I fear,
                    My dear;
               In a month you'll be going to sea,   70
                    Quite free,
               And all of my wishes
               You'll throw to the fishes
               As though they were never to be;
                    Poor me!   75
               As though they were never to be.
               And I shall be left all alone
                    To moan,
               And weep at your cruel deceit,
                    Complete;   80
               While you'll be asserting
               Your freedom by flirting
               With every woman you meet,
                    You cheat – Ah!
               With every woman you meet! Ah!   85

               Though I am such a smart little craft –
               Such a neat little, sweet little craft,
                    Such a bright little, tight little,
                    Slight little, light little,
               Trim little, prim little craft!   90

CHORUS.   Though she is such, etc.

(*Enter* ROBIN.)

ROB. Soho! pretty one – in my power at last, eh? Know ye not that I have
those within my call who, at my lightest bidding, would immure ye in an
uncomfortable dungeon? (*Calling.*) What ho! within there!   95

RICH. Hold – we are prepared for this (*producing a Union Jack*). Here is a
flag that none dare defy (*all kneel*), and while this glorious rag floats over
Rose Maybud's head, the man does not live who would dare to lay
unlicensed hand upon her!

ROB. Foiled – and by a Union Jack! But a time will come, and then —   100

ROSE. Nay, let me plead with him. (*To* ROBIN.) Sir Ruthven, have
pity. In my book of etiquette the case of a maiden about to be wedded to one
who unexpectedly turns out to be a baronet with a curse on him is not
considered. Time was when you loved me madly. Prove that this was no
selfish love by according your consent to my marriage with one who, if he   105
be not you yourself, is the next best thing – your dearest friend!

107–14 *In bygone days I had thy love*
Rose's ballad originally had a second verse which was cut after ten performances:

> My heart that once in truth was thine,
>> Another claims –
> Ah, who can laws to love assign,
>> Or rule its flames?
> Our plighted heart-bond gently bless,
> The seal of thy consent impress.
> Upon our promised happiness –
>> Grant thou our prayer!

135 *Oh, my forefathers*: When Henry Lytton was going through this speech after unexpectedly being called to fill in for the ill Grossmith (see the introduction), he was pulled up by Gilbert for hurrying it. In his memoirs Lytton recalls Gilbert as saying:

> That speech, 'Oh, my forefathers' is now a short speech, but originally it consisted of three pages of closely-written manuscript. I condensed and condensed. Every word I could I removed until it was of the length you find it today. Each word that is left serves some purpose – there is not one word too many. So when you know that it took me three months to perfect that one speech, I am sure you will not hurry it.

141 *The stage darkens for a moment*: Gilbert had first used the dramatic device of a picture gallery coming to life in his operetta *Ages Ago*, which had been put on at the Royal Gallery of Illustration in 1869. It was at a rehearsal of this work that Gilbert and Sullivan were introduced to each other by the composer Frederic Clay.

The scene in which the portraits become living people has always been difficult to stage effectively. It requires first of all a total blackout which can lead to difficulties for the orchestra as they try to follow an invisible conductor. In the original run this problem was overcome by giving the conductor an illuminated baton made out of a glass tube with fine platinum wires inside attached to batteries. I well remember the anguished cry of the pianist at one amateur performance of *Ruddigore* I attended when she found that her lamp was extinguished along with everything else.

The *Times* critic was singularly unimpressed by the way the scene was handled on the opening night:

> The ghost scene of the Second Act, representing the descent of the Murgatroyd ancestry from their picture frames, of which preliminary notices and the hints of the initiated had led one to expect much, was a very tame affair . . . A set of very ugly daubs, pulled up as you might a patent iron shutter to reveal a figure in the recess behind, can scarcely be called a good example of modern stage contrivance, especially when, as on Saturday night, one of these blinds or shutters comes down at an odd moment, while another refused to move.

BALLAD – ROSE.

In bygone days I had thy love –
Thou hadst my heart.
But Fate, all human vows above,
Our lives did part!　　　　　　　　110
By the old love thou hadst for me –
By the fond heart that beat for thee –
By joys that never now can be,
Grant thou my prayer!

ALL (*kneeling*).	Grant thou her prayer!　　　115
ROB. (*recitative*).	Take her – I yield!
ALL (*recitative*).	Oh, rapture!　　　(*All rising.*)

CHORUS.　　Away to the parson we go –
　　　　　　　Say we're solicitous very
　　　　　　That he will turn two into one –　　120
　　　　　　　Singing hey, derry down derry!
RICH.　　For she *is* such a smart little craft –
ROSE.　　Such a neat little, sweet little craft –
RICH.　　　Such a bright little –
ROSE.　　　　Tight little –　　　125
RICH.　　　　Slight little –
ROSE.　　　　Light little –
BOTH.　　Trim little, prim little craft!

CHORUS.　　For she *is* such a smart little craft, etc.

(*Exeunt all but* ROBIN.)　130

ROB. For a week I have fulfilled my accursed doom! I have duly committed a crime a day! Not a great crime, I trust, but still, in the eyes of one as strictly regulated as I used to be, a crime. But will my ghostly ancestors be satisfied with what I have done, or will they regard it as an unworthy subterfuge? (*Addressing Pictures.*) Oh, my forefathers, wallowers in 135 blood, there came at last a day when, sick of crime, you, each and every, vowed to sin no more, and so, in agony, called welcome Death to free you from your cloying guiltiness. Let the sweet psalm of that repentant hour soften your long-dead hearts, and tune your souls to mercy on your poor posterity! (*kneeling*).　　　　　　140

*(The stage darkens for a moment. It becomes light again, and the
Pictures are seen to have become animated.)*

143–6 *Painted emblems of a race*
The first seven notes of this chorus are the same as those of Sullivan's famous tune for the hymn 'Onward Christian Soldiers', the only difference being that 'Painted emblems' is in a minor key.

147–8 *march round the stage*: Sullivan originally wrote a thirty-two-bar march for the ghosts at this point, but it was cut during rehearsals after Gilbert complained that it was 'out of place in a comic opera. It is as though one inserted fifty lines of *Paradise Lost* into a farcical comedy'.

153 *poltroon*: A spiritless coward, a worthless wretch.

162 *Beware! beware! beware*: Sir Roderic's ghostly admonition was originally preceded by a passage for him and the chorus. It was sung on the first night but later cut. Here it is:

SIR ROD.	By the curse upon our race –
CHORUS.	Dead and hearsèd All accursèd!
SIR ROD.	Each inheriting their place –
CHORUS.	Sorrows shake it! Devil take it!
SIR ROD.	Must perforce, or yea or nay –
CHORUS.	Yea or naying Be obeying!
SIR ROD.	Do a deadly crime each day!
CHORUS.	Fire and thunder, We knocked under – Some atrocious crime committed Daily ere the world we quitted!

171 *Alas, poor ghost*: Compare *Hamlet*, Act I, Scene 5:

HAMLET.	Alas! poor ghost.
GHOST.	Pity me not.

Chorus of Family Portraits.

Painted emblems of a race,
    All accurst in days of yore,
Each from his accustomed place   145
    Steps into the world once more.

*(The Pictures step from their frames and march
round the stage.)*

Baronet of Ruddigore,
    Last of our accursèd line,   150
Down upon the oaken floor –
    Down upon those knees of thine.

    Coward, poltroon, shaker, squeamer,
    Blockhead, sluggard, dullard, dreamer,
    Shirker, shuffler, crawler, creeper,   155
    Sniffer, snuffler, wailer, weeper,
    Earthworm, maggot, tadpole, weevil!
    Set upon thy course of evil,
    Lest the King of Spectre-Land
    Set on thee his grisly hand!   160

(The Spectre of Sir Roderic *descends from his frame.)*

Sir Rod.   Beware! beware! beware!

Rob.   Gaunt vision, who art thou
    That thus, with icy glare
        And stern relentless brow,   165
        Appearest, who knows how?

Sir Rod.   I am the spectre of the late
        Sir Roderic Murgatroyd,
    Who comes to warn thee that thy fate
        Thou canst not now avoid.   170

Rob.   Alas, poor ghost!
Sir Rod.   The pity you
    Express for nothing goes:
    We spectres are a jollier crew
        Than you, perhaps, suppose!   175

Chorus.   We spectres are a jollier crew
        Than you, perhaps, suppose!

178–96 *When the night wind howls*
The words of this famous song, for which Sullivan provided one of his most effective and operatic settings, recall an early poem written by Gilbert for the magazine *Fun*:

> Fair phantom come!
> The moon's awake.
> The owl hoots gaily from its brake,
> The blithesome bat's a-wing.
> Come, soar to yonder silent clouds,
> The other teems with peopled shrouds:
> We'll fly the lightsome spectre crowds,
> Thou cloudly, clammy thing!

197 *you are the picture*: In keeping with his initial intention to make Sir Roderic a Lord Mayor (see the note to line 4), Gilbert originally wrote this line as 'You are the Lord Mayor that hangs etc.'. However, he changed it before the first night.

202 *as a work of art you are poor*: In the licence copy and the first edition the ghosts echo this remark as follows:

1ST GHOST. That's true.
2ND GHOST. No doubt.
3RD GHOST. Wants tone.
4TH GHOST. Not mellow enough.

205 *you spoke lightly of me*: In the pre-production libretto, the following exchange followed Sir Roderic's speech at this point:

ROB. How came you to be a Lord Mayor?
SIR ROD. I couldn't help it. It was part of my hideous doom.
ROB. Poor soul! And may I ask . . . [as now].

SONG – Sir Roderic.

When the night wind howls in the chimney cowls, and the bat in the
    moonlight flies,
And inky clouds, like funeral shrouds, sail over the midnight skies –
When the footpads quail at the night-bird's wail, and black dogs bay at the
    moon,   180
Then is the spectres' holiday – then is the ghosts' high-noon!
    CHORUS.   Ha! ha!
           Then is the ghosts' high-noon!

As the sob of the breeze sweeps over the trees, and the mists lie low on the
    fen,
From grey tomb-stones are gathered the bones that once were women and
    men,   185
And away they go, with a mop and a mow, to the revel that ends too soon,
For cockcrow limits our holiday – the dead of the night's high-noon!
    CHORUS.   Ha! ha!
          The dead of the night's high-noon!

And then each ghost with his ladye-toast to their churchyard beds takes
    flight,   190
With a kiss, perhaps, on her lantern chaps, and a grisly grim 'good-night';
Till the welcome knell of the midnight bell rings forth its jolliest tune,
And ushers in our next high holiday – the dead of the night's high-noon!
    CHORUS.   Ha! ha!
          The dead of the night's high-noon!   195
                  Ha! ha! ha! ha!

    ROB. I recognize you now – you are the picture that hangs at the end of
the gallery.
    SIR ROD. In a bad light. I am.
    ROB. Are you considered a good likeness?   200
    SIR ROD. Pretty well. Flattering.
    ROB. Because as a work of art you are poor.
    SIR ROD. I am crude in colour, but I have only been painted ten years.
In a couple of centuries I shall be an Old Master, and then you will be sorry
you spoke lightly of me.   205
    ROB. And may I ask why you have left your frames?
    SIR ROD. It is our duty to see that our successors commit their daily
crimes in a conscientious and workmanlike fashion. It is our duty to remind
you that you are evading the conditions under which you are permitted to
exist.   210

214 *Bank Holiday*: See the note to *Patience*, Act II, line 494.

230 *Yes, it seems reasonable*: This and the next line were dropped in recent D'Oyly Carte productions.

244 *I forged his cheque*: Originally this line was echoed by the ghosts as follows:

    1ST GHOST. That's true.
    2ND GHOST. Yes, it seems reasonable.
    3RD GHOST. At first glance it does.
    4TH GHOST. Fallacy somewhere!

251 *can I disinherit*: Another line originally taken up by the ghosts:

    1ST GHOST. That's right enough.
    2ND GHOST. Yes, it seems reasonable.
    3RD GHOST. At first sight it does.
    4TH GHOST. Fallacy somewhere!

ROB. Really, I don't know what you'd have. I've only been a bad baronet a week, and I've committed a crime punctually every day.

SIR ROD. Let us inquire into this. Monday?

ROB. Monday was a Bank Holiday.

SIR ROD. True. Tuesday?   215

ROB. On Tuesday I made a false income-tax return.

ALL. Ha! ha!

1ST GHOST. That's nothing.

2ND GHOST. Nothing at all.

3RD GHOST. Everybody does that.   220

4TH GHOST. It's expected of you.

SIR ROD. Wednesday?

ROB. (*melodramatically*). On Wednesday I forged a will.

SIR ROD. Whose will?

ROB. My own.   225

SIR ROD. My good sir, you can't forge your own will!

ROB. Can't I, though! I like that! I *did*! Besides, if a man can't forge his own will, whose will can he forge?

1ST GHOST. There's something in that.

2ND GHOST. Yes, it seems reasonable.   230

3RD GHOST. At first sight it does.

4TH GHOST. Fallacy somewhere, I fancy!

ROB. A man can do what he likes with his own!

SIR ROD. I suppose he can.

ROB. Well, then, he can forge his own will, stoopid! On Thursday I   235
shot a fox.

1ST GHOST. Hear, hear!

SIR ROD. That's better (*addressing Ghosts*). Pass the fox, I think? (*They assent.*) Yes, pass the fox. Friday?

ROB. On Friday I forged a cheque.   240

SIR ROD. Whose cheque?

ROB. Old Adam's.

SIR ROD. But Old Adam hasn't a banker.

ROB. I didn't say I forged his banker – I said I forged his cheque. On
Saturday I disinherited my only son.   245

SIR ROD. But you haven't got a son.

ROB. No – not yet. I disinherited him in advance, to save time. You see
– by this arrangement – he'll be born ready disinherited.

SIR ROD. I see. But I don't think you can do that.

ROB. My good sir, if I can't disinherit my own unborn son, whose   250
unborn son can I disinherit?

SIR ROD. Humph! These arguments sound very well, but I can't help
thinking that, if they were reduced to syllogistic form, they wouldn't hold
water. Now quite understand us. We are foggy, but we don't permit our

281–2 *anything like that*: Gilbert originally intended to make this the cue for a duet for Robin and Sir Roderic, to be followed by a chorus:

DUET AND CHORUS.

ROB.
Pray you, sir, excuse, in charity,
   Any act of impropriety
To my unfamiliarity
   With the rules of ghost society.
Pray withhold your animosity:
   Though it's awkward for a gentleman
To embark on wild ferocity
   Like a cut-throat Oriental man,
I'll forego my wild identity,
   So, without undue tautology,
Pray accept from this nonentity
   All appropriate apology!
Though the prospect does not fascinate,
   Like a baronet, bad but sensible,
I will murder – rob – assassinate –
   Everything that's reprehensible!

CHORUS.
Though the prospect, etc.

SIR ROD.
If you speak in all sincerity,
   And obey with due humility,
Pray forgive me my asperity
   Prompted by your imbecility.
Your obedience will gratify –
   We have gained a moral victory,
But before the terms I ratify,
   Hear my counsel valedictory.
Set to work with due rapidity,
   Make away with all impediment –
Naught will serve you, quip or quiddity,
   Pray believe that I said what I meant.
Poison, stab, defame and dissipate –
   Let your deeds be indefensible,
You'll commit, as I anticipate,
   Everything that's reprehensible!

CHORUS.
Poison, stab, defame, etc.

CHORUS.

Baronet of Ruddigore,
   Ere we seek our penal flames,
Your forgiveness we implore
   For miscalling you such names
As 'coward, poltroon, shaker, squeamer,
Blockhead, sluggard, dull-head, dreamer,
Shaker, shuffler, crawler, creeper,
Sniffler, snuffler, waiter, weeper,
Earthworm, maggot, tadpole, weevil',
All these names are most uncivil –
   This is our apology,
   Pardon – pardon us – or die!

ROB. (*in terror, on his knees*). I pardon you!
ALL.
He pardons us!
   Ha! Ha!

CHORUS.
Painted emblems, etc.

All the above is crossed out in Gilbert's hand in the pre-production libretto and the chorus 'He yields' substituted instead.

fogginess to be presumed upon. Unless you undertake to – well, suppose we 255
say, carry off a lady? (*Addressing Ghosts.*) Those who are in favour of his
carrying off a lady? (*All hold up their hands except a Bishop.*) Those of the
contrary opinion? (*Bishop holds up his hands.*) Oh, you're never satisfied! Yes,
unless you undertake to carry off a lady at once – I don't care what lady – any
lady – choose your lady – you perish in inconceivable agonies. 260

Rob. Carry off a lady? Certainly not, on any account. I've the greatest
respect for ladies, and I wouldn't do anything of the kind for worlds! No, no.
I'm not that kind of baronet, I assure you! If that's all you've got to say, you'd
better go back to your frames.

Sir Rod. Very good – then let the agonies commence. 265

(*Ghosts make passes.* Robin *begins to writhe in agony.*)

Rob. Oh! Oh! Don't do that! I can't stand it!
Sir Rod. Painful, isn't it? It gets worse by degrees.
Rob. Oh – Oh! Stop a bit! Stop it, will you? I want to speak.

(Sir Roderic *makes signs to Ghosts, who resume* 270
their attitudes.)

Sir Rod. Better?
Rob. Yes – better now! Whew!
Sir Rod. Well, do you consent?
Rob. But it's such an ungentlemanly thing to do! 275
Sir Rod. As you please. (*To Ghosts.*) Carry on!
Rob. Stop – I can't stand it! I agree! I promise! It shall be done!
Sir Rod. To-day?
Rob. To-day!
Sir Rod. At once? 280
Rob. At once! I retract! I apologize! I had no idea it was anything like
that!

CHORUS.

He yields! He answers to our call!
We do not ask for more.
A sturdy fellow, after all, 285
This latest Ruddigore!
All perish in unheard-of woe
Who dare our wills defy;
We want your pardon, ere we go,
For having agonized you so – 290

313 *Fly*: Observant readers of *Ruddigore* will have noticed that this opera lacks one of the essential ingredients of the Savoy repertoire, a patter song. In fact, there was originally a patter song for Robin at this point, preceded by a brief recitative. It went as follows:

RECITATIVE AND SONG – ROBIN.

Away Remorse!
   Compunction, hence!
Go, Moral Force!
   Go, Penitence!
To Virtue's plea
   A long farewell –
Propriety,
   I ring your knell!
Come guiltiness of deadliest hue,
Come desperate deeds of derring-do!

For thirty-five years I've been sober and wary –
My favourite tipple came straight from a dairy –
I kept guinea-pigs and a Belgian canary –
   A squirrel, white mice, and a small black-and-tan.
I played on the flute, and I drank lemon squashes –
I wore chamois leather, thick boots, and macintoshes,
And things that will some day be known as galoshes,
   The type of a highly respectable man!

For the rest of my life I abandon propriety –
Visit the haunts of Bohemian society,
Wax-works, and other resorts of impiety,
   Placed by the moralist under a ban.
My ways must be those of a regular satyr,
At carryings-on I must be a first-rater –
Go night after night to a wicked theayter –
   It's hard on a highly respectable man!

Well, the man who has spent the first half of his tether,
On all the bad deeds you can bracket together,
Then goes and repents – in his cap it's a feather –
   Society pets him as much as it can.
It's a comfort to think, if I now go a cropper,
I sha'n't, on the whole, have done more that's improper
Than he who was once an abandoned tip-topper,
   But now is a highly respectable man!

On the day after the opening performance, Gilbert wrote to Sullivan: 'I can't help thinking that the 2nd Act would be greatly improved if the recitation before Grossmith's song were omitted, and the song reset to an air that would admit of his singing it desperately – almost in a passion – the torrent of which would take him off the stage at the end.'

The recitative, in fact, remained, but a new patter song was written for the third edition of the libretto, published on 2 February, only eleven days after the opening night. It was dropped in the 1920 revival and has not been sung since professionally on stage, although it was included in two B.B.C. productions where it was sung by Peter Pratt and Derek Hammond-Stroud respectively. This second version went as follows:

Henceforth all the crimes that I find in the Times,
   I've promised to perpetrate daily;
To-morrow I start, with a petrified heart,
   On a regular course of Old Bailey.
There's confidence tricking, bad coin, pocket-picking,
   And several other disgraces –

So pardon us –
So pardon us –
So pardon us –
   Or die!

ROB.   I pardon you!   295
        I pardon you!

ALL.   He pardons us –
        Hurrah!

(*The Ghosts return to their frames.*)

CHORUS.   Painted emblems of a race,   300
      All accurst in days of yore,
     Each to his accustomed place
     Steps unwillingly once more!

(*By this time the Ghosts have changed to pictures again.*
    ROBIN *is overcome by emotion.*)   305

(*Enter* ADAM.)

ADAM. My poor master, you are not well —
ROB. Adam, it won't do – I've seen 'em – all my ancestors – they're just
gone. They say that I must do something desperate at once, or perish in
horrible agonies. Go – go to yonder village – carry off a maiden – bring her 310
here at once – any one – I don't care which —
ADAM. But —
ROB. Not a word, but obey! Fly!
        (*Exeunt* ADAM *and* ROBIN.)

(*Enter* DESPARD *and* MARGARET. *They are both dressed in sober black of* 315
 formal cut, and present a strong contrast to their appearance in Act I.)

DUET.

DES.   I once was a very abandoned person –
MAR.   Making the most of evil chances.
DES.   Nobody could conceive a worse 'un –
MAR.   Even in all the old romances.   320
DES.   I blush for my wild extravagances,
     But be so kind
     To bear in mind,

There's postage-stamp prigging, and then thimble-rigging
   The three-card delusion at races!
Oh! a baronet's rank is exceedingly nice,
But the title's uncommonly dear at the price!

Ye well-to-do squires, who live in the shires,
   Where petty distinctions are vital,
Who found Athenaeums and local museums,
   With views to a baronet's title –
Ye butchers and bakers and candlestick makers
   Who sneer at all things that are tradey –
Whose middle-class lives are embarrassed by wives
   Who long to parade as 'My Lady,'
Oh! allow me to offer a word of advice,
The title's uncommonly dear at the price!

Ye supple M.P.'s, who go down on your knees,
   Your precious identity sinking,
And vote black and white as your leaders indite
   (Which saves you the trouble of thinking),
For your country's good fame, her repute, or her shame,
   You don't care the snuff of a candle –
But you're paid for your game when you're told that your name
   Will be graced by a baronet's handle –
Oh! allow me to give you a word of advice –
The title's uncommonly dear at the price!

339 *penny readings*: Entertainments consisting of songs, dramatic recitations and readings held in church or village halls and for which the admission charge was a penny. George Grossmith was a dab at penny readings, particularly for the Young Men's Christian Association.

343 *A National School*: The name given in the nineteenth century to church schools, set up under the auspices of the National Society for the Education of the Poor in the Principles of the Established Church. In the first edition of the libretto this line appeared as 'A Sunday School' but it was never apparently sung as such, as the first-night review of the *Weekly Despatch* makes clear:

> Mr Gilbert is very respectful to the susceptibilities of the religious public. When Miss Jessie Bond, attired in Methodistical garments, dances her grotesque dance with Mr Barrington, she ought to sing, according to the book: 'And now we rule a Sunday School'. But she sings 'a National School' instead. No doubt the change was made at the last moment in deference to the feelings of Sunday-school teachers who are sure to be present in great numbers at the first morning performance of *Ruddygore*.

346 *This sort of thing takes a deal of training*: Indeed it does. Sir Despard and Margaret's dance is traditionally performed with the aid of a sharpened umbrella which is stuck into the stage. Peter Riley, for many years the D'Oyly Carte stage manager, recalls one terrible moment on tour when Kenneth Sandford realized that he was on a concrete stage, with no hope of performing the usual trick with the umbrella, and another when his umbrella disintegrated in mid-dance.

351 *So calm*: Various lines in this dialogue between Sir Despard and Margaret were cut when the Second Act was shortened early on in the initial run. After 'So calm!', for example, Margaret originally said 'So pure!' and Despard 'So peaceful!' before Margaret's 'So unimpassioned!'.

355 *Margaret, don't*: Another shortened passage. It originally went:

> DES. Margaret, don't. Pray restrain yourself. Be demure, I beg.
> MAR. Demure it is. (*Resumes her quiet manner.*)
> DES. Then make it so. Remember, you are now a district visitor.

MAR.   We were the victims of circumstances!

                                       (*Dance.*)   325

        That is one of our blameless dances.

MAR.   I was once an exceedingly odd young lady –
DES.   Suffering much from spleen and vapours.
MAR.   Clergymen thought my conduct shady –
DES.   She didn't spend much upon linen-drapers.   330
MAR.   It certainly entertained the gapers.
             My ways were strange
             Beyond all range –
DES.   Paragraphs got into all the papers.

                                       (*Dance.*)   335

DES.   We only cut respectable capers.

DES.   I've given up all my wild proceedings.
MAR.   My taste for a wandering life is waning.
DES.   Now I'm a dab at penny readings.
MAR.   They are not remarkably entertaining.   340
DES.   A moderate livelihood we're gaining.
MAR.   In fact we rule
             A National School.
DES.   The duties are dull, but I'm not complaining.

                                       (*Dance.*)   345

        This sort of thing takes a deal of training!

DES. We have been married a week.

MAR. One happy, happy week!

DES. Our new life –

MAR. Is delightful indeed!   350

DES. So calm!

MAR. So unimpassioned! (*wildly*). Master, all this I owe to you! See, I am no longer wild and untidy. My hair is combed. My face is washed. My boots fit!

DES. Margaret, don't. Pray restrain yourself. Remember, you are now a   355 district visitor.

MAR. A gentle district visitor!

DES. You are orderly, methodical, neat; you have your emotions well under control.

MAR. I have! (*wildly*). Master, when I think of all you have done for   360 me, I fall at your feet. I embrace your ankles. I hug your knees! (*Doing so.*)

DES. Hush. This is not well. This is calculated to provoke remark. Be composed, I beg!

MAR. Ah! you are angry with poor little Mad Margaret!

DES. No, not angry; but a district visitor should learn to eschew   365

371 *for a sick-room*: Despard originally continued at this point:

> Then again, as I've frequently told you, it is quite possible to take too much medicine.
> MAR. What, when you're ill?
> DES. Certainly. These are valuable remedies but they should be administered with discretion.
> MAR. How strange . . . [as now].

381 *Basingstoke*: Various explanations have been put forward as to why Gilbert chose the name of the rather undistinguished Hampshire town for the word which would bring Mad Margaret to her senses. Madge Terry in her book *An Operatic Glossary* suggests it was because there was a well-known mental hospital there but this was not, in fact, built at the time *Ruddigore* was written. A more convincing theory is perhaps that expounded by Geoffrey Wilson in the *Savoyard* for September 1978. He pointed out that the town had figured in a novel by Gilbert's father *The Doctor of Beauvoir*, and also that Gilbert's father and his sister lived at Salisbury, and so the dramatist must often have passed through Basingstoke on his way to visit them by train. It may be, in fact, that Basingstoke was not Gilbert's original choice for the 'word that teems with hidden meaning'. The magazine *Figaro* reported in December 1886 that reports from the rehearsals of the latest opera at the Savoy indicated there was a character called Mad Margaret 'with that blessed word Barnstaple'.

397 *a pure and blameless ratepayer*: The first-edition libretto continued at this point:

> ROB. That's all very well, but you seem to forget that on the day I reform I perish in excruciating torment.
> DES. Oh, better that than pursue a course of life-long villainy. Oh, seek refuge in death, I implore you!
> MAR. Why not die? Others have died and no one has cared. You will not be mourned.
> DES. True – you could die so well!
> ROB. You didn't seem to be of this opinion when *you* were a bad baronet.
> DES. No, because *I* had no good brother at my elbow to check *me* when about to go wrong.
> ROB. A home-thrust indeed! (*Aloud*) But I've done no wrong yet.

405 *your place*: The first edition continues here:

> ROB. Meaning you?
> DES. Meaning me.

407 *Wasn't he*: The cue for another line cut after the first edition:

> MAR. Desperate! Oh, you were a flirt!

melodrama. Visit the poor, by all means, and give them tea and barley-water, but don't do it as if you were administering a bowl of deadly nightshade. It upsets them. Then when you nurse sick people, and find them not as well as could be expected, why go into hysterics?

MAR. Why not? 370

DES. Because it's too jumpy for a sick-room.

MAR. How strange! Oh, Master! Master! – how shall I express the all-absorbing gratitude that – (*about to throw herself at his feet*).

DES. Now! (*warningly*).

MAR. Yes, I know, dear – it shan't occur again. (*He is seated – she sits on* 375
the ground by him.) Shall I tell you one of poor Mad Margaret's odd thoughts? Well, then, when I am lying awake at night, and the pale moonlight streams through the latticed casement, strange fancies crowd upon my poor mad brain, and I sometimes think that if we could hit upon some word for you to use whenever I am about to relapse – some word that teems with hidden 380
meaning – like 'Basingstoke' – it might recall me to my saner self. For, after all, I am only Mad Margaret! Daft Meg! Poor Meg! He! he! he!

DES. Poor child, she wanders! But soft – some one comes – Margaret – pray recollect yourself – Basingstoke, I beg! Margaret, if you don't Basingstoke at once, I shall be seriously angry. 385

MAR. (*recovering herself*). Basingstoke it is!

DES. Then make it so.

(*Enter* ROBIN. *He starts on seeing them.*)

ROB. Despard! And his young wife! This visit is unexpected.

MAR. Shall I fly at him? Shall I tear him limb from limb? Shall I rend 390
him asunder? Say but the word and —

DES. Basingstoke!

MAR. (*suddenly demure*). Basingstoke it is!

DES. (*aside*). Then make it so. (*Aloud.*) My brother – I call you brother still, despite your horrible profligacy – we have come to urge you to abandon 395
the evil courses to which you have committed yourself, and at any cost to become a pure and blameless ratepayer.

ROB. But I've done no wrong yet.

MAR. (*wildly*). No wrong! He has done no wrong! Did you hear that!

DES. Basingstoke! 400

MAR. (*recovering herself*). Basingstoke it is!

DES. My brother – I still call you brother, you observe – you forget that you have been, in the eye of the law, a Bad Baronet of Ruddigore for ten years – and you are therefore responsible – in the eye of the law – for all the misdeeds committed by the unhappy gentleman who occupied your place. 405

ROB. I see! Bless my heart, I never thought of that! Was I very bad?

DES. Awful. Wasn't he? (*to* MARGARET).

ROB. And I've been going on like this for how long?

413 *she trusted you*: At this point the original dialogue continued:

> ROB. Meaning *you*?
> DES. Nothing of the kind, sir. I was simply your representative.
> ROB. Well, meaning *us*, then. What a scoundrel we must have been! There, there . . . [as now].

431–63 *My eyes are fully open to my awful situation*
The 'matter trio' is one of the most difficult numbers to sing in the entire Gilbert and Sullivan repertoire. It should be taken at a breathtaking pace, and it is just as well that Gilbert made clear in the last lines that it doesn't really matter whether the words are heard or not.

The satirical magazine *Funny Folks* published a parody of the matter trio in its issue of 12 February 1887. It is entitled 'Randy in the South' and refers to the departure from English politics to the U.S.A. of Lord Randolph Churchill, father of Sir Winston:

> I am sitting 'neath a palm-tree, in an easy chair of wicker,
> In my mouth a prime Havanna, by my side a glass of 'licker',
> Something Yankeefied and coolish, in the which dissolving ice is,
> And the breeze is very balmy, and the sunshine very nice is.
> I can lounge and I can idle to day's end from its beginnin',
> In a helmet that is pithy, and a suit of snowy linen;
> Which is pleasanter than harking to the House's dreary chatter –
> To a load of doosid rubbish, which you know don't really matter.
> Which you know don't really matter, etc.

DES. Ten years! Think of all the atrocities you have committed – by attorney as it were – during that period. Remember how you trifled with this 410 poor child's affections – how you raised her hopes on high (don't cry, my love – Basingstoke, you know), only to trample them in the dust when they were at the very zenith of their fullness. Oh fie, sir, fie – she trusted you!

ROB. Did she? What a scoundrel I must have been! There, there – don't cry, my dear (*to* MARGARET, *who is sobbing on* ROBIN'S *breast*), it's all 415 right now. Birmingham, you know – Birmingham —

MAR. (*sobbing*). It's Ba – Ba – Basingstoke!

ROB. Basingstoke! of course it is – Basingstoke.

MAR. Then make it so!

ROB. There, there – it's all right – he's married you now – that is, *I've* 420 married you (*turning to* DESPARD) – I say, which of us has married her?

DES. Oh, *I've* married her.

ROB. (*aside*). Oh, I'm glad of that. (*To* MARGARET.) Yes, *he's* married you now (*passing her over to* DESPARD), and anything more disreputable than my conduct seems to have been I've never even heard of. But my mind 425 is made up – I *will* defy my ancestors. I *will* refuse to obey their behests, thus, by courting death, atone in some degree for the infamy of my career!

MAR. I knew it – I knew it – God bless you – (*hysterically*).

DES. Basingstoke!

MAR. Basingstoke it is! (*Recovers herself.*) 430

PATTER-TRIO.

ROBIN, DESPARD, *and* MARGARET.

ROB. My eyes are fully open to my awful situation –
    I shall go at once to Roderic and make him an oration.
    I shall tell him I've recovered my forgotten moral senses,
    And I don't care twopence-halfpenny for any consequences.
    Now I do not want to perish by the sword or by the dagger, 435
    But a martyr may indulge a little pardonable swagger,
    And a word or two of compliment my vanity would flatter,
    But I've got to die to-morrow, so it really doesn't matter!

DES.   So it really doesn't matter –

MAR.   So it really doesn't matter – 440

ALL. So it really doesn't matter, matter, matter, matter, matter!

MAR. If I were not a little mad and generally silly

457 *My existence*: In his pre-production copy, Gilbert crossed out 'existence' and substituted 'story'. The line appears in that form in the licence copy and the current
Macmillan edition, but 'existence' appears in the vocal score and is generally sung.

466 *Master – the deed is done*: In the pre-production libretto Robin had the following lines
before Adam's arrival:

> Yes, my mind is made up. I don't know what crimes I may not have committed by
> deputy, but since I've been the worst baronet that ever lived, my life has been practically
> blameless. Today I will commit no crime and consequently, tonight I perish!

473 *foiled again*: The pre-production libretto had the following exchange here:

> ROB. But I am foiled again – and by a stripling!
> ADAM. Nay, I am no stripling!
> ROB. Produce her – and leave us!

I should give you my advice upon the subject, willy-nilly;
I should show you in a moment how to grapple with the
    question,
And you'd really be astonished at the force of my suggestion.   445
On the subject I shall write you a most valuable letter,
Full of excellent suggestions, when I feel a little better,
But at present, I'm afraid I am as mad as any hatter,
So I'll keep 'em to myself, for my opinion doesn't matter!

DES.   Her opinion doesn't matter –   450

ROB.   Her opinion doesn't matter –

ALL.   Her opinion doesn't matter, matter, matter, matter, matter!

DES.   If I had been so lucky as to have a steady brother
Who could talk to me as we are talking now to one another –
Who could give me good advice when he discovered I was erring   455
(Which is just the very favour which on you I am conferring),
My existence would have made a rather interesting idyll,
And I might have lived and died a very decent indiwiddle.
This particularly rapid, unintelligible patter
Isn't generally heard, and if it is it doesn't matter!   460

ROB.   If it is it doesn't matter –

MAR.   If it is it doesn't matter –

ALL.   If it is it doesn't matter, matter, matter, matter, matter!

(*Exeunt* DESPARD *and* MARGARET.)

(*Enter* ADAM.)   465

ADAM (*guiltily*). Master – the deed is done!
ROB. What deed?
ADAM. She is here – alone, unprotected —
ROB. Who?
ADAM. The maiden. I've carried her off – I had a hard task, for she   470
fought like a tiger-cat!
ROB. Great heaven, I had forgotten her! I had hoped to have died
unspotted by crime, but I am foiled again – and by a tiger-cat! Produce her
– and leave us!

(ADAM *introduces* DAME HANNAH, *very much excited, and exits.*)   475

481 *difficult country*: In the pre-production libretto Hannah continued at this point:

> Prompted by I know not what infernal motive, he has carried me hither unprotected, save by the atmosphere of innocence that environs a pure and spotless woman, and left me helpless and trembling at your mercy.

485–6 *what I intended*: As originally performed, Robin and Hannah had a longer exchange at this point which went as follows:

> ROB. Circumstances of a delicate nature compelled me to request your presence in this confounded castle for a brief period – but anything more correct – more deeply respectful than my intentions towards you, it would be impossible for anyone – however particular – to desire.
> HAN. (*wildly*). Am I a toy – a bauble – a pretty plaything – to grace your roystering banquets and amuse your ribald friends? Am I a gew-gaw to while away an idle hour withal, and then be cast aside like some old glove, when the whim quits you? Harkye, sir, do you take me for a gaw of this description?
> ROB. (*appalled*). Certainly not – nothing of the kind – anything more profoundly respectable –
> HAN. Bah, I am not to be tricked . . . [as now].

The *Sunday Express* reviewer commented of this scene: 'Hannah's mock heroics and noisy defence of her virtue were not only ineffective – they were jarring. Whether they were too earnest, whether they were not sufficiently exaggerated, I cannot say: but they certainly missed the correct tone'. It was doubtless partly in response to such criticism, as well as in an effort to shorten Act II, that Gilbert cut down the dialogue.

495 *Dame Hannah*: Rosina Brandram, who created the role of Hannah, told the following story of an occasion when she could not find the dagger with which she had to make her Act II entrance:

> I absolutely refused to go on, as without it, it was quite impossible to play the scene. Everyone urged and implored me, and Mr Barrington, seeing the stage wait, went into the property-room and brought out something which he thrust into my hand, at the same time giving me a push which caused me to appear in sight of the audience; so, *nolens volens*, I had to proceed, knowing that in my hand I carried an insignificant gas key. I did the best I could to conceal this fact, and went on with the business. I had to rush and snatch a large dagger from a figure in armour and fling my supposed poignard to Mr Grossmith . . . Imagine my consternation when I saw by the expression on Mr Grossmith's face, as he stooped to pick up the key, that he meant mischief; my heart went right into my shoes, but I did not think he was going to give me away in the manner in which he did, for, holding up the gas key to the audience, he said: 'How can I defend myself with this?' Of course there was a laugh; my feelings may be better imagined than described. If ever I contemplated murder it was at that moment. I would willingly have slain both Mr Grossmith and Mr Barrington.

503 *Sir Roderic enters*: Originally Sir Roderic appeared through a trap-door in the stage with red flames rising around him. His method of entrance was changed to its present form in the first ten days of performance.

ROB. Dame Hannah! This is – this is not what I expected.

HAN. Well, sir, and what would you with me? Oh, you have begun bravely – bravely indeed! Unappalled by the calm dignity of blameless womanhood, your minion has torn me from my spotless home, and dragged me, blindfold and shrieking, through hedges, over stiles, and across a very difficult country, and left me, helpless and trembling, at your mercy! Yet not helpless, coward sir, for approach one step – nay, but the twentieth part of one poor inch – and this poniard (*produces a very small dagger*) shall teach ye what it is to lay unholy hands on old Stephen Trusty's daughter! 480

ROB. Madam, I am extremely sorry for this. It is not at all what I intended – anything more correct – more deeply respectful than my intentions towards you, it would be impossible for any one – however particular – to desire. 485

HAN. Bah, I am not to be tricked by smooth words, hypocrite! But be warned in time, for there are, without, a hundred gallant hearts whose trusty blades would hack him limb from limb who dared to lay unholy hands on old Stephen Trusty's daughter! 490

ROB. And this is what it is to embark upon a career of unlicensed pleasure!

(DAME HANNAH, *who has taken a formidable dagger from one of the armed figures, throws her small dagger to* ROBIN.) 495

HAN. Harkye, miscreant, you have secured me, and I am your poor prisoner; but if you think I cannot take care of myself you are very much mistaken. Now then, it's one to one, and let the best man win! (*Making for him.*) 500

ROB. (*in an agony of terror*). Don't! don't look at me like that! I can't bear it! Roderic! Uncle! Save me!

(SIR RODERIC *enters, from his picture. He comes down the stage.*)

ROD. What is the matter? Have you carried her off? 505

ROB. I have – she is there – look at her – she terrifies me!

ROD. (*looking at* HANNAH). Little Nannikin!

HAN. (*amazed*). Roddy-doddy!

ROD. My own old love! Why, how came *you* here?

HAN. This brute – he carried me off! Bodily! But I'll show him! (*about to rush at* ROBIN). 510

ROD. Stop! (*To* ROB.) What do you mean by carrying off this lady? Are you aware that once upon a time she was engaged to be married to me? I'm very angry – very angry indeed.

ROB. Now I hope this will be a lesson to you in future not to — 515

517 *Yes, uncle*: Originally Sir Roderic (who was still below the level of the stage on his trap-door), Hannah and Robin had the following exchange at this point:

> ROD. Has he treated you with proper respect since you've been here, Nannikin?
> HAN. Pretty well, Roddy. Come quite up, dear!
> ROD. No, I don't think I shall.
> ROB. No, I don't think you should.
> ROD. Hold your tongue.
> ROB. Yes, uncle.
> ROD. I'm very much annoyed. Have you given him any encouragement?

522 *to desire*: Again, there was originally a longer exchange between Hannah, Sir Roderic and Robin here, which – like the passage above – was cut early on in the first run:

> HAN. There now – come up, dear.
> ROD. (*reluctantly*). Very well, but you don't deserve it, you know (*comes up.*)
> ROB. Before we go any further, I am anxious to assure you on my honour as a gentleman, and with all the emphasis at my command, that anything more profoundly respectful –
> ROD. You go away.

530 *You don't deserve to be*: As originally performed, Hannah's speech began: 'You don't deserve to be, you bad, bad boy, for you behaved very shabbily to poor old Stephen Trusty's daughter. For I loved you all the while . . .'

551 *mickle*: This word properly means much, great or many, but Gilbert, following the usage of the Scottish proverb 'Many a mickle makes a muckle', gives it the opposite meaning. He uses it both here and in Phœbe's lines ''Tis but mickle/Sister reaps' in *The Yeomen of the Guard* (Act II, lines 567–8) to mean small or little.

ROD. Hold your tongue, sir.

ROB. Yes, uncle.

ROD. Have you given him any encouragement?

HAN. (*to* ROB.). Have I given you any encouragement? Frankly now, have I? 520

ROB. No. Frankly, you have not. Anything more scrupulously correct than your conduct, it would be impossible to desire.

ROD. You go away.

ROB. Yes, uncle. (*Exit* ROBIN.)

ROD. This is a strange meeting after so many years! 525

HAN. Very. I thought you were dead.

ROD. I am. I died ten years ago.

HAN. And are you pretty comfortable?

ROD. Pretty well – that is – yes, pretty well.

HAN. You don't deserve to be, for I loved you all the while, dear; and 530 it made me dreadfully unhappy to hear of all your goings-on, you bad, bad boy!

BALLAD – DAME HANNAH.

There grew a little flower
　　'Neath a great oak tree:
When the tempest 'gan to lower 535
　　Little heeded she:
No need had she to cower,
For she dreaded not its power –
She was happy in the bower
　　Of her great oak tree! 540
　　　　Sing hey,
　　　　Lackaday!
　　Let the tears fall free
For the pretty little flower and the great oak tree!

BOTH. 　　　　Sing hey, 545
　　　　Lackaday! etc.

When she found that he was fickle,
　　Was that great oak tree,
She was in a pretty pickle,
　　As she well might be – 550
But his gallantries were mickle,
For Death followed with his sickle,
And her tears began to trickle
　　For her great oak tree!

571 *Falls weeping*: In the first-night performance, 'There grew a little flower' was followed by this passage of dialogue between Sir Roderic and Hannah, which was later cut:

> ROD. Little Nannikin!
> HAN. Roddy-doddy!
> ROD. It's not too late, is it?
> HAN. Oh Roddy! (*Bashfully*).
> ROD. I'm quite respectable now, you know.
> HAN. But you're a ghost, ain't you?
> ROD. Well, yes – a kind of ghost.
> HAN. But what would be my legal *status* as a ghost's wife?
> ROD. It would be a very respectable position.
> HAN. But I should be the wife of a dead husband, Roddy!
> ROD. No doubt.
> HAN. But the wife of a dead husband is a widow, Roddy!
> ROD. I suppose she is.
> HAN. And a widow is at liberty to marry again, Roddy!
> ROD. Dear me, yes – that's awkward. I never thought of that.
> HAN. No, Roddy – I thought you hadn't.
> ROD. When you've been a ghost for a considerable time it's astonishing how foggy you become!

586 *Then I'm practically alive*: In the first-night performance Roderic said: 'We are all practically alive' and the dialogue and action thereafter continued:

> ROB. Every man jack of you!
> ROD. My brother ancestors! Down from your frames! (*The Ancestors descend*.) You believe yourselves to be dead – you may take it from me that you're not, and an application to the Supreme Court is all that is necessary to prove that you never ought to have died at all!
>
> (*The Ancestors embrace the Bridesmaids. Enter* RICHARD *and* ROSE, *also* SIR DESPARD *and* MARGARET.)
>
> ROB. Rose, when you believed . . . [as now].

The reappearance of the ancestral ghosts, which had not gone down well with the critics, was cut a few days after the opening performance and the present version, where the Bucks and Blades appear with the Bridesmaids, was substituted.

Sing hey,   555
Lackaday! etc.

BOTH.   Sing hey,
Lackaday! etc.

Said she, 'He loved me never,
                Did that great oak tree,   560
But I'm neither rich nor clever,
                And so why should he?
But though fate our fortunes sever,
To be constant I'll endeavour,
Aye, for ever and for ever,   565
                To my great oak tree!'
                Sing hey,
                Lackaday! etc.

BOTH.   Sing hey,
Lackaday! etc.   570

(*Falls weeping on* SIR RODERIC'S *bosom*.)

(*Enter* ROBIN, *excitedly, followed by all the characters
and Chorus of Bridesmaids*.)

ROB. Stop a bit – both of you.
ROD. This intrusion is unmannerly.   575
HAN. I'm surprised at you.
ROB. I can't stop to apologize – an idea has just occurred to me. A
Baronet of Ruddigore can only die through refusing to commit his daily
crime.
ROD. No doubt.   580
ROB. Therefore, to refuse to commit a daily crime is tantamount to
suicide!
ROD. It would seem so.
ROB. But suicide is, itself, a crime – and so, by your own showing, you
ought never to have died at all!   585
ROD. I see – I understand! Then I'm practically alive!
ROB. Undoubtedly! (SIR RODERIC *embraces* DAME HANNAH.) Rose,
when you believed that I was a simple farmer, I believe you loved me?
ROSE. Madly, passionately!

598 *My darling*: The first-night version continued at this point as follows:

CHORUS.

Hail the Bridegroom – hail the Bride!

RICH. (*Interrupting them*). Will you be quiet? (*To Robin.*) Belay, my lad, belay, you don't understand!

ROSE. Oh sir, belay, it's absolutely necessary.

ROB. Belay? Certainly not. (*To Rich.*) You see, it's like this – as all my ancestors are alive, it follows, as a matter of course, that the eldest of them is the family baronet, and I revert to my former condition.

RICH. (*Going to Zorah*). Well, I think it's exceedingly unfair!

ROB. (*To 1st Ghost*). Here, great uncle, allow me to present you. (*To the others.*) Baronet of Ruddygore!

ALL. Hurrah.

1ST GHOST. Fallacy somewhere!

FINALE.

602–31 *When a man has been a naughty baronet*

In the licence copy and the current Macmillan edition, the order of these verses is different, with Robin's coming first, then Rose's, then Richard's and finally Despard and Margaret's.

In the 1920 revival these verses were dropped and the finale was left consisting of the reprise of 'Oh, happy the lily'. It is printed in that version in the Oxford University Press edition of the operas and sung thus in the 1962 D'Oyly Carte recording. The original version was, however, reinstated by Royston Nash shortly after he joined the company as musical director in 1971, and was sung right up to the last performance in 1982.

ROB. But when I became a bad baronet, you very properly loved   590
Richard instead?

ROSE. Passionately, madly!

ROB. But if I should turn out *not* to be a bad baronet after all, how would
you love me then?

ROSE. Madly, passionately!   595

ROB. As before?

ROSE. Why, of course!

ROB. My darling! (*They embrace.*)

RICH. Here, I say, belay!

ROSE. Oh sir, belay, if it's absolutely necessary!   600

ROB. Belay? Certainly not!

FINALE.

ROSE.

When a man has been a naughty baronet,
And expresses deep repentance and regret,
   You should help him, if you're able,
   Like the mousie in the fable,   605
That's the teaching of my Book of Etiquette.

CHORUS.

That's the teaching in her Book of Etiquette.

RICH.

If you ask me why I do not pipe my eye,
Like an honest British sailor, I reply,
   That with Zorah for my missis,   610
   There'll be bread and cheese and kisses,
Which is just the sort of ration I enjye!

CHORUS.

Which is just the sort of ration you enjye!

ROB.

Having been a wicked baronet a week,
Once again a modest livelihood I seek.   615
   Agricultural employment
   Is to me a keen enjoyment,
For I'm naturally diffident and meek!

CHORUS.

For he's naturally diffident and meek!

DES. *and* MAR.

Prompted by a keen desire to evoke   620
All the blessed calm of matrimony's yoke,
   We shall toddle off to-morrow,
   From this scene of sin and sorrow,
For to settle in the town of Basingstoke!

ALL.

Prompted by a keen desire, etc.   625

For happy the lily, the lily
When kissed by the bee;
But happier than any,
But happier than any,
A lover is, when he
Embraces his bride.

630

CURTAIN

THE YEOMEN
OF
THE GUARD

OR

THE MERRYMAN AND HIS MAID

DRAMATIS PERSONÆ

SIR RICHARD CHOLMONDELEY (*Lieutenant of the Tower*)
COLONEL FAIRFAX (*under sentence of death*)
SERGEANT MERYLL (*of the Yeomen of the Guard*)
LEONARD MERYLL (*his Son*)
JACK POINT (*a Strolling Jester*)
WILFRED SHADBOLT (*Head Jailer and Assistant Tormentor*)
THE HEADSMAN
FIRST YEOMAN
SECOND YEOMAN
FIRST CITIZEN
SECOND CITIZEN
ELSIE MAYNARD (*a Strolling Singer*)
PHŒBE MERYLL (*Sergeant Meryll's Daughter*)
DAME CARRUTHERS (*Housekeeper to the Tower*)
KATE (*her Niece*)

Chorus of Yeomen of the Guard, Gentlemen, Citizens, etc.

ACT I. – Tower Green.
ACT II. – The same – Moonlight.
Time – Sixteenth century.

THE YEOMEN
OF
THE GUARD

The Yeomen of the Guard is the nearest that Gilbert and Sullivan got to a grand opera. Both librettist and composer had a high opinion of the work. Gilbert said that he regarded it as 'the best thing we have done', and Sullivan told the *Strand Musical Magazine* that it was his favourite opera.

After the relative failure of *Ruddigore*, which ended its run at the Savoy in November 1887, the morale of Gilbert, Sullivan and D'Oyly Carte was at a low ebb. There was no new opera to put on in its place, and *H.M.S. Pinafore* had to be revived as a stop-gap. Gilbert proposed yet another version of his beloved lozenge plot, and Sullivan once again rejected it.

The situation was saved by one of those chance incidents which inspired several of the best Savoy Operas. While waiting for a Metropolitan Line train one morning at Uxbridge Station Gilbert's eye was attracted by a poster advertising the Tower Furnishing Company, which showed a beefeater against a background of the Tower of London. 'I thought the beefeater would make a good picturesque central figure for another Savoy opera,' he later wrote, 'and my intention was to give it a modern setting, with the characteristics and development of burlesque – to make it another *Sorcerer*. But then I decided to make it a romantic and dramatic piece, and to put it back into Elizabethan times.'

Gilbert's decision to set his new opera in the great days of Tudor England was no doubt partly influenced by the wave of patriotism and nostalgia which swept Britain in the wake of Queen Victoria's golden jubilee. He seems to have taken as the basis for his plot a French play, *Don César de Bazan*, which told of a knight languishing in prison and condemned to die who married a gipsy dancer and, after escaping being shot, returned disguised as a monk. The story had already formed the basis of another opera, *Maritana* by Wallace.

Writing to Sullivan about the new work, Gilbert reassuringly pointed out: 'It is quite a consistent and effective story, without anachronisms or pathos of any kind, and I hope you will like it.' He was not to be disappointed. The composer's diary for Christmas Day 1887 reads: 'Gilbert read the plot of the new piece (The Tower of London): immensely pleased with it. Pretty story, no topsy-turvydom, very human and funny also.'

The new opera went through several changes of name. As Sullivan's diary indicates, it was originally called *The Tower of London*. This was later changed to *The Tower Warder* and then to *The Beefeaters*. However, Sullivan, perhaps with memories of *Ruddygore* in his mind, thought this a rather coarse and ugly name, and at his suggestion *The Yeomen of the Guard* was finally adopted.

The opera was composed and completed in a great rush. Sullivan wrote the overture in the auditorium during a final rehearsal and threw the parts to the players in the orchestra as he completed them, the ink on the paper scarcely dry. Tempers frequently flared between composer and librettist, and only an hour or so before the curtain went up on the first performance they had a somewhat stormy meeting to iron out some major production problems.

The first night, on 3 October 1888, was, however, an unqualified success. The *Daily Telegraph* spoke for critics and audience alike when it said of Sullivan's score: 'We place the songs and choruses in *The Yeoman of the Guard* before all his previous efforts of this particular kind. Thus the music follows the book to a higher plane, and we have a genuine English opera, forerunner of many others, let us hope, and possibly a sign of an advance towards a national lyric stage.'

The Yeomen of the Guard ran for 423 performances, ending its initial season on 30 November 1889. It was revived in 1897 and was subsequently seldom out of the D'Oyly Carte repertoire. In 1940 it became the first Savoy Opera to get a modern production and setting, and in 1962 and 1964 Anthony Besch staged a highly successful production at the Tower of London itself as part of the City of London Festival. This imaginative idea was repeated in July 1978 with Tommy Steele 'starring' as Jack Point. A videotape recording of this production has recently been issued, and another video of *The Yeomen* has been released with Joel Grey, the master of ceremonies in the film *Cabaret*, as the jester. There is every reason to suppose that the melodies of *The Yeomen of the Guard* will continue to delight audiences for as long as the Tower itself continues to keep its silent watch and ward over London town.

1 *Scene*: Until 1940 the D'Oyly Carte backcloth for *The Yeomen of the Guard* showed the White Tower in the middle background with the Cold Harbour (now the Guard House) and Lieutenant's house to the right of stage as seen by the audience. Peter Goffin's wartime production swept away this conventional representation in favour of a bare, angular set which showed none of the familiar features of one of London's best-known buildings. The critics were generally unhappy about this new look. The *Daily Mail* commented: 'Frankly the only adjective strong enough for this Tower of London is that which is traditionally associated with one of its towers'.

Another feature of the staging for the 1940 production which proved controversial was an interior set used to give the impression that Phœbe was sitting in a room. This set was 'flown' during the music preceding the entrance of the chorus (line 67) to reveal Tower Green. It was later abandoned.

This is not the only one of Gilbert's plays to open with a girl sitting spinning alone on the stage. His earlier work *Eyes and No Eyes*, an entertainment with music by Thomas German Reed, which was performed in 1875, began with a similar opening number in which the heroine, Clochette, sang 'As I at my wheel sit spinning'.

2–21 *When maiden loves*

The Yeomen of the Guard is the only Gilbert and Sullivan opera to begin with a solo rather than a chorus. This puts an added strain on the singer playing the role of Phœbe. Jessie Bond, who created the part, had to cope not only with her own first-night nerves but with Gilbert's anxieties as well, as she later recalled in her autobiography:

> I remember the first night of *The Yeomen* very well. Gilbert was always dreadfully overwrought on these occasions, but this time he was almost beside himself with nervousness and excitement . . . I am afraid he made himself a perfect nuisance behind the scenes, and did his best, poor fellow, to upset us all . . . It will be remembered that the curtain rises on Phœbe alone at her spinning-wheel; and Gilbert kept fussing about, 'Oh, Jessie, are you sure you're all right?' – Jessie this – Jessie that – until I was almost as demented as he was. At last I turned on him savagely. 'For Heaven's sake, Mr Gilbert, go away and leave me alone, or I sha'n't be able to sing a note!' He gave me a final frenzied hug, and vanished.

6 *heigho*: There is some doubt as to how this phrase should be pronounced: in early D'Oyly Carte productions it was sung 'Hi-ho' but latterly it was changed to 'Hay-ho'.

22 *Enter Wilfred*: In his book *The Secrets of a Savoyard*, Sir Henry Lytton, who played the part of Wilfred Shadbolt in the 1897 revival of *The Yeomen*, says that Gilbert based the character of the gaoler on 'a wicked, wizened little wretch who, in the sixteenth century, so legend says, haunted the Tower when an execution was due, and offered the unhappy felon a handful of dust, which was, he said "a powder that will save you from pain". For reward he claimed the victim's valuables.'

Shadbolt is not, however, usually played as a small and wizened character like King Gama, but rather as a big, stocky oaf. A note by A. F. Harris, a director of the theatrical costumiers Charles Fox Ltd, in a 1926 issue of the *Gilbert and Sullivan Journal* indicates his traditional costume: 'Wilfred Shadbolt's burly frame is attired in a dark green cloth jerkin, black ballet shirt, breeches to below the knee, puffed green stockings, heavy square-toed shoes, and large leather belt from which hangs a heavy bunch of keys. These should be made of wood to obviate the noise that might be made by metal keys rubbing together when Phœbe stealthily removes them.'

ACT I

SCENE. – *Tower Green.* PHŒBE *discovered spinning.*

SONG – PHŒBE.

When maiden loves, she sits and sighs,
    She wanders to and fro;
Unbidden tear-drops fill her eyes,
And to all questions she replies   5
    With a sad 'heigho!'
    'Tis but a little word – 'heigho!'
    So soft, 'tis scarcely heard – 'heigho!'
        An idle breath –
        Yet life and death   10
    May hang upon a maid's 'heigho!'

When maiden loves, she mopes apart,
    As owl mopes on a tree;
Although she keenly feels the smart,
She cannot tell what ails her heart,   15
    With its sad 'Ah me!'
    'Tis but a foolish sigh – 'Ah me!'
    Born but to droop and die – 'Ah me!'
        Yet all the sense
        Of eloquence   20
    Lies hidden in a maid's 'Ah me!' (*weeps*).

(*Enter* WILFRED.)

WIL. Mistress Meryll!
PHŒ. (*looking up*). Eh! Oh! it's you, is it? You may go away, if you like.
Because I don't want you, you know.   25
WIL. Haven't you anything to say to me?

28 *the Little Ease*: a dungeon in the Tower. Guy Fawkes, the perpetrator of the Gunpowder Plot to blow up Parliament, is said to have spent fifty days imprisoned there.

36 *Colonel Fairfax*: Although Fairfax is a well-known name in English history – its most famous bearer being Thomas Fairfax, the commander of Cromwell's New Model Army – the hero of *The Yeomen of the Guard* is purely fictitious.

40 *Beauchamp Tower*: Pronounced 'Beecham', this tower derives from Thomas Beauchamp, Earl of Warwick, who was imprisoned in it by King Richard II in 1397.

43 *at half-past seven*: The time of Fairfax's execution became progressively later in Gilbert's various drafts of the libretto. In the licence copy, it was set for 1.30, in the pre-production copy for 4.30, and in an early prompt-book it was changed to 6.30.

66 *Exit Wilfred*: Gilbert originally gave Wilfred a solo to sing before his exit. It appears in a pre-production prompt copy in the D'Oyly Carte archives but is not in the licence copy sent to the Lord Chamberlain. It may well have been written for Rutland Barrington, who was expected to create the role of Shadbolt, but cut when he suddenly announced he was leaving the D'Oyly Carte company to try his hand at theatrical management. The role had to be given instead to a newcomer, W. H. Denny, for whom this solo might have been regarded as a little too much. Here it is:

> When jealous torments reach my soul
> My agonies I can't control;
> Oh, better sit on red-hot coal
>   Than love a heartless jade!
> The red-hot coal will hurt, no doubt,
> But red-hot coals in time die out –
> But jealousy you cannot rout;
>   Its fires will never fade.
>   It's much less painful on the whole
>   To go and sit on red-hot coal
>   Till you're completely flayed –
>   Or ask some kindly friend to crack,
>   Your wretched bones upon the rack,
>   Than love a heartless jade!
>
> The kerchief on your neck of snow
> I look on as a deadly foe –
> It goeth where I may not go,
>   And stops there all day long!
> The belt that holds you in its grasp
> Is to my peace of mind a rasp,
> It claspeth what I may not clasp –
>   Correct me if I'm wrong!
>   It's much less painful, etc.
>
> The bird that breakfasts on your lip;
> I would I had him in my grip –
> He suppeth where I may not sip –
>   I can't get over that.
> The cat you fondle – soft and sly,
> He lieth where I may not lie,
> We're not on terms, that cat and I –
>   I do not like that cat!
>   It's much less painful, etc.

Phœ. Oh yes! Are the birds all caged? The wild beasts all littered down? All the locks, chains, bolts, and bars in good order? Is the Little Ease sufficiently uncomfortable? The racks, pincers, and thumbscrews all ready for work? Ugh! you brute!   30

Wil. These allusions to my professional duties are in doubtful taste. I didn't become a head-jailer because I like head-jailing. I didn't become an assistant-tormentor because I like assistant-tormenting. We can't *all* be sorcerers, you know. (Phœbe *annoyed*.) Ah! you brought that upon yourself.   35

Phœ. Colonel Fairfax is *not* a sorcerer. He's a man of science and an alchemist.

Wil. Well, whatever he is, he won't be one for long, for he's to be beheaded to-day for dealings with the devil. His master nearly had him last night, when the fire broke out in the Beauchamp Tower.   40

Phœ. Oh! how I wish he had escaped in the confusion! But take care; there's still time for a reply to his petition for mercy.

Wil. Ah! I'm content to chance that. This evening at half-past seven – ah!

Phœ. You're a cruel monster to speak so unfeelingly of the death of a young and handsome soldier.   45

Wil. Young and handsome! How do *you* know he's young and handsome?

Phœ. Because I've seen him every day for weeks past taking his exercise on the Beauchamp Tower.   50

Wil. Curse him!

Phœ. There, I believe you're jealous of *him*, now. Jealous of a man I've never spoken to! Jealous of a poor soul who's to die in an hour!

Wil. I am! I'm jealous of everybody and everything. I'm jealous of the very words I speak to you – because they reach your ears – and I mustn't go near 'em!   55

Phœ. How unjust you are! Jealous of the words you speak to me! Why, you know as well as I do that I don't even like them.

Wil. You used to like 'em.

Phœ. I used to *pretend* I liked them. It was mere politeness to comparative strangers.   (*Exit* Phœbe, *with spinning wheel*.)   60

Wil. I don't believe you know what jealousy is! I don't believe you know how it eats into a man's heart – and disorders his digestion – and turns his interior into boiling lead. Oh, you are a heartless jade to trifle with the delicate organization of the human interior!   65

(*Exit* Wilfred.)

(*Enter Crowd of Men and Women, followed
by Yeomen of the Guard*.)

69 *Tower Warders*: The Corps of Yeoman Warders of the Tower of London, known for short as the Tower Warders, was set up in 1548, i.e. four years after the death of Sir Richard Cholmondeley and therefore after the period in which this opera is set (see the note to line 257). The Yeomen of the Guard were a different body of men, established by Henry VII at his coronation in 1485 as a personal bodyguard for the sovereign. There is no evidence that they undertook duties as custodians of the Tower; they would more likely have been found at the monarch's residence at Windsor Castle. So, strictly speaking, Gilbert may be wrong on two counts in having Tower Warders or Yeomen of the Guard on duty in the Tower in the first half of the sixteenth century.

He is, however, quite right to have his chorus sing of their 'bygone days of daring'. Both the Yeomen of the Guard and the Tower Warders were made up of retired members of the Army and Royal Marines. They appear on stage in the full-dress Tudor outfit of red tunics reaching almost to the knees with large puffed sleeves trimmed in yellow and black and with the royal cypher (in this case H.R.) emblazoned on the front, with the Royal Crown above and the Rose of England below.

89–98 *This the autumn of our life*
This solo was given in early performances to Sergeant Meryll, who originally entered with the Yeomen.

CHORUS (*as Yeomen march on*).

Tower Warders,
Under orders,   70
Gallant pikemen, valiant sworders!
Brave in bearing,
Foemen scaring,
In their bygone days of daring!
Ne'er a stranger   75
There to danger –
Each was o'er the world a ranger;
To the story
Of our glory
Each a bold contributory!   80

CHORUS OF YEOMEN.

In the autumn of our life,
Here at rest in ample clover,
We rejoice in telling over
Our impetuous May and June.
In the evening of our day,   85
With the sun of life declining,
We recall without repining
All the heat of bygone noon.

SOLO – 2ND YEOMAN.

This the autumn of our life,
This the evening of our day;   90
Weary we of battle strife,
Weary we of mortal fray.
But our year is not so spent,
And our days are not so faded,
But that we with one consent,   95
Were our lovèd land invaded,
Still would face a foreign foe,
As in days of long ago.

CHORUS.   Still would face a foreign foe,
As in days of long ago.   100

PEOPLE.   YEOMEN.
Tower Warders,   This the autumn of our life, etc.
Under orders, etc.

(*Exeunt Crowd. Manent Yeomen.*)

105 *A good day to you*: In the pre-production prompt copy this line is 'A good day to you, corporal'. In early performances, it was 'A good day to you, sergeant', and Sergeant Meryll had the lines now given to the Second Yeoman.

111 *No. 14 in the Cold Harbour*: The Coldharbour Gate, with cells above it, was built by Henry III adjacent to the White Tower. The Coldharbour was demolished in the 1670s. In the licence and pre-production copies this line is 'No. 14 in the White Tower'.

124 *old Blunderbore*: The name of the giant in the fairy story *Jack the Giant Killer*, who grinds other men's bones to make his bread.

129–62 *When our gallant Norman foes*
The musical theme which introduces this song is the nearest that Sullivan gets in the Savoy Operas to a Wagnerian *Leitmotiv* used throughout the course of a work to suggest a particular mood or theme. It opens the overture and is heard again at the beginning of the finale to Act I.

137 *Though a queen to save her head should come a-suing*: Two queens of England, both wives of Henry VIII, were executed on Tower Green during the first half of the sixteenth century, Anne Boleyn in May 1536 and Catherine Howard in February 1542. A third queen, Lady Jane Grey, who ruled for just nine days, was executed in the Tower in 1554.

(*Enter* DAME CARRUTHERS.)

DAME. A good day to you! 105
2ND YEOMAN. Good day, Dame Carruthers. Busy to-day?
DAME. Busy, aye! the fire in the Beauchamp last night has given me work enough. A dozen poor prisoners – Richard Colfax, Sir Martin Byfleet, Colonel Fairfax, Warren the preacher-poet, and half-a-score others – all packed into one small cell, not six feet square. Poor Colonel Fairfax, who's 110
to die to-day, is to be removed to No. 14 in the Cold Harbour that he may have his last hour alone with his confessor; and I've to see to that.
2ND YEO. Poor gentleman! He'll die bravely. I fought under him two years since, and he valued his life as it were a feather!
PHŒ. He's the bravest, the handsomest, and the best young gentleman 115
in England! He twice saved my father's life; and it's a cruel thing, a wicked thing, and a barbarous thing that so gallant a hero should lose his head – for it's the handsomest head in England!
DAME. For dealing with the devil. Aye! if all were beheaded who dealt with *him*, there'd be busy doings on Tower Green. 120
PHŒ. You know very well that Colonel Fairfax is a student of alchemy – nothing more, and nothing less; but this wicked Tower, like a cruel giant in a fairy-tale, must be fed with blood, and that blood must be the best and bravest in England, or it's not good enough for the old Blunderbore. Ugh!
DAME. Silence, you silly girl; you know not what you say. I was born 125
in the old keep, and I've grown grey in it, and, please God, I shall die and be buried in it; and there's not a stone in its walls that is not as dear to me as my own right hand.

SONG WITH CHORUS – DAME CARRUTHERS *and* YEOMEN.

When our gallant Norman foes
  Made our merry land their own, 130
    And the Saxons from the Conqueror were flying,
At his bidding it arose,
  In its panoply of stone,
    A sentinel unliving and undying.
Insensible, I trow, 135
  As a sentinel should be,
    Though a queen to save her head should come a-suing,
There's a legend on its brow
  That is eloquent to me,
    And it tells of duty done and duty doing. 140

'The screw may twist and the rack may turn,
And men may bleed and men may burn,

143 *O'er London town*: This and the next line were originally written as:

> O'er London town and all its hoard
> I keep my solemn watch and ward.

154, 157 *all its beauty . . . of its duty*: The sole example in this opera of Gilbert's favourite rhyming combination (see the note to *H.M.S. Pinafore*, Act I, lines 247–58).

161 *I keep my silent*: In early performances this line was 'It keeps its silent watch and ward'.

166 *who, as a reward*: This line and the next down to 'hanged him' were cut from D'Oyly Carte performances in the 1970s. So also were the phrases 'brave' (line 173), 'a brave fellow, and' (line 191 – leaving just 'He's the bravest among brave fellows'), 'my brave boy' (line 195), 'Aye' (lines 197, 201 and 204), 'nay, my body' (line 202), 'the brave' (line 215), 'who saved his flag and cut his way through fifty foes who thirsted for his life' (lines 215-16), 'mind I say, I *think*' (line 221) and 'carefully' (line 226). These cuts were, however, substantially restored in Wilfred Judd's 1981 D'Oyly Carte production.

O'er London town and its golden hoard
I keep my silent watch and ward!'

CHORUS.   The screw may twist, etc.   145

Within its wall of rock
  The flower of the brave
    Have perished with a constancy unshaken.
From the dungeon to the block,
  From the scaffold to the grave,   150
    Is a journey many gallant hearts have taken.
And the wicked flames may hiss
  Round the heroes who have fought
    For conscience and for home in all its beauty,
But the grim old fortalice   155
  Takes little heed of aught
    That comes not in the measure of its duty.

'The screw may twist and the rack may turn,
And men may bleed and men may burn,
O'er London town and its golden hoard   160
I keep my silent watch and ward!'

CHORUS.   The screw may twist, etc.

(*Exeunt all but* PHŒBE. *Enter* SERGEANT MERYLL.)

PHŒ. Father! Has no reprieve arrived for the poor gentleman?
MER. No, my lass; but there's one hope yet. Thy brother Leonard,   165
who, as a reward for his valour in saving his standard and cutting his way
through fifty foes who would have hanged him, has been appointed a
Yeoman of the Guard, will arrive to-day; and as he comes straight from
Windsor, where the Court is, it may be – it *may* be – that he will bring the
expected reprieve with him.   170
PHŒ. Oh, that he may!
MER. Amen to that! For the Colonel twice saved my life, and I'd give the
rest of my life to save his! And wilt thou not be glad to welcome thy brave
brother, with the fame of whose exploits all England is a-ringing?
PHŒ. Aye, truly, if he brings the reprieve.   175
MER. And not otherwise?
PHŒ. Well, he's a brave fellow indeed, and I love brave men.
MER. *All* brave men?
PHŒ. Most of them, I verily believe! But I hope Leonard will not be too
strict with me – they say he is a very dragon of virtue and circumspection!   180
Now, my dear old father is kindness itself, and —

192 *he robbed the Lieutenant's orchard*: In the first performance this line was the cue for the following song, in which Sergeant Meryll extolled his son's virtues:

SONG – MERYLL.
A laughing boy but yesterday,
A merry urchin, blithe and gay!
　　Whose joyous shout
　　Came ringing out,
　　Unchecked by care or sorrow –
To-day, a warrior, all sun-brown,
Whose deeds of soldierly renown
Are all the boast of London Town:
　　A veteran, to-morrow!

When at my Leonard's deeds sublime
A soldier's pulse beats double time,
　　And brave hearts thrill,
　　As brave hearts will,
　　At tales of martial glory,
I burn with flush of pride and joy,
A pride unbittered by alloy,
To find my boy – my darling boy –
　　The theme of song and story!

Gilbert had not originally intended to have this song for Meryll – it does not appear in the pre-production copy and is written into the licence copy as a late insertion – and it seems that he never liked it. In a letter to Sullivan on the day of the first performance he wrote:

> I desire before the production of our piece to place upon record the conviction that I have so frequently expressed to you in the course of rehearsal, that unless Meryll's introduced and wholly irrelevant song is withdrawn, the success of the first act will be most seriously imperilled. Let me recapitulate:
> The Act commences with Phœbe's song – *tearful in character*. This is followed by the entrance of wardens – *serious and martial in character*. This is followed by Dame Carruthers' 'Tower' song – *grim in character*. This is followed by trio for Meryll, Phœbe and Leonard – *sentimental in character*. Thus it is that a professedly comic opera commences.

At a conference just an hour or so before the opening performance, composer and librettist agreed to cut the song but to keep it in just for the first night, largely for the benefit of Richard Temple, who was playing Meryll. It was restored for the 1962, 1964 and 1978 productions at the Tower of London but never reinstated in D'Oyly Carte stage performances.

MER. And leaves thee pretty well to thine own ways, eh? Well, I've no fears for thee; thou hast a feather-brain, but thou'rt a good lass.

PHŒ. Yes, that's all very well, but if Leonard is going to tell me that I may not do this and I may not do that, and I must not talk to this one, or walk with that one, but go through the world with my lips pursed up and my eyes cast down, like a poor nun who has renounced mankind – why, as I have *not* renounced mankind, and don't mean to renounce mankind, I won't have it – there!

MER. Nay, he'll not check thee more than is good for thee, Phœbe! He's a brave fellow, and bravest among brave fellows, and yet it seems but yesterday that he robbed the Lieutenant's orchard.

(Enter LEONARD MERYLL.*)*

LEON. Father!

MER. Leonard! my brave boy! I'm right glad to see thee, and so is Phœbe!

PHŒ. Aye – hast thou brought Colonel Fairfax's reprieve?

LEON. Nay, I have here a despatch for the Lieutenant, but no reprieve for the Colonel!

PHŒ. Poor gentleman! poor gentleman!

LEON. Aye, I would I had brought better news. I'd give my right hand – nay, my body – my life, to save his!

MER. Dost thou speak in earnest, my lad?

LEON. Aye, father – I'm no braggart. Did he not save thy life? and am I not his foster-brother?

MER. Then hearken to me. Thou hast come to join the Yeomen of the Guard!

LEON. Well?

MER. None has seen thee but ourselves?

LEON. And a sentry, who took but scant notice of me.

MER. Now to prove thy words. Give me the despatch, and get thee hence at once! Here is money, and I'll send thee more. Lie hidden for a space, and let no one know. I'll convey a suit of Yeoman's uniform to the Colonel's cell – he shall shave off his beard, so that none shall know him, and I'll own him as my son, the brave Leonard Meryll, who saved his flag and cut his way through fifty foes who thirsted for his life. He will be welcomed without question by my brother-Yeomen, I'll warrant that. Now, how to get access to the Colonel's cell? *(To* PHŒBE.*)* The key is with thy sour-faced admirer, Wilfred Shadbolt.

PHŒ. *(demurely)*. I think – I say, I *think* – I can get anything I want from Wilfred. I think – mind I say, I *think* – you may leave that to me.

MER. Then get thee hence at once, lad – and bless thee for this sacrifice.

240 *And shall I reckon*: In early libretti this and the next three lines were sung by Leonard.

244 *And shall we reckon*: In early libretti this and the next two lines were given to all, and lines 247–8 were then sung solo by Phœbe before being repeated by everyone.

257 *The Lieutenant enters*: The Lieutenant, listed in the *Dramatis personæ* as Sir Richard Cholmondeley, is the one real historical figure to appear as a character in the Savoy Operas. Sir Richard Cholmondeley (pronounced 'Chumley') was appointed Lieutenant of the Tower of London in 1513 and left the post in 1524, although he did not die until 1544. He was knighted after the battle of Flodden. In 1522 he had a tomb built for himself and his wife in the church of St Peter ad Vincula in the Tower, but he never occupied it, being buried at his country home in Cheshire. The action of *The Yeomen of the Guard* presumably takes place, therefore, some time during Cholmondeley's lieutenancy, i.e. between 1513 and 1524.

In his article already referred to on the costumes for *The Yeomen* (see the note to line 22), A. F. Harris comments:

> The Lieutenant of the Tower is most certainly striking in his plum velvet uniform, slashed blue velvet and trimmed gold, with black top boots, back and front plate, armhole robe and tight fitting hat with square top similar to a lancer's helmet.

PHŒ. And take my blessing, too, dear, dear Leonard!

LEON. And thine, eh? Humph! Thy love is new-born; wrap it up   225
carefully, lest it take cold and die.

TRIO – PHŒBE, LEONARD, MERYLL.

PHŒ.   Alas! I waver to and fro!
                Dark danger hangs upon the deed!

ALL.   Dark danger hangs upon the deed!

LEON.   The scheme is rash and well may fail,   230
                But ours are not the hearts that quail,
                The hands that shrink, the cheeks that pale
                      In hours of need!

ALL.   No, ours are not the hearts that quail,
                The hands that shrink, the cheeks that pale   235
                      In hours of need!

MER.   The air I breathe to him I owe:
                My life is his – I count it naught!

PHŒ. *and* LEON. That life is his – so count it naught!

MER.   And shall I reckon risks I run   240
                When services are to be done
                To save the life of such an one?
                      Unworthy thought!

PHŒ. *and* LEON. And shall we reckon risks we run
                To save the life of such an one?
                          245

ALL.   Unworthy thought!
         We may succeed – who can foretell?
         May heaven help our hope – farewell!

(LEONARD *embraces* MERYLL *and* PHŒBE, *and then exits.*
                     PHŒBE *weeping.*)   250

MER. Nay, lass, be of good cheer, we may save him yet.

PHŒ. Oh! see, father – they bring the poor gentleman from the
Beauchamp! Oh, father! his hour is not yet come?

MER. No, no, – they lead him to the Cold Harbour Tower to await his
end in solitude. But softly – the Lieutenant approaches! He should not see   255
thee weep.

(*Enter* FAIRFAX, *guarded. The* LIEUTENANT *enters,*
                - *meeting him.*)

276 *Thou and I*: This sentence (down to 'such goodly fashion') was cut from D'Oyly Carte productions in the 1970s.

281–302 *Is life a boon*

Sullivan produced three different settings for this song before Gilbert was satisfied that he had it right. He also took great trouble altering some of the notes so that they would be comfortably within the compass of Courtice Pounds, the new D'Oyly Carte lyric tenor, who was to create the role of Fairfax. His painstaking efforts were rewarded by the universally ecstatic reception that the song received from audience and critics alike.

When Sullivan died in 1900 Gilbert chose the first four lines of this song to be inscribed on his memorial, which can still be seen in the Embankment Gardens between the Savoy Theatre and the River Thames.

LIEUT. Halt! Colonel Fairfax, my old friend, we meet but sadly.

FAIR. Sir, I greet you with all good-will; and I thank you for the   260
zealous care with which you have guarded me from the pestilent dangers
which threaten human life outside. In this happy little community, Death,
when he comes, doth so in punctual and businesslike fashion; and, like a
courtly gentleman, giveth due notice of his advent, that one may not be
taken unawares.   265

LIEUT. Sir, you bear this bravely, as a brave man should.

FAIR. Why, sir, it is no light boon to die swiftly and surely at a given
hour and in a given fashion! Truth to tell, I would gladly have my life; but
if that may not be, I have the next best thing to it, which is death. Believe me,
sir, my lot is not so much amiss!   270

PHŒ. (*aside to* MERYLL). Oh, father, father, I cannot bear it!

MER. My poor lass!

FAIR. Nay, pretty one, why weepest thou? Come, be comforted. Such a
life as mine is not worth weeping for. (*Sees* MERYLL.) Sergeant Meryll, is
it not? (*To* LIEUT.) May I greet my old friend? (*Shakes* MERYLL'S *hand*.)   275
Why, man, what's all this? Thou and I have faced the grim old king a dozen
times, and never has his majesty come to me in such goodly fashion. Keep
a stout heart, good fellow – we are soldiers, and we know how to die, thou
and I. Take my word for it, it is easier to die well than to live well – for, in
sooth, I have tried both.   280

BALLAD – FAIRFAX.

Is life a boon?
   If so, it must befall
   That Death, whene'er he call,
Must call too soon.
   Though fourscore years he give,   285
   Yet one would pray to live
Another moon!
   What kind of plaint have I,
   Who perish in July?
   I might have had to die,   290
Perchance, in June!

Is life a thorn?
   Then count it not a whit!
   Man is well done with it;
Soon as he's born   295
   He should all means essay
   To put the plague away;

320 *a hundred crowns*: A crown was an old British coin worth a quarter of a pound, i.e. five shillings. Half-a-crown coins, worth two shillings and sixpence, were in circulation until the decimalization of the British coinage.

335 *Enter Jack Point*: Sir Henry Lytton, who played the role of Jack Point countless times between 1897 and 1934, had this to say in his *Secrets of a Savoyard* about the jester's first entrance:

> From the moment he enters the audience should know the manner of man that he is, and he must win their sympathy immediately. He is a poor strolling player who has been dragged from pillar to post. Footsore and weary though he is, Jack Point is anxious to please the crowd who have roughly chased him and Elsie Maynard in, for if he fails them have they not threatened to duck him in the nearest pond?

Traditionally, in D'Oyly Carte productions, on making his entrance Jack Point hit a citizen or two on the head with his pig's bladder. This essential item of a jester's equipment was for many years supplied by the meat department of the Savoy Hotel, but when this source of supply dried up, Peter Riley, the company's stage manager, turned to Harrods. On tour he was often forced to pump up balloons with a bicycle pump.

And I, war-torn,
  Poor captured fugitive,
  My life most gladly give –   300
  I might have had to live
Another morn!

(At the end, PHŒBE *is led off, weeping, by* MERYLL.)

FAIR. And now, Sir Richard, I have a boon to beg. I am in this strait for
no better reason than because my kinsman, Sir Clarence Poltwhistle, one of   305
the Secretaries of State, has charged me with sorcery, in order that he may
succeed to my estate, which devolves to him provided I die unmarried.
LIEUT. As thou wilt most surely do.
FAIR. Nay, as I will most surely *not* do, by your worship's grace! I have
a mind to thwart this good cousin of mine.   310
LIEUT. How?
FAIR. By marrying forthwith, to be sure!
LIEUT. But heaven ha' mercy, whom wouldst thou marry?
FAIR. Nay, I am indifferent on that score. Coming Death hath made of
me a true and chivalrous knight, who holds all womankind in such esteem   315
that the oldest, and the meanest, and the worst-favoured of them is good
enough for him. So, my good Lieutenant, if thou wouldst serve a poor
soldier who has but an hour to live, find me the first that comes – my
confessor shall marry us, and her dower shall be my dishonoured name and
a hundred crowns to boot. No such poor dower for an hour of matrimony!   320
  LIEUT. A strange request. I doubt that I should be warranted in granting
it.
  FAIR. There never was a marriage fraught with so little of evil to the
contracting parties. In an hour she'll be a widow, and I – a bachelor again for
aught I know!   325
  LIEUT. Well, I will see what can be done, for I hold thy kinsman in
abhorrence for the scurvy trick he has played thee.
  FAIR. A thousand thanks, good sir; we meet again on this spot in an hour
or so. I shall be a bridegroom then, and your worship will wish me joy. Till
then, farewell. *(To Guard.)* I am ready, good fellows.   330

(Exit with Guard into Cold Harbour Tower.)

  LIEUT. He is a brave fellow, and it is a pity that he should die. Now, how
to find him a bride at such short notice? Well, the task should be easy!
(Exit.)

(Enter JACK POINT *and* ELSIE MAYNARD, *pursued by a crowd of men and*   335
women. POINT *and* ELSIE *are much terrified;* POINT, *however, assuming an*
appearance of self-possession.)

341 *follify*: A Gilbertian invention, although there is a word 'folliful', meaning full of foolishness.

342 *vapidly*: Without animation.

CHORUS.

Here's a man of jollity,
 Jibe, joke, jollify!
Give us of your quality,
 Come, fool, follify!   340

If you vapour vapidly,
River runneth rapidly,
 Into it we fling
 Bird who doesn't sing!   345

Give us an experiment
In the art of merriment;
 Into it we throw
 Cock who doesn't crow!

Banish your timidity,   350
And with all rapidity
Give us quip and quiddity –
 Willy-nilly, O!

River none can mollify; –
 Into it we throw   355
Fool who doesn't follify,
 Cock who doesn't crow!

Banish your timidity, etc.

POINT (*alarmed*). My masters, I pray you bear with us, and we will
satisfy you, for we are merry folk who would make all merry as ourselves. 360
For, look you, there is humour in all things, and the truest philosophy is that
which teaches us to find it and to make the most of it.

ELSIE (*struggling with one of the crowd*). Hands off, I say, unmannerly
fellow!

POINT (*to 1st Citizen*). Ha! Didst thou hear her say, 'Hands off'? 365

1ST CIT. Aye, I heard her say it, and I felt her do it! What then?

POINT. Thou dost not see the humour of that?

1ST CIT. Nay, if I do, hang me!

POINT. Thou dost not? Now observe. She said, 'Hands off!' Whose
hands? Thine. Off whom? Off *her*. Why? Because she is a woman. Now, had 370
she *not* been a woman, thine hands had not been set upon her at all. So the
reason for the laying on of hands is the reason for the taking off of hands,
and herein is contradiction contradicted! It is the very marriage of *pro* with
con; and no such lopsided union either, as times go, for *pro* is not more unlike

375 *men and women marry every day*: This was originally 'men and women marry and are made one flesh', but Gilbert changed it to its present form before the first performance, perhaps because of the religious connotations of the first version.

377–8 *couplet . . . ballade*: Couplets are pairs of successive lines of verse rhyming with each other; triolets are stanzas of eight lines, much favoured by Hilarion and his friends in *Princess Ida*; quatrains are stanzas of four lines, usually with alternate rhymes; sonnets consist of fourteen lines; rondolets are short poems having only two rhymes throughout, and with the opening words used twice as a refrain; and ballades are poems consisting of one or more triplets of seven-lined stanzas, each ending with the same line as the refrain – and I bet Jack Point didn't know all that.

378–9 *saraband . . . Jumping Joan*: The saraband is a slow and stately Spanish dance in triple time; the gondolet is probably an English corruption of the Basque dance 'godalet'; the carole is a dance performed by men and women grouped in a ring and singing; the Pimpernel and Jumping Joan may well have been old English dances, or they may equally well be Gilbertian inventions – I can find no mention of them in any works of reference.

383–444 *I have a song to sing, O*

This is, perhaps, the best-loved of all Gilbert and Sullivan's songs. It was the one most constantly requested by ladies approaching the composer with their autograph albums. The *Morning Advertiser* echoed the views of many when it commented in its first-night review: 'Sir Arthur Sullivan has never written anything more delicately melodious and elegant than this; in fact of its kind he has never equalled it and probably never will'. In more recent times, the first line of the song has been used by the great D'Oyly Carte comic singer John Reed as the title both for a record and for a one-man show at the Savoy Theatre.

In fact, Sullivan found this song more difficult to set than any other he was given by Gilbert. It took him a fortnight to get the right tune. The main difficulty lay in what he called 'the House that Jack built' character about the number with an additional phrase being added to each verse. Eventually Gilbert came to his aid by humming him the tune of an old sea shanty which he had had in his mind when writing the words. Gilbert's account of how he helped Sullivan to get the tune, which throws much light on their working arrangements, is worth quoting in full:

> The verse always preceded the music, or even any hint of it. Sometimes – very rarely – Sullivan would say of some song I had given him, 'My dear fellow, I can't make anything of this' – and then I would rewrite it entirely – never tinker at it. But, of course, I don't mean to say that I 'invented' all the rhythms and stanzas in the operas. Often a rhythm would be suggested by some old tune or other running in my head, and I would fit my words to it more or less exactly. When Sullivan knew I had done so, he would say, 'Don't tell me what the tune is, or I shan't be able to get it out of my head.' But once, I remember, I did tell him. There is a duet in *The Yeomen of the Guard* beginning:

> I have a song to sing, O!
> Sing me your song, O!

> It was suggested to me by an old chantey I used to hear the sailors on board my yacht singing in the 'dog-watch' on Saturday evenings, beginning:

> Come, and I will sing to you –
> What will you sing me?
> I will sing you one, O!
> What is your one, O!

And so on. Well, when I gave Sullivan the words of the duet, he found the utmost difficulty in setting it. He tried hard for a fortnight, but in vain. I offered to recast it in another mould, but he expressed himself so delighted with it in its then form that he was determined to work it out to a satisfactory issue. At last, he came to me and said: 'You often have some old air in your mind which prompts the metre of your songs; if anything

con than man is unlike woman – yet men and women marry every day with   375
none to say, 'Oh, the pity of it!' but I and fools like me! Now wherewithal
shall we please you? We can rhyme you couplet, triolet, quatrain, sonnet,
rondolet, ballade, what you will. Or we can dance you saraband, gondolet,
carole, Pimpernel, or Jumping Joan.

    ELSIE. Let us give them the singing farce of the Merryman and his   380
Maid – therein is song and dance too.

    ALL. Aye, the Merryman and his Maid!

DUET – ELSIE *and* POINT.

POINT.   I have a song to sing, O!

ELSIE.   Sing me your song, O!

POINT.   It is sung to the moon   385
By a love-lorn loon,
Who fled from the mocking throng, O!
It's a song of a merryman, moping mum,
Whose soul was sad, and whose glance was glum,
Who sipped no sup, and who craved no crumb,   390
As he sighed for the love of a ladye.
Heighdy! heighdy!
Misery me, lackadaydee!
He sipped no sup, and he craved no crumb,
As he sighed for the love of a ladye.   395

ELSIE.   I have a song to sing, O!

POINT.   What is your song, O?

ELSIE.   It is sung with the ring
Of the songs maids sing
Who love with a love life-long, O!   400
It's the song of a merrymaid, peerly proud,
Who loved a lord, and who laughed aloud
At the moan of the merryman, moping mum,
Whose soul was sad, and whose glance was glum,
Who sipped no sup, and who craved no crumb,   405
As he sighed for the love of a ladye!
Heighdy! heighdy!
Misery me, lackadaydee!
He sipped no sup, etc.

POINT.   I have a song to sing, O!   410

ELSIE.   Sing me your song, O!

prompted you in this one, hum it to me – it may help me.' Only a rash man ever asks me to hum, but the situation was desperate, and I did my best to convey to him the air of the chantey that had suggested the song to me. I was so far successful that before I had hummed a dozen bars he exclaimed: 'That will do – I've got it!' And in an hour he produced the charming air as it appears in the opera. I have sometimes thought that he exclaimed 'That will do – I've got it' because my humming was more than he could bear; but he always assured me that it had given him the necessary clue to the proper setting of the song . . .

I remember it [the chantey] as my sailors used to sing it. I found out afterwards that it was a very much corrupted form of an old Cornish carol. This was their version of it:

FIRST VOICE.   Come, and I will sing you –
ALL.   What will you sing me?
FIRST VOICE.   I will sing you one, O!
ALL.   What is your one, O!
FIRST VOICE.   One of them is all alone,
                               And ever will remain so.

ALL.   One of them, etc.
SECOND VOICE.   Come, and I will sing you –
ALL.   What will you sing me?
SECOND VOICE.   I will sing you two, O!
ALL.   What is your two, O!
SECOND VOICE.   Two of them are lilywhite maids,
                               Dressed all in green, O!
ALL.   One of them is all alone,
                               And ever will remain so.

THIRD VOICE.   Come, and I will sing you –
ALL.   What will you sing me?
THIRD VOICE.   I will sing you three, O!
ALL.   What is your three, O!
THIRD VOICE.   Three of them are strangers.
ALL.   Two of them are lilywhite maids,
                               Dressed all in green, O!
                               One of them is all alone,
                               And ever will remain so!

And so on until twelve is reached.

THIRD VOICE.   Come, and I will sing you –
ALL.   What will you sing me?
THIRD VOICE.   I will sing you twelve, O!
ALL.   What is your twelve, O!
THIRD VOICE.   Twelve are the twelve apostles,
ALL.   Eleven of them have gone to heaven.
                               Ten are the Ten Commandments,
                               Nine is the moonlight bright and clear,
                               Eight are the eight archangels,
                               Seven are the seven stars in the sky,
                               Six are the cheerful waiters (!)
                               Five are the ferrymen in the boats,
                               Four are the gospel preachers,
                               Three of them are strangers,
                               Two of them are lilywhite maids,
                               Dressed all in green, O;
                               One of them is all alone,
                               And ever will remain so!

397 *What is your song, O*: In the first and second editions of the libretto this line was 'Sing me your song, O!'

404 *Whose soul was sad*: In the licence copy and early editions of the libretto this line began 'Whose soul was sore'. It was changed in the third edition to conform with the other verses.

POINT.
It is sung to the knell
Of a churchyard bell,
And a doleful dirge, ding dong, O!
It's a song of a popinjay, bravely born,   415
Who turned up his noble nose with scorn
At the humble merrymaid, peerly proud,
Who loved a lord, and who laughed aloud
At the moan of the merryman, moping mum,
Whose soul was sad, and whose glance was glum,   420
Who sipped no sup, and who craved no crumb,
As he sighed for the love of a ladye!

BOTH.
Heighdy! heighdy!
Misery me, lackadaydee!
He sipped no sup, etc.   425

ELSIE.
I have a song to sing, O!

POINT.
Sing me your song, O!

ELSIE.
It is sung with a sigh
And a tear in the eye,
For it tells of a righted wrong, O!   430
It's a song of the merrymaid, once so gay,
Who turned on her heel and tripped away
From the peacock popinjay, bravely born,
Who turned up his noble nose with scorn
At the humble heart that he did not prize: 435
So she begged on her knees, with downcast eyes,
For the love of the merryman, moping mum,
Whose soul was sad, and whose glance was glum,
Who sipped no sup, and who craved no crumb,
As he sighed for the love of a ladye!   440

ALL.
Heighdy! heighdy!
Misery me, lackadaydee!
His pains were o'er, and he sighed no more,
For he lived in the love of a ladye!

1st CIT. Well sung and well danced!   445
2ND CIT. A kiss for that, pretty maid!
ALL. Aye, a kiss all round.
ELSIE (*drawing dagger*). Best beware! I am armed!
POINT. Back, sirs – back! This is going too far.

436 *So she begged on her knees*: In the pre-production prompt copy, and therefore presumably as originally written by Gilbert, this and the next two lines ran:

> So she changed her tone and, with downcast eyes,
> She begged on her knees, with a heart forlorn,
> For the love of a merryman, etc.

508 *electuary*: A medicine made up with honey, syrup or some similarly sweet substance to disguise the taste.

517 *on this very spot*: In the pre-production copy this was 'on Tower Green'. It is, in fact, highly unlikely that Fairfax would have been executed within the precincts of the Tower on Tower Green. That place was reserved for the most exalted victims of the executioner's axe. Only six people were ever beheaded there: Anne Boleyn, Catherine Howard, Lady Jane Grey, the Earl of Essex, the Viscountess Rockford and the Countess of Salisbury. Commoners were executed on Tower Hill outside the Tower walls.

2ND CIT. Thou dost not see the humour of it, eh? Yet there is humour   450
in all things – even in this. (*Trying to kiss her.*)

ELSIE. Help! help!

(*Enter* LIEUTENANT *with Guard. Crowd falls back.*)

LIEUT. What is this pother?

ELSIE. Sir, we sang to these folk, and they would have repaid us with   455
gross courtesy, but for your honour's coming.

LIEUT. (*to Mob*). Away with ye! Clear the rabble. (*Guards push Crowd off,
and go off with them.*) Now, my girl, who are you, and what do you
here?

ELSIE. May it please you, sir, we are two strolling players, Jack Point   500
and I, Elsie Maynard, at your worship's service. We go from fair to fair,
singing, and dancing, and playing brief interludes; and so we make a poor
living.

LIEUT. You two, eh? Are ye man and wife?

POINT. No, sir; for though I'm a fool, there is a limit to my folly. Her   505
mother, old Bridget Maynard, travels with us (for Elsie is a good girl), but the
old woman is a-bed with fever, and we have come here to pick up some
silver to buy an electuary for her.

LIEUT. Hark ye, my girl! Your mother is ill?

ELSIE. Sorely ill, sir.   510

LIEUT. And needs good food, and many things that thou canst not
buy?

ELSIE. Alas! sir, it is too true.

LIEUT. Wouldst thou earn an hundred crowns?

ELSIE. An hundred crowns! They might save her life!   515

LIEUT. Then listen! A worthy but unhappy gentleman is to be
beheaded in an hour on this very spot. For sufficient reasons, he desires to
marry before he dies, and he hath asked me to find him a wife. Wilt thou be
that wife?

ELSIE. The wife of a man I have never seen!   520

POINT. Why, sir, look you, I am concerned in this; for though I am not
yet wedded to Elsie Maynard, time works wonders, and there's no knowing
what may be in store for us. Have we your worship's word for it that this
gentleman will die to-day?

LIEUT. Nothing is more certain, I grieve to say.   525

POINT. And that the maiden will be allowed to depart the very instant the
ceremony is at an end?

LIEUT. The very instant. I pledge my honour that it shall be so.

POINT. An hundred crowns?

LIEUT. An hundred crowns!   530

POINT. For my part, I consent. It is for Elsie to speak.

532–65 *How say you, maiden, will you wed*
The first edition of the libretto had a version of this song which was substantially different from the one substituted in the second edition and now sung. Here it is:

TRIO.

ELSIE, POINT, LIEUTENANT.

LIEUTENANT.

How say you maiden, will you wed
A man about to lose his head?
No harm to you can thence arise,
In half an hour, poor soul, he dies.
For half an hour
You'll be a wife,
And then the dower
Is yours for life.
This tempting offer why refuse?
If truth the poets tell,
Most men, before they marry, lose
Both head and heart as well!

ALL.

Temptation, oh temptation,
Were we, in truth, intended
To shun, whate'er our station,
Your fascinations splendid;
Or fall, whene'er we view you,
Head over heels into you!

ELSIE.

A strange proposal you reveal,
It almost makes my senses reel.
Alas! I'm very poor indeed,
And such a sum I sorely need.
Unfortunately,
Life and death
Have hung till lately
On a breath.
My mother, sir, is like to die;
This money life may bring.
Bear this in mind, I pray, if I
Consent to do this thing!

ALL.

Temptation, oh temptation, etc.

POINT.

Though as a general rule of life
I don't allow my promised wife,
My lovely bride that is to be,
To marry anyone but me,
The circumstances
Of this case
May set such fancies
Out of place;
So, if the fee is duly paid,
And he, in well-earned grave,
Within the hour is duly laid,
Objection I will waive!

ALL.

Temptation, oh temptation, etc.

538 *A headless bridegroom why refuse*: Keen to help Sullivan, Gilbert supplied him with two

TRIO – ELSIE, POINT, *and* LIEUTENANT.

LIEUT.	How say you, maiden, will you wed
	A man about to lose his head?
	For half an hour
	You'll be a wife,
	And then the dower
	Is yours for life.
	A headless bridegroom why refuse?
	If truth the poets tell,
	Most bridegrooms, ere they marry, lose
	Both head and heart as well!

535

540

ELSIE.	A strange proposal you reveal,
	It almost makes my senses reel.
	Alas! I'm very poor indeed,
	And such a sum I sorely need.
	My mother, sir, is like to die,
	This money life may bring.
	Bear this in mind, I pray, if I
	Consent to do this thing!

545

POINT.	Though as a general rule of life
	I don't allow my promised wife,
	My lovely bride that is to be,
	To marry any one but me,
	Yet if the fee is promptly paid,
	And he, in well-earned grave,
	Within the hour is duly laid,
	Objection I will waive!
	Yes, objection I will waive!

550

555

ALL.	Temptation, oh, temptation,
	Were we, I pray, intended
	To shun, whate'er our station,
	Your fascinations splendid;
	Or fall, whene'er we view you,
	Head over heels into you?
	Temptation, oh, temptation, etc.

560

565

(*During this, the* LIEUTENANT *has whispered to* WILFRED (*who has entered*). WILFRED *binds* ELSIE'S *eyes with a kerchief, and leads her into the Cold Harbour Tower.*)

versions of this and the next three lines with different metres. The second version, which the composer did not choose, went as follows:

> What matter, though
>   His head should fall?
> This trifling blow
>   Need not appal.
> Most men who wed,
>   So poets tell,
> Have lost both head
>   And heart as well!

581 *I've jibe and joke*: In the licence copy Jack Point's song began 'I've jest and joke'.

606 *gild the philosophic pill*: It was the custom of doctors in medieval and Tudor times to make their pills more attractive by gilding them with a thin coating of sugar. To gild the pill means to make something unattractive at least appear desirable.

Lieut. And so, good fellow, you are a jester?

Point. Aye, sir, and, like some of my jests, out of place.   570

Lieut. I have a vacancy for such an one. Tell me, what are your qualifications for such a post?

Point. Marry, sir, I have a pretty wit. I can rhyme you extempore; I can convulse you with quip and conundrum; I have the lighter philosophies at my tongue's tip; I can be merry, wise, quaint, grim, and sardonic, one by   575
one, or all at once; I have a pretty turn for anecdote; I know all the jests – ancient and modern – past, present, and to come; I can riddle you from dawn of day to set of sun, and, if that content you not, well on to midnight and the small hours. Oh, sir, a pretty wit, I warrant you – a pretty, pretty wit!   580

RECITATIVE and SONG – Point.

I've jibe and joke
      And quip and crank
For lowly folk
      And men of rank.
I ply my craft   585
      And know no fear,
But aim my shaft
      At prince or peer.
At peer or prince – at prince or peer,
I aim my shaft and know no fear!   590

I've wisdom from the East and from the West,
   That's subject to no academic rule;
You may find it in the jeering of a jest,
   Or distil it from the folly of a fool.
I can teach you with a quip, if I've a mind;   595
   I can trick you into learning with a laugh;
Oh, winnow all my folly, and you'll find
   A grain or two of truth among the chaff!

I can set a braggart quailing with a quip,
   The upstart I can wither with a whim;   600
He may wear a merry laugh upon his lip,
   But his laughter has an echo that is grim!
When they're offered to the world in merry guise,
   Unpleasant truths are swallowed with a will –
For he who'd make his fellow-creatures wise   605
   Should always gild the philosophic pill!

Lieut. And how came you to leave your last employ?

616 *the dignified clergy*: Those occupying senior positions in the hierarchy of the Church of England. Parish priests and curates were known as the undignified clergy.

619 *my jests are most carefully selected*: Compare this remark about Jester James, the subject of one of Gilbert's *Bab Ballads* published in *Time* magazine in 1879:

> His antic jokes were modelled on severely classic rules,
> And all his quips passed muster at the strictest ladies' schools.

630–31 *what is underdone cannot be helped*: This joke, and the one in line 638, first appeared in an earlier play by Gilbert, *Foggerty's Fairy*, which was performed at the Savoy Theatre in December 1881.

647 *my best conundrum wasted*: Sir Henry Lytton once asked Gilbert what the answer to this conundrum was and was told by the librettist that he would leave it in his will. Needless to say, when he died, it wasn't there. The truth is that Gilbert had never bothered about answering his own riddle. Many others have had a go at it, but no one has produced anything either plausible or even very amusing.

POINT. Why, sir, it was in this wise. My Lord was the Archbishop of Canterbury, and it was considered that one of my jokes was unsuited to His Grace's family circle. In truth, I ventured to ask a poor riddle, sir – Wherein 610 lay the difference between His Grace and poor Jack Point? His Grace was pleased to give it up, sir. And thereupon I told him that whereas His Grace was paid £10,000 a year for being good, poor Jack Point was good – for nothing. 'Twas but a harmless jest, but it offended His Grace, who whipped me and set me in the stocks for a scurril rogue, and so we parted. I had as 615 lief not take post again with the dignified clergy.

LIEUT. But I trust you are very careful not to give offence. I have daughters.

POINT. Sir, my jests are most carefully selected, and anything objectionable is expunged. If your honour pleases, I will try them first on 620 your honour's chaplain.

LIEUT. Can you give me an example? Say that I had sat me down hurriedly on something sharp?

POINT. Sir, I should say that you had sat down on the spur of the moment. 625

LIEUT. Humph! I don't think much of that. Is that the best you can do?

POINT. It has always been much admired, sir, but we will try again.

LIEUT. Well, then, I am at dinner, and the joint of meat is but half cooked.

POINT. Why, then, sir, I should say that what is *under*done cannot be 630 helped.

LIEUT. I see. I think that manner of thing would be somewhat irritating.

POINT. At first, sir, perhaps; but use is everything, and you would come in time to like it. 635

LIEUT. We will suppose that I caught you kissing the kitchen wench under my very nose.

POINT. Under *her* very nose, good sir – not under yours! *That* is where *I* would kiss her. Do you take me? Oh, sir, a pretty wit – a pretty, pretty wit! 640

LIEUT. The maiden comes. Follow me, friend, and we will discuss this matter at length in my library.

POINT. I am your worship's servant. That is to say, I trust I soon shall be. But, before proceeding to a more serious topic, can you tell me, sir, why a cook's brain-pan is like an overwound clock? 645

LIEUT. A truce to this fooling – follow me.

POINT. Just my luck; my best conundrum wasted!

(*Exeunt.*)

(*Enter* ELSIE *from Tower, led by* WILFRED , *who removes the bandage from her eyes, and exits.*) 650

651–6 *'Tis done! I am a bride*
The opening recitative which precedes Elsie's song was added at a late stage. It is missing from both the licence copy and pre-production prompt copy.

669 *Ah me! what profit we*: In early editions of the libretto, Elsie's song lacked lines 669–72 and 685–8. They were added in the third edition.

RECITATIVE and SONG – ELSIE.

'Tis done! I am a bride! Oh, little ring,
　　That bearest in thy circlet all the gladness
That lovers hope for, and that poets sing,
　　What bringest thou to me but gold and sadness?
A bridegroom all unknown, save in this wise,　　　　655
To-day he dies! To-day, alas, he dies!

　　　　Though tear and long-drawn sigh
　　　　　　Ill fit a bride,
　　　　No sadder wife than I
　　　　　　The whole world wide!　　　　　　660
　　　　　　　Ah me! Ah me!
　　　　　　Yet maids there be
　　　　Who would consent to lose
　　　　　　The very rose of youth,
　　　　　　　The flower of life,　　　　　665
　　　　　　To be, in honest truth,
　　　　　　　A wedded wife,
　　　　　　　No matter whose!

　　　　Ah me! what profit we,
　　　　　　O maids that sigh,　　　　　　670
　　　　Though gold should live
　　　　　　If wedded love must die?
　　　　Ere half an hour has rung,
　　　　　　A widow I!

　　Ah, heaven, he is too young,　　　　　675
　　　　Too brave to die!
　　　　　　Ah me! Ah me!
　　　　Yet wives there be
　　So weary worn, I trow,
　　　　That they would scarce complain,　　680
　　　　　　So that they could
　　　　In half an hour attain
　　　　　　To widowhood,
　　　　　　　No matter how!

　　O weary wives　　　　　　　　685
　　　　Who widowhood would win,
　　Rejoice that ye have time
　　　　To weary in.

　　　　(*Exit* ELSIE *as* WILFRED *re-enters.*)

696 *Now what could he have wanted*: Wilfred's remark in lines 696–7 was not in the first edition of the libretto. A note by Rupert D'Oyly Carte in 1923 says 'Not original – probably a gag by W. H. Denny approved by W.S.G.'

706 *a live ass is better than a dead lion*: This seems to mix up two traditional sayings, the biblical saw 'A living dog is better than a dead lion' (Ecclesiastes 9.4) and the Italian proverb 'A live ass is better than a dead doctor'.

716 *In the nice regulation of a thumbscrew*: Wilfred's demonstration of his grisly trade to Phœbe recalls the behaviour of Gilbert Clay, a gentle executioner who described his craft to his lover Annie Protheroe in a Bab Ballad which Gilbert contributed to *Fun* in October 1868:

> And sometimes he'd explain to her, which charmed her very much,
> How famous operators vary very much in touch,
> And then, perhaps, he'd show how he himself performed the trick,
> And illustrate his meaning with a poppy and a stick.

WIL. (*looking after* ELSIE). 'Tis an odd freak, for a dying man and his   690
confessor to be closeted alone with a strange singing girl. I would fain have
espied them, but they stopped up the keyhole. *My* keyhole!

(*Enter* PHŒBE *with* MERYLL. MERYLL *remains in the
background, unobserved by* WILFRED.)

PHŒ. (*aside*). Wilfred – and alone!   695
WIL. Now what could he have wanted with her? That's what puzzles
me!
PHŒ. (*aside*). Now to get the keys from him. (*Aloud.*) Wilfred – has no
reprieve arrived?
WIL. None. Thine adored Fairfax is to die.   700
PHŒ. Nay, thou knowest that I have naught but pity for the poor
condemned gentleman.
WIL. I know that he who is about to die is more to thee than I, who am
alive and well.
PHŒ. Why, that were out of reason, dear Wilfred. Do they not say that   705
a live ass is better than a dead lion? No, I don't mean that!
WIL. Oh, they say that, do they?
PHŒ. It's unpardonably rude of them, but I believe they put it in that
way. Not that it applies to thee, who art clever beyond all telling!
WILL. Oh yes, as an assistant-tormentor.   710
PHŒ. Nay, as a wit, as a humorist, as a most philosophic commentator on
the vanity of human resolution.

(PHŒBE *slyly takes bunch of keys from* WILFRED'S *waistband and hands them to*
MERYLL, *who enters the Tower, unnoticed by* WILFRED.)

WIL. Truly, I have seen great resolution give way under my persuasive   715
methods (*working a small thumbscrew*). In the nice regulation of a thumbscrew
– in the hundredth part of a single revolution lieth all the difference between
stony reticence and a torrent of impulsive unbosoming that the pen can
scarcely follow. Ha! ha! I am a mad wag.
PHŒ. (*with a grimace*). Thou art a most light-hearted and delightful   720
companion, Master Wilfred. Thine anecdotes of the torture-chamber are the
prettiest hearing.
WIL. I'm a pleasant fellow an I choose. I believe I am the merriest dog that
barks. Ah, we might be passing happy together —
PHŒ. Perhaps. I do not know.   725
WIL. For thou wouldst make a most tender and loving wife.
PHŒ. Aye, to one whom I really loved. For there is a wealth of love within
this little heart – saving up for – I wonder whom? Now, of all the world of
men, I wonder whom? To think that he whom I am to wed is now

741–82 *Were I thy bride*

This delightful song, which Gilbert reportedly said that he had written to show that English could be just as tuneful a language as Italian, has echoes of the Bab Ballad 'To Phœbe':

> 'Gentle, modest, little flower,
>   Sweet epitome of May,
> Love me but for half-an-hour,
>   Love me, love me, little fay'.
> Sentences so fiercely flaming
>   In your tiny shell-like ear,
> I should always be exclaiming
>   If I loved you, Phœbe, dear.
>
> 'Smiles that thrill from any distance
>   Shed upon me while I sing!
> Please ecstaticize existence,
>   Love me, oh, thou fairy thing!'
> Words like these, outpouring sadly,
>   You'd perpetually hear,
> If I loved you, fondly, madly; –
>   But I do not, Phœbe, dear.

A good deal of unofficial and unapproved D'Oyly Carte 'business' crept into this song, as an article by Jessie Bond in the December 1927 issue of the *Gilbert and Sullivan Journal* makes clear:

> What I hate is that senseless 'business' in 'Were I thy bride'. You know what I mean – the scratching of the jailer's chin, the ruffling of his hair, the ogling of the eyes, and all those 'comic' antics which, goodness knows why, are supposed to be funny.
> I think it is wicked that there should be this vulgarity in one of the loveliest of all the songs in the operas. Sir William Gilbert would not have endured it for a moment. He intended that the audience should hear this most beautiful lyric – and they never hear it today.
> During the rehearsals I remember that Gilbert asked me how I would wheedle Wilfred Shadbolt. 'Well Mr Gilbert', I answered, 'I might just gently stroke his chin, and I might . . .' He stopped me. 'That will do!' he exclaimed, 'that will be splendid'. You see what he meant! He wanted the wheedling suggested, but he did not want a lot of low comedy introduced, and still less did he want the action to mar the effect of the song.

alive and somewhere! Perhaps far away, perhaps close at hand! And I know   730
him not! It seemeth that I am wasting time in not knowing him.

WIL. Now say that it is I – nay! suppose it for the nonce. Say that we
are wed – suppose it only – say that thou art my very bride, and I thy cheery,
joyous, bright, frolicsome husband – and that, the day's work being done,
and the prisoners stored away for the night, thou and I are alone together –   735
with a long, long evening before us!

PHŒ. (*with a grimace*). It is a pretty picture – but I scarcely know. It cometh
so unexpectedly – and yet – and yet – *were* I thy bride —

WIL. Aye! – wert thou my bride —?

PHŒ. Oh, how I would love thee!   740

SONG – PHŒBE.

Were I thy bride,
Then all the world beside
Were not too wide
     To hold my wealth of love –
Were I thy bride!   745

Upon thy breast
My loving head would rest,
As on her nest
     The tender turtle dove –
Were I thy bride!   750

This heart of mine
Would be one heart with thine,
And in that shrine
     Our happiness would dwell –
Were I thy bride!   755

And all day long
Our lives should be a song:
No grief, no wrong
     Should make my heart rebel –
Were I thy bride!   760

The silvery flute,
The melancholy lute,
Were night-owl's hoot
     To my low-whispered coo –
Were I thy bride!   765

784 *No, thou'rt not*: Wilfred's speech was a late addition by Gilbert; originally he had
Wilfred exiting with Phœbe. Delivered by Kenneth Sandford, the last D'Oyly Carte
principal to play Shadbolt, who always repeated the last phrase 'Aye, if she die for it',
the speech never failed to win a round of applause.

800–801 *You make a brave Yeoman*: The earliest version of Gilbert's libretto contains no reference
at all to 'Yeoman' in the text – another word is always used instead. Thus in the pre-
production prompt copy this passage runs 'You make a brave Beefeater, sir! So – this
ruff is too high; So – and the belt should be thus. Here is your halbert, sir; carry it thus.
The warders come . . .'.

The skylark's trill
Were but discordance shrill
To the soft thrill
Of wooing as I'd woo –
Were I thy bride! 770

(MERYLL *re-enters; gives keys to* PHŒBE, *who replaces them at* WILFRED'S *girdle, unnoticed by him. Exit* MERYLL.)

The rose's sigh
Were as a carrion's cry
To lullaby 775
Such as I'd sing to thee,
Were I thy bride!

A feather's press
Were leaden heaviness
To my caress. 780
But then, of course, you see,
I'm not thy bride!

(*Exit* PHŒBE.)

WIL. No, thou'rt not – not yet! But, Lord, how she woo'd! I should be
no mean judge of wooing, seeing that I have been more hotly woo'd than 785
most men. I have been woo'd by maid, widow, and wife. I have been woo'd
boldly, timidly, tearfully, shyly – by direct assault, by suggestion, by
implication, by inference, and by innuendo. But this wooing is not of the
common order: it is the wooing of one who must needs woo me, if she die
for it! (*Exit* WILFRED.) 790

(*Enter* MERYLL, *cautiously, from Tower.*)

MER. (*looking after them*). The deed is, so far, safely accomplished. The
slyboots, how she wheedled him! What a helpless ninny is a love-sick man!
He is but as a lute in a woman's hands – she plays upon him whatever tune
she will. But the Colonel comes. I' faith, he's just in time, for the Yeomen 795
parade here for his execution in two minutes!

(*Enter* FAIRFAX, *without beard and moustache,
and dressed in Yeoman's uniform.*)

FAIR. My good and kind friend, thou runnest a grave risk for me!
MER. Tut, sir, no risk. I'll warrant none here will recognize you. You 800
make a brave Yeoman, sir! So – this ruff is too high; so – and the sword

808–17 *Oh, Sergeant Meryll, is it true*
    This chorus was not in early libretti and was only added in the third edition, which came out after the 1907 revival.

818 *Ye Tower Warders*: As sung on the first night this recitative began 'Ye Tower Yeomen'. The licence copy, however, has 'Warders', as now.

should hang thus. Here is your halbert, sir; carry it thus. The Yeomen come. Now remember, you are my brave son, Leonard Meryll.

FAIR. If I may not bear mine own name, there is none other I would bear so readily.   805

MER. Now, sir, put a bold face on it, for they come.

FINALE – ACT I.

(Enter Yeomen of the Guard.)

CHORUS.

Oh, Sergeant Meryll, is it true –
   The welcome news we read in orders?
Thy son, whose deeds of derring-do   810
Are echoed all the country through,
   Has come to join the Tower Warders?
If so, we come to meet him,
That we may fitly greet him,
And welcome his arrival here   815
With shout on shout and cheer on cheer –
Hurrah! Hurrah! Hurrah!

RECITATIVE – SERGEANT MERYLL.

Ye Tower Warders, nursed in war's alarms,
   Suckled on gunpowder, and weaned on glory,
Behold my son, whose all-subduing arms   820
   Have formed the theme of many a song and story!
   Forgive his aged father's pride; nor jeer
    His aged father's sympathetic tear!

                             (Pretending to weep.)

CHORUS.

Leonard Meryll!   825
Leonard Meryll!
Dauntless he in time of peril!
   Man of power,
   Knighthood's flower,
Welcome to the grim old Tower,   830
To the Tower, welcome thou!

835 *Have been prodigiously exaggerated*: This line was originally 'Are all prodigiously exaggerated'.

840 *Standard lost in last campaign*: In an article in the January 1978 edition of *The Savoyard* Charles Low suggested that Leonard Meryll's 'last campaign' was probably the battle at Jedburgh in the Scottish Border country in September 1523 in which the Earl of Surrey defeated the claimant to the Scottish throne, the Duke of Albany. In that case, Low suggests, the action of *The Yeoman of the Guard* should be dated to July 1524, at the end of Sir Richard Cholmondeley's period as Lieutenant of the Tower.

An earlier alternative might be the battle of Flodden in 1513, when an invasion of England by James IV of Scotland was beaten back. It is also possible, Low suggests, that Leonard Meryll lost his standard in the raids against France which were made in 1522–3.

855 *Oh! the tales that are narrated*: In early performances this line was sung: 'Oh! the facts that have been stated', and there was an additional line between lines 858 and 859: 'Monstrously exaggerated'. According to Peter Riley, the whole passage from lines 855–9 and the chorus which follows it were for many years dropped from D'Oyly Carte productions, being reinstated in the late 1960s. I have not been able to establish the exact period of this cut.

860 *They are not exaggerated*: The first edition of the libretto had additional couplets for the Third and Fourth Yeomen and another verse for Fairfax:

RECITATIVE – Fairfax.

Forbear, my friends, and spare me this ovation,
I have small claim to such consideration;
The tales that of my prowess are narrated
Have been prodigiously exaggerated!   835

Chorus.

'Tis ever thus!
Wherever valour true is found,
True modesty will there abound.

COUPLETS.

1st Yeoman.   Didst thou not, oh, Leonard Meryll!
    Standard lost in last campaign,   840
Rescue it at deadly peril –
    Bear it safely back again?

Chorus.   Leonard Meryll, at his peril,
Bore it safely back again!

2nd Yeoman.   Didst thou not, when prisoner taken,   845
    And debarred from all escape,
Face, with gallant heart unshaken,
    Death in most appalling shape?

Chorus.   Leonard Meryll faced his peril,
Death in most appalling shape!   850

Fair. (*aside*).   Truly I was to be pitied,
    Having but an hour to live,
I reluctantly submitted,
    I had no alternative!

(*Aloud.*)   Oh! the tales that are narrated   855
    Of my deeds of derring-do
Have been much exaggerated,
Very much exaggerated,
    Scarce a word of them is true!

Chorus.   They are not exaggerated, etc.   860

(*Enter* Phœbe. *She rushes to* Fairfax. *Enter* Wilfred.)

3RD YEOMAN.	You, when brought to execution, 　Like a demigod of yore, With heroic resolution 　Snatched a sword and killed a score!
CHORUS.	Leonard Meryll, Leonard Meryll Snatched a sword and killed a score!
4TH YEOMAN.	Then escaping from the foemen, 　Bolstered with the blood you shed, You, defiant, fearing no men, 　Saved your honour and your head!
CHORUS.	Leonard Meryll, Leonard Meryll Saved his honour and his head!
FAIRFAX.	True, my course with judgment shaping, 　Favoured, too, by lucky star, I succeeded in escaping 　Prison bolt and prison bar! Oh! the tales that have been stated 　Of my deeds of derring-do, Have been much exaggerated, etc.
CHORUS.	They are not exaggerated, etc.

Gilbert wrote to Sullivan on the morning of the first performance saying: 'The Warders' couplets in the finale are too long, and should be reduced by one half. This, you will observe is not "cutting out your music", but cutting out a *repeat* of your music. And may I remind you that I am proposing to cut, not only your music, but my words'. Sullivan's diary for 3 October records that he met Gilbert at the theatre shortly before the curtain went up and 'arranged to cut down second verse of couplets in Finale'; so it seems that they were never sung on stage.

RECITATIVE.

PHŒ.   Leonard!
FAIR. (*puzzled*).   I beg your pardon?
PHŒ.   Don't you know me?
        I'm little Phœbe!   865
FAIR. (*still puzzled*).   Phœbe? Is this Phœbe?
        What! little Phœbe? (*Aside.*) Who the deuce may *she* be?
        It can't be Phœbe, surely?
WIL.   Yes, 'tis Phœbe —
        Your sister Phœbe! Your own little sister!   870
CHORUS.   Aye, he speaks the truth;
        'Tis Phœbe!
FAIR. (*pretending to recognize her*).   Sister Phœbe!
PHŒ.   Oh, my brother!
FAIR.   Why, how you've grown! I did not recognize you!   875
PHŒ.   So many years! Oh, brother!
FAIR.   Oh, my sister!
WIL.   Aye, hug him, girl! There are three thou mayst hug —
        Thy father and thy brother and — myself!
FAIR.   Thyself, forsooth? And who art thou thyself?   880
WIL.   Good sir, we are betrothed. (FAIRFAX *turns inquiringly to*
        PHŒBE.)
PHŒ.   Or more or less —
        But rather less than more!
WIL.   To thy fond care   885
        I do commend thy sister. Be to her
        An ever-watchful guardian — eagle-eyed!
        And when she feels (as sometimes she does feel)
        Disposed to indiscriminate caress,
        Be thou at hand to take those favours from her!   890
CHORUS. Be thou at hand to take those favours from her!
PHŒ.   Yes, yes.
        Be thou at hand to take those favours from me!

TRIO — WILFRED, FAIRFAX, *and* PHŒBE.

WIL.   To thy fraternal care
                        Thy sister I commend;   895
                    From every lurking snare
                        Thy lovely charge defend:
                    And to achieve this end,
                    Oh! grant, I pray, this boon —
                        She shall not quit thy sight: 900

907 *From morn to afternoon*: This chorus was changed to its present version in the third edition of the libretto. Before that the chorus sang 'Oh! grant, I pray, this boon' etc. at line 907, 'So grant, I pray, this boon' etc. at line 921, and 'He freely grants that boon' at line 935.

918 *From two to eventide*: These lines were changed to their present form after the First World War. Before that they went:

> From two till day is done –
> From dim twilight to 'leven at night
> All kinds of risk I run!

936 *The bell of St Peter's begins to toll*: The bell of the church of St Peter ad Vincula, which stands within the precincts of the Tower of London adjoining Tower Green, was always rung during an execution.

Getting the right balance and rhythm for the tolling which accompanies the chorus 'The prisoner comes to meet his doom' is a difficult matter. J. M. Gordon, stage manager of the D'Oyly Carte Company for more than thirty years in the early part of this century, noted in his reminiscences that 'the Bell chorus was a great difficulty, it being a real bell of almost two hundredweights set behind the flats, and the slightest taps overpowering the chorus, it was moved more and more away, and eventually taken up to the fly tower where the conductor could be seen and the balance of tone correct with the chorus'.

Peter Riley, a more recent stage manager, found the tolling of the bell equally difficult to manage. 'We originally did it off stage but that proved unsatisfactory because it has to be tolled on every eighth beat and so the chap doing it really has to see the conductor, so we later transferred it to the orchestra pit. On the eleventh toll the headsman comes in'.

> From morn to afternoon –
>> From afternoon to night –
> From seven o'clock to two –
>> From two to eventide –
> From dim twilight to 'leven at night   905
>> She shall not quit thy side!

CHORUS.   From morn to afternoon, etc.

PHŒ.   So amiable I've grown,
>> So innocent as well,
> That if I'm left alone   910
>> The consequences fell
>> No mortal can foretell.
> So grant, I pray, this boon –
>> I shall not quit thy sight:
> From morn to afternoon –   915
>> From afternoon to night –
> From seven o'clock to two –
>> From two to eventide –
> From dim twilight to 'leven at night
>> I shall not quit thy side.   920

CHORUS.   From morn to afternoon, etc.

FAIR.   With brotherly readiness,
>> For my fair sister's sake,
> At once I answer 'Yes' –
>> That task I undertake –   925
>> My word I never break.
> I freely grant that boon,
>> And I'll repeat my plight.
> From morn to afternoon –   *(kiss)*
>> From afternoon to night –   *(kiss)*   930
> From seven o'clock to two –   *(kiss)*
>> From two to evening meal –   *(kiss)*
> From dim twilight to 'leven at night
>> That compact I will seal.   *(kiss)*

CHORUS.   From morn to afternoon, etc.   935

(The bell of St Peter's begins to toll. The Crowd enters; the block is brought on to the stage, and the Headsman takes his place. The Yeomen of the Guard form up. The LIEUTENANT *enters and takes his place, and tells off* FAIRFAX *and two others to bring the prisoner to execution.* WILFRED, FAIRFAX, *and two Yeomen exeunt to Tower.)*   940

944 *May Heaven have mercy on his soul*: Originally Dame Carruthers was given a solo verse between the chorus and Elsie's solo. It appears in the pre-production prompt copy and the licence copy:

> Thou solemn bell, whose iron tongue
>> So many a brave man's knell has rung,
> Of all that thou hast tolled away,
>> The bravest he who dies today!

945–8 *Oh, Mercy, thou whose smile has shone*
As sung in early performances, Elsie's solo was slightly different from the present version:

> Oh, Mercy, thou whose smile has shone
>> So many a captive on;
> Of all immured within these walls,
>> The very worthiest falls!

949 *Oh, Mercy, etc.*: In early performances, the chorus at this point repeated 'The prisoner comes to meet his doom' instead of the reprise of Elsie's solo which they now have.

CHORUS (*to tolling accompaniment*).

The prisoner comes to meet his doom:
The block, the headsman, and the tomb.
The funeral bell begins to toll –
May Heaven have mercy on his soul!

SOLO – ELSIE, *with* CHORUS.

Oh, Mercy, thou whose smile has shone   945
  So many a captive heart upon;
Of all immured within these walls,
  To-day the very worthiest falls!

CHORUS.   Oh, Mercy, etc.

(*Enter* FAIRFAX *and two other Yeomen from Tower in*   950
  great excitement.)

FAIR.   My lord! I know not how to tell
      The news I bear!
I and my comrades sought the prisoner's cell –
      He is not there!   955

CHORUS.   He is not there!
They sought the prisoner's cell – he is not there!

TRIO – FAIRFAX *and two Yeomen.*

As escort for the prisoner
  We sought his cell, in duty bound;
The double gratings open were,   960
  No prisoner at all we found!

We hunted high, we hunted low,
  We hunted here, we hunted there –
The man we sought with anxious care
  Had vanished into empty air!   965

(*Exit* LIEUTENANT.)

GIRLS.   Now, by my troth, the news is fair,
The man has vanished into air!

997–1004 *All frenzied with despair I rave*

In early performances Elsie and Point were given the following verses to sing in this ensemble, with everyone else singing the Lieutenant's verse with altered pronouns as now:

ELSIE.

All frenzied with despair I rave,
  My anguish rends my heart in two.
Unloved, to him my hand I gave;
  To him, unloved, bound to be true!
Unloved, unknown, unseen – the brand
  Of infamy upon his head:
A bride that's husbandless, I stand
  To all mankind for ever dead!

POINT.

All frenzied with despair I rave,
  My anguish rends my heart in two.
Your hand to him you freely gave;
  It's woe to me, not woe to you!
My laugh is dead, my heart unmanned,
  A jester with a soul of lead!
A lover loverless I stand,
  To womankind for ever dead!

ALL.　　　　As escort for the prisoner

　　　　　　We ⎫
　　　　　　　　⎬ sought his cell in duty bound, etc.　　　970
　　　　　　They ⎭

　　　　　　(*Enter* WILFRED, *followed by* LIEUTENANT.)

LIEUT.　　　Astounding news! The prisoner fled!
(*To* WILFRED.)　　Thy life shall forfeit be instead!
　　　　　　　　　　　　　(WILFRED *is arrested.*)

WIL.　　　　My lord, I did not set him free,　　　　975
　　　　　　I hate the man – my rival he!
　　　　　　　　　　　　(WILFRED *is taken away.*)

MER.　　　　The prisoner gone – I'm all agape!
　　　　　　Who could have helped him to escape?

PHŒ.　　　　Indeed I can't imagine who!　　　　　980
　　　　　　I've no idea at all – have you?

　　　　　　(*Enter* JACK POINT.)

DAME.　　　Of his escape no traces lurk,
　　　　　　Enchantment must have been at work!

ELSIE (*aside to* POINT).
　　　　　　What have I done! Oh, woe is me!　　　985
　　　　　　I am his wife, and he is free!

POINT.　　　Oh, woe is *you*? Your anguish sink!
　　　　　　Oh, woe is *me*, I rather think!
　　　　　　Oh, woe is *me*, I rather think!
　　　　　　Yes, woe is *me*, I rather think!　　　990
　　　　　　　　Whate'er betide
　　　　　　　　You are his bride,
　　　　　　　　And I am left
　　　　　　　　Alone – bereft!
　　　　　　Yes, woe is *me*, I rather think!　　　995
　　　　　　Yes, woe is *me*, I rather think!

ENSEMBLE – LIEUTENANT, PRINCIPALS, *and* CHORUS.

　　　All frenzied with despair I rave,
　　　　The grave is cheated of its due.
　　　Who is the misbegotten knave
　　　　Who hath contrived this deed to do?　　1000
　　　Let search be made throughout the land,

1003 *A thousand marks*: A mark was worth two thirds of a pound, i.e. thirteen shillings and fourpence.

Or $\left\{ \begin{array}{c} \text{his} \\ \text{my} \end{array} \right\}$ vindictive anger dread –

A thousand marks to him $\left\{ \begin{array}{c} \text{he'll} \\ \text{I'll} \end{array} \right\}$ hand

Who brings him here, alive or dead.

(*At the end,* ELSIE *faints in* FAIRFAX'S *arms; all the Yeomen and populace rush*   1005
off the stage in different directions, to hunt for the fugitive, leaving only the
Headsman on the stage, and ELSIE *insensible in* FAIRFAX'S *arms.*)

END OF ACT I

1–2 *Scene*: A note by Rupert D'Oyly Carte records: 'At the 1899 revival Act II was given a different setting to Act I, described as "The Tower from the Wharf". Nothing seemed to be gained by this and it was dropped later.'

3–10 *Night has spread her pall once more*
In early libretti this chorus, as now, was given to the women but with the men joining in to repeat all from 'He has shaken off his yoke' (line 7).

6 *Useless his dungeon key*: many editions have 'Useless now his dungeon key'.

22 *Pretty warders are ye*: This chorus was not sung in early performances.

ACT II

SCENE. – *The same.* – *Moonlight. Two days have elapsed. Women and Yeomen of the Guard discovered.*

CHORUS OF WOMEN.

Night has spread her pall once more,
   And the prisoner still is free:
Open is his dungeon door,   5
   Useless his dungeon key!
He has shaken off his yoke –
   How, no mortal man can tell!
Shame on loutish jailer-folk –
   Shame on sleepy sentinel!   10

(*Enter* DAME CARRUTHERS *and* KATE.)

SOLO – DAME CARRUTHERS.

Warders are ye?
   Whom do ye ward?
Bolt, bar, and key,
   Shackle and cord,   15
Fetter and chain,
   Dungeon of stone,
All are in vain –
   Prisoner's flown!
Spite of ye all, he is free – he is free!   20
Whom do ye ward? Pretty warders are ye!

CHORUS OF WOMEN. Pretty warders are ye, etc.

YEOMEN.   Up and down, and in and out,
              Here and there, and round about;

34 *reading from a huge volume*: Beti Lloyd-Jones, who was with the D'Oyly Carte Company as a contralto chorus member and soloist from September 1956 until the company folded in March 1982, acted as 'stage mother' to John Reed, the principal comedian for much of that time. She told me 'One of the little traditions we developed over those years was that before the Second Act of *Yeomen* I would always read a long screed to him from his book of jokes'.

39–40 *The councillor laughed hugely*: According to a note by Rupert D'Oyly Carte, George Thorne, who played Jack Point in D'Oyly Carte tours between 1888 and 1899, delivered this line as 'The sage was so pleased with this saw that he gave him a sausage'.

47 *Jailer that jailed not . . .*: The most alliterative passage in the Savoy Operas (see the note to *The Mikado*, Act I, lines 605–8).

Every chamber, every house,   25
Every chink that holds a mouse,
Every crevice in the keep,
Where a beetle black could creep,
Every outlet, every drain,
Have we searched, but all in vain.   30

ENSEMBLE.   Warders are $\begin{Bmatrix} ye \\ we \end{Bmatrix}$,

                       Whom do $\begin{Bmatrix} ye \\ we \end{Bmatrix}$ ward? etc.
                                                    (*Exeunt all.*)

(*Enter* JACK POINT, *in low spirits, reading from a huge volume.*)

POINT (*reads*). 'The Merrie Jestes of Hugh Ambrose. No. 7863. The Poor   35
Wit and the Rich Councillor. A certayne poor wit, being an-hungered, did
meet a well-fed councillor. "Marry, fool," quoth the councillor, "whither
away?" "In truth," said the poor wag, "in that I have eaten naught these two
dayes, I do wither away, and that right rapidly!" The councillor laughed
hugely, and gave him a sausage.' Humph! The councillor was easier to   40
please than my new master the Lieutenant. I would like to take post under
that councillor. Ah! 'tis but melancholy mumming when poor heart-broken,
jilted Jack Point must needs turn to Hugh Ambrose for original light humour!

(*Enter* WILFRED, *also in low spirits.*)

WIL. (*sighing*). Ah, Master Point!   45
POINT (*changing his manner*). Ha! friend jailer! Jailer that wast – jailer that
never shalt be more! Jailer that jailed not, or that jailed, if jail he did, so
unjailerly that 'twas but jerry-jailing, or jailing in joke – though no joke to
him who, by unjailerlike jailing, did so jeopardize his jailership. Come, take
heart, smile, laugh, wink, twinkle, thou tormentor that tormentest none –   50
thou racker that rackest not – thou pincher out of place – come, take heart,
and be merry, as I am! – (*aside, dolefully*) – as I am!
WIL. Aye, it's well for thee to laugh. Thou has a good post, and hast
cause to be merry.
POINT (*bitterly*). Cause? Have we not all cause? Is not the world a big butt   55
of humour, into which all who will may drive a gimlet? See, I am a salaried
wit; and is there aught in nature more ridiculous? A poor, dull, heart-broken
man, who must needs be merry, or he will be whipped; who must rejoice,
lest he starve; who must jest you, jibe you, quip you, crank you, wrack you,
riddle you, from hour to hour, from day to day, from year to year, lest he   60
dwindle, perish, starve, pine, and die! Why, when there's naught else to
laugh at, I laugh at myself till I ache for it!

73–137 *Oh! a private buffoon*

An undated prompt copy in the possession of Dame Bridget D'Oyly Carte has a note pencilled against the first verse of this song: 'This verse is now omitted at the Savoy'. The prompt copy in the British Library has the first verse stroked out. I have been unable to discover the dates when this verse was cut and when reinstated. In the 1910 D'Oyly Carte recording C. H. Workman sang the first verse, but not the third!

WIL. Yet I have often thought that a jester's calling would suit me to a hair.

POINT. Thee? Would suit *thee*, thou death's head and cross-bones?   65

WIL. Aye, I have a pretty wit – a light, airy, joysome wit, spiced with anecdotes of prison cells and the torture-chamber. Oh, a very delicate wit! I have tried it on many a prisoner, and there have been some who smiled. Now it is not easy to make a prisoner smile. And it should not be difficult to be a good jester, seeing that thou art one.   70

POINT. Difficult? Nothing easier. Nothing easier. Attend, and I will prove it to thee!

SONG – POINT.

Oh! a private buffoon is a light-hearted loon,
   If you listen to popular rumour;
From the morn to the night he's so joyous and bright,   75
   And he bubbles with wit and good humour!
He's so quaint and so terse, both in prose and in verse;
   Yet though people forgive his transgression,
There are one or two rules that all family fools
   Must observe, if they love their profession.   80
      There are one or two rules,
        Half a dozen, maybe,
      That all family fools,
        Of whatever degree,
      Must observe, if they love their profession.   85

If you wish to succeed as a jester, you'll need
   To consider each person's auricular:
What is all right for B would quite scandalize C
   (For C is so very particular);
And D may be dull, and E's very thick skull   90
   Is as empty of brains as a ladle;
While F is F sharp, and will cry with a carp
   That he's known your best joke from his cradle!
      When your humour they flout,
        You can't let yourself go;   95
      And it *does* put you out
        When a person says, 'Oh,
      I have known that old joke from my cradle!'

If your master is surly, from getting up early
   (And tempers are short in the morning),
An inopportune joke is enough to provoke   100
   Him to give you, at once, a month's warning.

112 *D.D.*: Doctor of Divinity. This distinguished species of clergyman also gets a mention in *The Sorcerer* (Act II, line 18) and in *The Pirates of Penzance* (Act I, line 432).

Then if you refrain, he is at you again,
    For he likes to get value for money;
He'll ask then and there, with an insolent stare,   105
    'If you know that you're paid to be funny?'
        It adds to the tasks
        Of a merryman's place,
        When your principal asks,
        With a scowl on his face,   110
    If you know that you're paid to be funny?

Comes a Bishop, maybe, or a solemn D.D. –
    Oh, beware of his anger provoking!
Better not pull his hair – don't stick pins in his chair;
    He don't understand practical joking.   115
If the jests that you crack have an orthodox smack,
    You may get a bland smile from these sages;
But should they, by chance, be imported from France,
    Half-a-crown is stopped out of your wages!
        It's a general rule,   120
        Though your zeal it may quench,
        If the family fool
        Tells a joke that's too French,
    Half-a-crown is stopped out of his wages!

Though your head it may rack with a bilious attack,   125
    And your senses with toothache you're losing,
Don't be mopy and flat – they don't fine you for that,
    If you're properly quaint and amusing!
Though your wife ran away with a soldier that day,
    And took with her your trifle of money;   130
Bless your heart, they don't mind – they're exceedingly kind –
    They don't blame you – as long as you're funny!
        It's a comfort to feel,
        If your partner should flit,
        Though *you* suffer a deal,   135
        They don't mind it a bit –
    They don't blame you – so long as you're funny!

POINT. And so thou wouldst be a jester, eh?

WIL. Aye!

POINT. Now, listen! My sweetheart, Elsie Maynard, was secretly wed to   140
this Fairfax half an hour ere he escaped.

WIL. She did well.

161-94 *Hereupon we're both agreed*
This spirited song was originally sung as an ensemble, with Point and Wilfred singing together throughout rather than, as now, dividing up some of the lines between them.

175 *a tale of cock and bull*: A 'cock and bull story' is a long, rambling and generally incredible yarn. The origins of the term seem to lie in an old fable about cocks, bulls and other animals discoursing in human language.

POINT. She did nothing of the kind, so hold thy peace and perpend. Now, while he liveth she is dead to me and I to her, and so, my jibes and jokes notwithstanding, I am the saddest and the sorriest dog in England!   145

WIL. Thou art a very dull dog indeed.

POINT. Now, if thou wilt swear that thou didst shoot this Fairfax while he was trying to swim across the river – it needs but the discharge of an arquebus on a dark night – and that he sank and was seen no more, I'll make thee the very Archbishop of jesters, and that in two days' time! Now, what   150
sayest thou?

WIL. I am to lie?

POINT. Heartily. But thy lie must be a lie of circumstance, which I will support with the testimony of eyes, ears, and tongue.

WIL. And thou wilt qualify me as a jester?   155

POINT. As a jester among jesters. I will teach thee all my original songs, my self-constructed riddles, my own ingenious paradoxes; nay, more, I will reveal to thee the source whence I get them. Now, what sayest thou?

WIL. Why, if it be but a lie thou wantest of me, I hold it cheap enough, and I say yes, it is a bargain!   160

DUET – POINT *and* WILFRED.

BOTH.   Hereupon we're both agreed,
                        All that we two
                        Do agree to
                   We'll secure by solemn deed,
                        To prevent all   165
                        Error mental.

POINT.   You on Elsie are to call
                        With a story
                        Grim and gory;

WIL.   How this Fairfax died, and all   170
                        I declare to
                        You're to swear to.

POINT.   I to swear to!
WIL.   I declare to!

BOTH.   Tell a tale of cock and bull,   175
                   Of convincing detail full,
                        Tale tremendous,
                        Heaven defend us!
                   What a tale of cock and bull!

197 *Two days gone*: In the first edition this line began 'A day and a half gone'.

BOTH.	In return for { your / my } own part	180
	You are } making I am }	
	Undertaking	
	To instruct { me / you } in the art	
	(Art amazing, Wonder raising)	185

POINT.	Of a jester, jesting free.
	    Proud position –
	    High ambition!	

WIL.	And a lively one I'll be,
	    Wag-a-wagging,
	    Never flagging!
		190

POINT.	Wag-a-wagging!	
WIL.	Never flagging!	
BOTH.	Tell a tale of cock and bull, etc.	

(Exeunt together.)   195

(Enter FAIRFAX.*)*

FAIR. Two days gone, and no news of poor Fairfax. The dolts! They seek him everywhere save within a dozen yards of his dungeon. So I am free! Free, but for the cursed haste with which I hurried headlong into the bonds of matrimony with – Heaven knows whom! As far as I remember, she should 200 have been young; but even had not her face been concealed by her kerchief, I doubt whether, in my then plight, I should have taken much note of her. Free? Bah! The Tower bonds were but a thread of silk compared with these conjugal fetters which I, fool that I was, placed upon mine own hands. From the one I broke readily enough – how to break the other! 205

BALLAD – FAIRFAX.

Free from his fetters grim –
    Free to depart;
Free both in life and limb –
    In all but heart!
Bound to an unknown bride   210
    For good and ill;
Ah, is not one so tied
    A prisoner still?

216 *Gyves*: Leg-irons.

218 *Although a monarch's hand*: In the licence and pre-production prompt copies this line appears as 'Although King Henry's hand', a clear indication that Gilbert envisaged the opera as being set during the reign of Henry VIII (1509–47).

> Free, yet in fetters held
>   Till his last hour,   215
> Gyves that no smith can weld,
>   No rust devour!
> Although a monarch's hand
>   Had set him free,
> Of all the captive band   220
>   The saddest he!

(*Enter* MERYLL.)

FAIR. Well, Sergeant Meryll, and how fares thy pretty charge, Elsie Maynard?

MER. Well enough, sir. She is quite strong again, and leaves us   225
to-night.

FAIR. Thanks to Dame Carruthers' kind nursing, eh?

MER. Aye, deuce take the old witch! Ah, 'twas but a sorry trick you played me, sir, to bring the fainting girl to me. It gave the old lady an excuse for taking up her quarters in my house, and for the last two years I've   230
shunned her like the plague. Another day of it and she would have married me! (*Enter* DAME CARRUTHERS *and* KATE.) Good Lord, here she is again! I'll e'en go. (*Going.*)

DAME. Nay, Sergeant Meryll, don't go. I have something of grave import to say to thee.   235

MER. (*aside*). It's coming.

FAIR. (*laughing*). I'faith, I think I'm not wanted here. (*Going.*)

DAME. Nay, Master Leonard, I've naught to say to thy father that his son may not hear.

FAIR. (*aside*). True. I'm one of the family; I had forgotten!   240

DAME. 'Tis about this Elsie Maynard. A pretty girl, Master Leonard.

FAIR. Aye, fair as a peach blossom – what then?

DAME. She hath a liking for thee, or I mistake not.

FAIR. With all my heart. She's as dainty a little maid as you'll find in a midsummer day's march.   245

DAME. Then be warned in time, and give not thy heart to her. Oh, *I* know what it is to give my heart to one who will have none of it!

MER. (*aside*). Aye, *she* knows all about that. (*Aloud.*) And why is my boy to take heed of her? She's a good girl, Dame Carruthers.

DAME. Good enough, for aught I know. But she's no girl. She's a married   250
woman.

MER. A married woman! Tush, old lady – she's promised to Jack Point, the Lieutenant's new jester.

DAME. Tush in thy teeth, old man! As my niece Kate sat by her bedside to-day, this Elsie slept, and as she slept she moaned and groaned,   255

264 *kirtle*: A skirt or outer petticoat. In the pre-production prompt copy this phrase reads 'or I'll swallow my farthingale'.

and turned this way and that way – and, 'How shall I marry one I have never seen?' quoth she – then, 'An hundred crowns!' quoth she – then, 'Is it certain he will die in an hour?' quoth she – then, 'I love him not, and yet I am his wife,' quoth she! Is it not so, Kate?

KATE. Aye, aunt, 'tis even so.   260

FAIR. Art thou sure of all this?

KATE. Aye, sir, for I wrote it all down on my tablets.

DAME. Now, mark my words: it was of this Fairfax she spake, and he is her husband, or I'll swallow my kirtle!

MER. (*aside*). Is it true, sir?   265

FAIR. (*aside to* MERYLL). True? Why, the girl was raving! (*Aloud.*) Why should she marry a man who had but an hour to live?

DAME. Marry? There be those who would marry but for a minute, rather than die old maids.

MER. (*aside*). Aye, I know one of them!   270

QUARTET.

FAIRFAX, SERGEANT MERYLL, DAME CARRUTHERS, *and* KATE.

> Strange adventure! Maiden wedded
>   To a groom she's never seen –
>   Never, never, never seen!
> Groom about to be beheaded,
>   In an hour on Tower Green!   275
>   Tower, Tower, Tower Green!
> Groom in dreary dungeon lying,
> Groom as good as dead, or dying,
> For a pretty maiden sighing –
>   Pretty maid of seventeen!   280
>   Seven – seven – seventeen!
>
> Strange adventure that we're trolling:
>   Modest maid and gallant groom –
>   Gallant, gallant, gallant groom! –
> While the funeral bell is tolling,   285
>   Tolling, tolling, Bim-a-boom!
>   Bim-a, Bim-a, Bim-a-boom!
> Modest maiden will not tarry;
> Though but sixteen years she carry,
> She must marry, she must marry,   290
>   Though the altar be a tomb –
>   Tower – Tower – Tower tomb!

(*Exeunt* DAME CARRUTHERS, MERYLL, *and* KATE.)

298 *Enter Elsie*: Gilbert originally gave Elsie a recitative and song at this entrance. It is printed in the pre-production copy and in the licence copy, where it is crossed out.

RECITATIVE – Elsie.

Unloved, unseen, unknown, the brand
Of infamy upon his head!
A bride all husbandless I stand,
To all mankind for ever dead!

SONG – Elsie.

There's many a maid
In best arrayed
Comes tripping, tripping over the lea,
And many, and more,
Rare tales can tell
Of gallants a score
Who spoke them well,
And left them jilted – sorry, but free.
A tripping, tripping over the lea;
But never a maid that you'll espy
Can tell so sorry a tale as I!
Ah me! how merry a maid may be
A-tripping, tripping over the lea!

Oh maidens fair,
Who, free from care,
Come tripping, tripping over the lea,
Pity the bride
All husbandless,
What sorrows betide
No one can guess!
Oh maidens, maidens, happy are ye
A-tripping, tripping over the lea!
For though I'm a wife, the wife of none!
Than maid and widow and wife in one,
'Tis better a jilted maid to be,
A-tripping, tripping over the lea!

FAIR. So my mysterious bride is no other than this winsome Elsie! By my hand, 'tis no such ill plunge in Fortune's lucky bag! I might have fared worse 295 with my eyes open! But she comes. Now to test her principles. 'Tis not every husband who has a chance of wooing his own wife!

(Enter ELSIE.*)*

FAIR. Mistress Elsie!
ELSIE. Master Leonard! 300
FAIR. So thou leavest us to-night?
ELSIE. Yes, Master Leonard. I have been kindly tended, and I almost fear I am loth to go.
FAIR. And this Fairfax. Wast thou glad when he escaped?
ELSIE. Why, truly, Master Leonard, it is a sad thing that a young and 305 gallant gentleman should die in the very fullness of his life.
FAIR. Then when thou didst faint in my arms, it was for joy at his safety?
ELSIE. It may be so. I was highly wrought, Master Leonard, and I am but a girl, and so, when I am highly wrought, I faint. 310
FAIR. Now, dost thou know, I am consumed with a parlous jealousy?
ELSIE. Thou? And of whom?
FAIR. Why, of this Fairfax, surely!
ELSIE. Of Colonel Fairfax?
FAIR. Aye. Shall I be frank with thee? Elsie – I love thee, ardently, 315 passionately! (ELSIE *alarmed and surprised.*) Elsie, I have loved thee these two days – which is a long time – and I would fain join my life to thine!
ELSIE. Master Leonard! Thou art jesting!
FAIR. Jesting? May I shrivel into raisins if I jest! I love thee with a love that is a fever – with a love that is a frenzy – with a love that eateth up my heart! 320 What sayest thou? Thou wilt not let my heart be eaten up?
ELSIE *(aside).* Oh, mercy! What am I to say?
FAIR. Dost thou love me, or hast thou been insensible these two days?
ELSIE. I love all brave men.
FAIR. Nay, there is love in excess. I thank heaven there are many brave 325 men in England; but if thou lovest them all, I withdraw my thanks.
ELSIE. I love the bravest best. But, sir, I may not listen – I am not free – I – I am a wife!
FAIR. Thou a wife? Whose? His name? His hours are numbered – nay, his grave is dug and his epitaph set up! Come, his name? 330
ELSIE. Oh, sir! keep my secret – it is the only barrier that Fate could set up between us. My husband is none other than Colonel Fairfax!
FAIR. The greatest villain unhung! The most ill-favoured, ill-mannered, ill-natured, ill-omened, ill-tempered dog in Christendom!
ELSIE. It is very like. He is naught to me – for I never saw him. I was 335

355 *arquebus*: A very up-to-date reference – the *Oxford English Dictionary* dates the first recorded use of the word as being in 1532, eight years after Sir Richard Cholmondeley's departure from the Tower. It goes on to define an arquebus as 'The early type of portable gun, varying in size, and, when used in the field, supported on a tripod, trestle or other carriage, or upon a forked rest. The name in German meant literally "hook-gun", from the hook, cast along with it, by which it was attached to the carriage'.

blindfolded, and he was to have died within the hour; and he did not die –
and I am wedded to him, and my heart is broken!

FAIR. He was to have died, and he did *not* die? The scoundrel! The
perjured, traitorous villain! Thou shouldst have insisted on his dying first, to
make sure. 'Tis the only way with these Fairfaxes.   340

ELSIE. I now wish I had!

FAIR. (*aside*). Bloodthirsty little maiden! (*Aloud.*) A fig for this Fairfax! Be
mine – he will never know – he dares not show himself; and if he dare, what
art thou to him? Fly with me, Elsie – we will be married to-morrow, and thou
shalt be the happiest wife in England!   345

ELSIE. Master Leonard! I am amazed! Is it thus that brave soldiers speak
to poor girls? Oh! for shame, for shame! I am wed – not the less because I
love not my husband. I am a wife, sir, and I have a duty, and – oh, sir! thy
words terrify me – they are not honest – they are wicked words, and
unworthy thy great and brave heart! Oh, shame upon thee! shame upon   350
thee!

FAIR. Nay, Elsie, I did but jest. I spake but to try thee — (*Shot heard.*)

(*Enter* MERYLL *hastily.*)

MER. (*recitative*). Hark! What was that, sir?

FAIR.   Why, an arquebus –   355
Fired from the wharf, unless I much mistake.

MER.   Strange – and at such an hour! What can it mean?

(*Enter* CHORUS.)

CHORUS.

Now what can that have been –
    A shot so late at night,   360
    Enough to cause a fright!
What can the portent mean?

Are foemen in the land?
    Is London to be wrecked?
    What are we to expect?   365
What danger is at hand?
    Let us understand
    What danger is at hand!

(LIEUTENANT *enters, also* POINT *and* WILFRED.)

393 *Colonel Fairfax and no other*: In early editions of the libretto, this and the next line were
first repeated by Fairfax before the chorus took them up as follows:

> Colonel Fairfax and no other
> > Was the man to whom he clung!
> Yes – they closed with one another
> In a rough-and-tumble smother;
> Colonel Fairfax and no other
> > Was the man to whom he clung!

RECITATIVE.

LIEUT.	Who fired that shot? At once the truth declare!	370
WIL.	My lord, 'twas I – to rashly judge forbear!	
POINT.	My lord, 'twas he – to rashly judge forbear!	

DUET AND CHORUS – WILFRED *and* POINT.

WIL. Like a ghost his vigil keeping –

POINT. Or a spectre all-appalling –

WIL. I beheld a figure creeping – 375

POINT. I should rather call it crawling –

WIL. He was creeping –

POINT. He was crawling –

WIL. He was creeping, creeping –

POINT. Crawling! 380

WIL. He was creeping –

POINT. He was crawling –

WIL. He was creeping, creeping –

POINT. Crawling!

WIL. Not a moment's hesitation – 385
 I myself upon him flung,
 With a hurried exclamation
 To his draperies I hung;
 Then we closed with one another
 In a rough-and-tumble smother; 390
 Colonel Fairfax and no other
 Was the man to whom I clung!

ALL. Colonel Fairfax and no other
 Was the man to whom he clung!

WIL. After mighty tug and tussle – 395

POINT. It resembled more a struggle –

WIL. He, by dint of stronger muscle –

POINT. Or by some infernal juggle –

WIL. From my clutches quickly sliding –

POINT. I should rather call it slipping – 400

405 *Down he dived into the river*: This line and the chorus's repeat in line 409 were originally sung: 'He plunged headlong in the river'.

417 *With an ounce or two of lead*: This line was not sung in early performances, everyone merely repeating line 416.

423 *He discharged it without winking*: This and the next three lines were not in the first edition of the libretto used for early performances.

429 *Anyhow, the man is dead*: In early performances Wilfred had this line only to himself, with everyone then joining him to finish the song thus:

> ALL.　　　Whether stone or lump of lead,
> 　　　　　Arquebus from sentry seizing,
> 　　　　　With the view his king of pleasing,
> 　　　　　　Wilfred shot him through the head,
> 　　　　　　And he's very, very dead.
> 　　And it matters very little whether stone or lump of lead,
> 　　It is very, very certain that he's very, very dead!

The chorus then sang the refrain 'Hail the valiant fellow' (lines 448–51).

WIL.   With a view, no doubt, of hiding –

POINT.   Or escaping to the shipping –

WIL.   With a gasp, and with a quiver –

POINT.   I'd describe it as a shiver –

WIL.   Down he dived into the river,
                And, alas, I cannot swim.   405

ALL.   It's enough to make one shiver –
            With a gasp and with a quiver,
            Down he dived into the river;
                It was very brave of him!   410

WIL.   Ingenuity is catching;
                With the view my king of pleasing,
            Arquebus from sentry snatching –

POINT.   I should rather call it seizing –

WIL.   With an ounce or two of lead   415
                He despatched him through the head!

ALL.   With an ounce or two of lead
                He despatched him through the head!

WIL.   I discharged it without winking,
            Little time I lost in thinking,   420
            Like a stone I saw him sinking –

POINT.   I should say a lump of lead.

ALL.   He discharged it without winking,
            Little time he lost in thinking.

WIL.   Like a stone I saw him sinking –   425

POINT.   I should say a lump of lead.

WIL.   Like a stone, my boy, I said –

POINT.   Like a heavy lump of lead.

WIL.   Anyhow, the man is dead,
            Whether stone or lump of lead!   430

ALL.   Anyhow, the man is dead,
                    Whether stone or lump of lead!
            Arquebus from sentry seizing,

448–51 *Hail the valiant fellow*
    In early libretti this chorus was sung twice: once, as noted above, before the
    Lieutenant's recitative, and then again, as now, after it. On both occasions it was sung
    without line 452.

With the view his king of pleasing,
  Wilfred shot him through the head,   435
  And he's very, very dead.
And it matters very little whether stone or lump of lead;
It is very, very certain that he's very, very dead!

RECITATIVE – Lieutenant.

The river must be dragged – no time be lost;
The body must be found, at any cost.   440
To this attend without undue delay;
So set to work with what despatch ye may!

               (*Exit.*)

ALL.   Yes, yes,
We'll set to work with what despatch we may!   445

  (*Four men raise* WILFRED, *and carry him off on
      their shoulders.*)

CHORUS.

Hail the valiant fellow who
Did this deed of derring-do!
Honours wait on such an one;   450
By my head, 'twas bravely done!
Now, by my head, 'twas bravely done!

  (*Exeunt all but* ELSIE, POINT, FAIRFAX, *and* PHŒBE.)

POINT (*to* ELSIE, *who is weeping*). Nay, sweetheart, be comforted. This
Fairfax was but a pestilent fellow, and, as he had to die, he might as well die 455
thus as any other way. 'Twas a good death.

ELSIE. Still, he was my husband, and had he not been, he was
nevertheless a living man, and now he is dead; and so, by your leave, my
tears may flow unchidden, Master Point.

FAIR. And thou didst see all this?   460

POINT. Aye, with both eyes at once – this and that. The testimony of one
eye is naught – he may lie. But when it is corroborated by the other, it is good
evidence that none may gainsay. Here are both present in court, ready to
swear to him!

PHŒ. But art thou sure it was Colonel Fairfax? Saw you his face? 465

POINT. Aye, and a plaguey ill-favoured face too. A very hang-dog face –
a felon face – a face to fright the headsman himself, and make him strike

496 *His twig he'll so carefully lime*: In medieval and Tudor times people caught birds by smearing twigs with a sticky substance called bird-lime. The phrase 'to lime a twig' came to be used figuratively, as in Shakespeare's 'Madam, myself have limed a bush for her' (*Henry VI, Part 2*, Act I, Scene 3).

awry. Oh, a plaguey, bad face, take my word for 't. (PHŒBE *and* FAIRFAX *laugh.*) How they laugh! 'Tis ever thus with simple folk – an accepted wit has but to say 'Pass the mustard,' and they roar their ribs out!   470

FAIR. (*aside*). If ever I come to life again, thou shalt pay for this, Master Point!

POINT. Now, Elsie, thou art free to choose again, so behold me: I am young and well-favoured. I have a pretty wit. I can jest you, jibe you, quip you, crank you, wrack you, riddle you —   475

FAIR. Tush, man, thou knowest not how to woo. 'Tis not to be done with time-worn jests and thread-bare sophistries; with quips, conundrums, rhymes, and paradoxes. 'Tis an art in itself, and must be studied gravely and conscientiously.

TRIO – ELSIE, PHŒBE, *and* FAIRFAX.

FAIR. A man who would woo a fair maid   480
Should 'prentice himself to the trade,
   And study all day,
   In methodical way,
How to flatter, cajole, and persuade;
He should 'prentice himself at fourteen,   485
And practise from morning to e'en;
   And when he's of age,
   If he will, I'll engage,
He may capture the heart of a queen!

ALL. It is purely a matter of skill,   490
Which all may attain if they will:
   But every Jack,
   He must study the knack
If he wants to make sure of his Jill!

ELSIE. If he's made the best use of his time,   495
His twig he'll so carefully lime
   That every bird
   Will come down at his word,
Whatever its plumage or clime.
He must learn that the thrill of a touch   500
May mean little, or nothing, or much:
   It's an instrument rare,
   To be handled with care,
And ought to be treated as such.

ALL. It is purely a matter of skill, etc.   505

535 *That's not true, but let it pass*: In early performances Point said 'That's not true, but let it pass this once'.

PHŒ.   Then a glance may be timid or free,
                      It will vary in mighty degree,
                          From an impudent stare
                          To a look of despair
                      That no maid without pity can see!   510
                      And a glance of despair is no guide –
                      It may have its ridiculous side;
                          It may draw you a tear
                          Or a box on the ear;
                      You can never be sure till you've tried!   515

ALL.   It is purely a matter of skill, etc.

FAIR. (*aside to* POINT). Now, listen to me – 'tis done thus – (*aloud*) – Mistress Elsie, there is one here who, as thou knowest, loves thee right well!

POINT (*aside*). That he does – right well!

FAIR. He is but a man of poor estate, but he hath a loving, honest heart. 520 He will be a true and trusty husband to thee, and if thou wilt be his wife, thou shalt lie curled up in his heart, like a little squirrel in its nest!

POINT (*aside*). 'Tis a pretty figure. A maggot in a nut lies closer, but a squirrel will do.

FAIR. He knoweth that thou wast a wife – an unloved and unloving 525 wife, and his poor heart was near to breaking. But now that thine unloving husband is dead, and thou art free, he would fain pray that thou wouldst hearken unto him, and give him hope that thou wouldst one day be his!

PHŒ. (*alarmed*). He presses her hands – and he whispers in her ear! Ods bodikins, what does it mean? 530

FAIR. Now, sweetheart, tell me – wilt thou be this poor good fellow's wife?

ELSIE. If the good, brave man – *is* he a brave man?

FAIR. So men say.

POINT (*aside*). That's not true, but let it pass. 535

ELSIE. If the brave man will be content with a poor, penniless, untaught maid —

POINT (*aside*). Widow – but let *that* pass.

ELSIE. I will be his true and loving wife, and that with my heart of hearts!

FAIR. My own dear love! (*Embracing her.*) 540

PHŒ. (*in great agitation*). Why, what's all this? Brother – brother – it is not seemly!

POINT (*also alarmed, aside*). Oh, I can't let *that* pass! (*Aloud.*) Hold, enough, Master Leonard! An advocate should have his fee, but methinks thou art over-paying thyself! 545

FAIR. Nay, that is for Elsie to say. I promised thee I would show thee how to woo, and herein lies the proof of the virtue of my teaching. Go thou, and apply it elsewhere! (PHŒBE *bursts into tears.*)

549–84 *When a wooer/Goes a wooing*
François Cellier, musical director of the D'Oyly Carte Company from 1880 until 1913, disclosed in an interview with the *Westminster Gazette* the reason why this much-loved song never received an encore:

> In 'The Yeomen of the Guard' we always have a passionate demand for a repetition, which I avoid with the utmost care. All lovers of this opera will remember the quartette towards the end 'When a lover [*sic*] goes a-wooing' – a very sad number for Phœbe and Jack Point. The latter retires in distress at the loss of Elsie, and Phœbe is left on the stage to mourn the loss of Fairfax. Not only have Fairfax and Elsie to change too quickly to allow of the encore being taken, but Sir Arthur Sullivan expressly desired that a repetition should not be given, on the ground that the dramatic effect would be utterly spoiled.

567 *mickle*: The word mickle properly means much or a lot. It is used both here and by Dame Hannah in *Ruddigore* (Act II, line 551) erroneously to mean little.

QUARTET – ELSIE, PHŒBE, FAIRFAX, *and* POINT.

ELSIE.
  When a wooer
    Goes a-wooing,   550
  Naught is truer
    Than his joy.
FAIR.
  Maiden hushing
    All his suing –
  Boldly blushing –   555
    Bravely coy!

ALL.
  Oh, the happy days of doing!
  Oh, the sighing and the suing!
  When a wooer goes a-wooing,
    Oh, the sweets that never cloy!   560

PHŒ. (*weeping*).
  When a brother
    Leaves his sister
  For another,
    Sister weeps.
  Tears that trickle,   565
    Tears that blister –
  'Tis but mickle
    Sister reaps!

ALL.
  Oh, the doing and undoing,
  Oh, the sighing and the suing,   570
  When a brother goes a-wooing,
    And a sobbing sister weeps!

POINT.
  When a jester
    Is outwitted,
  Feelings fester,   575
    Heart is lead!
  Food for fishes
    Only fitted,
  Jester wishes
    He was dead!   580

ALL.
  Oh, the doing and undoing,
  Oh, the sighing and the suing,
  When a jester goes a-wooing,
    And he wishes he was dead!

        (*Exeunt all but* PHŒBE, *who remains weeping.*)   585

PHŒ. And I helped that man to escape, and I've kept his secret, and

624 *Enter Leonard hastily*: In the 1978 Tower of London production, Leonard made this entrance on a white charger, which was then left to swish its tail at the back of the orchestra pit during the finale.

Originally, Gilbert had intended Leonard's entrance to come later in Act II. The pre-production prompt copy in the D'Oyly Carte archives has Meryll and Dame Carruthers entering at this point. They then have the dialogue which now appears in lines 657–85. After the singing of 'Rapture, rapture' Phœbe and Wilfred appear to have the following conversation after seeing Meryll and Dame Carruthers going off together:

> PHŒ. There – see what has come of thine intermeddling! I am to have thee as a husband and that cackling old hen wife as a mother!
> WIL. And thou hast lost a brother, eh?
> PHŒ. Aye, a very loving brother!
> WIL. To the devil with his love! It maddens me to think of it. Why, who is this?

At this point Leonard enters, as now, and the dialogue continues from line 625 to line 652, at which point the finale begins.

pretended that I was his dearly loving sister, and done everything I could
think of to make folk believe I *was* his loving sister, and this is his gratitude!
Before I pretend to be sister to anybody again, I'll turn nun, and be sister to
everybody – one as much as another!   590

(*Enter* WILFRED.)

WIL. In tears, eh? What a plague art thou grizzling for now?

PHŒ. Why am I grizzling? Thou hast often wept for jealousy – well, 'tis
for jealousy I weep now. Aye, yellow, bilious, jaundiced jealousy. So make
the most of that, Master Wilfred.   595

WIL. But I have never given thee cause for jealousy. The Lieutenant's
cook-maid and I are but the merest gossips!

PHŒ. Jealous of thee! Bah! I'm jealous of no craven cock-on-a-hill, who
crows about what he'd do an he dared! I am jealous of another and a better
man than thou – set that down, Master Wilfred. And he is to marry Elsie   600
Maynard, the little pale fool – set that down, Master Wilfred – and my heart
is wellnigh broken! There, thou hast it all! Make the most of it!

WIL. The man thou lovest is to marry Elsie Maynard? Why, that is no
other than thy brother, Leonard Meryll!

PHŒ. (*aside*). Oh, mercy! what have I said?   605

WIL. Why, what manner of brother is this, thou lying little jade? Speak!
Who is this man whom thou hast called brother, and fondled, and coddled,
and kissed! – with my connivance, too! Oh Lord! with my connivance! Ha!
should it be this Fairfax! (PHŒBE *starts*.) It is! It is this accursed Fairfax! It's
Fairfax! Fairfax, who —   610

PHŒ. Whom thou has just shot through the head, and who lies at the
bottom of the river!

WIL. A – I – I may have been mistaken. We are but fallible mortals, the
best of us. But I'll make sure – I'll make sure. (*Going.*)

PHŒ. Stay – one word. I think it cannot be Fairfax – mind, I say I *think* 615
because thou hast just slain Fairfax. But whether he be Fairfax or no Fairfax,
he is to marry Elsie – and – and – as thou hast shot him through the head,
and he is dead, be content with that, and I will be thy wife!

WIL. Is that sure?

PHŒ. Aye, sure enough, for there's no help for it! Thou art a very brute 620
– but even brutes must marry, I suppose.

WIL. My beloved! (*Embraces her.*)

PHŒ. (*aside*). Ugh!

(*Enter* LEONARD, *hastily.*)

LEON. Phœbe, rejoice, for I bring glad tidings. Colonel Fairfax's   625
reprieve was signed two days since, but it was foully and maliciously kept
back by Secretary Poltwhistle, who designed that it should arrive after the
Colonel's death. It hath just come to hand, and it is now in the Lieutenant's
possession!

632 *Ods bobs*: Short for 'ods bodkins', a corruption of 'God's body' – a common oath from the sixteenth to the nineteenth centuries.

637 *cockatrice*: A grotesque mythical creature with the head, wings and feet of a cock and the tail of a dragon or serpent. The word came to be used as a term of reproach for a woman.

638 *cleave thee to the chine*: Split you to the backbone. Gilbert used the phrase in his Bab Ballad 'Sir Conrad and the Rusty One':

> Ho! stand, Sir Knight, if thou be brave,
> And try thy might with mine,
> Unless you wish this trusty glaive
> To cleave you to the chine!

PHŒ. Then the Colonel is free? Oh, kiss me, kiss me, my dear! Kiss   630
me, again, and again!

WIL. (*dancing with fury*). Ods bobs, death o' my life! Art thou mad! Am *I*
mad? Are we *all* mad?

PHŒ. Oh, my dear – my dear, I'm wellnigh crazed with joy! (*Kissing*
LEONARD.)   635

WIL. Come away from him, thou hussy – thou jade – thou kissing,
clinging cockatrice! And as for thee, sir, devil take thee, I'll rip thee like a
herring for this! I'll skin thee for it! I'll cleave thee to the chine! I'll – oh!
Phœbe! Phœbe! Who is this man?

PHŒ. Peace, fool. He is my brother!   640

WIL. Another brother! Are there any more of them? Produce them all at
once, and let me know the worst!

PHŒ. This is the real Leonard, dolt; the other was but his substitute. The
real Leonard, I say – my father's own son.

WIL. How do I know this? Has he 'brother' writ large on his brow? I   645
mistrust thy brothers! Thou art but a false jade!

(*Exit* LEONARD.)

PHŒ. Now, Wilfred, be just. Truly I did deceive thee before – but it was
to save a precious life – and to save it, not for me, but for another. They are
to be wed this very day. Is not this enough for thee? Come – I am thy Phœbe   650
– thy very own – and we will be wed in a year – or two – or three, at the
most. Is not that enough for thee?

(*Enter* MERYLL, *excitedly, followed by* DAME CARRUTHERS,
who listens, unobserved.)

MER. Phœbe, hast thou heard the brave news?   655

PHŒ. (*still in* WILFRED'S *arms*). Aye, father.

MER. I'm nigh mad with joy! (*Seeing* WILFRED.) Why, what's all this?

PHŒ. Oh, father, he discovered our secret through my folly, and the price
of his silence is —

WIL. Phœbe's heart.   660

PHŒ. Oh dear, no – Phœbe's hand.

WIL. It's the same thing!

PHŒ. *Is* it?

(*Exeunt* WILFRED *and* PHŒBE.)

MER. (*looking after them*). 'Tis pity, but the Colonel had to be saved at any   665
cost, and as thy folly revealed our secret, thy folly must e'en suffer for it!
(DAME CARRUTHERS *comes down.*) Dame Carruthers!

DAME. So this is a plot to shield this arch-fiend, and I have detected it.
A word from me, and three heads besides his would roll from their
shoulders!   670

686–718 *Rapture, rapture*

This song was added to the opera to give Elsie and Fairfax time to change into their wedding garments. It was subsequently dropped when it was found that there was, in fact, enough time for the costume change without it. Wilfred Judd reinstated it in his 1981 D'Oyly Carte production.

MER. Nay, Colonel Fairfax is reprieved. (*Aside.*) Yet, if my complicity in his escape were known! Plague on the old meddler! There's nothing for it – (*aloud*) – Hush, pretty one! Such bloodthirsty words ill become those cherry lips! (*Aside.*) Ugh!

DAME (*bashfully*). Sergeant Meryll! 675

MER. Why, look ye, chuck – for many a month I've – I've thought to myself – 'There's snug love saving up in that middle-aged bosom for some one, and why not for thee – that's me – so take heart and tell her – that's thee – that thou – that's me – lovest her – thee – and – and – well, I'm a miserable old man, and I've done it – and that's me!' But not a word about Fairfax! The 680 price of thy silence is —

DAME. Meryll's heart?

MER. No, Meryll's *hand*.

DAME. It's the same thing!

MER. *Is* it! 685

DUET – DAME CARRUTHERS *and* SERGEANT MERYLL.

DAME.
    Rapture, rapture!
      When love's votary,
    Flushed with capture,
      Seeks the notary,
        Joy and jollity 690
        Then is polity;
        Reigns frivolity!
    Rapture, rapture!

MER.
    Doleful, doleful!
      When humanity, 695
    With its soul full
      Of satanity,
        Courting privity,
        Down declivity
        Seeks captivity! 700
    Doleful, doleful!

DAME.
    Joyful, joyful!
      When virginity
    Seeks, all coyful,
        Man's affinity; 705
        Fate all flowery,
        Bright and bowery,
        Is her dowery!
    Joyful, joyful!

730 *Enter . . . Elsie as Bride*: In early performances, before 'Rapture, rapture' was out, Elsie appeared before the chorus 'Comes the pretty young bride'.

Gilbert wrote to Richard D'Oyly Carte:

> Elsie should change her dress to something like a wedding dress at the end of the piece. It should not be a wedding dress of a modern type (of course), but a dress of Henry VIII time that will suggest something of a matrimonial nature to the spectator. White silk or satin, and white bars, and a wreath of white flowers would do – but kept 'bourgeoise' in cut.

731–8 *'Tis said that joy in full perfection*
In the licence copy this is given to Elsie as a solo.

MER.   Ghastly, ghastly!   710
          When man, sorrowful,
        Firstly, lastly,
          Of to-morrow full,
           After tarrying,
           Yields to harrying –   715
           Goes a-marrying.
        Ghastly, ghastly!

BOTH.   Rapture, etc.

               (*Exeunt* DAME *and* MERYLL.)

FINALE.

(*Enter Yeomen and Women.*)   720

CHORUS OF WOMEN.
(ELEGIACS.)

Comes the pretty young bride, a-blushing, timidly shrinking –
Set all thy fears aside – cheerily, pretty young bride!
Brave is the youth to whom thy lot thou art willingly linking!
 Flower of valour is he – loving as loving can be!
   Brightly thy summer is shining,   725
   Fair as the dawn of the day;
    Take him, be true to him –
    Tender his due to him –
   Honour him, love and obey!

(*Enter* DAME, PHŒBE, *and* ELSIE *as Bride.*)   730

TRIO – PHŒBE, ELSIE, *and* DAME CARRUTHERS.

  'Tis said that joy in full perfection
   Comes only once to womankind –
  That, other times, on close inspection,
   Some lurking bitter we shall find.
  If this be so, and men say truly,   735
  My day of joy has broken duly.

   With happiness $\left\{ \begin{array}{c} \text{my} \\ \text{her} \end{array} \right\}$ soul is cloyed –

   This is $\left\{ \begin{array}{c} \text{my} \\ \text{her} \end{array} \right\}$ joy-day unalloyed!

739 *Yes, yes*: In early performances the chorus sang:

> Yes, yes
> This is her joy-day unalloyed!

746 *No! no*: In early performances Elsie had a longer solo here:

> No! no! recall those words – it cannot be!
> Leonard, my Leonard, come, oh, come to me!
> Leonard, my own – my loved one – where art thou?
> I knew not how I loved thine heart till now!

747–54 *Oh, day of terror*
In early performances this ensemble was sung as follows:

ELSIE *and* PHŒBE.	CHORUS *and others.*
Oh, day of terror! day of tears!	Oh, day of terror! day of tears!
What fearful tidings greet mine ears?	What words are these that greet our ears?
Oh, Leonard, come thou to my side,	Who is the man who, in his pride,
And claim me as thy loving bride.	So boldly claims thee as his bride?

LIEUTENANT *and* POINT.
Come, dry these unbecoming tears,
Most joyful tidings greet thine ears.
The man to whom thou art allied
Appears to claim thee as his bride.

757 *All thought of Leonard Meryll*: The pre-production prompt copy, the licence copy, and the draft manuscript have the following lines at this point, crossed out in Gilbert's hand and changed to the present version:

FAIR. (*sternly*). All thought of Leonard Meryll set aside.
  Thou art mine own! I claim thee as my bride.
ALL. Thou art his own – his own!
  Alas, he claims thee as his own!

Repeat Ensemble.

ELSIE. A suppliant at your feet I kneel,
  Thy heart will yield!
FAIR. (*sternly*). I have a heart that cannot feel,
  It is a heart of tempered steel
  Three times annealed!
ELSIE. My piteous cry, oh, do not mock,
  But set me free.
FAIR. (*sternly*). Mine is a heart of massive rock,
  Unmoved by sentimental shock,
  Come thou with me!
CHORUS. He has a heart of tempered steel,
  That cannot feel.
  He has a heart of massive rock,
  That naught can shock:
  Thy husband he!
ELSIE. Leonard, my loved one, etc.

ALL.　　　　　Yes, yes, with happiness her soul is cloyed!
　　　　　　　This is her joy-day unalloyed!　　　　　　　740

(Flourish. Enter LIEUTENANT.*)*

LIEUT.　　　　Hold, pretty one! I bring to thee
　　　　　　　　News – good or ill, it is for thee to say.
　　　　　　　Thy husband lives – and he is free,
　　　　　　　　And comes to claim his bride this very day!　　745

ELSIE. No! no! recall those words – it cannot be!

ENSEMBLE.

KATE *and* CHORUS.	DAME CARRUTHERS *and* PHŒBE.
Oh, day of terror! Day of tears!	Oh, day of terror! Day of tears!
Who is the man who, in his pride,	The man to whom thou art allied
Claims thee as his bride?	Appears to claim thee as his bride.
Day of terror! Day of tears!	Day of terror! Day of tears!　　750

LIEUT., MERYLL, *and* WILFRED.	ELSIE.
Come, dry these unbecoming tears,	Oh, Leonard, come thou to my side,
Most joyful tidings greet thine ears,	And claim me as thy loving bride!
The man to whom thou art allied	Day of terror! Day of tears!
Appears to claim thee as his bride.	

(Flourish. Enter COLONEL FAIRFAX, *handsomely dressed,*　　755
and attended by other Gentlemen.)

FAIR. *(sternly).*　All thought of Leonard Meryll set aside.
　　　　　　　Thou art mine own! I claim thee as my bride.
CHORUS.　　　Thou art his own! Alas! he claims thee as his bride.
ELSIE.　　　　A suppliant at thy feet I fall;　　　　　　　760
　　　　　　　Thine heart will yield to pity's call!
FAIR.　　　　 Mine is a heart of massive rock,
　　　　　　　Unmoved by sentimental shock!
CHORUS.　　　　Thy husband he!
ELSIE *(aside).*　Leonard, my loved one – come to me.　　765
　　　　　　　　They bear me hence away!
　　　　　　　But though they take me far from thee,
　　　　　　　　My heart is thine for aye!
　　　　　　　　　My bruisèd heart,
　　　　　　　　　My broken heart,　　　　　　　　770
　　　　　　　Is thine, my own, for aye!

(To FAIRFAX.*)*　Sir, I obey!
　　　　　　　　I am thy bride;

But ere the fatal hour
  I said the say   775
That placed me in thy power
  Would I had died!
Sir, I obey!
  I am thy bride!

(*Looks up and recognizes* FAIRFAX.) Leonard!   780

FAIR.   My own!

ELSIE.   Ah! (*Embrace.*)

ELSIE *and* {With happiness my soul is cloyed,
 FAIR.   {This is our joy-day unalloyed!

CHORUS.   Yes, yes!   785
  With happiness their souls are cloyed,
  This is their joy-day unalloyed!

(*Enter* JACK POINT.)

POINT.   Oh, thoughtless crew!
   Ye know not what ye do!   790
  Attend to me, and shed a tear or two –
   For I have a song to sing, O!

CHORUS.   Sing me your song, O!

POINT.   It is sung to the moon
    By a love-lorn loon,   795
  Who fled from the mocking throng, O!
 It's the song of a merryman, moping mum,
 Whose soul was sad, and whose glance was glum,
 Who sipped no sup, and who craved no crumb,
  As he sighed for the love of a ladye! 800

CHORUS.   Heighdy! heighdy!
   Misery me, lackadaydee!
 He sipped no sup, and he craved no crumb,
  As he sighed for the love of a ladye!

ELSIE.   I have a song to sing, O!   805

CHORUS.   What is your song, O?

810 *It's the song of a merrymaid*: Gilbert at first gave Elsie a much less sympathetic parting song. During the first run she sang:

> It's the song of a merrymaid, peerly proud,
> Who loved a lord and who laughed aloud
> At the moan of the merryman moping mum,
> Whose soul was sad and whose glance was glum, etc.

The words were changed by Gilbert to the present version for the first revival in 1897.

821 *Point falls insensible at their feet*: The question of whether Point is meant to die at the end of the opera, or merely to faint, is one that has long exercised Savoyards, and no doubt it always will. The fact is that different actors have interpreted Gilbert's final direction in different ways, and Gilbert himself seems to have been content to leave Jack Point's fate to the audience to decide on as they wished.

According to Sir Henry Lytton, admittedly a somewhat biased source, George Grossmith, who created the role of Point, played the final scene for laughs, falling down in a way that was 'irresistibly funny'. It was even said that when the curtain went down on the first-night performance the 'insensible' jester, lying prostrate on the stage, raised a leg and waggled it in the air. The review in *The Era* certainly commented 'The finale . . . ends the opera brightly . . . and all ends happily'. However, another critic who saw Grossmith in the role of Point on several occasions said 'The pathos of [his] final fall struck me as being very fine indeed'.

The first artist to make Jack Point 'die' at the end of the opera was George Thorne, who played the role in the first provincial tour of *The Yeomen*, which opened in Manchester on 1 November 1888. A fortnight later Henry Lytton, playing in another D'Oyly Carte touring company, introduced a similarly tragic ending at a performance in Bath.

Lytton continued his tragic interpretation of the final scene right through until his last appearance with the D'Oyly Carte Company, appropriately playing the role of Point, in Dublin on 30 June 1934. In his book *The Secrets of a Savoyard* he maintained that Gilbert had always intended Point to die and had only toned down the ending in response to Grossmith's reputation as a great jester and his feeling that, whatever he did at the end, the audience would laugh.

Lytton says in his book that he once asked Gilbert if his tragic portrayal of Point should be modified in any way. 'No' was the dramatist's reported reply. 'Keep on like that. It is just what I want. Jack Point should die and the end of the opera should be a tragedy.'

That supposed remark, however, almost certainly gives a false impression of Gilbert's feelings about this scene. He had plenty of opportunities in successive editions of the libretto to change the word 'insensible' to 'dead' if he wanted to make absolutely clear that he meant the ending to be tragic. Yet he never did so. Nor are his early directions in the licence copy or pre-production prompt-book any stronger on this point. The only direction which appears in these early editions of the libretto, and not subsequently, is that 'As Point falls all *except* Warders point towards him'.

The best guide to Gilbert's intentions in this scene is the remark which he made to J. M. Gordon, the D'Oyly Carte stage manager after Lytton had 'died' on stage: 'The fate of Jack Point is in the hands of the audience, who may please themselves whether he lives or dies'. Gordon adds in his manuscript reminiscences, *The Making of a Stage Manager and Producer*, 'This is the only direct statement from Gilbert on the subject and confirms the directions on the libretto'.

ELSIE.

It is sung with the ring
Of the songs maids sing
Who love with a love life-long, O!
It's the song of a merrymaid, nestling near,   810
Who loved her lord – but who dropped a tear
At the moan of the merryman, moping mum,
Whose soul was sad, and whose glance was glum,
Who sipped no sup, and who craved no crumb,
As he sighed for the love of a ladye!   815

CHORUS.

Heighdy! heighdy!
Misery me, lackadaydee!
He sipped no sup, and he craved no crumb,
As he sighed for the love of a ladye!
Heighdy! Heighdy! Heighdy!   820

(FAIRFAX *embraces* ELSIE *as* POINT *falls insensible at their feet.*)

CURTAIN

MORE ABOUT PENGUINS, PELICANS AND PUFFINS

For further information about books available from Penguins please write to Dept EP, Penguin Books Ltd, Harmondsworth, Middlesex UB7 0DA.

In the U.S.A.: For a complete list of books available from Penguins in the United States write to Dept DG, Penguin Books, 299 Murray Hill Parkway, East Rutherford, New Jersey 07073.

In Canada: For a complete list of books available from Penguins in Canada write to Penguin Books Canada Ltd, 2801 John Street, Markham, Ontario L3R 1B4.

In Australia: For a complete list of books available from Penguins in Australia write to the Marketing Department, Penguin Books Australia Ltd, P.O. Box 257, Ringwood, Victoria 3134.

In New Zealand: For a complete list of books available from Penguins in New Zealand write to the Marketing Department, Penguin Books (N.Z.) Ltd, P.O. Box 4019, Auckland 10.

In India: For a complete list of books available from Penguins in India write to Penguin Overseas Ltd, 706 Eros Apartments, 56 Nehru Place, New Delhi 110019.

THE ANNOTATED
GILBERT AND SULLIVAN

H. M. S. PINAFORE

THE PIRATES OF PENZANCE

IOLANTHE

THE MIKADO

THE GONDOLIERS

Their best-loved operas
introduced and edited by Ian Bradley

What were the 'cherished rights' enjoyed on Friday nights by the House of Lords? Who was the modern Major-General? And why was Koko's little list changed in 1948?

The explanations are all here, alongside the full libretto text, in a fascinating commentary on the five most popular Gilbert and Sullivan operas. It covers:

* contemporary and historical allusions
* obscure words and references
* 'lost' songs and dialogue originally written for the operas but later cut
* the sources and backgrounds of Gilbert's characters and plots
* the major production points based on the practices of the D'Oyly Carte Opera Company

With Gilbert and Sullivan's operas gaining a new lease of life in the theatre, on film and on television, this book provides the ideal companion – as well as a source of innocent merriment – for audiences both new and old.

Also published by Penguins

FULL CIRCLE

Janet Baker

'Some people call it genius, others empathy, and some "star" quality. Whatever it is called, Janet Baker possesses it . . .' – Harold Rosenthal in the *Listener*

Janet Baker's diary, kept during the last year of her tremendous stage career, is both the most fascinating glimpse yet of opera behind-the-scenes, and a marvellously candid self-portrait.

Details of day-to-day preparation for her farewell performances – in *Alceste* at Covent Garden, *Maria Stuart* with the ENO and *Orfeo* at Glyndebourne, are interspersed with brief, illuminating comments on music and musicians, and anecdotes about her family, marriage and life in London. And throughout this enjoyable year of autobiography, the faith, stamina and indefinable 'star' quality that have endeared Dame Janet to a huge audience are all very much in evidence.

'Wholeheartedly honest . . . in print here, she is herself in the raw' – Susan Hill in the *Daily Telegraph*

'The book tells us more about Dame Janet than any biographer or critic could have done, and explains just why she is the great artist we know and love' – *Opera*

With the first full discography, specially compiled for this Penguin edition, and with photographs by Zoë Dominic.